# PROGRAMS OF THE BRAIN

# PROGRAMS OF THE BRAIN

BASED ON THE GIFFORD LECTURES, 1975–7

**J. Z. YOUNG**, F.R.S.

*Emeritus Professor of Anatomy, University College, London*

1978

OXFORD UNIVERSITY PRESS

*Oxford University Press, Walton Street, Oxford* OX1 6DP

OXFORD   LONDON   GLASGOW
NEW YORK   TORONTO   MELBOURNE   WELLINGTON
KUALA LUMPUR   SINGAPORE   JAKARTA   HONG KONG   TOKYO
DELHI   BOMBAY   CALCUTTA   MADRAS   KARACHI
IBADAN   NAIROBI   DAR ES SALAAM   CAPE TOWN

© *J. Z. Young 1978*

**British Library Cataloguing in Publication Data**

Young, John Zachary
  Programs of the brain.
  1. Psychology, Physiological  2. Brain
  I. Title
  152   QP360   78–40443

ISBN  0–19–857545–9

*Printed in Great Britain
by Fletcher Son Ltd, Norwich*

# Preface

Anyone who writes a book dealing with such fundamental themes as this one would be a fraud if he did not feel the need to apologize for his ignorance and temerity. Can it be right for one person to try to cover so many important topics? The result is bound to irritate those who really know about them and could mislead those who don't.

These apologies are made to warn, not to make excuses. I believe that the ideas expressed here are partly new and will be found useful. They are an attempt to show how with recent knowledge we can improve the way we think about ourselves. In particular we can see how the aims and purposes of our own lives are related to the operations of nature of which we are part. Biological facts, from genetics to neuropsychology, show that living things can properly be said to act in pursuit of particular aims. Each tries to achieve certain standards appropriate to its way of life. The result of this continual striving, choosing and deciding, through millions of years, has been a progressive accumulation of information about how best to live. Contrary to what is often said the facts of biology show both purpose and progress in life.

To understand human life we must look for the basis of its standards. We can find it in the operations of the brain by considering how all its millions of cells work together to produce the programs of our actions. This is not yet a very precise conception but it allows us to talk about the contributions of the various parts of the brain to the many human activities listed in the chapters of this book, whether practical, such as eating, or abstract, such as thinking.

Our brains, like those of any other species, allow us to learn those things that are appropriate to our way of life, which is social. A child comes into the world with a constitution pre-programmed to allow it to learn how to get on with other people. A main aim in this book has been to show how various parts of the brain work together to produce a unified operating system, centred on the model or hypothesis that the most important acts of human life are responses to other people. The concept of programs directed to this end can be useful to human biologists at all levels from physiology to sociology. It may seem at first to be too simple for detailed technical use, but it forces attention to the combined actions of millions of nerve cells. Its simplicity is an advantage for the layman, who can understand something about how this mysterious organ his brain operates during his perceptions and actions and the varying moods of his inner life.

The way the concept of programs can be used is illustrated in the Glossary. Here I have re-defined familiar words such as 'knowledge' or 'thinking' in terms of *Programs of the brain*. The ideas behind the definitions may seem strange at first, as will other parts of the book. I believe they will prove useful.

This book is based on the Gifford Lectures given in 1975–7 in the University of Aberdeen. I am most grateful to the Vice-Chancellor and members of that University for the invitation, for the welcome that I found there, and for the stimulus from the audience and their questions. I am especially grateful to Professors George Dunnet, Fred Holliday and Vero Wynne-Edwards and to the Staff of the Department of Zoology, where the lectures were given.

Preparation of the lectures and the book has been very greatly helped by Dr. Marion Nixon, who has researched for me endlessly in libraries and helped with every phase of preparation of the manuscript. I could never have covered such a wide field without her. Parts of the manuscript were read at some stage by Professors Richard Gregory, Stuart Sutherland, and Pat Wall, and Drs. Ted Honderich and Samir Zeki, and I have greatly profited from their help. But I have persisted in my own versions of many problems of physiology, psychology, and philosophy.

The Wellcome Institute for the History of Medicine has provided me with workspace and for this I am most grateful to its Director Dr. Edwin Clarke and his staff. The Wellcome Trust has provided support for Dr. Nixon and for working expenses. Finally I owe a great debt to Raye and Kate Young for their encouragement and help throughout the preparation of the lectures and of the book, and to Raye for drawing Figure 20.8. The Oxford University Press has, as usual, provided continual help and advice.

J.Z.Y.

*London*
*February 1978*

# Contents

. . . a good environment is not a luxury,
it is a necessity.'
*Richard Wollheim, 1978*

# 1 What's in a brain?

## *What can be learned from brains?*

Most people if asked to describe their brains would be puzzled how to begin. We all know at least something about our hearts, stomachs, and kidneys, but even at school we learn little about brains. Everyone can recognize a brain on the butcher's slab or in a museum jar, but what is the connection between such stuff and that person we admire because 'he has a good brain'? Even the most able physiologist has no real answer to the question. He can tell us a lot about nerve cells and nerve fibres, the messages that they carry, and the reflexes they produce, but there is no generally satisfactory way of describing the operations of whole masses of nervous tissue. The theme of this book is that a good method may be to say that brains contain programs that regulate our lives.

A great deal has been found out about brains in recent years and we can use this new knowledge to make useful statements about many puzzling aspects of human life. No one will doubt that information about the brain is valuable, for example in cases of nervous disease and perhaps in much illness that is called mental. But how far can such knowledge help with normal daily life? I hope to show that it can give new views of the problems raised by our habits and appetites, our work and play, our loves and hates —in fact with a good part of all our life as adults. It can guide us in planning the education of children, and sometimes help to make wise decisions about social and political problems, for instance about questions of population and race.

If we can learn something from neuroscience about these matters, is it possible that knowledge of the brain can go still further and help with the study of philosophy and the theory of knowledge, aesthetic appreciation, moral judgement, conscience, ethics, and religion? This question has obviously been in the thoughts of philosophers, though some of them indignantly reject any such idea. Indeed when one has pursued the enquiry only a short way the most serious difficulties appear. We have first to decide what is 'knowledge of the brain', then what it is we want to know about these other subjects and how we propose to relate the two sets of knowledge. As soon as we begin to ask the questions we find that we have to investigate the very study with which we hope to answer them. This is a circular course indeed, and it is typical of the problem that will present itself over and over again. How are we to define the procedure by which to study human procedures? How can man study himself? Can the brain be said to study the brain? These are very fundamental problems. If all speech is influenced by the particular social system of the speaker can there be any metasociety, standing outside all the others? Can there be a metalanguage with which to describe languages? Is there an escape from what has been called 'the prison house of language'? (Jameson 1972). The biologist may be able to help even with such very difficult problems of the nature and limits of knowledge (epistemology).

## The language of the brain

The key we shall try to use to unlock the prison door is to say that a brain contains knowledge and information, written in its own language. This is actually a very complicated statement. We may all think that we know what is meant by 'information', but it is really a very subtle concept, not easy to analyse. The word is of course borrowed from ordinary speech, but we shall try to give it a more precise meaning that will allow us to say that all life depends on a flow of information. Information is carried by physical entities, such as books or sound waves or brains, but it is not itself material. Information in a living system is a feature of the order and arrangement of its parts, which arrangement provides the signs that constitute a 'code' or 'language' (Chapter 7). The essential feature is that when the signs of the code are transmitted along suitable channels they provide the control that helps to *maintain the order that is the essence of life* (Chapter 3). So the concepts of signs and information, and of coding and language, are closely related to the nature of life itself, and like life they are not simple at all. We shall return several times to discuss them (Chapters 3, 7, and 15).

For the present we can work with the idea that to understand a strange language means to be able to translate the sounds heard or the words written into one's own language (although 'translation' is not at all a simple concept either, see Steiner 1975). So to understand the language of the brain we must learn to recognize and interpret the elements of the script and the meanings of the signs in which it is written. Neuroscience is beginning to do this. In this book I hope to show how the organization of the brain can be considered as the written script of the programs of our lives. So the important feature of brains is not the material that they are made of but the information that they carry.

What neuroscience can do is to translate the language in which the brain programs are written into ordinary language. Since these are the programs that produce the phenomena of human language we are not really escaping from our prison, but are as it were enlarging it. We are using the analogies of language and of writing to understand the entities that produce them. As so often in the past, man, having invented an artefact (in this case writing) to help him with his life (by carrying information), is now trying to describe himself in terms of his artefact.

However much wisdom we acquire, we shall remain limited human creatures. But I believe that such new knowledge of the brain of man enables us greatly to expand our understanding of fundamental problems. We can give new meaning to concepts such as value, choice and decision, and even provide some help with problems of the aims and ends of life that trouble many people. We hope to gain from the discussion the power to give richer, fuller use to such words. It may be that some of our deepest difficulties about the nature of mind, matter, and consciousness will turn out to be products of the very structure of the brain (Chapter 22).

These may seem excessive claims to make for results from study of the brain, which some people may think to be a subject that is pedestrian, material, complicated, and even faintly disgusting. I hope to be able to reverse this view and to show that study of the brain reveals outstandingly beautiful and intricate patterns, not only of matter but of information and of action, patterns whose significance we can still perceive only dimly.

## Do brains think?

As we come to know more it may even be that we shall arrive at an answer to the question 'how does the brain produce our sayings?' But is this a good or even proper question to ask? A philosopher may insist that 'sayings' are produced by 'people' or by 'minds'. Brains, he will say, are only the agents (in some way) of the production of speech: they do not 'make' language any more than does a record player. Do brains think? Some people would say it is a confusion of categories: 'Persons think' they might say and persons are not brains. I should be inclined to agree with these critics, but only in part and largely because of our current ignorance about brains. At present the word 'brain' means only a little more than a reference to a convoluted whitish mass of stuff. Is it possible to change all that and to give so full a meaning to the word 'brain' that it will no longer be a semantic mistake to say that brains think? My thesis is that we can already partly answer that question. By looking carefully at the brain we have learned to decipher something of its language.

We cannot tell in what direction future knowledge will carry us. But at least I hope you will agree to reject what we might call the 'keep off the grass' view of the place of science. Some people hold that those who study 'mere matter', such as brains, should leave the study of 'fundamentals' to experts who are concerned primarily with man and the 'humanities'. I shall firmly repudiate this view because it involves a false dichotomy of knowledge. Of course there are great advantages in specialisation, and nearly all cultures have their specialists and theoreticians. The biologist must greatly regret that he is ignorant about the history of human thought and anything he says on these general topics is bound to be weakened by this lack. He will also probably not be familiar with relevant recent philosophical techniques such as symbolic logic, let alone know much relevant mathematics. He probably knows little of the work of those who specifically study man—anthropologists and sociologists.

For these and other reasons biological study cannot possibly replace others, it must remain conscious of its weakness as well as its strength. For example, biology can show some of the prerequisites for the development of human culture, but is quite unfitted to follow the full richness of its development. The idea of a sort of take-over bid by science is as dangerous and distasteful as is the opposite, the rejection of the use of scientific knowledge to help to answer fundamental questions because that would involve a 'naturalistic fallacy' (Moore 1903). Knowledge is obtained in many ways and knowledge about man is in many ways different from knowledge about any other subject. But to reject scientific facts impoverishes discussion, even of the most abstract problems. The question of the proper place of different types of knowledge continues to be disputed. But surely we have advanced from the position that man and his cultures are as it were 'outside nature' (p. 133). As we learn to recognize the weaknesses of our language we can at least question the claims that any of its categories are final and absolute.

What we have to try to do is to create new signs and symbols, which will carry meanings and evoke responses that are more satisfactory than those we use at present. We are all uneasy over some of the great questions such as the relations of mind and body or the meaning of our existence. I think that scientific facts, properly told, can help towards removing this unease. We may even be able, by study of our nature, to discover the basis for this need for belief in meanings and certainties.

# 2  Programs of the brain

## How can the actions of the brain be described?

The idea is, then, to use the facts recently discovered about the brain to develop ways of speaking and thinking that will help with our ordinary lives. To do this we need some system by which to organize the great mass of information that has been collected from experiments and observations on brains and nerve cells. We have to put together the work of anatomists who study pathways in the brain, physiologists who record its electrical responses, and biochemists who investigate its endless chemical activities. Clinical neurologists and neurosurgeons tell us much about it in health and disease and psychologists of various sorts assess the performances of men and animals under different conditions. The list of those whose work is involved in the study of the brain is indeed long and confusing. What do all these people do? The very number of disciplines involved makes the organization of brain research difficult, and few are ready even to give a name to the whole study. 'Neuroscience' is perhaps the most general label and is becoming widely used. We are not concerned with these difficulties of organization and nomenclature but with the problem of how to unite the mass of facts about the brain into a form that is easily understood. Neuroscientists themselves have been rather slow in devising ways of organizing the knowledge already gained about how the numerous neurons and chemical processes combine when we act as we do. How do the cells work together in the production of language, or when we become loving or aggressive, when we agree or disagree? Still less is all this knowledge so arranged as to tell us what goes on within us while we appreciate beauty of form or sound, or ourselves create a useful new machine or a work of art. Nevertheless all these things, and much more, come *through* the brain, even if we still hesitate to say that they come *from* it. Certainly we should not decry such a wonderful bearer of good things by labelling it 'merely material'. In any case if such words as 'merely material' have any meaning they cannot be applied to the brain, as we shall shortly find out.

## What form can an understanding of the brain take?

If the essential feature of the brain is that it contains information then the task is to learn to translate the language that it uses. But of course this is not the method that is generally used in the attempt to 'understand the brain'. Physiologists do not go around saying that they are trying to translate brain language. They would rather think that they are trying to understand it in the 'ordinary scientific terms of physics and chemistry'.

Biophysics and biochemistry have indeed shown us an immense amount of detail about the messages that pass along nerves and the chemicals that they secrete. All this information is of the greatest value, for example in medicine and for the development of drugs and the treatment of nervous diseases. But it is inconceivable that we should be able to describe how the brain operates by giving all the details of how these processes go on while we lead our daily lives. There are at least 50 thousand million cells in the brain, and each of these has many parts and connections. How could we follow the messages along all or even many of these pathways? Millions are acting together for each second as I write.

It may be answered 'well then, let us use statistics in treating them, as we do for, say, the molecules in a gas. Let us describe the aggregate of their behaviour'. This is indeed what we shall have to do, but the difficulty is that the nerve cells are *not all alike*. Their very differences constitute the coding system by which the brain processes information (p. 44). We shall meet this multichannel problem over and over again, it is the secret of the nervous system and differentiates it from all our communication artefacts such as the telephone or television, or from computers.

## The enchanted loom

We must, therefore, seek for ways to describe the joint operations of many differing nerve cells. There have been many such attempts. The father of neuroscience, Sir Charles Sherrington, in his Gifford Lectures of 1937, spoke of an 'enchanted loom' with lights that flashed as messages weaved around the brain. The image has proved appealing to physiologists, but is perhaps not really very revealing of the interacting activities of millions of communication channels (1940). It illustrates that we may have to be ready to use comparisons that are evocative, even poetic. Sherrington was indeed a man of vivid imagination and published a volume of poetry called *The assaying of Brabantius* (1925). In my Reith Lectures of 1950 I used the comparison of the brain with ten thousand million bureaucrats telephoning each other about the plans and instructions for keeping a country's affairs going (Young 1951). The image is not attractive, but at least it suggests the concept of operations planned and conducted with a purpose, just as the brain plans actions to keep the body alive.

Pictures of this sort are much too general and vague to have any real explicative value. However, it is unwise to denigrate the use of simple models. Think only what a revolution was begun when Johannes Kepler

said that the universe is not like a person but like a clock! Descartes'
comparison of the operations of the brain with those of automata worked
by hydraulics embodied at least something of the right principle.

## Systems theories

With the advent of computers to assist our brains, and theory to go with
them, many mathematical models have been produced that are much more
precise. Indeed most of them are so precise that they do not come anywhere
near to describing the *variety* of operations of the brain, which is its outstanding characteristic. Engineers who deal with the automatic systems that
are used to control sophisticated factories have devised 'systems theories',
which show how variables in each of the many parts of a complicated set of
machines affect all the others, and the whole operation. These methods have
obvious applications to description of the varied parts of living things
(Arbib 1972). For instance all the changes that influence the flow of blood
around the different organs of the body have been modelled in a system of
some three hundred 'boxes'. Systems theories such as these may well prove
very useful for neuroscience and these elaborate models will probably
gradually come into more general use as we become more numerate and less
literate. Fortunately or unfortunately none of them is yet either complete
enough or familiar enough to serve our present purpose. We want to be able
to talk about how recent knowledge of the actions of all these millions of
cells in the brain can help our daily lives.

## Programs

For this purpose I suggest the humble analogy of a *program*, and I propose
to say that the lives of human beings and other animals are governed by sets
of programs written in their genes and brains. Some of these programs may
be called 'practical' or physiological and they ensure that we breathe, eat,
drink, and sleep. Others are social, and regulate our speaking and other
forms of communication, our agreeing, and our loving or hating. We also
have long term programs, those that ensure continuing not of ourselves
but of the race, programs for sexual activity and mating, programs for
growth, adolescence, and, indeed, for senescence and dying. Perhaps the
most important programs of all are those used for the activities that we call
mental, such as thinking, imagining, dreaming, believing, and worshipping.
We may properly say that there are programs also for these if we agree that
our actions and thoughts all come through the brain, though this makes it
still more difficult to leave the question of whether they come *from* it. You
may ask whether I am saying that these brain programs think our thoughts.
I am indeed saying that, but only 'in a certain sense'. This is not meant to be

evasive. It is important to try to be clear about the relations of mind and brain, but this is not easy! I am proposing that if we look closely at what we wish to convey by using these two words *together* we shall come to a single view of human beings as persons. The brain operates in certain organized ways that may be described as programs, and the actions of these programs constitute the entity that we call the mind of a person.

The concept of a program may not seem very romantic or satisfactory for describing all of these wonderful things that we do. Indeed I am not very enamoured of it myself and do not want it to be thought of in the connotation of the glossy brochure one buys in a theatre. This sense of the word is a Victorian addition to the earlier use, meaning a plan decided beforehand to achieve some end. Indeed the spelling that I am using is the original seventeenth-century one and the form 'programme' is an affected nineteenth-century adoption from the French. I have in mind also the modern use of the word in 'computer program', although brain programs are only partly like the algorithms of computer software in which every step is logical (p. 41).

## The long history of our programs

The emphasis that I wish to adopt is that a program is a plan of action selected from a set arranged beforehand to meet particular types of situation, and written down in a notation or language. *Webster's Third New International Dictionary* defines a program as 'a plan of procedure; a schedule or system under which action may be taken towards a desired goal'. The concept is thus of a plan of action that is *chosen* from a set of possible plans and with specific objectives (see Mayr 1976). I want especially to emphasize the importance of selection of objectives and of the historical influence on everything that we do. Some of the influences on selection of plans are recent, depending on what has happened in the last few minutes, hours, or day. Other influences stretch back through selections made in the years of our life, in childhood, and in prenatal life and of the DNA of our genes by natural selection over countless generations.

And so backward through time we must trace the selective agencies that have composed the programs. The culture into which we are born is of course the product of 'history' in the sense that we use the word at school. The programs provided for us by the society in which we find ourselves are indeed major determinants of our lives, including religion, law, politics, art, ethics, and, above all, language. As a biologist I am not really suited to discuss these in detail, but it is evident that all of them, like the rest of our life, depend not only on the proper functioning of our 'lower' organs, say the heart, but on the specific features of our brains and glands that enable us to learn and to respond in these human ways (Chapter 8). There is evidence that the human brain is programmed to allow communication by language (Chapter 6), and also for much social behaviour. Because of our brain organization we are able to love and to hate, to command and to obey, to create beautiful things and to enjoy them, and also to believe and to worship.

The programs in man are largely written by a process of learning. We shall have therefore to examine particularly what is known of the mechanisms of memory and whether it has specific facilities and limitations in man (Chapter 10). The symbolism of nearly all our culture is enshrined in language, which certainly comes through the brain, by the benefit of certain inherited capacities for learning (p. 78). Similarly with our emotions and loves, hates and fears. There is no doubt that like our pre-human ancestors we have parts of the brain that serve to produce these (p. 140). To understand the various contributions to the programs of our lives we must look at the selective influences that have been at work, both recently and back to the very origin of life. Selection has brought our ancestors from the pre-biotic soup first into single cells (Chapter 5), then through many stages to fishes, newts, reptiles, early shrew-like mammals and on to monkeys, apes, and early men. All these stages still have their influences, even if faint, in determining the programs of what men can do. Of course anyone today may feel that the effect of the fact that his ancestors were newts is indeed faint compared to the facts that his father was a dustman or a duke, or that there is now a world economic depression. But the oldest influences are in some ways the most potent of all. The strongest motive for each of us from day to day is the urge to live. That urge must be the result of the events that first brought life into being. There would be no language, no culture, no signs or symbols, or world crises, if men and women were not driven on by the basic needs of life. To study how these needs arose and how they operate today should surely help us to see our place in a wider framework.

## The languages of life

Our conception is then that we can say that life is guided by programs and that programs are written in languages. The neuroscientist will therefore ask what is this language that he is expected to find in the brain? The question of the nature of language is a fundamental problem that underlies all discussions of knowledge, whether scientific or philosophical. Languages consist of sets of signs and there are those who believe that the study of signs, semiotics, is close to the centre of any theory of knowledge (see Sebeok 1977). Indeed our thesis is that the faculty of communication pervades all of living. We are not simply using the 'analogy' of linguistics to explain life; on the contrary the enthusiast for semiotics will say that life consists of signs and that semiotics includes linguistics rather than the reverse. Charles Peirce (1839–1914) who originated the modern study of signs answered the question 'What is a man?' with 'Man is a symbol'. (*Collected works* 1931–5).

This may sound mysterious, even nonsensical, but it contains a very important truth that can be stated quite clearly. The essence of a living thing is that it is organized and acts to maintain its organization (Chapter 3). It can only do this because it receives from its past history the plan or, as we shall say, *program*, of what to do to keep alive.

The information in this program must have a physical embodiment as a system of signs. To produce the right actions these signs must in some way correspond to the environment, they are symbolic representations of what goes on around (p. 60). The essence of each type of living thing therefore persists as a system of signs. Our general definition of a language is thus that it is a system of relations of parts constituting the signs that organize the actions necessary for the self-maintenance of a living system (see also Chapter 7).

Each individual mammalian life follows a program written in two main languages (or four in man) embodied in distinct media.

1. The fundamental program is inherited, written in the triplets of bases of the DNA code. This is transcribed and translated during development and throughout life to produce the living individual, able to react appropriately with the world.

2. The second language in a mammal is embodied in the structure of the brain. Its units are the groups of nerve cells, so organized as to produce the various actions at the right times. Our task throughout this book is to learn to understand this language. We shall not have much difficulty with the simpler parts, those that deal with say sleeping or breathing or eating. But we can only state in outline how the brain carries the information that allows men to see or to talk, or to think.

3. Speech and culture represent the third level of the human life program, largely embodied in the organized sounds of spoken language. This is, of course, the sort of program that is most obvious and which is most familiar. Linguists, anthropologists, and sociologists all describe the forms and structures of the systems of language and society that regulate human lives. Our purpose in this book is in a sense to try to discover what relationship there may be between knowledge of these linguistic and cultural programs and knowledge of the brain.

4. These programs find their physical expressions and codes not only in human habits and speech sounds but also in writing and other forms of *recorded* speech. These provide a fourth level of coding, also peculiar to man, enabling some of the information for living to be recorded outside of any living creature.

The proposal is to use the analogy of the encoding of information by writing to speak about the way in which the brain contains the scripts of the programs that issue in human action. This is not merely to use a picturesque metaphor. Discoveries made by physiologists in recent years show the detailed characteristics of the cells in the brain that provide the code signs for features of the world, such as a particular line or sound, or the colour red (Chapters 12 and 16).

## The origin of codes

One of the fundamental questions about any code is how its signs have come to have their meanings. Linguists are agreed that with a few exceptions words are arbitrary signs, there is nothing 'lion-like' about the word lion. The Morse code has been specifically designed so that the more frequently occurring letters have the shorter signs. Some linguists wish to distinguish between 'signs', which are purely arbitrary, and 'symbols' which indicate some of the properties of that which they designate, though the distinction is drawn differently by various workers (Chapters 8 and 20).

How have the living codes arisen? There have been suggestions that the DNA code is not wholly arbitrary; some of its triplets may have special chemical relationships with the amino-acids that they represent (Crick 1968). The nerve cells that detect horizontal and vertical contours in an octopus are themselves orientated in these directions (Young 1960). But there is little information about how the main patterns of organization of the brain have arisen. It is a fascinating subject for enquiry and an important clue is that the nerve cells that analyse the information of the senses are laid out on the brain to make actual physical maps of the surface of the body or the retina (Chapters 11 and 12). What goes on in the brain must provide a faithful representation of events outside, and the arrangement of the cells in it provides a detailed model of the world. But the function of this model is to provide actions suitable for survival, so this topographically organized representation somehow provides a set of hypotheses about what is likely to happen, and of programs for dealing with these events. The task is to show how the brain cells provide the code in which these hypotheses and programs are written.

This, put very briefly, is the case for considering the theory of signs as the basis for all knowledge. We need some way to talk about the factors that organize our lives. They are a most intricate set of plans and arrangements, programs, which have been constructed from influences, some recent, some from long, long ago. Throughout the book we shall try to discover something more about where these influences come from, and how they guide our lives from day to day.

# 3 Living and choosing

## Selecting what to do

The thesis will be that the human activities of choosing are a special case of procedures that are fundamental to all living processes. Living involves using whatever information is available to make choices between alternatives, with the aim of achieving the goal of the continuation of life. Every organism carries in its DNA the 'instructions' for doing this by dealing with various eventualities that may arise. Each individual and indeed each separate cell must make choices from moment to moment of those operations that are required to meet the particular situation. Study of the principles that are involved in this sequence of selections shows how human conscious choosing is a special development of this general property of living things.

The core of this thesis is that living organisms depend upon an organization or 'structure' that regulates all their operations. This is often called a system of 'instructions' or 'information', inherited from the past, and we shall discuss how to interpret these ideas. Similarly all human life depends upon the information that is used for the continual sequence of choices that are made as we conduct the elaborate system of relations needed in society. In all cultures from the most primitive to the most sophisticated people are continually faced with situations where they must choose; what to do, what to say, what to ask for, what to buy, what to give, and so on. Of course their choices depend upon all sorts of individual and temporary needs, preferences, and cultural influences. But it may be that all of these are subordinate to a fundamental method of acting that is embodied in the programs of the brain, inherited and learned.

Structuralist anthropologists believe that they can recognize some such deeper system, which has been defined as 'the unconscious superstructure, value system or systems of representation which orders social life at any of its levels and against which the conscious social acts and events take place and become comprehensible' (Lévi-Strauss 1963). The whole gamut of social interaction is interpreted in terms of such a structure, with a particular dialectic formula in which each act is related to its opposite. The structuralist system is considered by some other anthropologists to be far-fetched and even to be based partly on faulty ethnographic data. For us it suggests the possibility that human activities are governed by a basic brain organization that depends upon making certain types of selection from the possible sets of actions. The model draws strongly on the analogy of language. In selecting the items of social intercourse, whether it be wives, money, food, or clothes, the individual, for the structuralist, is using 'words' to communicate with his fellows. In making his selections he is constrained by a grammar, just as he is in speech.

For the biologist the analogy can be drawn much wider (if analogy is the word). He can see these selections as strictly comparable to those that have been made in living processes throughout their entire history. Life continues because organisms make repeated choices among previously established sets of possible alternative actions. A rabbit must choose whether to go out and feed or stay at home. As it runs out or back the brain must make the lungs and heart work at just the right rates. And as the food goes down, the stomach must secrete the appropriate digestive juices, and so on. In each case a choice is made from the possible levels of each activity. The very essence of living is the presence of varied possibilities of action, allowing selection or choice of those that ensure that the organism remains alive. Before we deal with the objection that the word 'choice' should be used only of conscious processes and creatures, we must examine more closely this biological choosing. It is curious that understanding of this apparently theoretical, almost literary, question has been expanded enormously as a result of the analysis of DNA by *physical* science, as applied by molecular biologists. Using essentially the methods of physics and chemistry they have shown the fundamental basis of information transfer and so the way to a wider interpretation of our own life and daily choices. They have given new evidence on the old questions of what is life and how did it begin. With this knowledge of the physical basis of the inheritance of information we can now understand much better how to interpret the mysterious properties of living things and their relation to human capacities for free individual choice.

## Vitalism

Biologists no longer believe that living depends upon some special non-physical agency or spirit. The concept that it does so is a relic of the strong tendency to describe phenomena in terms appropriate to persons. I propose to argue that there is indeed an inherited tendency for the brain to work like this (p. 31). Children and people in unsophisticated cultures usually speak of all natural events as 'caused by' some conscious agent or person (Piaget 1971). Obviously the fact that such animistic interpretations are made by humans is no guarantee that they are true. But perhaps if we are honest we shall all admit that we find it difficult not to use them when thinking of 'ultimate' causes, if we do so at all. Can we really pretend to think about the originator of the universe except in personal terms? We shall return to this question later (Chapter 5). However, in thinking about the nature of life, biologists in this century have not paid much attention to vitalists such as Bergson (1907) who postulated an *élan vitale*, or Driesch (1927) with his mysterious force of 'entelechy'. It is curious that philosophers on the other hand have spent much time discussing Bergson, who is especially admired in his native France. This difference in evaluation is a good example of the difficulties in reaching agreement between disciplines and cultures. Are the biologists right to neglect Bergson, or is it, as the philosophers and the French might say, that any explanation without an *élan* is incomplete?

Prominent vitalists today are mostly physicists, such as Polanyi (see Polanyi and Prosch 1975) and Elsasser (1975), who are professionally disturbed at the 'extraordinary' behaviour of living things. Elsasser believes that this can only be explained by the addition to ordinary physics of what he calls 'biotonic laws'. If there are such influences operating for life in general then they may indeed well act within the brain and our search for programs will surely meet them (see Popper and Eccles 1977). For this reason alone it is important to examine how the more orthodox biologist explains the 'unusual' behaviour of living matter.

Much the most influential form of vitalism today is, paradoxically, dialectical materialism, as developed by Marx and Engels following Hegel. This holds that the fundamental law of all action is a dialectic of opposites. Mind is the only permanent and authentic reality and it reflects life. Thought, it is alleged, proceeds by antitheses and these reflect the dialectic of matter and life. Such wordy generalizations will seem to the scientist so wide as to lack real content, and as applied to biology by Engels they are frankly ridiculous. He puts it like this: when a grain of barley develops it is negated and the plant arises and produces the flower, which in its turn is negated when it makes the seed. Such a simple doctrine of opposites seems wholly vacuous to a western biologist, and has presumably been abandoned by intelligent Marxists.

## Choosing the living materials

These 'idealist' analyses (if that is the word for vitalism) stand in sharp contrast to the biology that has been based upon physical science. The beginning of this is traditionally dated from the discovery by Friedrich Wöhler in 1828 that the organic compound urea could be made from inorganic constituents. The result of showing that living things are composed of the same constituents as the rest of the earth has been to revolutionize biology and medical science, producing both the population explosion and the revolution in agricultural science by which it has been contained (so far). We are not now concerned with whether this revolution has been a good or bad thing, but to see whether it allows us to give a satisfactory description of life and especially of human life.

When I was young we were taught a song:

> Nor you nor I nor nobody knows
> How oats and beans and barley grows.

It is hardly an exaggeration to say that now we *do* know. Using the language of physics rather than that of Engels we can describe nearly all living phenomena in the same terms as non-living. The qualification 'nearly' is important as we shall see in discussing origins (Chapter 5). We know of course that living things contain no special elements but are made out of some 16 of the 92 elements that occur naturally on earth. The fact that not all elements are used by living things introduces us at once to the concepts of 'selection' and 'choice'. Not only are these elements a very special set but they are combined together to make molecules more complicated than any others known in the universe. This does indeed point to life as 'peculiar' or 'extra-ordinary', and no wonder that physicists become vitalists.

## The steady state of life, homeostasis

But we have to face even odder features of life than this. These large molecules are organized into living organisms, which are not closed systems in equilibrium but in a steady state of continual interchange with their surroundings, maintained only by continual intake of fuel and expenditure of energy. The great extent of these interchanges has been recognized only since atomic physics made radioactive isotopes available for biological experiments. Thus there is a special form of carbon ($^{14}C$) not usually present in carbon compounds except in minute amounts, which has chemical properties identical to normal carbon ($^{12}C$) but can be readily identified by the radiation it emits. So you can make a lump of sugar with this $^{14}C$ and when it is eaten then follow it as it goes through the stomach and intestines, into the blood and from there perhaps to muscle where it acts as fuel and is 'burnt' when the muscle contracts. Before long it will be breathed out of the lungs as radioactive carbon dioxide, perhaps only an hour or two after it was eaten.

By similar methods it can be shown that in most parts of the body there is a quite rapid 'turnover'. The stuff of the cells does not remain the same for long but is broken down and eliminated, its place being taken by new molecules. And in many tissues the cells themselves live for only a few days and are then replaced. So living consists as it were of a continual death and re-birth. And yet as all these interchanges go on the integrity of the whole is preserved. This process of self-maintenance was called *homeostasis* by the American physiologist Walter B. Cannon in a book published in 1932 with the interesting title *The wisdom of the body*. Cannon was referring to the maintenance of the constancy of the blood in a mammal. For example if the level of sugar falls even slightly the brain cells cease to function and you faint. Similarly the oxygen, calcium, and many other constituents are kept constant, by elaborate controlling and regulating mechanisms. But homeostasis should not mean only constancy of the blood, it is the essential property of all life, which continues only because there are countless control systems at work. A man is continually expending energy to prevent the dissolution of his body, which would inexorably follow as it does in all non-living systems. What is it then that prevents this from happening? Surely, says the vitalist, there must be some special principle at work, a vital force that flies away when we die. Biology can nearly meet this challenge—not quite because we do not yet know for certain how life arose, nor can we make life without the assistance of previously living matter (Chapter 5).

## Teleology

Nevertheless we can now say that we understand how it comes about that organisms behave in this way as if all their actions were directed towards an aim or goal. It has been curiously unfashionable among biologists to call attention to this characteristic of living things. This has been largely because until recently it was not understood that organisms contain *standards* and that their actions are adjusted until each standard is met. In this sense the ends or aims are indeed the 'causes' of living actions. Another objection has been that the conception of 'teleology' has been associated with that of a final aim of life, implying metaphysical or religious beliefs. To avoid this, recent authors have used the word 'teleonomy' to describe the directional character of living activities (see Pittendrigh 1958; Mayr 1961, 1976; Monod 1972). But words of this sort confuse many people and one is enough, let us keep to 'teleology'. An excellent discussion of it is given by Wright (1976, and see also Taylor 1964). We shall deal later with the further question of whether teleological explanation unavoidably invokes conscious purpose.

The point is that living things *do* act in a directed way, whatever words we like to use to say so. They are able to continue to do this because they are not isolated systems, which would inevitably dissipate, but are influenced and regulated by the record, stored in their DNA, of an immense past sequence of events, some that occurred recently, some a very long time ago. Selections made throughout this long past continue to influence each one of us for each moment of our lives. Their results are embodied in the highly stable DNA molecules, which serve as the centre of a system that regulates all the tissues. They give us what we can only call instructions and information, providing standards indicating what to do (Phillips 1978).

The instructions of the genes provide, during embryonic development, the system of reference standards at which to aim. For example the cells of the hypothalamus ensure that the right amount of food and drink are taken and the right amount is incorporated to allow the body to grow to its proper size (Chapter 4). These hypothalamic centres, with other parts of the brain, provide standards throughout life. They stimulate the need for what is lacking, for instance of food, sex, or sleep, and they indicate satisfaction when enough has been obtained. The instructions of the DNA are basically responsible for setting these standards in the brain. But this of course is only part of their action, throughout life the genes continue to operate in every cell of the body, giving instructions to the cells as to how to select the right chemical action to meet the eventualities that are likely to cause the body to disintegrate.

The discovery of the structure and properties of these stable instruction-carrying molecules of DNA has shown how this information is embodied in an enormous long string that we describe as code words, provided by the sequences of three nucleotide bases. It is not possible here to describe the details of the system but important for us to have some understanding of its nature (see Young 1971). It is particularly necessary to analyse what is involved in the concept that any system carries 'information'. This is considered further in connection with the codes of the nervous system (Chapter 7). The properties embodied in these systems of organization of the living materials serve to provide representations of the environment, by which the organism can guide its decisions.

## Goals and standards

Objective study of living organisms shows clearly that they *do* indeed have targets and take actions that ensure survival. It is extraordinary that by many biologists 'the most distinctive feature of living systems was treated as unmentionable' (Sommerhoff 1974, p. 74). How many biologists can swear that they have never criticized an argument as 'teleological'? Botanists are particularly liable to do this, I suppose because obviously a plant can't tell us about its aims. This controversy brings out strongly the need to allow change and development in the use of words.

It has been argued that to say that survival is the aim or goal of organisms is tautologous, because, except in man, we do not know that choices are made 'with the goal in mind'. It is true that we cannot ask an animal about its goals. But we now find that every organism contains systems that literally embody set points or reference standards. The control mechanisms operate to ensure that action is directed to maintaining these standards (Chapter 13).

To say that all living things have the purpose and aim of survival is therefore not an *ex post facto* tautology. To quote Monod 'one of the fundamental characteristics common to all living beings without exception: [is] that of being *objects endowed with a purpose or project*' (1972, p. 20). Moreover every organism 'achieves it with efficiency rarely approached in man-made machines, by an apparatus entirely logical, wonderfully rational and perfectly adapted to its purpose, to preserve and reproduce the structural man.'

The discovery of these reference standards in the brain and indeed in all organisms gives an entirely new and unsuspected view of the whole question of aims and purposes in the life of men as well as of other creatures. The patterns of nerve cells of the hypothalamus of the brain are the physical embodiments of fundamental standards. The patterns of their actions are set originally during embryonic development, under the control of the inherited DNA. Throughout life they are basic parts of our choices, though often concealed. They influence our wants and desires, our satisfactions and revulsions, our longings, and our fears. Or course these are not the only or even the main influences. The standards that we try to use in human life include very many further subtleties derived from our cultures. We do not follow only the hypothalamus. But we shall have to enquire carefully how what are ordinarily called standards of conduct are related to the settings of these physical standards in the brain.

## Choosing

The nucleus of the fertilized egg contains the instructions needed to make all the different proteins of all the types of cell in the body. Of course only some of the instructions will be needed for each type of cell, some to make a liver cell, different ones for a nerve cell and so on. Embryologists are only just beginning to find out how in higher animals the selection of the right set for each of the various cell types is made. Already quite a good understanding has been reached about how simple organisms such as bacteria make selection from the much fewer possible courses of action with which they are endowed by heredity. We may therefore first follow the process of selection as it is conducted in bacteria.

Like every other living cell a bacterium is provided with a range of things that it can do. It can make different enzymes, which are the 'miracle-workers' that allow organisms to perform chemical changes that a chemist can only do at high temperatures. For instance enzymes make sugar 'burn' to give out energy without first heating it. The enzymes can do this because they are very long protein molecules, which fold up to form complicated masses of atoms. Among these folds are variously shaped pits and holes and into these cracks and crannies other substances are squeezed together and so forced to interact as they would if heated. By making a different enzyme when conditions change, bacteria can meet a new situation. The classic example of this is the bacterium *Escherichia coli*, which lives in our intestines. If a culture of these, living in glucose solution as its source of energy, is given a new sort of sugar, lactose, then within a few minutes the bacteria will begin to produce the enzyme called β-galactosidase, which was not there before but is necessary if this new sugar is to provide them with energy. In their normal life in our intestines they must be ready to change quickly to deal with whatever sort of sugar we send down to them. The bacteria are thus selecting or choosing just that one from the several enzymes that their DNA would allow them to produce.

Most of the steps involved in the choice are now understood and they provide a classic example of the sequence of events in any communication channel. The genes of the bacterium that are not being used are held suppressed. When the new sugar arrives it must first somehow be detected by some 'sensory' system at the surface of the cell. Then a signal is passed through the cell, a process of de-repression is set into action, and the special enzymes around the DNA begin to transcribe the new set of relevant sequences so that β-galactosidase is produced. What is important for us is to see that the whole cell is involved in a process of detection, communication, and then selection from a set of possible actions. This process is similar in principle to the vastly more complex acts of choice that we ourselves make. All choice depends upon selecting among a set of possible actions. We can do far more things than a bacterium, which is provided with DNA sequences that would allow the manufacture of enzymes suitable only for certain conditions. Their choice is not unlimited and has been determined in the past by natural selection, acting upon chance mutations.

## Progress in the evolution of choices

When we make 'choices' they involve selection from a vast set of possible actions, for example in speaking. The difference in scale is so great that the comparison of human choice with that of the bacterium may well seem ridiculous. But there is a complete set of intermediates between them and us. All life involves selection between alternative possibilities, and as evolution has proceeded creatures have acquired ever fresh ways of acting and so a greater range of choice of possibilities, thus enabling animals and plants to survive in an ever-widening range of habitats. This is one of the senses in which there has been a progress in evolution (contrary to what one often reads). The 'higher' organisms have become able to live in conditions that would have been impossible for their ancestors. To give one example, when animals and plants came to colonize the land they needed special devices to prevent loss of water and to obtain it. Every species depends upon thousands of such devices, especially if it lives in what we may call a 'difficult' environment, as was pointed out long ago (Young 1938). As organisms have become more complicated they have come to need a larger and larger variety of possible actions in order to avoid dissolution. This has meant that choice has become continually wider and more difficult and we could well say that this reaches its maximum in humans. They can live almost anywhere on Earth—or even outside it—if they choose well enough.

It will be objected that although human choice indeed involves selection it differs from these biological examples in that it is conscious. This is of course the great problem of the relation of mind and body. For the present we are seeking to show that biological language can be usefully applied even to the more specifically human attributes. We are looking now for similarities that can be revealing in spite of differences. To me it is significant that all organisms by virtue of their past history must make selections from sets of possible courses of action. I have come to realize the importance of this continual selection only in recent years and probably it is not widely appreciated. It seems to me that the parallel with human choice is quite close. If you like to say 'It is only a metaphor' I shall not quarrel over the words. Much of language depends upon metaphors, '. . . it is neither accident nor affliction that we use them so much' (Wright 1976, p. 13). We are enquiring whether it is useful to enlarge the language we use about ourselves by making comparisons with what other organisms do. 'Choice' implies an organized chooser, a set of alternatives, and an aim or objective, and all of these are present even in bacteria. The similarity is there, whether or not our consciousness alters its relevance. Of course we are not saying that by studying bacteria we can learn much about what decisions to take in human problems. The choices we are called upon to make are the ones peculiar to the human condition. The study of other organisms will only give us general ideas about our nature, just as the study of history of humans in the past will only give hints of what to do today. The point is that choosing between possibilities is the special endowment of all living things (perhaps a unique endowment) and specific mechanisms are provided for it. Life depends upon choice among various possibilities. All living things *must* choose. Human beings have a greater number of possibilities of action than any other creature and therefore the widest burden or privilege of choice. The quantitative difference is indeed so great as almost to suggest the use of a separate terminology for man, but the temptation to do this is just what we are trying to avoid, because emphasizing the differences obscures significant similarities.

## Determinism

This brings us face to face with the problem of determinism. Another objection to saying that bacteria choose is that the reactions by which they select what enzymes to make are chemical reactions and therefore fully 'determinate' and allowing no real choices such as humans make. It is true that the nature of the inducing substance (the lactose in our example) determines what shall be made. As Monod puts it, 'the exclusive *choice* of a substrate [is] determined by its steric structure' (1972). (Note that he uses the word choice, *choise* is the original French.) This statement seems to mean that the bacterial cell recognizes which sugar is present and sets up a chain of chemical reactions which can now be fully described. But is this really true? What one tends to forget is that describing the chemistry of DNA and its reactions does *not* completely describe the process. The bacterial cell can produce the appropriate enzyme, say β-galactosidase, only because it is endowed by its past history not only with DNA but with a very particular composition and organization. The cell must have receptors at the surface to detect the new sugar and a communication system to transmit the information to the DNA. Then there is an elaborate system of polymerase enzymes, which allow the selection of the new set of instructions and their 'transcription' and 'translation' to make a new enzyme. It is the presence of this elaborate *individual*, with a history, acting as a chooser with an 'aim', that makes the whole process so *unlike* all known chemical reactions except those of other living things. We must note specially that every individual must be assumed to have some differences from all others, both by the effects of its environment and heredity. How then can we be *sure* what it will do (p. 23)? We shall have to see later whether we can 'explain' how life arose and came to this present state, with such a store of information. For the moment we shall not be deterred from speaking of choice just because we can describe some of the final stages of the process in chemical detail. The problem is to find the best terms to describe the whole system.

The idea that scientific study shows that living things operate under a principle of compulsion implies that 'determinism' is a precise conception. In fact the very opposite is the case. As Austin says, he is '. . . inclined to think that determinism itself is still a name for nothing clear' (1956). A recent discussion of the problem in relation to ethics concludes 'The suggestion that either psychological or social theory . . . confronts us with a deterministic picture of human behaviour is a sheer myth' (Mackie 1977, p. 217). An opposite view is that 'it follows from these three premises, about states of the brain as effects, as correlates and as causes, that on every occasion when we decide or choose we can only decide or choose as in fact we do' (Honderich 1978). This certainly seems to be a subject where further discussion and clarification of ideas and terms are still needed.

Physicists of course have their own sort of indeterminism, in dealing with very small systems. Some people have supposed that this might be relevant to the question of the interaction of mind and body. For the present we are concerned with the determinacy of the chemical reactions in macroscopic systems such as whole bacteria or men. If there is a *principle* of determinacy it presumably states something like 'given stated initial conditions a particular chemical reaction will always follow a particular course'. A principle of this sort may be defined as 'a highly general or inclusive law . . . exemplified in a multitude of cases' (*O.E.D.*). Any principle of determinacy therefore must depend upon a long series of experiments and observations with systems sufficiently simplified *so that their initial conditions are fully known*. But the essential features of each living organism is its *history*, and this is at best partly unknown, moreover each animal consists of a great number of parts, all different and all changing rapidly. This past history, variation, and rapid change are the very factors that make the continuation of life possible, but they equally make it impossible to fulfil the conditions needed to establish a principle of determinacy (see Mayr 1976). No two organisms are exactly alike and even the parts within them are mostly different. Thus any two mitochondria or other cellular component will have minor differences. There are no known methods by which the behaviour of such a complex system with a long history can be *precisely* described or forecasted. To say that we could do so 'in principle' is most unscientific and misleading. There can be no 'multitude of cases' in which such systems have been studied, and no such principle has been experimentally established in any complex creatures.

Under these conditions it is impossible to find sufficiently large sets or runs of similar circumstances to establish the 'principle' of determinism. This does not mean that we are wholly ignorant or unable to make any forecasts about the future. Of course we can forecast *statistically* the limits within which a group of living things have been found to behave, whether they are mitchondria or Moslems. What we cannot do is to extrapolate from this to assert that we understand the meaning of any *principle* of determinism as applied to living things. 'Principles', such as those of chemistry, apply to classes that are relatively homogeneous, say acids and bases. Of course it can be argued that even there we are using statistics of large samples of molecules. If the reaction of an acid with a piece of chalk can only be forecast statistically, why do we not assert that there is an element in it of 'choice'? What, if anything, is the specific sort of indeterminacy found in living things? It is surely that the variation which makes precise forecasting of living reactions impossible is inherent in the making of choices that is the condition of living. There is nothing peculiar about the individual chemical components of a living system but no two organisms contain precisely the same set of them. Every creature begins with an endowment of varied possible actions. We can never be sure what these are because they are continually subject to mutation so the genetic make-up of an organism cannot be known with the same 'certainty' as the composition of a chemical substance. Even more serious is the difficulty that each individual experiences a different sequence of events during its life and reacts appropriately to these. There is therefore no set of identical creatures about which predictions can be made. 'The problem of preparing two electrons in precisely the same state is exactly the same problem confronting the biologist of breeding two ducks with the same hereditary characteristics' (Thom 1975, p. 16). Living organisms are able to continue only because they are subject to this variation and adaptation. If they are relatively simple and very numerous, such as bacteria, we can of course forecast their behaviour statistically with some accuracy. But their variation and the capacity to choose and so to change is essential for their continuity. From minute to minute they change their operations to keep themselves on the target, which is to maintain the constancy of their internal environment.

## Free will

The conclusion of this discussion is that the conception of 'causation' and hence of determinism is not absolute but relative to the degree of detail that is known about the behaviour of a system. Seeking for causes is an empirical, practical matter and we can establish them with various degrees of probability. In this sense we can establish the 'causes' of the actions of bacteria with some accuracy but human beings are vastly more variable. The causes of the actions of a given man will include not only all the genetic variables and the choices made in his past but also all those operations of the brain that go on as he exercises the special human capacities of choice between many alternatives, which we ordinarily call his free will. We can make some forecasts about these operations but the very fact that we call them 'free' indicates that too many factors enter for the forecast to be precise. Neither he himself nor anyone else can foresee exactly what the results of his brain actions will be.

## Conclusion

We may incorporate what this chapter has shown in a series of statements.

1. Living organisms contain a selected set of all the chemical elements present in other material systems.
2. These elements are organized in a way that is not only unusual but unique so far as we know. The class 'living organisms' is a set of one.
3. In particular they act so as continually to change the matter they contain (the process of turnover) but yet maintain their organization. They thus act with an aim or end, they show homeostasis (teleology or teleonomy).

4. They can do this because they are not closed systems but carry a system of *instructions* inherited from the past.
5. This enables them to select among possible sets of actions. This we compare with our human faculty of choice.
6. Selection goes on continually in every living cell in a manner that is very complicated and defies precise prediction by any means yet known. Statistical forecasts of behaviour are possible, but there is no sense in saying that organisms are in principle determinant.

# 4  Growing, repairing, and ageing

## The human life cycle

The human way of life is essentially social. To get the things needed to keep alive we cooperate with other people. This requires special programs of the brain and the whole pattern of human lives is organized around social activities. The sequence of human development, early helplessness, long childhood, late adolescence, and long adult life, is designed to allow the brain to develop and to acquire and use a set of programs for the skills of a social life. In the earlier stages of a baby's existence it is so totally dependent on hereditary instructions that it seems obvious to refer to it as pre-grammed. The instructions as to how to remain alive come from its DNA and there is nothing much the baby can do about it. The great question is when and how far does this situation change? It has been conventional for many people to regard the newborn child as a blank sheet, a *tabula rasa*, upon which anything can be written. This view is often associated with John Locke and the empiricist tradition, in contrast to so-called rationalists such as Leibniz and Descartes and many others, who have emphasized in effect the *restrictions* that are imposed by intrinsic features of human nature (see Hacking 1975). This is obviously a question to which the biologist can contribute a great deal, indeed it is largely a question of fact. He will not wish, however, to distinguish too sharply between the parts of the program that unfold before and after the crisis of birth. It is true that from its earliest days the child begins to learn in a way it could not do in the womb, but it is able to do so only by virtue of the neural equipment with which it is provided by heredity (see Szentágothai and Arbib 1974). And this equipment is not a static machine, provided complete and finally at birth. It is true that in man the full number of nerve cells is already laid down at that time. But they are far from their final form, either in structure or function. Each of them has the capacity to develop in a certain general direction, but with a wide margin of possibilities, *which are determined by experience*. Without suitable experience many of the nerve cells will not develop at all but will fade away and disappear. The capabilities of many parts of the nervous system continue to change and mature for many years after birth and at each stage suitable inputs are required for this maturation.

## Critical periods of development

These critical periods have been investigated in detail recently by Hubel and Wiesel (1977) at Harvard and Blakemore and Cooper (1970) in Cambridge, England. In order to be sure that they were dealing with *inborn* characteristics Hubel and Wiesel delivered baby monkeys by Caesarian operation. They found cells in the brain that responded in nearly all essential ways like those of adults (see p. 50). The English workers found the same in kittens who had not yet opened their eyes. The cells respond typically to characteristic features such as orientated contours, though they differ from those of adults in being more likely to stop responding on successive trials. Furthermore Hubel and Wiesel found, also in kittens, that there are *critical* periods at which deprivation of vision (by an eye shade) will prevent the cells achieving their final state. There is a period of 4–6 weeks after birth when exposure for only a few hours to lines of one orientation results in a brain in which there are only cells sensitive to that direction, the others having all disappeared.

So the genetic programs of intrauterine development become the genetic programs for the acquisition of information and can then interact with the environmental and cultural situations that the individual meets. The result produces what we shall call the programs of the model in the brain that guide adult behaviour.

## Learning by selection

The evidence that many detailed features are already present at birth agrees with the conception that learning consists largely of *selection* among the many possible pathways in the brain (Young 1974). Many biological processes, from evolution to immunization, have been found to depend upon such selection among sets, rather than by shaping by *instruction*. This is indeed the difference between Darwinian and Lamarckian interpretations of evolution. Our traditional methods of education seem to depend so much on instruction that many people find it hard to understand how selection could have produced all the wonders of living form. Similarly it may be difficult to believe that the acquisition of the wonderful powers of our brains, such as language, depend upon selection of certain pathways at critical times and the loss of others. It is not possible yet to be sure how far this is true. Probably both processes operate, unwanted pathways are suppressed and wanted ones are improved by use. We probably learn both by selection *and* instruction (Chapter 10).

The task is therefore to disentangle these processes of nature and nurture, so as to help towards providing the best inputs at each stage. The subject is a very old one, but has been advanced greatly in recent decades by the work both of physiologists and anatomists studying the function and structure of the brain, mainly of animals, and of psychologists investigating human and animal behaviour. With these various sources of evidence we begin to be able to recognize a series of critical or sensitive periods in development, at each of which, with appropriate input, the brain develops certain of the features that are characteristic of the species. The evidence is of course easiest to come by for the earlier stages, but it may well be that the emergence of new potentialities, requiring new stimuli, continues far on into life. The question of whether it continues even to our final decades leads us to look now at the whole span of life and hence at the problem of its duration and so of senescence. If we are to understand how the child acquires programs we must know for how long they are to be expected to act. Is their acquisition part of a major program that decrees that life shall cease after a certain time and how has this limitation been determined?

## What determines senescence?

It has been pointed out by Medawar (1952) and Williams (1957) that effects of genes appear at different times. Some, as we have seen, appear early and influence the whole lifetime and power of survival of the individual. Other genetic factors manifest their effects only later in life and are, therefore, subject to a correspondingly weakened influence of natural selection (Medawar and Medawar 1977). This is interpreted to mean that genes manifesting lethal or unfavourable effects later in life will not be removed from the population, because individuals carrying them will have reproduced before they appear. This would mean that we become decrepit because of the effects of this 'genetic dustbin'. But is the converse also true? Could genes appearing late be selected if they *benefit* relatives or the whole population? There is considerable doubt among geneticists as to the circumstances that allow for selection to act upon a whole population rather than on individuals (Chapter 19). So it is not certain whether groups that benefit from the advice of elderly sages will have a selective advantage, perhaps only if it is given to relatives. Commonsense as well as one's ageing preference suggests the hope that they may do so. However others feel compelled to believe that the failure to select against later appearing *defects* must lead inevitably to senescence (see Williams 1957). But if this pessimistic view is the whole story how does it come about that animals have characteristic lengths of life—differing by nearly 100 times even among mammals? One year for mice and a hundred for humans.

## The human life span

This does rather suggest that some later appearing genes may have proved advantageous in the species with longer lives. In any case it can hardly be that senescence is simply a running out of life's program, nor is it a failure of this program to provide the repairs necessary for a longer span. It has recently been shown that even the cells in tissue culture have a capacity for division that is approximately proportional to the length of life of the species. Cells from older animals or men are capable of fewer divisions than those from younger ones. This proves that senescence is itself a programmed terminus. Death is a part of the program of life. And this should not be considered an absurd, paradoxical, or pessimistic view. We are all familiar with programmed death for other organisms—from annual plants to mayflies. We know that it is appropriate for them to die at the right time. Moreover death of cells occurs abundantly during normal child development especially in the brain. Further, death occurs at each moment in each one of us throughout life, thousands of blood cells and cells of the intestine die every second. Indeed the turnover by which matter passes continually in and out of the body is a kind of continual birth and death. The question is therefore not why should life discontinue but how long can it best continue in order to promote a given type of life—whether it be as part of the intestine of a man or the whole of his life, or the life of a leaf or of a mayfly.

So if there is a genetically determined life-span for each cell or each species how are we to interpret our own life history? There is no doubt that the human pattern of a long non-reproductive childhood is genetically determined. Other mammals become sexually mature immediately they have stopped growing. Only in man and apes is there a long period of immaturity, followed by a rapid pre-adolescent growth spurt, greater in the males. This childhood is obviously correlated with the presence of a large brain, well able to learn. In apes the pattern is presumed to be correlated with the social and sexual system, the growth at adolescence serving to give the adults their dominant position. It seems likely that extension of the period of childhood in man is related to the acquisition of social skills, which will only be learned if the child is submissive to his elders. Probably specially sensitive or critical periods of learning therefore continue to become manifest under genetical control at least until puberty, which is a phase that certainly appears through an inherited hormonal program.

Given this understanding of childhood what are we to make of the problem of the span of adult life? First it is long—longer than that of any other mammal. Yet the end of life is by a definite process of senescence, which should be distinguished from disease (even though some of its manifestations lead to disease). It is calculated that if all deaths due to cancers were eliminated, only 2 years would be added to the average life (in the U.S.A.). The question is whether there is an optimum duration for the persistence of individuals for a given initial span of education. It is clearly not efficient for the species for its individuals to spend a long time learning skills that are then used only for a short time. In general the mammals with better and more educable brains are the longer lived, one thinks of elephants, apes, and horses and perhaps whales. But such comparisons and judgements are very hazardous, dogs are intelligent too and they do not live so long.

The problem of the human life-span is presumably connected with that of the menopause, which is certainly a specifically human feature that is genetically programmed to occur rather late, around 45 years of age. The number of children reared by a woman is about ten in communities that seek to maximize reproduction (e.g. the religious sect of the Hutterites). Is there, or was there, some feature making this the optimum, and is the traditional three score years and ten the life-span that allows the last of the ten children to be reared? It seems to be rather too long. The matter remains a mystery.

## Who repairs the repairer of the repairer . . .?

Granted that there can be selection to determine the life-span of a species there must presumably also be selection for mechanisms of repair that allow the attainment of that age. For example there are known to be specific enzymatic mechanisms by which DNA can be repaired. If a piece of one of the two chains functions in an aberrant way it is removed, and a new stretch of DNA is then synthesized, using the other chain as a template. Specific enzymes, the ligases, then join the new pieces into the old chain. Moreover there is evidence that more new DNA is made in this way in older organisms.

Repair mechanisms such as this themselves need repairing, and obviously the regress of what repairs the repairer cannot be indefinitely avoided. This seems to set a limit on the possible length of survival of any individual homeostatic device. Living organisms avoid this dilemma only by evading or by-passing it. The individuals do not live for ever but are replaced after the appropriate time by others, shuffling the instructions to make a slightly different program. In this sense death is truly the secret of life.

But this does not in my view mean that there is no possibility of improvement in repair processes and prolongation of life. As we have seen there must be more efficient repair mechanisms in the longer lived species. It follows that selection to improve them *can* occur. There are doubts among geneticists as to the circumstances that make this possible, but something has done it in the past, and might continue to do so. Presumably if there *is* a premium on longevity then longer lived populations will replace the others. It would be difficult to prove whether this is or is not happening today. The idea of much longer lives is not altogether pleasing, even to those of us who are already older.

The purpose of this discussion is to emphasize that there is evidence that genetic programs unfold at very different times of life, some even towards its end. Each new genetic manifestation takes its course according to the environmental situation and the action of the individual, as determined by his previous condition. We shall later return to the early stages of the life-cycle and watch the early unfolding of a few of these potentialities.

# 5 Beginning

## Why do we ask about origins?

An important fact about the human brain is that difficult questions such as 'how did the world begin?' come to be asked. Even chimpanzees don't ask that sort of question. The fact that we want to know about origins may tell us much about the way our brains work. It emphasizes that we try to develop comprehensive schemes by which the antecedents of all events are explained and future events forecast. This characteristic separates us from animals almost as much as does language, to which of course our particular sort of model-making is related. Humans have a special tendency to apply their brains to the formation of elaborate schemes or 'models' with which they, as we say, 'explain' what goes on around them. And this is not an activity only of learned professors. All men and women are apt to demand explanations and meanings for life. (Incidentally, for the scientist these general questions often seem unimportant and he may seem unwilling to try to provide answers.) This need for explanations seems so natural that we forget how odd it is and that there must be some reason for it, and moreover that there must have been a time, perhaps one or two million years ago, when our ancestors had brains that did *not* work like this. Or could they have *partly* worked like this? How did this sort of thinking *begin*? Is there any evidence with which to try to answer these questions?

Living things differ from non-living things in being continually influenced by information inherited from the past. By virtue of those instructions they are able to maintain a steady state of interchange with the environment, keeping their identities intact or passing them on to others like themselves. Where does this flow of information come from and when did it first begin?

## Theories of creation

In trying to find explanations for origins the technique that has been used by men almost universally until recently has been to postulate the operation of some form of super-person or god. Instead of dismissing this as a primitive notion we should rather use it as evidence of how the brain works. I believe that it is the result of an inherited human propensity to pay special attention to the actions of other people. We shall follow later the sequence by which the child first uses this tendency in all his 'explanations' and then partly frees himself from it (Chapter 9). There are still plenty of people in the world who believe in the operation of gods and spirits. The biologist should ask why. The answer may in turn also tell us something about how both the theistic and scientific beliefs may have arisen.

There is now information that suggests rather strongly that life arose on earth by the operation of forces similar to those that are still at work today. Although we cannot be sure of this, many scientists will none the less prefer to *believe* in some such *natural* origin (p. 34). Darwin himself expressed it 'that the principle of continuity renders it probable that the principle of life will hereafter be shown to be a fact or consequence of some general law'.

## The origin of the universe

Meanwhile we should perhaps remind ourselves that we are even more ignorant about the origin of the universe than about the origin of life. Astronomers are beginning to propound theories that sound as if they substitute for the action of a creator. The earliest event of which they can find evidence may have been a Big Bang. But does that really tell us about the Origin? According to Weinberg (1977) there was 'an explosion . . . filling all space from the beginning with every particle of matter reaching away from every other particle.' But where were the space and the particles before the bang? What astronomers show us is that we are surrounded by a universe of dimensions that seem so stupendous that it is hard to contemplate them. But the important word here is 'seem'. Perhaps it is really that our brains and the language produced by them have been developed for dealing only with literally *mundane* matters. The times and distances involved may make us feel small ('la silence de ces vastes espaces m'effraie', Pascal). But the electron microscopist can show us structures within ourselves that are about as many times smaller than our whole self as the Earth is than our galaxy. Discovery is indeed giving us the means to contemplate some of these questions of magnitude without quite so much difficulty as formerly. No doubt astronomers find it easier than the rest of us. But for me this does not solve the problem of origins. I feel simply that no one has given me any clear information of how the universe began. I am not clear if indeed there is any meaning in asking that question. In fact the thought that it may be the wrong question is perhaps as near as I can come to answering it. The very concept of a beginning is perhaps applicable only to earthbound affairs. I sometimes feel inclined to agree with the sentiment said to have been expressed by Lord Rutherford, 'Don't let me catch anyone talking about the universe in my laboratory.' But then neither would he allow anyone to talk about nuclear energy, and Bernal's comment on Rutherford's statement is that it 'was probably due only to his native caution and the British empirical tradition' (1967). People have certainly not been prevented from further discussion of the origin of the universe, but it is obviously not the subject of a strictly empirical science. We can analyse the universe but we cannot conceivably 'make' it. By contrast it is just possible to imagine the synthesis of life (p. 35).

## Can we imagine an impersonal creator?

The conventional concept of a creator is so obviously a product of our anthropocentric method of brain-working that one suspects it as ingenuous. Yet to replace the idea of God as something like a man by a wholly impersonal entity is so mysterious and indeed terrifying that I personally really cannot seriously contemplate it. The brain simply will not work with such concepts, in spite of all the efforts of science and science-fiction. These are problems that theologians have debated through the centuries and modern knowledge has not solved them. Only in one sense do we perhaps begin to approach a solution. In the light of discoveries of the very large and the very small, and of such questions as relativity, we begin to see that this problem is not at all what simple language suggests. In questions about the infinite commonsense is non-sense (as indeed it often is in mundane matters too). We should perhaps consider that the real question is not 'what is the universe and who made it?', but 'what are we humans and what is it possible for us to know?' These are more humble questions, to which we already have some answers and are rapidly finding more. I hope to show that by exploring these answers we may even be able to find some evidence about the meaning of life and its direction, which people so badly need as guidelines for the conduct of their lives. Scientists have been content for too long with the widespread view that they have no evidence on these questions of value. Study of life seems to me to show that it does have an aim, a direction, and a purpose. We shall find these best by looking at present and past actions of man and his living relatives (Chapter 6).

I venture to think that further attention to the limitations of human capacity may also be of help to physicists and astronomers in their attempts to find general interpretations of their observations of the very great and the very small. There is increasing agreement that many of these fundamentals are questions about the status of observations and therefore of observers. In particular they are questions about the status of description and therefore of language. Once again we find ourselves faced with this question of whether we can find a language to describe languages. Is it possible to ask metaquestions? This is in a sense the theme of our whole investigation and we shall not try to draw conclusions yet. Let us rather return to the problem of how life began on Earth.

## The beginning of living programs

There is much evidence that all the living things on Earth had one common origin. For instance all use the same DNA code and similar amino-acids. There seem to be three possible general hypotheses about how this form of organized matter arose on Earth. It might have come from some other part of the universe. It might have begun here by the operation of God as a special creative agency on Earth or, thirdly, it might have arisen on Earth by the operation of what we may call the ordinary physical and chemical laws as we see them at work today. We know enough now to discuss this last possibility rationally, though not conclusively, so let us deal with it first. The really significant feature of the giant molecules that are found in all living things, is that the nucleic acids carry *information*, which enables the proteins to act as enzymes, which are the catalysts that make life possible. The sequences of the amino-acids in proteins make the chains fold up to produce those crannies and corners in which molecules like sugar are made to 'burn' without a match, by being brought close together with oxygen (Chapter 3). What we need to find out is how these *specific* sequences arose—where did the *information* come from? As I understand it chemists have not yet been able to bridge this crucial gap. (For further references see Bernal 1967; Young 1971; Dose *et al.* 1974; and Weinberg 1977, Yockey 1977.)

Until we are sure, theories for a 'natural' origin for the genetic code, though very suggestive, are not based on complete scientific premises. I am afraid that we have to admit that we do not know for certain how specific sequences arose. This means that we cannot answer the question of how 'collections of matter came to produce their own description' (Pattee 1961). How we react to this disappointment is another question about human nature, to which we shall return in considering belief (Chapter 21). Some may wish to consider the alternative that life came here from some other region of space—but this of course does not tell us how it arose. Others will wish to use the time-honoured belief in a Creator, exercising special powers to produce the language of life on Earth, perhaps 3500 million years ago. Finally there will be those who prefer to use the scientific belief in the orderliness of nature that we mentioned before (p. 32). They will hope that although we cannot fully see the solution, yet it is there and will be found. It seems to me that we have reason to adopt such a belief and it is the solution that I should accept. This of course also involves the belief, now widely held, that it is probable that matter also became so organized many times to form life-like systems elsewhere in the universe. The discussion of this interesting probability does not really help us with our task of describing the programs of the brain (see Sagan, 1973).

No one has yet synthesized a living cell in the laboratory. Attempts to do it are being made in various ways. For instance mixtures of amino-acids when heated produce 'proteinoids'. These are not true proteins, but when treated with water make 'microspheres' that have membranes and some of the properties of cells (Fox 1976). True living cells are much more complicated, and it is still not possible to say whether they will ever be made artificially—personally I believe that it will be done. At least we know now in some detail what the various substances involved are. This is a very big step towards bringing them together. But the components of even a simple bacterium are very numerous and it will not be at all easy to assemble them. Chemists have been able to go much further in this direction than seemed possible even a few decades ago. It is quite likely that they will succeed in making some form of self-maintaining, self-replicating systems that might be regarded as living things. What will they be like? Not, I am afraid, anything very interesting. Perhaps just little drops of jelly that imitate some of the synthetic actions of bacteria. Not very impressive indeed, but intellectually it will be a big step, if it is ever taken. It may perhaps be a very important industrial tool as well, the artificial cells might be useful for making all sorts of chemicals.

For our own discussion the important point is that we can get so close to thinking realistically about the origin of life and its artificial synthesis. Yet it is serious that we cannot understand how the language that ensures living continuity arose. For we cannot repeat too often that the centre of all our problems is the study of codes, signs, and languages. We shall know the origin of life only when we understand how its code of instructions began.

# 6 Evolving

## The origin of man

In any study of the origins of brain programs, the question of when and how man arrived on the earth is obviously central. On balance it is reasonable to suppose that life arose by physical processes not fundamentally different from those at work in the non-living world today (Chapter 5). The problem is then to ask whether the species *Homo sapiens* arose in the same way as all other creatures. The method of speaking about ourselves that we commonly adopt implies that in each person there is an entity the mind, somehow interacting with the brain. If man arose by the same evolutionary process as other organisms, then it cannot be that this entity is some special spirit borne by humans alone and breathed into all or each of us by some special agent. If the characteristics we ascribe to mind are then the outcome of a normal evolutionary process we shall be warned to suspect our tendency to regard them as in some way distinct from those of the rest of the living world. We may be more inclined to re-examine our attitude to these questions and to ask how far the properties we ascribe to minds and hence also to brains are a result of linguistic conventions.

As anthropological discoveries are made they continually increase the evidence that man reached his present state by a slow process of change. There can hardly be such a thing as absolute proof of this, because we can never have a complete series of all the remains of all the men and pre-men who have ever existed. But it is striking how, as further evidence accumulates, the continuity of our ancestry becomes more evident. Human beings and other mammals do not commonly leave fossil remains. The animals that fossilize most readily live in water and have shells that are regularly preserved in the sediments washed down by rivers. So oysters provide some of the best series of fossils. The shells of minute protozoans (Foraminifera) are better still and are used by geologists studying the strata in search of oil. Human fossils are mostly from caves or have been buried under the ash from volcanoes, as in the famous deposits investigated by the Leakeys at Olduvai in Tanzania and Lake Turkana (formerly Lake Rudolph) in northern Kenya (Leakey and Lewin 1977).

Considering the improbabilities of fossilization, it is remarkable that we have a number of specimens that are near to our ancestry extending back for some 2½ million years, and a few others more remote from further back still. As the evidence accumulates, it becomes in fact more confusing, which is inevitable in any set of evolving populations. We run into the problem that there may have been several parallel lines of rather man-like creatures. Indeed, as we find more and more fossils, we are forced to face some worrying questions about our identity. We have been talking about the origin of 'man', but what is man? It is usual to hold that all those alive today belong to one species and subspecies *Homo sapiens sapiens*. A few people believe that the different modern races have evolved separately (Coon 1963). Even if this is not true, it is certain that we are not all descended from one primeval pair, but from a *population*, which like all populations must have been heterogeneous. Recent discoveries in Africa, especially by R. Leakey and his colleagues, show that between say 3 million and 1 million years ago there were several distinct lines of creatures evolving in a somewhat human direction (Leakey and Walker 1976). They had left the forest life of our ape-like ancestors and begun to walk on two legs, probably hunting game on the open plains.

## Evolution of the brain

These recent discoveries have given further evidence that the brain evolved gradually to its present condition. Unfortunately we cannot from fossil evidence say much about changes in its outward form and of course nothing of internal structure. But the *size* of the brain at least tells us something about it and this can be estimated from the fossils. The brains of apes have a volume of rather less than 500 ml, whereas modern human brains average about 1500 ml. Our ape-like ancestor in the Miocene period, say 15 million years ago, probably had a brain of about modern ape size.

The Australopithecines were fossil hominids living in Africa as recently as 2 to 1 million years ago whose brains were little bigger than those of apes. They walked on two legs though with a gait different from ours, but opinions now tend to the view that they were not on the direct line of human descent. The earliest pebble tools have been associated with them, but may have been used by other hominids living at the same time. A skull recently found by Richard Leakey (1976) was larger and more human, than that of *Australopithecus*, with a capacity of about 800 ml and its owner lived about 2½ million years ago. So far the only name given to it is its museum number KNMR 1470. Rather larger skulls are those referred to as *Homo erectus*, found first in Java, then at Peking and more recently in Europe and Africa. Dating of the specimens is not easy but none are known to be more than one million or less than half a million years old. The skulls were not quite human, with a volume of about a litre, and the leg bones found with them show that these people walked fully erect. The cave at Peking showed evidence that they had fires and made flint hand-axes.

The question of when individuals of modern human form arose is complicated, as would be expected if they appeared gradually. The skull found at Swanscombe in Kent and dated at 250 000 years ago has mostly modern features and it was of human volume. Neanderthal man, *Homo sapiens neanderthalensis*, living from perhaps 1000 000 to 50 000 years ago had rather large skulls, with a brain volume of 1600 ml, but different in some ways from modern skulls. Fully human skulls, *H. sapiens sapiens*, have been found only from 40 000 years ago onwards. If the brain has evolved slowly in this way it seems likely that human society, language, and consciousness emerged gradually too. This has important implications, both for the way we think about ourselves and for the methods we can use to learn more. It emphasizes not only that we are physically a part and parcel of the rest of the organic world, but that we should look there too, even for the antecedents of what we call our cultural and spiritual world. Man is certainly outstanding in his powers of gathering and communicating information, but one of our greatest mistakes is to act continually as if these powers of information transfer are wholly unlike anything in the rest of nature. They are indeed to be found in some form throughout the living world. They have become gradually developed by natural selection in our ancestors because they were valuable for survival. The powers that we have today are similarly there for *use*. We should not be ashamed to look at the usefulness even of our most treasured cultural activities, say religious belief or the pleasure we take in painting and music. To say that religion or art or music are useful seems to me not in the least to devalue them but on the contrary it improves our estimation of their value. I believe that these 'spiritual' and creative activities are even *more important*, in the literal, practical sense, than the more mundane ones that are the concern of politics, business, and industry (Chapters 20 and 21). I shall argue that such satisfactions of our emotional needs provide the motivation that keeps us alive and at work. These are the things that together ensure the continuity and survival of human communities, even more than do the provision of food and shelter. The teaching that 'man does not live by bread alone' is perhaps needed more than ever today. I believe that a proper study of how the brain operates will enable us to see more clearly the place that so-called cultural and spiritual activities play in human homeostasis.

## Did mind appear gradually?

If the human brain and behaviour have evolved gradually, it seems likely that the features that seem to separate men from animals have also been gradually acquired. In particular, it is most unlikely that human beings suddenly began to have consciousness or minds distinct from their bodies. What may perhaps have happened was that as language developed, people began to employ the symbols used to indicate actions of other people to refer to themselves. Animals obviously recognize others, but the critical human stage was the acquisition of the power to make symbolic representation by language of concepts indicating the distinction between self and other. This allows expression to oneself as well as to others of the experiencing of the self and of the world, which we call being conscious. An insight to this question comes from children who are born blind. They only begin to refer to themselves as 'I' or 'me' after they have learned to play with dolls. 'The acquisition of personal pronouns is closely united with the capacity for symbolic representation of the self, and vision normally plays a central facilitating role in each of these achievements' (Fraiberg and Adelson 1973). Perhaps some of the problems that worry us about such concepts as mind and body and consciousness may resolve themselves if we examine how we have come to use them, both during individual development and in evolution. If we knew more about the origins of language we might be able to work out how the categories of mind and of consciousness developed *gradually*. And the same applies of course to all our other concepts. An interesting example is the belief in the operation of spirits. One often reads that 'primitive people' interpret natural phenomena as due to the operation of spirits. But surely this is really a very sophisticated notion. It cannot have been the mode of operation of our 'primitive' ape-like ancestors. How did they come to adopt this interpretation? The question leads back to that of the origin of the concepts of mind and soul and of course of religion.

As development of a child proceeds a symbolic model, composed of hypotheses about the world, is built in the brain, and later used to decide upon programs of action that maintain life. We want to know all we can about this model. It depends partly on programs of inherited instructions as to how to investigate the world and how to learn from it. Our ancestors before they were men must have already had such capacities, and have made hypotheses that were suitable for *their* lives. What would these early 'minds' have been like, and how have they become changed to produce our present characteristics? Before we can even attempt to answer these questions, we need much better definitions of what these characteristics are today. As so often we find ourselves caught in a dilemma, if we knew how consciousness and mind began, we might be able to define better what we mean by them—or should it be the other way round?

# 7 Controlling, coding, and communicating

## The brain as a controller

All organisms are active systems, choosing to do those things that may keep them alive. In higher animals the most significant selections between possible courses of action are made by the brain, which is the agent that regulates the whole life of the individual. The nervous system is therefore continually *doing* things. It is much more than a simple set of conduction channels. Perhaps we have been too ready to emphasize its communicative function, using the analogies of our own artefacts such as telephones or radio. Communication is indeed essential for control and we shall have much to say about how nerves carry information. But much more is involved than this. That is why we are trying to think in terms of *programs*. The brain contains the very instructions that serve to organize what we do, in the light of incoming information. In particular it contains the reference system of standards, departure from which sets us off in pursuit of those things that are necessary for the continuance of our lives.

Why should we seek to understand control, coding, and communication? One of the ways of acting that humans adopt, through their brains, is to make general schemes or models of the world, to help in the prediction of suitable courses of action. It seems likely that the human brain is programmed to allow the devising of such *general* schemes, indeed this is one of its special talents. Even a gorilla or a whale, clever though he is, does not refer to a religious or political world-view for the conduct of his life. We shall try to find out something of the way human brains make such schemes, from childhood onwards. One clue is that the brain contains mechanisms by which external events are compared with the actions of other human beings, which are the entities with which it is chiefly called upon to deal. So if communication is the essential feature of all social intercourse it is surely no accident that we are now moved to borrow these concepts of control, communication, and coding from social activities, in order to talk about the brain. These features that seem so characteristically human turn out to be properties of all living activity. The very concept of control implies an agent doing things, with specific aims, and this we have seen to be characteristic of all life (Chapter 3).

Whatever type of model is used for the brain it must include the conception that it is an *active* agent. As the Russian neurologist Luria (1973) puts it, the analogy of the brain as a responding device would mean that its work is entirely determined by the past. But, he says, 'It has become abundantly clear that human behaviour is active in character, it is determined not only by past experience but also by plans and designs formulating the future, and that the human brain is a remarkable apparatus which cannot only create these models of the future, but also subordinate its behaviour to them.' Notice that Luria does not hesitate to speak of the *brain* as the agent that 'creates' models of the future. Some will smile at his so dismissing the problem of 'mind'. He is more interested in the question of how we are to talk about the brain, and he passes on to consider how we may best deal with the realization that the nervous system is more than a simple passive conductor. This leads him to deny that computer analogies can be useful. Indeed he believes that they '. . . hinder the advancement of truly scientific knowledge of the brain as the organ of the mind'. I should disagree with him about this. Truly all models are inadequate and we are ourselves going to use the rather rough non-mechanical analogy of programs. However, this does not mean dispensing with machine analogies, which are essential as well. Luria does not tell us what sort of terms will be used by the new science of neuropsychology that he proposes. He refers to 'morphology, physiology, psychology and clinical medicine', but all of these sciences continually use analogies from artefacts. When we speak of 'structure' we refer to buildings and in 'function' to machines. It is indeed difficult to decide what terms to use to describe ourselves and our brains.

The history of biology shows that as man devises tools to substitute for the function of his body he also creates new language to describe these very functions (see Young 1951). The history of our knowledge of our hearts, lungs, stomach, muscles, and now brains bear witness to this sequence of discovery. One powerful method to acquire understanding of ourselves is to make artefacts that imitate ourselves. But we can agree with Luria that even the most sophisticated computers provide a hopelessly inadequate means of speaking about say, the creativity of humans. In any case computers use principles that are different in many ways from those of the brain. We cannot hope to describe in detail how the brain works by looking at the bits of metal and minerals inside a computer. What we have to use is the understanding of the *principles* of information transfer, and the 'software' or system of programs that have been devised by computer scientists (see p. 62).

## Information

The biologist and the computer scientist both use for their general terminology terms borrowed from the language of social relations. Living, we say, continues because all the actions are 'controlled' by the giving of 'instructions', based upon 'communication' of 'information' in a 'code'. 'Order' is maintained by 'orders'. The conceptions of code and language are particularly important. They involve a set of physical events (say spoken sounds or written words) that have been chosen in the past as signs to represent other sets of events (Chapter 2). If we are to use such words as these wisely in biology we must specify as precisely as possible what we propose to mean by them in relation to the structures and activities of living tissues.

Engineers need to define the amount of information that can be passed along wires or other communication channels. They emphasize that the essence of information is that it controls decisions. Accordingly one 'bit', the unit of information, is defined as the operation needed to make a decision between two equi-probable events (Quastler 1965). As applied to language or any code this means that the amount of information in a letter, word, or sentence is inversely proportional to the frequency with which it occurs. The word 'and' contains less information than 'ant'. In choosing names for me my parents fortuitously selected those with almost the rarest initial letters, thus carrying the maximum information—which is quite a help in life (once one has left school!).

Systems of measurement of amounts of information can be very useful in biology, where codes are so important as the controllers of life. Control implies reference to a source of order, information or instructions, and the organism inherits this in its DNA. Using these instructions the embryo produces organs and actions appropriate to its way of life. We have seen how this reference to the DNA is achieved in a bacterium when a new sugar is first detected by a receiver at the surface (p. 18). Information about it is then transmitted across the bacterium by some physical process, though it is not known how it is done. Arriving at the central agent (the DNA) the information initiates action appropriate to meet and compensate for the external change (making a new enzyme). So the word is being used in two senses. The 'information' in the DNA is the basic source of order of the individual transmitted along the channel of heredity. For these instructions to be used 'information' about what is needed must be transmitted from the outside world. Similarly in an animal or man behaviour is controlled by the information or instructions included in the brain (which has developed under the influence of the DNA). But this set of standards in the brain is consulted by the other sort of information coming from the outside through channels provided by the nerves.

This apparent paradox of two channels and two sorts of information points us to the complicated relationship between organisms and their past history and present environment. A wonderfully complex order has been produced by the aeons of natural selection. This ensures that every organism is so carefully matched to its environment that its actions tend to keep it alive. To describe this matching is the central task of biology. To do it we propose to use the analogy of human communication and speak of information in languages and codes. The whole organism can be considered as a coded representation of its environment. We can say that the wings of a bird 'represent' the air and the legs of man the land, and similarly that their brains contain representations in code that allow them to fly or walk, and their nerves carry code messages about relevant features of the world.

This conception of organisms as symbolic representations of their environments may seem fanciful. In fact it gives a much deeper insight into life than the usual talk about 'structures' and 'functions', which use analogy with machines. Thom has put it that information equals form (1975). To understand this way of thinking we can examine the coding of information in the nervous system.

## Coding

So far we have not spoken about the nature of the changes that convey information along a communication channel. Some physical events in the nerve must provide the units of a code, which together stand for or represent the events in the outside world to which the organism must react. Evidently this correspondence must be a *pre-established* property of the communication system. We notice again that organisms are systems dependent upon their history. The correspondence of the words of a human language with what they are to signify, however it becomes established, is mostly arbitrary (Chapter 2). But somehow in the process of production of effective communication channels there must be correspondence with what is to be communicated. We have therefore to enquire what are the units of the neural code and how did they come to represent events in the world. Descriptions of how the nervous system encodes information usually begin by showing how signals pass along nerves and how they are set up in sense organs, say the eyes or ears. We shall indeed examine these signals, but this is starting at the wrong end. The essential function of communication is to enable a controller to issue the right instructions from its set of possible actions. The essence of speech sounds is that they are *understood*, which assumes that appropriate action follows.

## The brain as an active controller

The brain then is an agent issuing instructions, after it has decoded (understood) the signals it receives about what is going on around it. Its units, the nerve cells, are essentially capable of *activity*. They are the agents that initiate most of our actions. We sleep or wake, go walking or eating or reading because our brains contain active cells that operate when we choose to do these things. Notice that we are working gradually towards our discussion of whether the cells of the brain make us do these things or allow some other agent, the mind, to work through them (p. 266). No one argues that the mind enters directly into many reflex actions, triggered from outside, as when we touch a hot object or our mouth waters when we smell our favourite food. But what about when tears spring to our eyes at a touching scene in a film, as they readily do to mine? More of this later, for the present we are reminding ourselves that the brain is not a passive agent, subject only to information from outside. There are influences *from within* that can provide the programs for our lives.

I propose to illustrate the activities of the nervous system so far as possible from experiments that I have done myself. To show that the nervous system is an active agent I choose an observation that Gerard and I made long ago (1937). We found that rhythmical electrical changes continue in a frog's brain *even after it has been removed from the head.* It is not understood how these waves are related to the frog's behaviour. Indeed not much is known about the significance of the somewhat similar 'brain waves' that can be recorded from a human head, and which change when we sleep (Chapter 18). We are concerned now to note that nerve cells are able to do something active. They constitute an *agent*, something whose past history has left it in a state of continual activity and interaction with its surroundings. A living thing is not a passive system, resting in equilibrium, but is continually doing things. And, as we have seen for living actions in general, the things done are so organized as to guide the organism to its objectives, which are to stay alive and to perpetuate its kind. These are the actions that are undertaken by the controller of the behaviour, using of course, from moment to moment, the information that is coming to it from the outside to determine which of its set of programs shall be used to issue instructions.

## Nerve cells. The dictionary and grammar of the brain

How is the brain able to produce all the complex actions of an animal or man? The essence of this power lies in the great number and variety of nerve cells, and of their activities and of their connections. This makes it possible for there to be such a vast set of alternative actions. There are said to be about ten thousand million nerve cells in the human cerebral cortex ($10^{10}$) (Fig 7.1). But the really important fact is that probably no two of them are exactly alike. Simplifying the matter grossly we shall show that each one of these cells corresponds to one of the following: (1) a small part of one particular feature of change going on in the outside world; (2) some small part of a memory record of a past external change; or (3) to some small part of the instructions for an action that can be done by the body, say to initiate the movement of a few fibres of one muscle. The combination of the actions of the cells that represent the outside with those that represent events in the

surface of brain

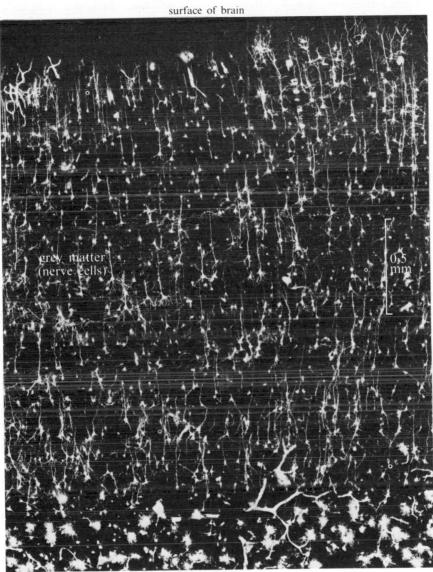

grey matter
(nerve cells)

0.5
mm

white matter, with glia cells and nerve fibres

FIG. 7.1. Section of the cerebral cortex from the frontal lobe of a human brain. Stained with
Golgi–Cox silver method by which about one out of every hundred cells is stained.

past initiates the actions appropriate from moment to moment. This is indeed a ridiculous simplification and our whole later discussion must serve to elaborate it—we venture on it here to show how the nerve cells or systems are, as it were, the letters of the cerebral alphabet. Combinations of them compose the words, sentences, paragraphs, chapters, and books that constitute the programs that produce our patterns of behaviour. To understand the language of the brain it is necessary to know how the nerve cells combine, like letters or the phones of speech, to produce units that have meaning, like words. The words, when used in proper combinations represent events in the outside world or issue appropriate instructions to the muscles or glands. Since spoken or written language is used by people to attain their aims and ends it follows that the language of the brain is in a sense more fundamental because it contains components that actually determine those ends. If grammar is the system that regulates the proper use of language we might say that the brain operates a sort of metalanguage with a metagrammar, which regulates the proper conduct of life, including speech.

So the brain contains a huge number of units, each capable of some activity in combination with others. Our analysis into three sorts suggests that the activities of each nerve cell, with its neighbours, somehow represents either some present or past event in the outside world or some action that the creature can perform. We must now explain what it means to say that some cells 'represent' events in the world and others 'represent' actions that the body can do to influence the world.

## The electrical signals in nerves

The wonderful calculations that brains perform depend on the power of nerve cells to produce certain electrical and chemical changes. We can hardly hope to explain these fully in a short time but to have any understanding of the brain at all one must appreciate something of their nature. The nerve fibres are very extended strands of protoplasm stretching away from a central nerve cell body (Fig. 7.2). This contains the nucleus, whose DNA is responsible for controlling the actual physical state of the nerve cell and its parts. It presides over the workshop, as it were, that produces the actual material of the cell, making it ready to perform its particular function of sending appropriate messages.

The 'messages' take the form of signals passing along the nerve fibres and a great deal is known about the physical and chemical changes by which they are transmitted. Mammalian nerve cells and fibres are rather small and hard to investigate. So in the 1920s and 1930s some of us looked for larger ones whose activities would be easier to study. I was lucky enough to find some of the biggest of all nerve fibres, those of the squid (Fig. 7.3). These are beautiful transparent threads, showing as clear channels among a lot of

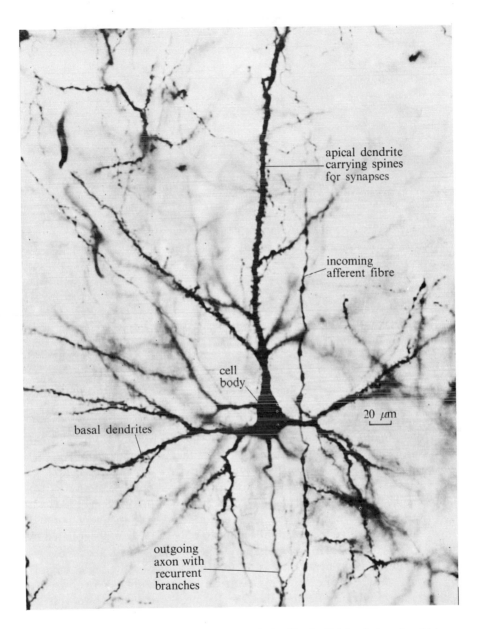

apical dendrite
carrying spines
for synapses

incoming
afferent fibre

cell
body

20 μm

basal dendrites

outgoing
axon with
recurrent
branches

FIG. 7.2. Single nerve cell from the cerebral cortex. Stained by the Golgi technique, by which only a few cells are coloured while others all around are left unstained.

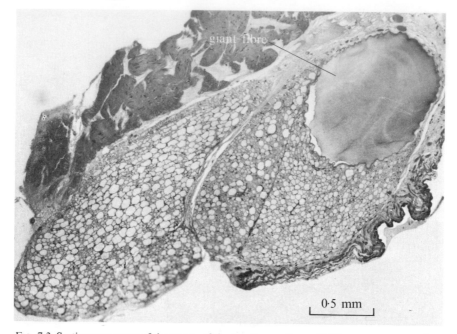

FIG. 7.3. Section across one of the nerves of the mantle sac of a squid. There are many small nerve fibres and one enormous one, which carries the fast signals that activate the jet propulsion muscles.

smaller fibres in the nerve bundles. When I first saw them I did not realize that they were nerve fibres, indeed I thought that they were veins. It was necessary to convince myself and others that they really did conduct nerve messages. Figure 7.4 shows one of the very first records of the signals carried by a giant nerve fibre. This shows one of the most fundamental characteristics of the nervous system. The signals in the nerve fibres are all alike. Of course the nature of these signals, known as nerve impulses or action potentials, had been studied long before, especially by the work of Keith Lucas and Lord Adrian. The squid's nerve fibres made it possible to find out much more about these signals, possibilities that have been brilliantly exploited by Cole, Katz, Hodgkin, Huxley and many other workers (see Katz 1966).

Each squid's giant nerve fibre is up to 1 mm across, quite big enough to put a wire inside to measure any electrical events. Doing this shows that there is an electrical potential difference of nearly one-tenth of a volt between the inside and outside of the fibre. Similar voltages across the surfaces of all of our millions of nerve cells provide the means by which messages are sent and decisions made in the nervous system. Each nerve fibre is a charged system, it has a source of energy available to allow the propagation of messages. If the fibre is suitably stimulated a sort of electrical explosion

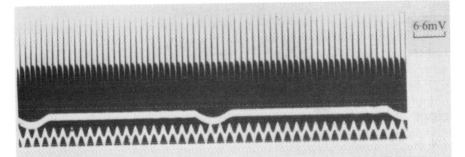

Fig. 7.4. A series of action potentials set up in a giant nerve fibre of a squid by depolarizing one end with oxalic acid. As recorded by an oscillograph. The time-markers show 1/5 or 1/100th sec.

spreads all the way along its whole length. This is the *nerve impulse* which is the signal that travels along nerve fibres. After the signal has passed there is a 'refractory period' before the next impulse can pass. Each action potential is thus complete, and they are all identical. It is as if there was a train of gunpowder, where each explosion sets off the next. The size of the 'impulse' depends only on the charge at each point. The signal comes out as strong at the end as at the beginning. Such *conduction without decrement* is obviously a very safe way of conveying information.

The two important points to notice are first that the impulse goes along without decreasing or fading away, and second that all impulses in any one nerve fibre are alike. This conduction without decrement constitutes the 'all-or-nothing' law of nervous conduction and it determines the whole character of the nervous system. It differs fundamentally from signalling by artefacts such as telephone or radio where the different sounds are registered or coded by altering the signal itself, so that it varies, for instance, to follow the changes of the human voice. This cannot happen in a nerve fibre. The only variation that is possible is in the number and distribution of the pulses that go along. This 'frequency modulation' does indeed allow any one nerve fibre to carry different patterns of impulses. They can be few or many and they can be spaced with different patterns of intervals. These patterns might be used to transmit different messages but the nervous system in general uses differences in frequency only to indicate different intensities—for instance the loudness of a given tone.

The nerve impulses are thus the basic units of the language, comparable to the phones of speech or to letters. They do not themselves convey meaning. Certain groupings of them may do so (by their frequencies) but the meaningful units or words of the brain language are the individual nerve cells. Differences of quality, such as different tones or visual contours, are encoded in the nervous system by *having a different nerve cell and nerve fibre for each quality*. That is why we have such a vast number of nerve cells. The brain is essentially a *multichannel system*. Its method of coding is to make up messages by putting each item of information into a separate channel is rather like the system that electrical engineers call line labelling, but its name to physiologists is the doctrine of specific nerve energies. When this was first enunciated in 1848 by J. Müller, he noted that it was actually adumbrated by Thomas Young in 1802, who suggested that we detect colour by various combinations of three primary channels, for red, green, and blue.

So we have to learn to think about something that works quite differently from our telephones or radio, which depend upon modulation of the signals themselves. It is a hard lesson for anyone and even some of those who study the brain find it difficult to remember.

## Encoding in the nervous system

Just as each nerve fibre carries only one sort of signal so, with some simplification, we can say that each cell of the brain usually represents one word of information indicating the presence of certain limited features, say a blue rectangle with a given slope. Similarly a motor nerve cell may provide the command for one small action by a muscle. The work of D. H. Hubel and T. N. Wiesel, from 1959 onwards, at Harvard have shown this very clearly for the process of seeing by a cat or monkey, and no doubt our own vision is similar (Hubel and Wiesel 1977). Their method was to pass an electrode into the part of the cerebral cortex of the brain that receives the nerve fibres that are activated by light falling on the retina (Fig. 7.5). If the electrode is connected with a suitable amplifier it will record on the face of an oscilloscope any electrical changes that are produced by a nerve cell near to its tip. Will any visual change serve to stimulate every visual cell? If not, what type of visual event would we expect to provide the stimulus? What was actually found was that each cell of the primary visual cortex responds only to a moving boundary between light and dark, set at one particular angle. The cells do not respond to simple changes of brightness, even when it is greatly increased or decreased in intensity. Nor do they respond to a moving spot of light, but only when a bright or dark edge or contour, with a particular orientation, is moved in a particular part of the visual field. If the electrode is now pushed a little way obliquely through the brain it meets a cell that responds to a contour with a slightly different orientation. The cortical nerve cells are arranged in columns, at right angles to the cortical surface, each of about a hundred cells (Figs. 7.6 and 7). All the cells in one of the columns through the thickness of the cortex react to the same contour. Thus the primary visual cortex contains hundreds of thousands of columns of cells, each composed of cells tuned, as it were, to detect a particular contour

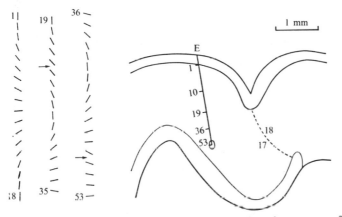

FIG. 7.5. Experiment by Hubel and Wiesel (1968) to show the responses of cells of the visual cortex of the monkey. The animal is anaesthetized and an electrode (E) introduced through the surface of the cortex. It is connected to an amplifier and oscilloscope, which records the action potentials of the cells as shown in Fig. 7.6. Each cell responds only when a dark bar set at a particular angle is moved in the visual field of the opposite eye.

The electrode was pushed through the cortex and cells 1–53 were encountered, giving responses to the orientations shown on the left. (From Hubel & Wiesel 1968.)

(Chapter 12). For the present the point is that visual information is encoded by putting certain items, such as contours or redness, each into a separate channel. The 'meaning' of the activity of any one cell is that one simple type of visual change has occurred, say movement of a contour with a particular orientation in one particular way. The actions of all the cortical visual cells together must then provide the information that somehow allows for decision as to what action shall be taken—or as we should say 'what the person sees'. The problem posed by such multichannel coding is to understand how so many cells interact to form representations that come to serve as symbols for events in the outside world.

It was known already from the work of Vernon Mountcastle (1957) of Johns Hopkins University that essentially the same system of 'coding' is found in the sense of touch, and it is so also for hearing and the other senses. But to complete our brief study of coding into the words of the neural language we must show that outgoing information is also broken up in the same way. Figure 12.4 shows the impulse firing pattern of a single cell of the part of the cortex that controls movement of the eye of a monkey that has learned to follow the track of a moving light.

If the nerve cells are the words of the code we can compare the problem of how they represent the world to understanding how a grammar allows the combination of words to make meaningful statements. Unfortunately this is where present knowledge fails us, because we have no physiological

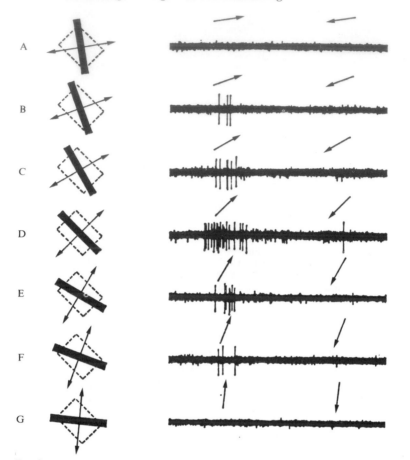

FIG. 7.6. Responses of a single cell of the visual cortex in the experiment described for Fig. 7.5. The cell produced its signals (nerve impulses) only with the bar moved to the right, at the angle shown in D. (From Hubel and Wiesel 1968.)

technique for studying the actions of many nerve cells at once. But there is a clue from the anatomical fact that the information from the sensory surfaces of the retina, or skin, or from the ear is laid out in a topographically precise way on the surface of the brain (Chapters 11 and 12). Moreover for each sense there is a series of such maps, each recombining in a new way the words of information provided by the cells. So the grammar of this language has something to do with spatial relations. It communicates meanings by topological analogies. This illuminates many questions about the means by which we think, often using spatial analogies (Chapter 16).

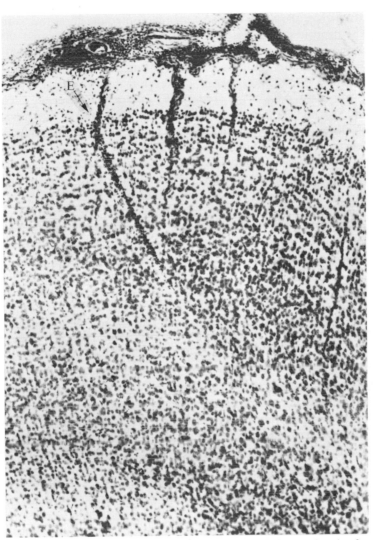

FIG. 7.7. Section of the visual cortex of the monkey. This is the actual section from the experiment shown in Fig. 7.5. E is the track of the electrode. It can be seen to cross the vertical columns of cells. The section has been stained with a dye that colours the nuclei, so all the cells are shown (compare with Fig. 7.1). Field width is 1 mm. (From Hubel and Wiesel 1968.)

## Deciding by the nervous system. The synapses

The signals set up by a pattern of light on the retina, or by an object held in the hand thus provide a coded message about the world. It is understood or decoded where the impulses in the different nerve fibres converge and activate other nerve cells. Each cell of the brain or spinal cord has a number of receptive branches, the dendrites, and a single outgoing fibre, the axon (Fig. 7.2). The dendrites are spread through a limited volume around the cell body and they serve to initiate activity in the cell so that it sends signals along its axon, reaching to a greater or lesser distance. Each fibre entering the nervous system from a sense organ branches many times and makes connections with many cells in the spinal cord or brain. Conversely each central cell receives the endings of many incoming fibres and of the fibres arising from cells elsewhere within the brain. The points where the endings of the axon of one cell meet the dendrites of another are known as *synapses* (Fig. 7.9). We must look at them to see how messages are passed on. At the synapse the membranes of the two nerve cells are pressed against each other, but the contents of the fibres are not continuous. There is therefore a barrier between the inside of the incoming (pre-synaptic) fibre and that of the post-synaptic cell. This barrier makes it impossible (usually) for the electrical nerve impulse to spread from one to the other. The transmission is effected by the release from the pre-synaptic fibre of a chemical, such as acetylcholine, to which the post-synaptic surface is especially sensitive. The response to the chemical serves to amplify the effect of impulses arriving, so that they influence the post-synaptic cell.

These chemical transmitters have become well known only in recent years. They are found in the knobs (known as boutons) at the ends of the pre-synaptic fibres (Figs. 7.8 and 7.9). The transmitter chemical is enclosed in little sacs, the synaptic vesicles. When nerve impulses arrive along the pre-synaptic fibre, some of these vesicles are released and discharge their contents into the gap between the two surfaces at the synapse. The contents of the vesicles then produce changes of the post-synaptic membrane, which acts just as if it had been electrically stimulated. This initiates a local electrical depolarization, and a flow of current through the dendrite to which the bouton is attached. But the bouton is only small and this current, produced by a small area of post-synaptic membrane is not usually sufficient to set off an action potential in the axon of the cell. However, there are many other boutons all over the surface of the dendrites. There may be up to 50 000 of these little knobs attached to the surface of a single cell of the cerebral cortex (Cragg 1967). They will include branches of several different incoming nerve fibres. The currents produced under the different boutons will summate. If they are sufficiently close together in space and in time, then they will set up an action potential, travelling away down the axon of the post-synaptic cell to its ending in contact with yet another nerve cell, or with a muscle or gland. This process of summation of the effects of the boutons is thus the means by which *decisions* are reached in the nervous system.

The signals arriving in various combinations along the sensory nerve fibres will activate particular nerve cells. A set of signals in the optic nerve

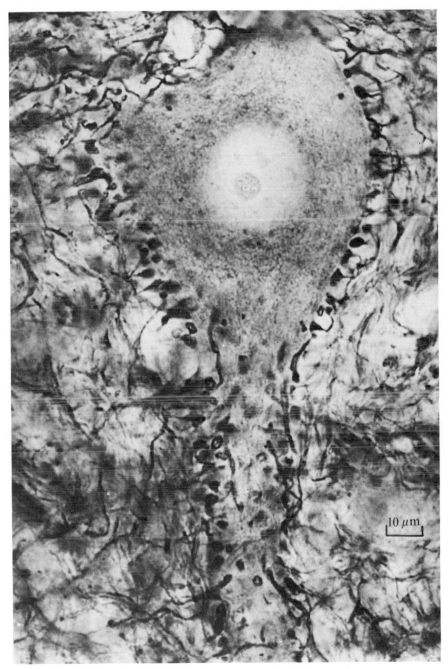

10 μm

FIG. 7.8. Part of a cell from the spinal cord of a cat, stained with silver to show many presynaptic endings of nerve fibres on the cell body and one of the dendrites.

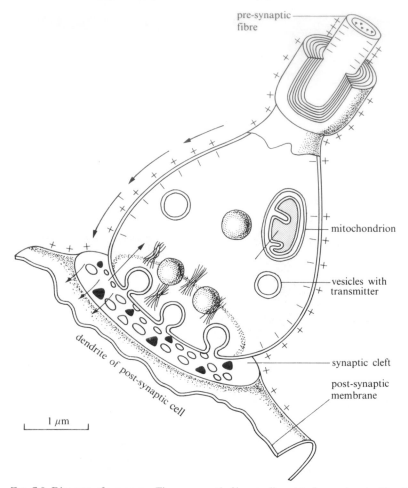

FIG. 7.9. Diagram of a synapse. The presynaptic fibre swells out to form a terminal bouton. This contains various bodies, mitochondria, fibrils, and little sacs or vesicles, which contain the chemical transmitter. The membrane of the bouton is polarized (negative inside). When an action potential arrives it depolarizes the membrane and this allows the transmitter to pour out from some of the vesicles over the post-synaptic membrane. The transmitter reacts with receptors there (black triangles) and this depolarizes the membrane of the dendrite. (After Gray 1973.)

represents the presence of a cup in the visual field. A set of signals in the nerves from the hand will occur when a cup is held. In each case certain groups of cortical nerve cells will be activated. But it is not known how the meaning of 'cup' is obtained from the signals. We do not even know whether the same set of cells is active when the cup is recognized by sight or by touch. But evidence about how this decoding is achieved is beginning to accumulate (Chapter 12). For the present the point is that the first stage of what may be called the decoding of the signals in a set of nerve fibres is by the activation of certain particular cells of the brain by the synapses.

Though it can be useful to speak of 'coding' and 'decoding' in this way we must be careful to avoid the conception that there is some final stage where the message is 'understood'. There is no central place in the brain where this occurs. The 'decoding' is completed only by action. A dog recognizes a bone by gnawing it. Even in ourselves the understanding of a meaning implies preparation for action. The very word 'understand' is the same as 'hypothesis' from the Greek 'to stand under'. The brain is continually making hypotheses that prepare for useful actions.

## Nervous control and communication

Studies of electrophysiology have given some idea of how information is coded, transmitted, and decoded by the nervous system. But animals and men are not activated only by stimuli from outside. We must return therefore to the conception that the brain is an active agent exercising control. The nerve cells are not necessarily inactive until they are stimulated from outside. Many of them never come to rest, but go through continual cycles of activity or changes in sensitivity. The effect of incoming impulses is then to alter their frequency of discharge. Whole sections of the nervous system never cease their activities. To take the simplest example, the cells of the respiratory centres send out nerve impulses regularly every few seconds to the muscles of the chest, from our first breath to our last (Chapter 8). Some of these rhythms are due to inherent properties of the membranes of the cells. Others are the result of cyclical chains of nerve cells, so arranged that they continually re-excite each other. If we decide that we are justified in holding that the brain produces behaviour we shall say that the control of all that we do comes from the combined operations of this vast set of internal rhythms with the inflow of information from the sense organs. Our task would then be to try to understand how all these millions of cells, acting together, produce the programs of human action.

The basic outlines of the patterns of connection are laid down by heredity. These are our pre-programs, such as that for breathing. Nearly all of our activities include a part that is hereditary and can be referred to as 'instinctive'. Much more interesting is the question of how these basic patterns come to be combined with other patterns of action of the nerve cells by the process of learning. This is how we acquire language and the socially transmitted programs that dominate so much of our lives. Even more interesting is the question of how new programs can arise within us, as they certainly do if we are even minimally creative. These are some of the problems that we hope to face later.

It is indeed a tremendous task to conceive such intricate operations.

'Anyhow,' you may say, 'why worry? I am not conscious of what goes on in my brain and indeed it is "I" who exerts control, not all these nerve cells.' For much of life it is indeed best not to worry. Ordinary language does well enough for most purposes of control, coding, and communication. But our endeavour is to see whether by study of the brain we can improve upon it as an instrument for philosophical understanding, and for management of ourselves in sickness and in health.

# 8  Repeating

## Rhythmical programs

The classical units by which nervous action is described are the nerve cells and their connections. These are organized into the higher assemblies of neurons that operate reflex actions, such as blinking or drawing away the hand from a flame. But nearly everyone is agreed that the behaviour even of simple animals cannot be described as the consequence only of reflexes, as if they were puppets performing a series of movements dictated by the environment. In man, as indeed in all animals, much of the impetus to act comes from within. We may gain an insight into brain programs by looking first at some rhythmic actions that are generated within the nervous system. The conduct of life in a complex environment such as our own involves an elaborate hierarchy of controls, many operating rhythmically to produce the pattern of our days.

## Living rhythms

A jellyfish is almost the simplest of animals that has a nervous system. It beats its umbrella continuously and so stays near the surface. The simple nerve network that is its 'brain' drives it to this repeated action. What do we want to find out that would help us to 'understand' the jellyfish? Obviously we want to know where the rhythm comes from. Old work by Romanes (1882) and new work by Horridge (1968) has found the answer in the marginal ganglia, which are placed at intervals around the edge of the bell. They are connected by two nerve networks, one bringing nerve signals from the surface and the other carrying them away to the muscles. If the marginal bodies are cut away one by one, the bell continues to beat until the last has gone. So the nerve cells of these ganglia are the pacemakers of the beat. They initiate the fundamental program of the life of the jellyfish. But their rhythm can be altered by messages coming from various sense organs that lie both within them and elsewhere on the body. The sense organs and nerve nets also serve to initiate feeding reactions by which the stinging tentacles carry food that they have caught towards the mouth. So the medusa has a few simple programs that keep it afloat and seeking for food. The modulation of the beat has some effect in bringing it into suitable food conditions, but I do not know of detailed studies of its behaviour and ecology. No doubt it is more complex than I have suggested.

The ongoing contraction of the bell is an outward and visible sign of the rhythmic program of the medusa. Mammals such as ourselves do not show such simple external rhythms. There are, however, internal rhythmical activities going on all the time. Quite a lot of animals much more elaborate than jellyfishes also show continual external activity. Thus a squid or a dogfish, being heavier than water, must swim continually throughout their lives. The point to stress is that all brains are continually active, producing actions that are directed to maintaining life. Various programs can be elicited by external change as modifications of the ongoing continuous activities.

## Symbolism

The programs of the brain are physically embodied in the organizational features of the nervous system from which the action patterns proceed. These structural and functional characteristics of the nervous system must therefore, as it were, reflect the environment in which the organism operates. In this sense, we can say that the features of living structures and their activities symbolize the features of the world around. This brings us again to the question of language and symbolization (Chapters 2, 7, and 20). Perhaps it gives clues as to how to think more clearly about what constitutes a symbol and how it is materially embodied or instantiated (if that is the word). We say that a sign is symbolic when it somehow corresponds to features of the surroundings in such a manner that it communicates a lot of information that is used by an organism in its business of keeping alive. The concept (like this definition) is not simple, and the concept of symbolism is used in various ways. But the key to the concept as we are using it is that a symbol is a special sort of signal because it represents the features of the surroundings in such a way that the organism immediately recognizes its significance and acts accordingly. The figure ♀ is the sign for female, but the figure of Mae West is a symbol of femininity. If the beating of the jellyfish bell is important for its life we can say that the activities of the nerve cells in its marginal bodies symbolize the sea. This may seem far-fetched and poetical, but why not? Much language is symbolic and poets teach us how to use words with special force. We may need their help in finding new ways to talk about brains. We are trying to find how to describe the correspondence between the structure and actions of the nerve cells and the life that they make possible. We can gain help by saying that the nerves in the marginal bodies of the jellyfish have a structure and organization that represents or symbolizes the sea. Furthermore these activities themselves depend on the symbol system of heredity, the code of the DNA. Symbols are indeed the core of life (p. 42). They provide the 'knowledge' of what the world is like, which is essential for survival, 'written' in the structure and organization of animals and men.

So the programs of the brain symbolize the environment in the sense that they provide actions that correspond to, or represent it. Some of the programs do this because of heredity and many of them are built up by the results of experience of the environment, recorded in the memory.

## The program for breathing

Some programs are performed with basic rhythms that are intrinsic to a cell group in the brain. From our first breath to our last gasp, the nerve cells of the respiratory centres go through rhythmical changes that provide us with oxygen by breathing. These are nerve cells that never come to rest, incidentally showing that repose and sleep, whatever they are for, are not essential for basic nervous functions (Chapter 18). Of course, these respiratory centres can vary their activity to suit the needs of the body. It would be very inefficient to provide the maximum of oxygen all the time, so we pant only after exercise. Such increases are provided partly by the direct influence on the neurons of increased carbon dioxide in the blood. Also there are sense organs in the lungs and in certain sites along the arteries that measure the amounts of oxygen and carbon dioxide in the blood and send messages to the respiratory centres, producing an increase or decrease in the rate of breathing. So this whole system can be said to be a representation of the demand for oxygen and its supply. The representation is not a 'picture' but a whole set of nerves and muscles provided by heredity with certain properties. These are the programs of respiratory behaviour. We shall try to seek for the anatomical features and functional properties that provide the programs for all the other living activities. Many of them seem much more exciting than respiration—say the program for speaking or for loving. But let us not despise breathing, after all it is essential and has provided us with a simple example of understanding the brain.

Other nerve cells only go into action when suitably excited by an external change, which we call a stimulus. Such reflex responses are also programmed. For instance the nervous system is so planned by heredity that we perform the actions of withdrawal from a pin-prick (flexor reflex), or swallowing of food, and many other such reflexes, at the appropriate moments. The mechanisms for these provide, then, programs for avoiding, for swallowing, and so on. These are not initiated rhythmically but are brought into action at the right moments as parts of rhythms of longer periodicity, such as those for feeding or sleeping.

Nearly all the more important programs are compounds of rhythms with periodicities initiated within the organism and stimuli provided from outside. When we eat, drink, or reproduce ourselves, we use programs that involve internal rhythms, manifesting themselves as 'needs' or 'wants'. These set the system searching for stimuli that lead to actions that meet the need, and produce the satisfaction of consummation or fulfilment. Both the internal changes and external stimuli are essential for the satisfactory action and so for the conservation of the individual and the species. The programs are written, we may say, in the features of bodily and nervous anatomical and physiological organization that ensures the performance of these vital actions.

## The hierarchy of controls of the pattern of life

We are looking for some scheme or system with which to talk and think usefully about the brain. We may build upon the question 'Why do we want to find such a scheme?' The answer must surely be that in some sense the brain *needs* such schemes to work with. Since the purpose of its operations is to produce actions that keep the individual alive it must have in it some model or set of hypotheses or programs that are relevant to the complicated world in which we have to live. It is easy enough to say this, but the neurologist wants to know what these models are and how they are built out of nerve cells and their actions. Another clue is that we find words for ourselves in the language that we develop for the artefacts we make (p. 41).

Computers are in a sense artificial brains. Can we frame the descriptions that we want of brain function in the language used for computers? Computers are as it were a sort of new experimental animal that we can use for our studies, just as we use *Escherichia coli* or the giant nerve fibres of a squid. Clearly we are not made of transistors and it is the *principles* of computer software that we should consider. The analogy of computer programs can indeed be helpful—but only in the most general sense. Since we do not know how information is stored in the brain we cannot expect to use the detailed analogies of addressing and storing information, which is probably not done on the same principles in brains and computers (p. 95). What can be useful is the concept of a hierarchy of controls. It is a general finding of those who study the control of complicated organizations, say of armies or factories, that it is essential to separate functions at different levels. Each level can thus operate with a minimum of information and memory, whether it be the general in command of an army, the major of a battalion, the captain of a company, or a humble corporal of his section.

Computers and brains use the hierarchical system extensively. The incoming signals pass through a series of centres, each extracting information of a more abstract or general nature. Similarly on the motor side, general indications of courses of action are produced at the highest levels and passed to lower ones, such as the spinal cord, where details of execution are organized. There is a beautiful example of this in the octopus brain where the functionally higher centres lie physically above the lower (Figs. 8.1 and 10.3). At the lowest level there are more nerve cells in the arms than in all the rest of the nervous system and they regulate the detailed movements of the individual suckers. Then there are lower motor centres, controlling the

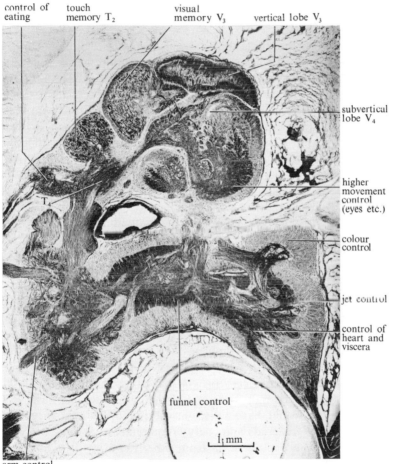

control of eating

touch memory $T_2$

visual memory $V_3$

vertical lobe $V_3$

subvertical lobe $V_4$

higher movement control (eyes etc.)

colour control

jet control

control of heart and viscera

$T_4$

funnel control

1 mm

arm control

FIG. 8.1. Section through the middle of the brain of an octopus to show the hierarchy of control centres. The cells in the lower parts provide the programs that regulate movements of the arms, funnel, jaws, etc. Higher motor centres ensure proper tracking and other controls. The highest centres, including the vertical lobe, provide memories that allow selection of appropriate programs of attack or retreat. The brain here is stained with silver, which colours especially the fibres at the centre of each lobe, leaving the cell bodies round the outsides less stained. See also Fig. 10.3.

actions of all the arms together and of the jaws, and of the mantle and funnel that make the jet and of the mucles controlling the colour. Above these are centres that are rather like our own cerebellum and ensure that movements are on target, well-timed and steady. Finally on top there is only a relatively small part of the brain concerned with deciding what to do, and this contains appropriate memory records to help in making these decisions.

The question of whether the human brain can be considered as a hierarchy has been much debated. There is a series of centres that are physically placed one above the other (Fig. 11.6). The cerebral cortex exercises a great deal of overriding control. Yet we can recognize many lower levels. The spinal cord contains the basic reflex mechanisms for the control of movements of the body and limbs. The cerebellum among other functions ensures that the movements are steady and properly timed. The reticular system at the centre of the brain has a central function in activating all the rest, for instance by the control of sleep and waking (Chapter 18). The hypothalamus and neighbouring regions contain the reference system or standards, which ensure that the whole brain takes the actions that are needed for continued life (p. 134). The cerebral cortex, much the largest part of the brain, is concerned with analysis of incoming information and deciding what to do in the light of memory records stored from the past. Although the arrangement is hierarchical yet the cortex exerts much detailed control, for instance of the movement of individual muscles (p. 125). This emphasizes the extent to which the operations of the human brain constitute one whole, more fully integrated than in other species. This very fact that there is so little 'delegation' of control may be reflected in the unity of the individual mind, being the program of a unified brain.

An alternative way of considering nervous organization is to make comparison with a set of computer programs brought together for the continual automatic regulation of some process, say of chemical manufacture. Imagine a regulation system so complete that it would take charge of a whole factory, not only for a day but for years. Its daily operations would be controlled by clocks and thermometers that allowed each part of the process to continue for the right time and at the correct temperature. For continual working it would have to set in motion operations to ensure supplies of all the raw materials and energy requirements, in spite of cyclic variation of supplies and competition from other factories. It would also have to have ways of estimating the demand for its products, and, for the really long term, the programs would have to undertake not only the repair of the factory but the building of new ones, with of course new programs. To do all this it would have to have systems capable of anticipating many eventualities in the world. However, somewhere there would have to be what we might call a 'motivating system' and it is difficult to think of this factory operating indefinitely unless the motivation was human.

What we may learn from all this is that the model or scheme we are looking for in the brain is a way of conducting life, including the motivation to do so. Animals and men live out patterns of activity, following programs of instructions partly inherited and partly learned. These programs are written or instantiated in the hierarchical structure and activities of the nervous system. These serve to model the world in the sense of producing actions that keep the organism and the species alive in spite of the hazards of the environment.

We are likely to find the program of the brain then, by looking at the pattern of life of the species. The study of such patterns is, or should be, the aim of ethologists and psychologists, looking beyond the simple features of sign–signals and stimulus–response situations. An essential feature is that the patterned activity is generated from within. The programs unfold themselves, without waiting for stimuli, although they often need those for their fulfilment.

## Living clocks

Many features of human life operate with periodicities of seconds, minutes, days, weeks, months or years (see Halberg 1977). The brain and glands between them generate these rhythmic programs and there has been a great advance in recent decades in understanding of how they do it. This knowledge may serve as an example of what may be meant in 'understanding the brain' at a simple level. Interest in internal clocks was especially stimulated by the independent discoveries that bees and birds can use the position of the sun (azimuth) as a compass for steering (von Frisch 1950; Kramer 1950; and see Pittendrigh 1974). This implies that they must have internal chronometers to compensate for the movement of the sun throughout the day, just as seamen need one to navigate by the stars (incidentally some migrating birds can use the stars too). To make a clock that is useful in this way it is necessary to have some system that will behave in a rhythmic manner at a frequency that can be set to correspond to appropriate external conditions. Many animal and plant activities can be entrained in this way, often to follow a diurnal cycle—hence circadian rhythms (from the Latin *circa, dies*; 'about a day'). If the animal is then left in constant light or darkness it will continue this oscillation, at least for some time. In one of my own investigations I studied the daily change of colour by larval lampreys. These are especially interesting because the entraining is done through the pineal organ, which in these animals is an eye with a retina. Even in mammals the pineal still continues to influence rhythms, though it is no longer an eye (p. 67).

These free-running circadian rhythms are not necessarily very exact. For example starlings have been trained to first find their food by a compass reaction, flying in a certain direction, using the sun. Then they were kept in constant light and continued to show daily activity-cycles, but with a periodicity of about 23·5 hours. After several days in the light they were again given the opportunity to use the sun as a compass and made the errors that would be expected because their watches had been running half an hour a day fast (Hoffmann 1960).

The basic oscillators that provide such clocks are probably the metabolic processes that go on in individual cells. Indeed there are many known examples of single cell rhythms both in protozoa and in metazoan cells. Thus the parasites that cause malaria (which are single protozoan cells) are carried from person to person by mosquitoes, and these may have different flight patterns, some sorts of mosquito fly at dusk others at dawn. The parasites come out into the blood of the vertebrate host at the times of flight of the *insect* vector. They are not entrained to the cycle of the vertebrate host. This is presumably a case where the cycle is genetically determined. Each type of malaria parasite has been selected for carriage by a particular species of mosquito. There is evidence that at least in some cells the basic cyclic process is synthesis of protein, determined by the read-out of information from the DNA.

In the nervous system individual cells can set the rhythmic program. Indeed nerve cells when transplanted from one insect species to another can reset the rhythm of the host (Truman 1974). In the sea-hare *Aplysia* one cell of the parieto-visceral ganglion shows an oscillatory rhythm of discharge, which continues for many days in isolation and even in tissue cultures (Strumwasser 1974). This animal is active in the day and sleeps at night, but it continues this rhythm even after removal of that particular cell. There are other rhythmic cells near to the eyes and it is these that entrain and maintain the daily activity cycle. This introduces us to the very important fact that there are several distinct pacemakers even in a sea-hare—how many more must there be in our brains to control the complicated programs of our lives? Another interesting feature of the brain of *Aplysia* is that there are neurons that produce a peptide whose injection into another animal induces egg-laying. The setting of long-term programs such as those of reproduction requires that signals set up by the nervous system be somehow *added together* to compute the time of year and forecast when breeding should occur. Production of a secretion is a good way to do this adding, and we may now follow a similar process in mammals.

## Cyclic reproduction

In animals that breed in the spring, such as ferrets and hamsters, the gonads are quiescent in both males and females throughout the summer and autumn. As the days shorten the ovary and testis ripen, ready for reproduction in the new year. This maturation is produced by an influence of the decreased amount of light signals, coming from the eye, upon the pineal gland. This organ produces a hormone, melatonin, which inhibits the gonads. Removal of the inhibition allows maturation. This mechanism is of special interest to us because it is probably the basis of one of our own most fundamental programs, the lengthening of childhood and delayed onset of reproduction. Certain rare tumours of the pineal gland produce precocious maturity at the age of 3 or 4 (Chapter 4). So it may be that a genetic mechanism that keeps the pineal gland active for about 14 years is responsible for one of the most fundamental features of our whole life system. It is significant that in adult humans there is little or no melatonin in the blood, and the pineal becomes calcified. It is no longer needed for its original purpose, since our reproduction is not cyclic like that of ferrets. Incidentally it is suggested that the reason for the recent tendency to an earlier age of puberty in developed countries is the increased amount of illumination. This explanation is not certain, but it is possible and no better reason has been found.

## Hormonal rhythms

Basic rhythms are a very fundamental feature of our human programs and several of them arise by cells in the hypothalamus acting as clocks and controlling the pituitary gland. This gland is described as the 'conductor of the orchestra' of internal secretions. But this conductor uses a 'score' that is written in the brain. For the operations of the pituitary are themselves controlled by the overlying hypothalamus, which is a small but very important part of the brain, influenced by many other parts, including the cerebral cortex. The pituitary gland produces some dozen different hormones, which control many medium- and long-term functions such as sex, reproduction and lactation, growth, metabolism, and thyroid activity. It is significant that the fibres leading from the nerve cells of the hypothalamus, besides carrying electrical nerve signals, also control the pituitary by the production of special active chemical substances, the process known as neurosecretion. Once again we see that control of longer term programs involves chemical mechanisms, allowing for accumulation and so for computing long times by addition. If we are to understand the brain it is not enough to know only about nerve cells and their connections and activities. We have to appreciate all the manifold influences that determine what we may call our moods and so all the operations of the brain.

A particularly interesting example is the control of the daily rhythm of secretion of the hormones of the cortex of the adrenal gland, which have fundamentally important actions on every cell of the body. These adrenal secretions are produced in man mainly just before dawn, as if to be ready for their job of toning us up throughout the day. Conversely in nocturnal animals such as the rat the maximum adrenal secretion is in the early evening. These rhythms are produced partly by changes in the amount of the adrenocorticotropic hormone (ACTH) released by the pituitary, partly by an intrinsic periodicity in the cells of the adrenal gland itself. This example reminds us that there are complicated interacting feedback systems even in these rather slow-going parts of the program. In the brain they must be far more complicated. Indeed brain processes of course enter into the control of the adrenal. The hypothalamus sends an ACTH-releasing factor from its nerve cells to the pituitary. These nerve cells are no doubt influenced by all sorts of cerebral activities—including alterations of our daily schedules due to east–west flying or going to night-clubs. There is indeed evidence that alteration of these circadian rhythms may have very profound effects on metabolism, perhaps including influences on the length of life.

This brings us finally to the sleeping–waking rhythm, which is controlled from a different part of the brain, the neurons of the raphe, the strip of cells near the mid-ventral line. These produce the substance serotonin (5-hydroxytryptamine (5-HT)) whose injection into cats produces the electrical activities characteristic of so-called paradoxical sleep (Chapter 18). Injection of a drug that prevents 5-HT synthesis produces insomnia, which can be reversed by 5-hydroxytryptophan, the precursor of 5-HT. Destruction by surgery of the neurons of the raphe also makes the cat stay continually active. In antagonism to the 5-HT there is another set of substances the catecholamines, such as adrenaline, which produce awakening. Probably these effects are produced by action upon different parts of the reticular system, whose nerve cells and fibres control the activity of large parts of the brain (p. 111).

These are some examples of brain programs that are performed rhythmically. This gives us an easy introduction to our plans to understand the brain, because we can readily agree that these sets of events are programmed and this may help to see how the concept of a program can be used. Heredity provides the foundation of capabilities both to perform certain actions and to modify them to suit environmental conditions. Animals and men are provided by their genes with clocks and also with the equipment needed to entrain these rhythms to the length of the day. What is thereby achieved is a state of the animal or man that represents or symbolizes the actions it must take to ensure survival under those particular conditions. This symbolic state is what we are calling for convenience a program. It is a physical system of nerve cells whose organization constitutes a coded store of instructions, compounded both of heredity and learning. It is obvious that such programs regulate many of our more routine actions throughout our lives, making us wake and sleep, eat and reproduce, grow and age. In our further chapters we shall have to see whether we can identify similar information stores as the basis for the more complicated things that we do, including loving and hating, knowing and thinking, and even believing and worshipping. We do these things only in part rhythmically, but they are actions coming from within the system. All living action comes essentially from within, as a result of the operation of the programs, part inherited, part acquired. These programs co-operate with the signals coming from the sense organs, but even these are not simply imposed on us. What we see and hear is largely the result of our own programs of search, some of them following habitual rhythms (Chapter 12).

# 9 Unfolding

## The first programs

Every animal is provided at birth with a large set of detectors for events that are likely to be relevant to its life (Chapter 5). Those that it uses become developed, while the unused ones disappear. It is not known how large the initial set may be in man, but it seems likely that the child starts with a great redundancy of connections, which is later reduced as he learns. As he matures, further potentialities become available and are in turn developed, if they are put to good use (Chapter 10).

So the program of heredity unfolds and experience makes use of it. Study of the stages of development will help very much in determining what functional features we must look for if we are to frame a reasonably adequate model of how the brain works. We should be able to find the components that are present from the beginning and how additions are made as behaviour develops towards that of the adult.

Two fundamental facts are obvious from the crying of a child's first day, that he is a communicating creature, and that he experiences something that can be called emotion or feeling—namely discomfort or pain. Charles Darwin (1872) followed carefully the sequence of development of facial expression in his own children, and more recent studies have in the main confirmed his findings (Charlesworth and Kreutzer 1973). The expressions of emotion do not all appear from the beginning, but gradually, following a hereditary program. One of the earliest is the smile. In its first stages the baby smiles mainly when it is drowsy and there is some difference of opinion as to how and when the smile becomes 'social', that is to say elicited by a human face or voice sounds. There is some agreement however that from about two months onwards a human face, seen from in front (not profile) is the stimulus that easily elicits a smile. From then on it becomes an important part of the communication system for controlling parent–child behaviour (in both directions). Laughter seems gradually to develop later, usually from four months onwards and then at five months in response to tickling, and only later in social situations. The expression of smiling is certainly much older than mankind, in monkeys it is used for submission, that is, in a sense, for agreement. The capacity to be submissive and agreeable with the group has evidently become exaggerated in man.

Darwin found that anger developed later than smiling. He put it at four months, indicated by red face and screams of rage and frustration. Full temper tantrums, however, come later still, in the second year. Nearly everyone will have seen a child in such a state, it is an unmistakable protest. But surely the child cannot have *learned* to throw tantrums by observation of his elders. The capacity to do so was inborn and then developed and matured. It must involve specific actions of the brain, and study of aggression in animals suggests which part of the brain it comes from (Chapter 15). Like smiling it certainly has a history long preceding our own appearance on the earth.

As behaviour becomes more complicated it is increasingly difficult to separate the inborn and acquired elements, but it seems likely that both are present even in more complicated actions, for instance amusement. Darwin recorded at 3½ months that a child laughs at a game of peek-a-boo. More complicated came jealousy at 15 months, when Darwin pretended to caress a large doll. Then shyness, when he returned after an absence and the child hesitated and lowered his eyes. It would be difficult to say how much of such responses is innate and how much learned. But the response of blushing when ashamed must be innate and so also probably is the expression of grief with turned down mouth.

Blushing is especially interesting since the sense of shame involves some of the most human social characteristics. It develops rather late (only at 2–4 years according to Darwin) and more readily in girls. Earlier, the child is unselfconscious and not shy. But the capacity to blush is inborn. Indeed only by long training do the wicked learn not to blush when they lie! Can blushing be one of our later evolutionary developments? Perhaps it was advantageous to evolve, after speech, an anti-misinformation device. Surely the incapacity *not* to show shame is a powerful aid to the moral practices that are close to the centre of civilized religion and social organization (Chapter 19).

There are various ways of investigating which responses are innate. For instance, blind children at first smile, cry, laugh, and show the usual signs of joy, anger, annoyance, and sulkiness. But these manifestations decrease with age. Like so many other inborn responses they atrophy if not used. Other evidence about the innateness of expressive behaviour comes from feral ('wolf') children who showed the capacity of anger, joy, shyness, impatience, and depression (Maclean 1977). Other evidence is that expressions of emotion are recognized by people in very distinct cultures when shown by photographs.

The importance of these perhaps rather obvious facts for us is that humans are born with certain capacities for communication of emotional and even moral attitudes. This is not surprising since such expressions constitute the language of animals—such as it is. Can we recognize any similar stage of progressive development of more distinctively human characteristics?

## Growing skills of the infant

Stages of the appearance of physical operations by children have been studied by many workers but we shall use especially the observations of J. Bruner, formerly of Harvard, now at Oxford (1974). A child is born with a large set of actions that it can already perform perfectly well, including those that it needs to maintain its life such as sucking, swallowing, and breathing. It can do these things almost at once and without instruction, moreover it avoids trying to do more than one of them at a time. These are actions performed with little information and this implies that they are 'hard-wired' and cannot be varied or recombined in any subtle ways.

But the skills that the child is about to learn are quite different from these. Bruner lists five competences that will be acquired by the end of the first year—*feeding, attending, perceiving, manipulating*, and *interacting with others*. Each of these has a background of species-typical genetic instructions, but the neurons able to perform these tasks are also capable of adaptational changes. All capacity to adapt and to learn depends upon the possession of particular sorts of nerve cell and their metabolic operations (see Chapter 10). We do not know what these learning mechanisms are and cannot say how far they limit the variation in performance that can be learned. Certainly these skills do not mature in fixed or invariant ways, but flexibly, to suit the particular conditions that are encountered. Like other memory processes these are partly achieved by suppression of unwanted actions, limiting originally redundant sets of possibilities, which is the scheme that I suggest for memory mechanisms in general (Chapter 10).

These early skills are not isolated units, to be later replaced, or ones to which others will later be added. On the contrary they form the very centre and core of all subsequent behaviour and personality, the centre of the brain-program of action. They 'become the constituents for new patterns of action directed at more remote or complex objectives' (Bruner 1974, p. 298). These skills thus become generative, in the sense that they can be combined and recombined—they are open and lead on to the use of tools and of language.

From the very start we can recognize in the acquisition of such skills the elements of much of human behaviour. The same fundamental program is at the base of the processes that make culture possible. They are characterized by Bruner as *intention, skill, attention*, and *integration*. We can illustrate these by the growth of the power of the child to integrate the action of eye and hand. By intention we mean in this case the capacity to direct anticipatory orientating action towards an object, say in the visual field, with the aim of putting it in the mouth.

There are considerable differences in the situations to which infants will direct their gaze, and in the age at which they will do so. The earliest visually attractive objects in Bruner's studies included circles with features resembling the human face or, alternatively, bright sparkly objects. The action of following objects with the eyes is perhaps the earliest of all anticipation or intention movements. It must involve a process by which distinction is made between movements produced by the individual and those initiated in the outside world. We shall follow the mechanisms for this later. It is probably largely predetermined in the infant and such activity is soon performed smoothly and with skill (Bruner 1974, p. 272). The capacity to make this distinction between self and other is thus fundamentally linked with *intention*, the aim of reaching a particular situation and achieving satisfaction therefrom.

## Searching for what to see

For its first six weeks or so the child is very easily distractable but then for a while becomes so readily attached to visual targets that it cannot leave them. Gradually it adopts what Piaget might call a schema of moving the eyes around, searching for targets rather than being caught by them (Chapter 12). This is an excellent example of a program in the sense we are using it. Partly by inheritance and partly by learning the brain has come to produce a set of operations that is switched on whenever the conditions are appropriate. When we come to examine the process of seeing we shall be able to trace the neurological mechanism that is used and knowledge of it is a great help to pediatricians in the care of children's eyesight.

## Learning to explore

Meanwhile at about 6–8 weeks the earliest manipulations begin. At first when an attractive object appears the child swipes crudely towards the midline, at the same time opening its mouth. If a hand happens to hit the object it may be grasped and brought to the mouth. Bringing the hand alone to the mouth is accomplished in very early days and seeing an attractive object will at first itself be followed by mouth opening. Perception of any-thing is indeed an *act*, or at least clearly accompanied by an act. This is a very important thought, with many implications.

Gradually manipulative skill improves, at first there is rivalry between the two hands, then they come to be used together. The movements become more and more anticipatory, by feed forward, for instance the hand is opened as the arm moves towards an object. If the object and hand are covered at the moment of contact a 7-month child will not take it but will pull his hand out and search again. At 9 months he will bring the object out. The full achievement of the skill of exploring objects involves eliminating various sorts of irrelevance. At first the child tenses his whole body and makes movements of arms and shoulders, as well as hands, often in competition. All this becomes sorted out at about 8 months as successive stages are simplified and ordered, each one or two steps ahead, so that the object does not have to be followed intensely at each step. The action becomes ballistic, fully planned from the start to stop at the right point. The whole process gradually becomes freed from the mouth as its aim. The child now explores the object visually or tactually, or by the action of banging with it. So another phase of visual and manual exploration begins, ready to lead on to the capacities that have allowed production of tools of all sorts from hand axes to aeroplanes.

## Later development of the brain

The period of maturation that we have been following with Jerry Bruner is approximately what Piaget calls the period of sensori-motor intelligence— from birth to about 2 years old (1971). We have now to see whether we can gain any insights into what happens next as the child's brain develops further. Inevitably it becomes more difficult to do this as he approaches the mature human condition. Experiments with kittens will not tell us much about the skills that are acquired by children in the periods Piaget calls pre-operational thought and concrete operations. They include first, language, then the later acquisition of the capacity to understand conservation of quantity, cause and effect, and much else.

It is worthwhile to examine the changes that take place, and for educational theory it is fundamental. As neuroscience develops we shall certainly come to understand more. There is some indirect evidence that these later developments are accompanied by physical changes in the brain. For example if a child up to about 10 years old unfortunately loses the usually dominant left cerebral hemisphere it will none the less be able to acquire language in the right hemisphere, which would normally not possess this facility. So evidently the use to which the brain is put fundamentally influences its later development.

## Learning about conservation

In what Piaget calls the pre-operational stage 2–7 years the child is dependent on concepts involving spatiotemporal continuity. For example his classification categories may change from moment to moment. Asked to put together similar objects from several sets mixed together he may first choose a red square and red triangle, saying they are alike because both are red, Then instead of adding another red he will add a yellow triangle 'because it has the same shape', and then back to colour with a yellow circle and so on. Similarly with language, spatial concepts must be preserved. Shown a toy truck pushing a car he can say 'truck pushes car', but not 'car is pushed by truck'—the pusher must come first and the passive language of reversibilities is simply not available. The well-known experiments of failure of conservation concepts are similar. The child judges quantity by the level of liquid it can see in a jar. The concept of a given quantity (that is of object conservation) simply has no meaning for him apart from what he can see (Beard 1969). He has no conception of measuring or of series. Similar problems arise over comparisons. Take the question, Edith is fairer than Susan, Edith is darker than Lily: Who is the darkest? Most young children cannot solve this. They consider each relationship separately. I confess to finding the problem difficult myself!

How then does a child come to the concepts of conservation and relationships as he passes through the period of concrete operations (7–12 years)? It seems that this cannot be 'taught'. A child can be shown conservation and reversibility and even do it for himself but still not be able to make the reversal in his head. Experience must play a part, but there is little account in the literature of intermediate stages, and teachers seem to avoid the attempt to teach such skills as understanding of reversibility. It seems likely that what is involved is largely a process of maturation of a program by which the brain comes to be able to combine distinct experiences in new ways. In the pre-operational stage the child's thinking is described by Piaget as like a slow-motion film, representing one static frame after another but lacking a simultaneous encompassing view of all the frames (Schwebel and Raph 1974, p. 10).

## The unified model in the brain

Later, therefore, there is a unification of previously distinct processes, either by the overall interaction of the parts or by a dominating superior control. Workers in the subject often speak of this appearance of a unified approach, as if the child now truly begins to operate with a *single model*, which it lacked before. The characteristic achievements of this stage all provide capacities for such a general view. Classification, seriation, conservation, number and space all begin to enter into judgements, behaviour, and speech. The child now has 'something flexible and plastic and yet consistent and enduring, with which he can structure the present in terms of the past without undue strain and dislocation, that is, without the ever-present tendency to tumble into the perplexity and contradiction which mark the preschooler' (Flavell 1963, p. 165).

This is a good way to think about the model in the brain, but what does the change involve neurologically and what external influences are required for this maturation to occur? One guess is that the integrated action of the various parts of the cortex may depend upon maturation of long pathways between areas, which develop relatively late. But this is much too simple and anyhow few of such pathways are known. There must be much more to it than this. Emotional factors are certainly involved, for one pronounced feature is that at this time the child is becoming more socialized and less egocentric. The interaction with others may be a requirement for the maturation. The child begins to consider his own actions, to get beyond individual acts and words, in fact to pass from personal forms of representation to socialized forms with more general meaning.

## Cognition and emotion

At all times the child is acting out its own life in the immediate present—not preparing for some undiscernable future. His own homeostasis is his primary interest in these early years, and for long after, and meeting his own emotional and physical needs may be at all stages actually a requirement for maturation. And '. . . before and beyond the three R's—more precisely beneath the three R's—exists a human being who is not partly cognitive and partly emotional but in being and substance is both of these all of the time and indivisibly' (Schwebel and Raph 1974, p. 30). We have to think of all brain programs of activity as compounded in this way. Similar considerations come into play far beyond the stage of the three R's into the period when the child begins to conduct formal operations in its head, beyond 12 years and indeed throughout the life of the adult. Cognition and emotion are never wholly separate, because of the interaction of brain processes. It is difficult to know how far it is wise to try to separate cognitive skills from their emotional background. Academic purity frowns upon emotion and believes that it need not enter into learned logical discourse. Certainly we do not want emotion in every phase of discussion, but attempts to elucidate fundamentals without considering why we are doing so are bound to fail to satisfy (Chapter 17).

## The program for adolescence

To emphasize the place that emotion plays in the unfolding of the program consider what happens at adolescence. Here a clock that has been ticking in the hypothalamus sends chemical signals to the pituitary to release more gonadotropic hormones (Fig. 9.1). The individual has no control over this clock and the evidence is that environmental factors such as climate or food do not have much effect either. Yet sex hormones now released from the ovary or testis produce a dramatic change in her or his physical and emotional condition. It is easy to dismiss this as a crude example of an unfolding program but there is every reason to think that all nervous activities are influenced by the changes at puberty. And the individual will

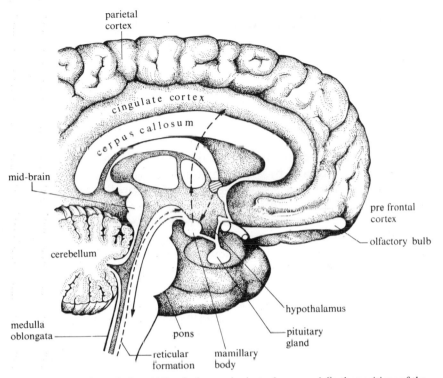

parietal
cortex

cingulate cortex

corpus callosum

mid-brain

pre frontal
cortex

olfactory bulb

cerebellum

hypothalamus

medulla
oblongata

pituitary
gland

pons

reticular
formation

mamillary
body

FIG. 9.1. Section through the middle of a human brain to show especially the positions of the hypothalamus, pituitary body, and the reticular formation. (From Young 1971.)

continue to be so influenced for every day of his life, indeed, as one sadly learns, there are physical and emotional changes hardly less profound towards its end. If the biologist is called crude to emphasize that many emotional as well as rational factors influence all thinking he may reply that no system that claims to show what is meant by knowledge should neglect them. For the very concept of receiving information depends upon the presence of a receiver who is able to produce acts that in some way correspond to the signals that are sent (p. 42). And such actions are the property so far as we know only of systems like ourselves that are motivated by inner urges to ensure life's continuance. The sustained effort to do this is somewhere near to the root of all acquisition of knowledge.

# 10 Learning, remembering, and forgetting

## What's in a memory?

It might seem to be contradictory to speak of a program for learning, since this is one of the processes by which programs are written in the brain. But of course we learn only because we are provided by heredity with programs that enable us to do so. Indeed, the situation is even more complicated, there are programs for learning to learn. These inborn mechanisms are not infinitely powerful, we cannot learn *any* thing or *every* thing. The power to learn will obviously vary between individuals and there may be limits to what it is possible for any person to learn. This is the problem of the *tabula rasa*, which still bedevils philosophy and politics 200 years after John Locke (see p. 25). To what extent is the brain at birth a blank sheet that can learn anything? Are we all endowed with almost unlimited learning power that could be made the basis of any desired social, political, and educational policies? Should we aspire to sufficient knowledge and skill to mould all human beings to a satisfactory pattern of life? Or, alternatively, does the learning program differ in each of us, and does it always carry limitations, imposed by its ancestry as a tool suitable for use by our hunter–gathering or ape-like ancestors? These are momentous questions indeed, in the literal sense of their relevance to world politics today. This is one of the points at which biological knowledge is needed to help with our most important decisions.

Certainly we can say that a brain is not a general-purpose computer into whose memory *any* information can be placed. It is more like one that already has a system of programs within it. In a digital computer, each item of information is stored at a particular location as the answer to a particular question that has been arranged by the program. Even to record the numbers beyond 8, four such points must be consulted (8 = 1000, 9 = 1001, 10 = 1010, and so on). The system works only because the 'address' of the points can be found in order and very fast. The information from each point is then sent to one or a few central processers, where the calculations are done. The information at each point of a computer memory is thus determined wholly by the programmer (though some computers include programs for search of the environment). Information can be added to the store very rapidly and it can be equally quickly totally erased and replaced by quite different information. Obviously, brains are not like this. Can you imagine total erasure of all the information in your head and its replacement? Bernard Williams (1956–7) and other philosophers have indeed seriously discussed the implications of doing this. If my information was put into your brain would you be you or me? To a biologist, this theoretical question seems simply absurd and irrelevant. The memory of a person or animal is something that is constructed and grows, the result of a unique series of experiences and actions from conception onwards. It can be added to, but never wholly remade. Indeed, its very existence is only possible as part of that program of events that we call a lifetime. But here we must ask what sort of entity is a memory; is it indeed a thing?

It is interesting that until the publication in 1976 of the second volume of the *Supplement*, the *Oxford English Dictionary* did not mention the use of the word 'memory' for an *instrument*. This usage has grown up only since the invention of computers in the 1940s. In the earlier edition of this dictionary, memory is the 'faculty of remembering'. The use of the word faculty indeed shows a sort of pre-scientific attempt to describe an agent. A 'faculty' seems to be a sort of immaterial machine, but it would distract us to follow this piece of history. As so often happens, human invention of a useful assistant for a natural function has led to clarification of the language with which we talk about that function in ourselves. I propose that we use the word memory essentially as the computer scientist does for the physical agent or system that allows for the setting up of programs of action effective for survival, modified to suit the experience of the individual. (This does not mean that we use computer methods of coding or addressing, though sometimes there are similarities between brain programs and computer software.) Memories are thus physical systems in brains, whose organization and activities constitute records or representations of the outside world, not in the passive sense of pictures but as action systems. The representations are accurate to the extent that they allow the organism to re-present appropriate action to the world. This brings us into head-on collision with daily use, where 'memory', besides indicating the faculty of remembering, is also the word we use for our personal conscious experiences. I might say that I have a memory of the house my parents lived in, or a memory of what I ate for breakfast this morning. As before, I propose that at this stage of our enquiry, we should evade this problem, promising to return to it later (p. 215). Let us see what categories of memory there may be that do *not* require the use of a concept of consciousness.

## Memory for skills

William James (1890) recognized two categories or components of memory, primary and secondary, which have often been noticed since. Indeed there have been numerous attempts to divide memory (often dichotomously, as the human brain seems to like to do). Pavlovians recognize two sorts of conditioned reflexes—classical or associational and operant or instrumental—sometimes called Types 1 and 2. If we are to have a dichotomy I prefer that suggested by Gregory (1969, p. 236), who distinguishes stored information of two sorts, memory for skills and memory for events. The memory for skills is certainly not strictly conscious. For a wide range of physical actions we learn to perform certain behavioural acts and strategies, and psychologists have made careful study of the course of such learning. It is characteristic of acquiring a skill, say to type or to play the piano, that at first there is little progress, then there is advance by jumps to new plateaux of achievement. Skill may allow apparently impossible feats, as in playing arpeggios, which can be much faster than the half second which is the minimum human decision time. How has the brain acquired a system that can produce such a performance? Probably the answer is that there has been laid down a model, or as I prefer to say, a program, that dictates the performance to be produced as certain fixed groups of input features occur. A typist or pianist reading at top speed will make mistakes over *unusual* letters or notes. He achieves his results by prediction, whole large sequences of action are released by simple signals. Similar systems of prediction are used in other skilled performances, for instance in speaking and the understanding of language. To understand how skills are learned, we shall have to try to find how such an action system can be developed and especially what coding system allows reading of outside instructions and performance of actions that represent them.

All *animal* memories can be considered as stored information for the performance of skills. We only know that an animal has learned by studying its actions. I will not say that this disposes of Gregory's second category, of memory for events. We humans certainly do have the facility to recall single events that occurred both recently and long ago. Capacity to do this may be one of our unique features and some workers would recognize two categories here, semantic memory, for meanings of words and concepts, and episodic memory for personal experiences (Tulving 1972). In order to find out what the memory system of the brain is like it is probably wiser to begin by studying the memory for skills rather than events. This, of course, does not mean that the two sorts of memory are unrelated, nor that we must restrict ourselves to animals.

## Three theories of memory

A physical event outside the body provides 'information' only if the nervous system identifies it as a symbol, a sign that something is likely to have a particular relevance for life, which may be good or bad. The smell of food is not eatable, nor do nerve impulses in the olfactory nerve provide calories, but an adult animal or man can learn to go towards those smells that are likely to yield food but to avoid others. What we now want to know is what changes occur in the brain during such adult learning. How do particular patterns of nerve impulses come to have symbolic meaning?

An animal or man will only learn if he tries to do things. A creature that sits still and does nothing cannot learn anything. Put the other way round, this reminds us once again that whatever the memory is, it is certainly a part of an action system. It is not a passive structure nor a picture, nor a model in any literal representational sense. It is particularly important to stress this because, following Bartlett (1932) and Craik (1943), many people, including myself, have developed the concept that by learning we build a model in the brain (Young 1964). I am using now the concept of programs or hypotheses or plans partly because people are so apt to consider a model as a static thing. We have defined the programs of the brain as plans for action and we are now asking how these are learned. But of course whether we speak of models or programs or plans, they must have a physical basis. Even if human memory records are set up 'in our minds', I think all scientists at least would agree that when we learn there must also be a change in our brains.

Out of all the immense amount of work that has been devoted to memory, there have emerged three types of theory about the nature of the change that establishes a memory record. There might be (1) a change of standing pattern of activity, or (2) a change of some specific chemical molecules, such as the instructional molecules of RNA, or (3) a change in the pathways between neurons within the nervous system. This last is probably the main basis for stable memory records, but all three methods are worth examining.

## Does memory depend upon self-re-exciting activity?

The brain is continually active and one sign of this is its electrical activities, whether action potentials or slower potential changes such as can be seen in electroencephalograms (Chapter 18). Several workers have shown that as an animal learns there are changes in the electrical activity of the brain. The late J. Olds (1977) and his colleagues at the California Institute of Technology developed a technique by which after implanting electrodes in the brain of a rat, they could follow the electrical activity of various regions before, during, and after learning a simple task such as pressing a lever to obtain a pellet of food. The whole experiment can be done in two or three days. Changes in electrical activity were found in many parts of the brain. Very interestingly, the earliest signs were in certain regions near the hind end of the brain, including the medial forebrain bundle, which we shall later identify as a possible reward pathway (Chapter 13). Changes in the thalamus come later in the learning process, and changes in the cerebral cortex later still.

Unfortunately, we do not yet know how these electrical changes operate to produce the new behaviour of the animal. An early suggestion was that learning sets up cycles of activity in the brain and that these serve to maintain a particular pattern of activity. The importance of self-re-exciting chains of nervous action was first realized, I think, by Alexander Forbes of Harvard in 1922, dealing with the spinal cord, and then by Lorenté de No in 1933 for the control of eye movements. I learned of it from Lorenté during a visit to St Louis in 1936. I then noticed that in the brains of cuttlefishes there are very beautiful self-re-exciting circuits (1938). We found that cuttlefishes show an interesting simple sort of memory. When their prey, say a prawn, disappears out of sight, they will follow it. But they cannot do this if the circuit has been interrupted by a cut (Sanders and Young 1940). So it may be that the nerve impulses going round the circuit serve as it were to keep the representation of the prawn acting upon the cuttlefish, even when the image is no longer on the retina. This has never been proved to be the explanation of this case, but the circuit arrangement is very striking and there is more evidence for such a mechanism in octopuses (p. 90).

Many workers have since used the concept of self-re-exciting chains as parts of their theories of memory (e.g. Hebb 1949, who is often cited as the originator of the concept). It is unlikely that this is the main basis for long-term memory, but such circuits may play an important part in setting up the record. Shocks to the brain received immediately after an event prevent the establishment of a long-term memory record of it. This is a fact that is well attested by those who suffer accidents, and is confirmed by many experiments with electrical shocks given to men or animals. A shock received say one hour later has no such effect on the memory. Footballers questioned immediately after they had been concussed were able to give information about what happened, but half an hour later could remember nothing. There had been no transfer to the long-term store. So the conception has grown up that the record is formed in two stages (perhaps more). In the first or *short-term memory*, the record is maintained by an ongoing activity, perhaps of the cyclic form I have discussed. Thereafter, a process known as consolidation takes place and the record is firmly established. This *long-term memory record* surely must involve some stable physical change, for records of single events can remain for up to 100 years in man. Cyclic activity could not last for a fraction of this time without becoming distorted. Moreover, procedures that must upset activity, or retard or even stop it, such as shock, anaesthesia, or cooling nearly to freezing point, do not disrupt the memory in an animal.

## Is the memory record stored in macromolecules?

I shall not spend long on this hypothesis, which has been very popular with biochemists. There have been various fantastic reports of the transfer of records between flat worms that eat each other, or by injection of brain extracts and so on. There is no doubt that following such ingestions or injections, the behaviour of the recipients may be changed. For instance, after certain injections animals may jump away faster to avoid a shock, as in the experiments of Ungar (1972). Changes in the tendency to respond are indeed a simple form of learning, known as sensitization, which is common in simpler animals, which have no discriminative memory mechanism. But the memory records that we are really interested in are discriminative and *specific*. The animal must do one thing in response to one stimulus and another to a related one   not merely to give one avoidance response. There have been no convincing experiments showing that such discrimination depends upon specific molecules, or that it can be transmitted by injections. Domagk of Göttingen and his colleagues recently enlisted our help in Naples to see whether they could find evidence of the presence of specific memory molecules in brain extracts from trained octopuses (1976). Animals were trained to take a rough sphere but reject a smooth one (or the reverse) (p. 84). The injection of brain extracts from the trained animals produced no effect on the behaviour of untrained recipients, nor did they increase (or decrease) the subsequent speed of learning. Of course, it can be said that these were the wrong extracts and so on, but the fact is that no experiments of this sort in any animal have yet succeeded in showing transfer of capacity to discriminate.

In any case, it is most unlikely that the coding system of the brain involves specific chemical molecules since there is no sign of them from any physiological experiments. A great range of chemical substances is of course involved in the action of the nervous system, including for instance, acetylcholine, adrenaline, serotonin, and various amino-acids. But these are all relatively simple substances, they are not at all like the gigantic informational molecules of DNA and RNA. Everything known about the nervous system suggests that its coding depends upon the use of very numerous distinct channels, each carrying a slightly different feature of the information. New behaviour is therefore likely to be the result of new connections, not of the formation of specific molecules.

## Memory by selection between pathways

The majority of neuroscientists probably believe that this is the basis of the memory mechanism, which indeed seems an inevitable conclusion if the brain is essentially a multichannel system. Yet there is really no single piece of hard evidence for this 'belief' that the memory depends upon changed connections. Several workers have shown that anatomical and biochemical features of nervous tissue change with increased or decreased use (see Rosenzweig *et al.* 1972). But no one has found a situation suitable for the study of the detailed form and function of nerve cells before and after the learning of a discrimination. This is serious and could be seen as a great criticism of those of us who have spent much of our lives in the study of memory. The 'belief' is probably sound and historians of science will perhaps see in the future why we have failed so far. It may be that the discovery of the specific nucleotides has actually hindered neuroscience. Many able biochemists and biophysicists have come to work in biology but have been led astray by the macromolecules.

Electron microscopy has brought the possibility of visualizing changed synapses, and hence of changed connections but has revealed that there are so many synapses on each cell that looking for those changed by learning is worse than trying to find the needle in a haystack. My own view is that what is needed is to concentrate attention on parts of the brain that are likely to reveal the change, even if that means using animals that do not show such elaborate memory records as our own.

## The two memories of the octopus

It has been for this reason that we have studied the octopus. I first turned to this animal because its nervous centres are of a suitable level of complexity to allow discriminative memory. It turns out that octopuses have not one but *two* distinct discriminative memory systems, as well as some simpler memory capacities. There is a visual memory system that ensures that the animal attacks things that look like providing food and avoids those that give shocks (Fig. 10.1). In addition there is a touch memory system that ensures that the arms draw in only those objects it touches that have in the past been associated with food, and rejects those that give shocks (Fig. 10.2). We have not succeeded in showing what changes are involved in the memory mechanism, yet from the results that the octopuses have yielded, we can draw various conclusions that help considerably in the search for useful lines of attack on the memory problem.

## The memory record is localized

The changes involved in adult learning take place in specific parts of the brain that have evolved for this particular function. In octopuses there are distinct sets of lobes serving to make the programs that are visual and tactile memory records. Each memory system includes four separate centres and these are similar in the two sets (Figs. 8.1 and 10.3). The two systems are almost completely separate, so that removing one of them does not interfere

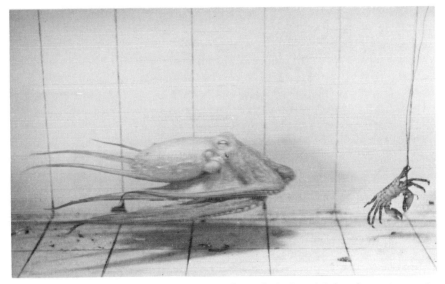

FIG. 10.1. An octopus swimming forward to attack a crab, the funnel, below the eye, is turned backwards. In escape reactions the jet propels the animal backwards.

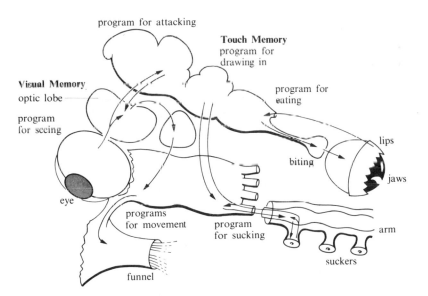

FIG. 10.2. The two discriminative memory systems of an octopus. Both of these are developments of the part of the brain that controls eating. The touch memory contains the program that ensures drawing in food, in the visual memory are the programs that produce attack on likely food objects.

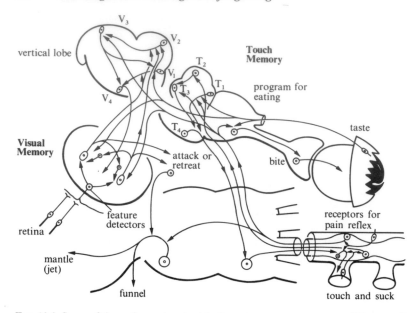

Fɪɢ. 10.3. Some of the pathways involved in the octopus memory systems. Fibres sending signals from the eyes, suckers (touch), lips (taste), and skin (pain) make local connections to operate reflex programs and then pass on to the memory centres. They pass through four similar areas in each of the memories, marked $V_{1-4}$ and $T_{1-4}$. The actual appearance of these areas can be seen in Fig. 8.1.

with the other (Bradley and Young 1975). This finding of localizable memory systems may seem to contradict the experience in mammals, where changes occur widely throughout the brain during learning (p. 92). It may be that this difference is a misleading result of the fact that mammalian action systems make use of information from many sensory systems at once. The design of the cerebral cortex is indeed partly based on the principle of bringing signals together. The records for particular sorts of learning may nevertheless be localized within the whole. There is certainly much evidence of specific types of defect from localized cortical lesions. But the cortex is an enormous haystack and we are more likely to find our needles in some smaller bundle.

## Mnemons, the units of memory

In order to clarify our ideas about the changes that take place in the memory it is useful to think about how the feature detectors of the sense organs come to have appropriate connections with motor systems. An untrained octopus will come out slowly to attack either a vertical or a horizontal rectangle. If it is given shocks for the vertical rectangle and a piece of fish for the horizontal one it learns in a few trials to come out quickly to the latter but to stay at home when the vertical shape appears. It could also learn the reverse discrimination. It follows that before training there must have been potential connections of both sorts of feature detectors with both of the action systems (Fig. 10.4). An exactly similar situation exists in the touch memory system of the octopus. It can be taught either to draw in a rough object and to reject a smooth one, or the reverse.

In these relatively simple situations therefore the learning consists of altering the probabilities of the effects of the feature detectors (Fig. 10.4). This could be done either by increasing the effectiveness of the pathways that are wanted, or by decreasing those that are not. We shall assume that *both* methods are adopted (p. 91). The result is that after learning, each feature detector comes to initiate a program producing one action, whereas initially it could have played a part in either of two (or more) actions. Each feature detector with its attendant neurons thus constitutes a unit of memory or *mnemon*. It is the entity that records one bit of information, namely the decision which of two actions shall follow when one particular external change occurs.

Of course in practice the outputs of many feature detectors work together and the situation is very complicated. Nevertheless it is conceptually useful to consider mnemons as logical units, perhaps actually realized in the way shown in Fig. 10.4 in relatively simple situations such as that of the octopus. It is convenient to suppose that these units become 'switched' completely and irreversibly as soon as they are activated by appropriately associated external stimuli and rewards. Gradual learning then consists in the accumulation of sufficient units to ensure reliable response. The concept of a

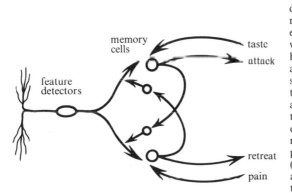

FIG. 10.4. A mnemon or single memory unit. The feature-detector cell records the occurrence of a particular type of event (say presence of an object with a vertical outline). The cell has two outputs allowing for alternative actions. There is a slight bias in favour of one of these, producing say a slow attack on the object. Signals will then arrive indicating the results of the action and will either reinforce what was done or produce the opposite action (retreat). Side branches will then activate the small cells, making them produce an inhibitory transmitter that blocks the unwanted pathway. Thereafter this feature detector can produce only one response.

mnemon has been developed on the basis that units are switched irreversibly in this way, mainly by switching off the unwanted pathway. But the basic principle remains the same if the switching mechanism proves to operate gradually, requiring several exposures, and if it involves increase of the wanted as well as decrease of the unwanted pathways. It is very likely that the change occurs in both directions. The question of *how* the changes in probability are produced is discussed later.

## Rewards for learning

In order to learn the symbolic significance of signals that come in from the outside world an animal or man must be able to relate them to its own life and needs, by the subsequent satisfaction or pain that results when it acts in a certain way. Learning most obviously takes place when an animal *does* something, and receives a positive or negative reward for the act. This is a controversial subject, because association between stimuli may occur without obvious reward, at least in higher animals, and of course in humans. Rather than engage in this controversy over reinforcement, I prefer the concrete evidence that some systems that learn do indeed include pathways by which signals of reinforcement from inside an animal can be combined with those from outside and so give them symbolic meaning. Knowledge even of such simple learning from rewards would be a great step towards understanding of learning without obvious rewards. Human beings do of course have powerful reward systems, but they involve prizes more difficult to discuss than simple food or shock.

In octopuses, the system shown in Fig. 10.3 allows for signals of taste from the lips, or of pain from all over the body to come into relation with signals from the eyes or from the arms. Even in mammals we begin to know something of how rewards operate. Figure 10.5 shows a pathway characterized by the chemical transmitters in its fibres. It leads from the locus coeruleus in the medulla oblongata to the hypothalamus and so to the cingulate cortex and other fore-brain areas. The nucleus coeruleus lies close to the place of entry of the nerve fibres that bring sensations of taste from the tongue. Crow and his colleagues of Aberdeen, showed that rats from which the locus coeruleus had been removed could not learn to run in a maze for a food reward (Anlezark *et al.* 1973). Moreover, with electrodes planted in this nucleus, rats will learn to press a lever repeatedly to stimulate themselves (Chapter 13). Finally, the hippocampus is a part of the brain deeply implicated in learning in man, in ways that we shall later discuss. The locus coeruleus also sends fibres to the cerebellum and various schemes have been suggested for the involvement of the cerebellum in learning (Mark 1974, Gilbert 1975). On the other hand this subject is very new and controversial and more recently it has been denied that either the locus coer-

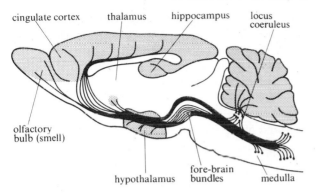

cingulate cortex    thalamus    hippocampus    locus
                                            coeruleus

olfactory
bulb (smell)

hypothalamus    fore-brain    medulla
            bundles

FIG. 10.5. Diagram of some aminergic pathways in a rat's brain. They lead forwards from the cells of the locus coeruleus and other centres in the medulla oblongata, which are close to the entry of fibres of taste. These pathways carry signals indicating good food forwards to the hypothalamus, hippocampus and cingulate cortex. All these areas are involved in the programs regulating eating, including learning what is good to eat. (After Ungerstedt 1971.)

uleus or the cerebellum are involved in learning of movements in rats (Routtenberg 1976). Such contradictions are common during the opening up of new fields of research in a complex subject. The patient investigator or student has to use his judgement as he watches the evidence unfold and has the pleasure of discovering that each new controversy deepens his knowledge of the intricacies of his subject.

## A short-term memory to hold the address

Learning thus consists of a change in the probabilities of conduction in certain pathways. Therefore the signals indicating rewards (e.g. taste or pain) must somehow be brought to act upon the pathways between specific detectors and effectors. But there will often be a delay of at least several seconds between the moment when an animal sees or hears something and moves off to investigate it, and the moment when he reaches it and receives a taste or pain. Some holding device is therefore needed to keep a short-lasting memory of the earlier situation until the reward arrives. In an octopus, this is probably one of the functions of the vertical lobe system ($V_{1-4}$ in Fig. 10.3). This could provide a re-exciting circuit by which whatever cells are active in the optic lobe when an animal first sees are maintained in an active state until the reward arrives. There is evidence of this holding of the address from experiments with octopuses from which the vertical lobes had been removed. If they are repeatedly shown a crab and given a shock if they approach it, such operated animals cannot readily learn not to attack it at a subsequent showing, as a normal octopus will do. But if instead of taking the crab out of sight, it is left in view of the operated octopus, then after a shock few further attacks are made. We have as it were substituted for the absent vertical lobes by leaving the crab in view (J. J. Barlow and G. D. Sanders, personal communication). Presumably, the short-term memory that is known in higher animals has similar functions, it keeps the address of the cells initially stimulated until the reward signals arrive and perhaps then also for a rather longer period while consolidation is taking place (p. 82). The maintaining of the address may be done by a simple lowering of the threshold of the neurons concerned, so that when the reward signals arrive they have a greater effect upon them than on other cells.

## Generalization in the memory

Memories would be of little use if they only allowed establishment of a connection between a *few* receptors and the nerve cells that activate the appropriate muscles. For example it would be very inefficient for an octopus to have to learn every tactile response eight times over. Any effective neural memory system must have a mechanism for *generalization*. What is learned by one part of the receptor surface should be performed equally by other parts. The mechanism providing this facility (as the engineers would say) can also be seen in an octopus. In both the visual and tactile memory systems there are lobes in which the fibres from different parts of the sensory surface interweave with those bringing signals from the taste receptors of the lips and mouth (lobes $V_2$ and $T_2$ in Fig. 10.3). Here the topographical arrangement of the receptor surface is not preserved, and presumably the reinforcement signals are enabled to reach to all the appropriate cells. This function is thus in a sense the opposite of the last, now no *one* address is respected, the signals are sent to all relevant addresses. This must indeed involve a complicated pattern of connectivity. Presumably it is to ensure this that these lobes contain their characteristic weaving bundles of fibres. Experiments show that these lobes do in fact serve for this function. If they are bisected, an octopus that has learned only with one eye, cannot choose correctly between shapes shown to the other eye (Muntz 1961). After a similar operation to the inferior frontal lobe, what is learned with one arm (or the arms of one side) cannot be performed by the others (Wells and Young 1966).

## Inhibition of unwanted programs

If learned programs of action depend upon certain pathways in the nervous system, it is essential that the others, which are not wanted, shall be suppressed. Indeed, such inhibition must be a fundamental feature even in artificial multichannel systems (Taylor 1964). In an octopus this seems to be another function of the vertical lobe system. Animals from which it has been removed are in some respects over-reactive. They are not able to prevent the operation of programs for actions that lead to damaging results. Animals without these lobes still show signs of learning to discriminate, but they make numerous mistakes—especially in taking the negative or unwanted action. It is significant that fibres bringing signals from all parts of the surface reach into the vertical lobes, and they are presumed to carry signals of pain (nocifensors). The failure to inhibit reactions is also a feature of mammals with certain brain lesions. In man, such inhibition may be an important function of the frontal lobes, one of the latest parts to be developed in evolution (p. 202).

## The memory mechanism involves microneurons

Finally, we can say something from our octopus studies about the possible nature of the change that is involved in learning. In the touch memory system, the only part that *must* be present for learning to take place involves a region with a mixture of large nerve cells with very small ones ($T_4$). The large neurons probably serve to operate the actions either of drawing in or pushing away by the arms. The small ones may be involved in producing the changes in probability that link each type of feature detector with the appropriate action program. My own hypothesis is that these small neurons, amacrine cells, begin to produce a chemical substance that acts as an inhibitory transmitter, blocking the unwanted pathway (Fig. 10.4). This hypothesis assumes that the nervous system in early life has a vast redundancy of connections. Learning then consists, in the first instance, of the inhibition of the unwanted ones, leaving their opposites open for use. No doubt they in turn later become more fully established. The programs are thus initially organized by inhibition of some of the possible pathways, leaving the others open for use and further strengthening.

## The evolution of memory

A great advantage of this hypothesis is that it helps to explain how memory mechanisms may have arisen. Reflex systems often make use of reciprocal inhibition of antagonistic muscles. When we bend an arm at the elbow the flexor muscles contract, but the extensors are inhibited. Evidence in the spinal cord of mammals shows that this effect is produced by collateral pathways, activating small cells (Renshaw cells) that liberate an inhibitory transmitter. This could be considered as a very short-term inhibitory memory. What I am suggesting is that longer-term memories have as their basis an increase in this period of inhibition. This would have become useful as the discriminative powers of the receptor sensory systems improved and so made more alternative programs possible. If the inhibition is sufficiently prolonged the alternative action is repeatedly performed and the connections of its pathways are increased by use. In earlier accounts I have emphasized mainly the inhibitory aspect of the process, but there is good evidence also that use of pathways leads to the development both of the nerve fibres and of the cells and dendrites and synapses that are involved. But the initial inhibition of the unwanted path is an essential preliminary to use of the other one.

The cephalopods provide us with a final bonus in that they show evidence that a memory system has evolved in approximately the manner suggested. Squids and cuttlefishes have excellent brains and a visual memory probably as good or better than that of octopuses. But they have no need for a tactile memory system. They locate their prey with the eyes and use the arms only to seize it. They do not explore with the arms. Correspondingly, they lack all the complex apparatus of the octopus' tactile memory, which must be a relatively recent acquisition. Squids and cuttlefishes presumably have a reciprocal inhibitory system to ensure that they do not draw in creatures that have bitten them. The more elaborate tactile memory of octopuses may well have evolved by elaboration of this simple short-term memory (Fig. 10.6).

## Human memory

These various insights derived from animal experiments can help us a little to understand the immensely complicated question of human memory. The concept of a distinction between short- and long-term memory has been used extensively by neurologists and psychologists. Its validity is strongly indicated by the results of surgical removal of tissue of the temporal lobes and hippocampus of the brain for the relief of epilepsy. After removal of the hippocampus on both sides there has been found to be a very severe impairment of the capacity to set up long-lasting information stores. The now classical case of one patient, H.M., has been investigated in detail over many years by Dr. Brenda Milner in Montreal (1970). His I.Q. actually increased from 103 to 115 after operation. He remembers things before the operation very well, but is now unable to remember anything that occurred even a few minutes previously, unless he recites it over and over again. He can hold a number for many minutes by such rehearsal, but if distracted forgets at once, and can't even remember that he had been given a number. Thus his short-term memory is normal but there is a defect in setting up the consolidation process. There is still however some capacity for long-term storage. If he was given a complex maze task he could not remember it, because the later parts interfered with the earlier. But a very simple maze could be learned after long practice and there was quite good retention even two years later, even though he could not remember having had the training

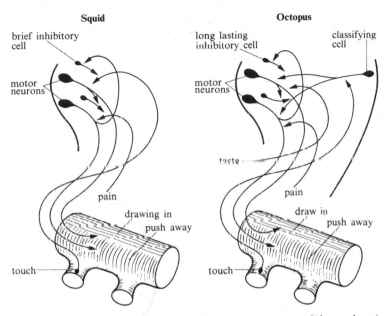

FIG. 10.6. Diagram of the touch learning system of an octopus and the non-learning avoidance system from which it perhaps evolved and which is still found in a squid.

sessions. Evidently the defect is neither in the short memory system nor in the longer storage system itself but in *acquisition in the latter*, perhaps in transfer from one to the other, if that is the way long-term storage occurs. Furthermore H.M. has some capacity to learn motor skills such as manual tracking.

At present we can only begin to use these fascinating observations in the formulation of theories about human memory. A valuable clue is that the hippocampus receives projections from the ascending pathways of the medial forebrain bundle, which include pathways that signal reward (p. 88). It also receives, via the cingulate and entorhinal regions of the cerebral cortex signals from all the main exteroceptive senses, bringing information from the outside world. It is therefore very well placed for the job of giving to incoming signals the symbolic significance that makes them memorable. We do not know how it does it, but a further clue is that changes in the pattern of its electrical activities lasting several days can be induced in a cat by electrical stimulation (Bliss and Gardner-Medwin 1973).

## Strategies of memorizing

Before we can find out how long-lasting memories are built up we must discover how they are related to the basic programs for activity strategies that have been growing in the brain since childhood (p. 72). There is probably no discontinuity between acquisition of the earliest social skills and the memorizing of information by an adult. Young children seem not to have deliberate strategies for this—they do not 'try to remember', nor do they use cues. We can say that the young child has no metamemorial capacity, he does not know about knowing, nor know what it is to remember (Flavell 1977). Techniques of retrieval and rehearsal begin to be detectable at about four years old. From then on information seems to be as it were processed at different levels and retention depends upon how far it is related to the existing operational schemata discussed by Bruner (1974) and Piaget (1971). The mature memorizer transforms the information to give it meaning.

## Re-coding for memory

There have been many attempts to understand the process of encoding. Thus we can distinguish between 'taxonomic and conceptual coding' or 'episodic and semantic' (Tulving 1972). Psychologists are actively engaged in trying to discover the systems that are used to register information and make it available for recall. One suggestion is that each unit to be remembered is accompanied by some ancillary information that acts as a retrieval cue (Tulving 1972). An example of such cues would be 'time tags' or 'place tags'—'when did I hear that name?' or 'where did I hear it?'

There is as yet no agreement, in spite of much work, as to how this process of re-coding for storage occurs (see Baddeley 1976). The early work of Ebbinghaus concentrated on study of the capacity to memorize strings of nonsense syllables (1885). Increasingly however it has been realized that storage depends greatly on meaning and on relating new information to what Bartlett (1932), following Head (1926), called a schema or model. This is essentially the conception we are following, but the worry is that no one has been able to provide any clear notions about the neuronal organization that constitutes the building of a schema or program. My hypothesis is that it will be found to involve the introduction of limitations into an initially redundant network. The model may thus be formed on the analogy of a statue, by *removal* of unwanted material, leaving relevant connections. Memory is a selective process.

Much evidence about coding for memory comes from experiments on the accuracy of recall when different types of cue are available. Short-term memory is greatly influenced by acoustic similarity. In memorizing sequences of consonants it was found that mistakes were especially frequent between letters that *sound* similar (e.g. B and T, M and N) even when they were presented *visually* (Conrad 1964). Sequences such as DCBTPV gave more errors than LWKFRT. So it may be that short-term retention involves some form of acoustic coding. It is the order that is disrupted when the letters are similar, acoustic similarity actually *helps* retention of the letters themselves. Further studies showed the same effect with words, acoustic similarity (mad, map, man) produced more errors of ordering than dissimilar ones (pen, day, rug) (see Baddeley 1976). On the other hand long-term memory seems to depend more on semantic similarity. Experiments of the same sort showed that words with similar meanings (huge, big, great, etc.) had a larger effect on long-term memory than those with dissimilar meanings (foul, old, deep, etc.), but there was only a slight difference in short-term memory.

The evidence thus suggests that the long-term storage system is what we might call 'content addressed' as in some computer systems, rather than 'list addressed'. Each item is not stored at a particular place in the memory by column and row, but as part of a very elaborate system of symbolic meanings. The meanings indicate parts of action systems that are, or have been, important for the life of the individual. But not all long-term memory is 'semantic', we readily remember sounds such as the slamming of a door.

Some slips of the tongue provide evidence that the storage system includes associative addressing indices. For example, consider 'It didn't bother me in the sleast'. In the search for 'least' the word 'slightest' was also activated, and 'the brain failed to complete its choice between them before the program was articulated' (Laver 1970) Incidentally it is interesting that the author (a linguist) uses here the words 'choice' and 'program' with which we have been so much concerned.

Unfortunately all this does not take us far to understanding the neural base of human memory. Visual factors certainly enter into much of it. Words are easy to remember in proportion to the ease with which they evoke visual images (Paivio 1969). But ease of pronouncing, and familiarity are also powerful factors. The relationship of visual and semantic coding is well shown by recent evidence that subjects make size judgements more readily if they are presented with pictures than with words. Also it takes longer to decide whether a leopard is bigger than a tiger than whether a buffalo is bigger than a mouse 'just as if the subject were comparing self-generated images or scale models of the animals' (Baddeley 1976, p. 232).

Further evidence about the importance of meaning in memory comes from those suffering from some forms of aphasia. Concrete words may be more easily read by these patients than abstract ones—'inn' is easier than 'in', 'witch' than 'which', and so on. As Baddeley says, 'This phenomenon should surely have implications for theories of reading, but the great mass of educational research on reading seemed to have no model that was sufficiently detailed to draw any clear conclusions: it was not even clear what questions should be asked' (Baddeley 1976, p. 376).

These few examples may illustrate the richness, difficulty, and importance of work on the human memory system. The long-term store can perhaps at present best be described as 'a single semantic abstract memory system which contains both linguistic and pictorial information and which can be accessed equally well by words or pictures' (Baddeley 1976, p. 234). One might add 'or by any sounds, smells or tastes, or by touches or pains'. Blind and deaf people still have memories. Whatever system is involved must have a large component of association, whether between sights or sounds or meanings or emotional feelings.

By studying the clusters of associations that people actually use some moderately effective computer models of human memory have been constructed (Anderson and Bower 1972). Studies of memory for pictures and sentences suggests that what we learn are fragments, making up clusters of features. Any fragment acts as clue for the whole cluster (G. V. Jones 1975, see Baddeley 1976, p. 346). This very interesting 'fragmentation hypothesis' agrees with ideas we have developed from the evidence of physiological studies of the cortex (p. 51). The information received from the feature detectors serves to gain access to a whole section of the program. Perhaps after all we are not so very far from an understanding of the coding system and this may help us to find how alterations in the network produce records in the memory. The switching of a few thousand mnemons may be sufficient to form a new link.

## Forgetting

If learning involves the formation of new connections how does it come about that we forget? The easiest answer is that we don't. Perhaps once something has passed into long-term memory at least part of its effect may be there for ever. There is a good deal to be said for this. Most people agree that early influences in childhood remain with us, at least to some extent, and psychoanalysts will say that there are many buried 'unconscious' memories that can yet be recalled. It is quite likely that what we call forgetting is in fact the interference of subsequent learning. If the memory involves a whole complex of records of semantic, visual, and other matters it may indeed be that changes of the complex to form the basis of further learning make recall of earlier events more difficult. Psychologists in spite of many experiments are still undecided as to how far forgetting can be explained by such interference. It is assumed that 'memory traces' show some exponential decay with time, perhaps due to quasi-random neural activity—but there is little physiological basis for this. We have no other means to measure the 'strength' of a memory trace than by mapping its apparent decay by the ease of recall. In experimental situations the effects of interference or forgetting certainly depend upon the similarity between material learned and what is interposed. But recall in ordinary life depends upon an elaborate process of search and reconstruction, say when one is seeking the name of a man one met last week. The assumed decaying trace has first to be located and then discriminated from noise and intervening material. It is difficult to believe that all parts of the memory system are equally liable to decay by some random process and of course the more fundamental parts are continually being reinforced, because they are parts of our daily life programs.

## Prodigies of memory

There are great variations between individuals in capacity to remember, and a few people have memories that seem quite fantastic. People with 'iconic memories' can study a page for a few moments and then recite everything written there. They can even read off the words backwards, reporting that they have the page as it were literally before their eyes. This faculty is somewhat disturbing to our scheme for understanding the brain model as a semantically organized system. These people seem to have a literally photographic memory.

Other memorizers report that they do in fact use programs that involve meaning. In his study, *The mind of a mnemonist*, Luria (1968) records that his subject memorized strings of items, even of nonsense, by placing each of them in some spot on a walk he would conduct in his head around a familiar place. He could then recall them several years later. He evidently had some special freak of brain structure or activity that gave him the capacity to use place codes in far greater detail than is normal. The case will serve as a reminder that what we do in memorizing is to add to our set of programs of suitable actions. We give symbolic significance to external stimuli by relating them to the action patterns that we have built up for the conduct of our lives. When we say that something becomes a symbol we mean that it has acquired significance. Human beings, like octopuses, have the power to continue to learn the symbolic significance of external signals, even when they are adult. To our shame we do not yet know what changes in the nervous system enable them to do this, but we are beginning to recognize the characteristics of some of the complex stages that are necessary for the process.

# 11   Touching, feeling, and hurting

## Programs for touching

This chapter considers some of the brain programs that organize the relations between an individual and the surrounding world. The various sensations of touch give information about the immediate environment and also tell us something about the surface of our own bodies. Touch and pain are thus 'near senses' while seeing or hearing are 'distance senses' received by distance receptors. When the skin is damaged we feel pain, which though generated outside we refer to ourselves, so the contrast between touching the outer world and feeling the inner is not sharp. The programs of action that are selected from moment to moment are determined by the symbolic significance attributed to the nerve impulses that have arrived. The signals may come from events far away, in seeing, or at the surface of the body as by touching, or actually within it as when feeling pain.

Animals and men do not wait passively to receive stimulation, they continually seek it by exploratory programs. If the tactile information that comes in suggests something 'good' we explore for more. Other information indicates damage and is called 'painful' and initiates a program of withdrawal. An adequate account of brain processes should provide interpretations of how the different signals from the skin acquire the different symbolic values. Signals become symbolic when they acquire 'importance' for the individual by reference to the systems that determine his aims. We shall show that signals that are 'painful' are indeed referred to the reward centres of the core brain. The symbolic significance of signals of touch, indicating the shapes of objects, are determined by much more complicated systems of reference, after they have passed through the thalamus to the cerebral cortex.

In the receptor systems of the skin, therefore, there are all the stages between signals about the state of the outer world and those that indicate ones own pain. A difference between touch and pain, however, is that there are active programs for gaining information by touch. We learn to recognize the feel and shape of things, whereas pain is basically inflicted upon us and is formless. Correspondingly there is for touch a cortical map of the surface of the body (p. 107), whereas pain has no cortical representation. Nevertheless the realities of masochism show that at least in man there can be programs for the pursuit of pain. There is also evidence of whole systems whose function is to switch off pain and some pain-killers such as morphine imitate these natural programs (p. 112).

## Programs for avoiding damage

The concept of pain has caused much difficulty to philosophers, moralists, and theologians, but the biologist cannot see what all the trouble is about. Pain is harsh, but no Creator could produce viable organisms without it, at least of anything like the human type. Every animal must have programs to ensure withdrawal from harmful situations. Even sedentary creatures such as worms that live in tubes shoot back into their holes when they are threatened. Indeed in one of these worms, *Myxicola*, the nervous system consists largely of a single huge nerve fibre, which ensures that nerve impulses go rapidly from the crown of feeding tentacles to the muscles, to produce a withdrawal when the animal is shadowed (as by a predator) or touched. No very elaborate program is needed in *Myxicola*'s nervous system to produce such responses. Nor does their existence raise any serious philosophical problems. We are content to see that such mechanisms have obvious advantages for survival.

The code value of the nerve impulses in the worm's giant nerve fibre are built in by heredity; which has provided all the appropriate connections. Nevertheless some variation is possible. If the worm is repeatedly shadowed it soon *stops* withdrawing, by the process called habituation. So the nerve impulses which at first symbolized 'Danger—perhaps this shadow is a dogfish' now symbolize 'Only passing clouds, keep feeding'. In every animal particular patterns and sequences of nerve impulses represent forecasts of the probable relevance for survival of some inner or outer event, in the light of past experiences, both remote and recent.

There is an immense gap between such simple protective responses of worms and the complex pains that we suffer. Yet these too are devices necessary for survival, made complicated by the elaborate pattern of life that human beings have adopted. I hope to show that it is useful to say that we develop programs that estimate the gravity of pain and devise means for avoiding it. Many such reactions of course are inherited, but some can be modified by learning. The enquiry will help us to gain further ideas of what is involved in a complex brain system. First the input that is collected by the brain's action programs from the periphery provides a human being with much more information about occurrences than is available to simple animals. Secondly, the brain interprets the battery of signals that reach it in the light of its needs and of the programs that are already stored in its memory. Thirdly, the brain is itself a very active system, seeking for information and sending out signals serving to select from all that goes on around it, items that its programs indicate that it needs to receive.

## Subjective experience of pain

Of course even the highest organisms have some simple withdrawal responses. A child does not have to learn to draw away its hand from a hot object. The flexor reflex ensures that it pulls it away at once and then howls. But the child soon learns not to do it again, and it also learns the value of howling. What interests us now is not the flexor reflex and withdrawal process, which we understand and accept as readily as the withdrawal of the worm—it is the pain that we want to know about. Being by definition a 'subjective state', you may say that neither biology nor any other material science can study pain. But all sensations are in a sense subjective, what is so special about pains and pleasures? Experiences of pain are sensations, like the associated experiences of the material events that accompany them, burns, nerve fibres, avoidance responses, etc. The difference is that pains and pleasures are intimate and personal to oneself. They cannot strictly be shared because they are signals that carry warning or reward to that particular individual. We may learn something by looking at the variations of the pain phenomenon, with the hope that its special features may help to show what it is that makes it somehow different from physical events.

First, notice that pain varies a great deal between individuals. 'How do you know that it varies?', one may ask, and this shows us at once another characteristic of mental occurrences, we each feel that we know about our own, but can only learn of those of others indirectly by their behaviour and especially by their speech. The responses that people give to presumably painful situations certainly vary a great deal, both between individuals and in the same person at different times. Immediately after an injury there is sometimes little indication of pain. Military surgeons have often reported that men dreadfully wounded seem to feel no pain, perhaps partly because they are thinking how glad they are to be alive and out of the battle. However, the point is that severe pain usually comes some time after injury (or of course from a chronic internal disturbance). It is a signal that things are wrong and it sets off the search for a remedy. Dentists report that patients often say that their pains have gone away when they reach the safe care of the man who will relieve them. Conversely we all know of people whose pains we feel may be exaggerated in an attempt to gain sympathy and attention.

This tells us a lot about another very general characteristic of these phenomena—they are greatly dependent on the social situation. Is it possible that what we call our personal feelings are in some way actually a *product* of man's deeply social way of life and dependence on communication? This seems a contradiction, and we must be careful to avoid any suggestion that to call pains social would be to pretend that they are 'unreal'. Almost nothing is more real for a human being than his reactions to those around him, and of them to him. Not only are responses of pain social but they are also at least partly learned, often according to the practices of the culture in which the individual grows.

## Variations in response to pain

Evidence has been collected about the lowest threshold of skin sensation in people of different genetic stocks. Using a weak electric shock Sternbach and Tursky (1965) tested American women of Italian, Irish, Jewish, and old American ethnic groups to find the weakest shock they could feel. There was a similar threshold in all of them. As Melzack (1973, p. 25) put it, 'the sensory conductory apparatus, in other words, appears to be essentially similar in all people so that a given critical level of input always elicits a sensation'. Yet in another study differences in *pain* threshold were found. The levels of radiant heat that were said to be painful by Italians and Jews, were only called warm by northern Europeans. Again, the *maximum* shock that would be tolerated was found to be much less in Italian women than in those of old American or Jewish descent (Sternbach and Tursky 1965). These differences seem to go with differing cultural attitudes to pain. In still another study Zborowski found that Jewish and Italian women cry out when in pain and expect sympathy, whereas women of old American stock were more stoical and tended to withdraw when hurt and to suffer in silence (see Melzack 1973).

Such differences in expression of pain have been studied even in dogs. Scottish terriers raised from birth in isolation, so that they did not suffer the knocks and scrapes of normal puppies, when grown up did not react fully to nervous stimuli. They would withdraw when they touched a lighted match but then would immediately touch another one. When pricked with a pin they drew away a paw but showed none of the signs of 'emotion' that were present in their litter mates who had a normal upbringing and who would not allow further approaches with flame or pin (Melzack and Scott 1957).

Melzack interprets this interesting result as due to the failure of the dogs to recognize what is important. Having been reared in isolation they found all stimuli equally relevant (or irrelevant). Every individual brain has to acquire its own store of information, to make its own programs and learn which actions and emotional responses are appropriate. Pavlov long ago showed that if a strong electric shock is given to a paw shortly before feeding, a dog soon stops reacting against it and begins to salivate, wag its tail, and turn towards the food dish.

Many other examples show that the expression of pain depends upon past experience and culture. There is every reason to suppose that the pain actually felt (as we say) shows similar variations. Should we interpret this to mean that pain is more 'real' for some people than others? The problem shows how difficult it is to be precise in the use of subjective concepts. Perhaps more helpfully we may say that this shows that past experience has a great influence on what we feel and suffer, as it obviously does upon what we know.

## Pain and suffering

Such laboratory studies and thoughts are very interesting but they do not seem to touch the questions raised by really serious pain. Obviously it is useful to have avoidance responses and to learn what to avoid. But what is the value to the individual or the species of the intractable pains of cancer or neuralgia? Persistent and terminal pains seem only to be an added burden, 'There is no merit to this suffering, no lesson to be learned' (Melzack 1973, p. 202). But is this all that can be said? The human way of life would not be what it is without the threats that pain imposes. Should we recognize sin if there were no pain? This obviously raises theological echoes. Religions have faced the problem that seems at first a mystery for biology. How big a part does pain play in our moral and social system? Perhaps it does have some beneficial effects. A surgeon has said of the care of long-term unconscious patients that those who attend them 'have been helped to adjust to life and understand sacrifice' (Lewin 1976).

The trouble is that neurological sciences have hardly begun to consider the complications that are involved in the cerebral programs of the social, speaking creatures that we are. Quite a large part of our suffering comes from the information we have about the possible or probable unhappy outcome of a painful situation, social as well as personal. Other animals knowing less also suffer less. We should not expect to have it both ways. We are proud to be far-seeing, to have programs that take account of many contingencies. We must also learn to develop programs that mitigate the anxieties that go with this knowledge and canalize them in useful directions. Psychiatrists are indeed engaged in doing just this and using knowledge of how peoples brains operate to assist in providing adequate programs, aided also by drugs. The question of intractable terminal pain is linked with that of senescence, which we have already considered in Chapter 4. Granted that there is an inevitable end to individual lives and that we have largely avoided death by accident, we need to use our brains to develop programs to meet the situation. Euthanasia is obviously a possibility, when all else fails, in spite of the problems it raises.

## Phantom limbs

Some of the most serious and intractable pains come from amputations, the pains of phantom limbs and related phenomena. These are trials indeed, but at least they have served to show us a great deal about the nature and cause of pain. After an amputation most patients report feelings as if the limb was there, often in some particular position. Usually the feeling goes away, but it may persist for years and the phantom may be intensely painful. The cut ends of the severed nerves form a lump of tissue known as a neuroma. The nerve fibres do not die (at least for a very long time) and indeed they sprout and grow for a short distance, forming all sorts of spirals and other figures among the surrounding tissues. The capacity for growth and regeneration is a very important property of nerves. It operates daily in our fingers and elsewhere to repair the fine nerves of small areas of skin that have been damaged by burns, bruises or cuts. Even whole nerves can make effective new connections after being severed. Injuries to nerves are a common feature among war wounds, and during the Second World War some of us were engaged in seeking for ways to improve the treatment of damaged nerves and to enable the outgrowing fibres to become connected with the proper parts of the skin or muscles. But when a limb has been amputated there is of course nowhere for the growing nerve fibres to go to. The tips of the sensory nerve fibres are still liable to be stimulated, say by jarring of the neuroma by a knock on the end of the nerve, they are indeed especially sensitive to changes of temperature or other conditions. When these nerves conduct signals to the brain they inevitably send a very disordered set of messages, compared to the pattern of discharge that the nerves usually carry from the skin. It is really quite surprising that nerve impulses provoked in this way are interpreted by the brain as indicating anything at all about a whole phantom limb. Indeed this shows the general point that when even a few signals arrive at the brain they act as symbols that can arouse the very elaborate and well ordered response that we call 'sensation of a limb'. This is important evidence that the coding system does not depend upon some elaborate patterning of frequencies among the nerve impulses. The code is provided by the variety of the nerve fibres and their connections. Any signals in the nerve fibres from, say, a thumb, when they arrive at the brain symbolize 'thumb'. The brain has special capacities for 'making sense' of the sets of signals it receives. It is not a passive receiver like a camera but an active creator of meaning (Chapter 12).

Nevertheless the impulses do usually arrive in certain patterns. There are various different sorts of sense organs in the skin (Fig. 11.1) and they are not normally all activated together, as may happen to the nerve fibres in a neuroma. It is not surprising that after amputation the pattern is not as well ordered as it should be, and this gives us a great hint as to the meaning of pain. It may be that pain is a condition in which nerve impulses arrive in a set of nerve fibres that are not usually stimulated together. They come in combinations that were not expected on a basis of previous experience. One patient reported by Livingston (1943), who has made classical studies of

touch corpuscles free nerve endings

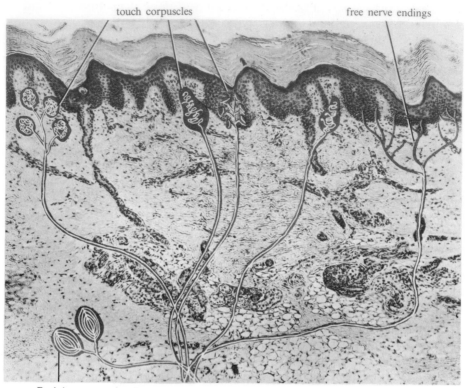

Pacinian corpuscles (? pressure)

FIG. 11.1. Receptor organs seen in a section of the skin. The hairs and their nerve fibres are not shown. (Montagna from McCloy 1964, from *The Science of Man 2*, © BBC 1964, with kind permission.)

these matters, had a painful phantom hand, tightly clenched. To explain the pains he told Dr. Livingston to clench his own fist and hold it tightly bent. After five minutes the doctor was sweating with pain and the patient allowed him to let go. 'But you *can* let down your hand', he said 'I cannot'. So once again we see how the *concept of action* comes even into the feeling of pain, which seems to be definitely something imposed on a person from without. Something wrong with the pattern of input from the patient's severed nerve made the brain act as if to perform impossible movements. The attempted action is conducted within the brain and its impossibility initiates the program associated with feeling pain. This pain should lead to corrective movements, but there is no program by which these actions can be performed. And so the cycle of errors continues. 'With what profit?' you may say. Perhaps it at least teaches us to be careful. Is it fantastic to think that the unhappy victim is playing some useful social role?

Other clues interesting to us, come from the fact that the pain of phantom limbs is not evoked only or directly from the neuroma in the stump itself. There are often 'trigger zones' elsewhere in the body. Even a pin prick on the head or on another limb will set off a severe pain in the phantom. Pain elsewhere in the body, for example from angina pectoris, may produce pain in the phantom limb that was not there before. The trigger that sets off phantom-limb pains may be 'emotional', in the sense that when such patients are upset by circumstances or by friends or relatives they develop the pain. This has led some people to suppose that the whole phenomenon is 'psychological'. The very use of the word in this connection shows how confused and feeble such concepts are. These patients indeed have emotional disturbances, as would anyone suffering unremitting pain and anxiety about whether they are alienating everyone around them by their complaints. But there is very good evidence that the pain does not have what is usually called a psychiatric basis (Chapter 15). A careful statistical study showed that amputees who have painful phantoms are not more liable to neuroses than those who have no pain (see Melzack 1973, p. 60).

Even more important is the fact that phantom pain can very often be relieved by blocking the nerve leading from the neuroma with an anaesthetic drug. A surgical operation cutting off the neuroma also has the same effect and many cases of phantom pain have been treated in this way. Unfortunately the pain often returns as a new neuroma forms on the cut end of the nerve. So a new operation has to be performed and the process has been repeated several times in the attempt to help some patients. Other expedients have been to cut the sensory nerve roots themselves, close to the spinal cord. A third method is to interrupt the presumed 'pain pathway' further along on the way to the brain, by an operation on the spinal cord itself. But the astonishing thing is that my colleague Pat Wall has discovered that the most effective way of abolishing these pains has been not to cut or anaesthetize the nerves but to stimulate them! To explain how he came to this discovery we must go back to consider the pathways that bring information from the skin.

Many investigators have sought for a special set of nerve fibres carrying signals of pain, but no one has ever been able to prove that there is any particular type of nerve ending in the skin that generates 'pain', as the rods and cones generate 'vision', the organs of the ear 'hearing', or those of the nose 'smell'. Those are all 'distance receptors', and the signals that they send serve to symbolize events far away. Pain, however, is essentially in or on the body, it indicates that there is derangement of some sort in the bodily activities. In order to find the nature of this derangement what we should look for is not specific pain sense organs but the disordered activity of other sense organs. To a large extent this is what in fact has been found by recent studies of the physiology of pain.

## The sense organs of the skin

The skin contains several different sense organs, which between them serve the various senses that we call touch, pressure, temperature, and pain (Fig. 11.1). Some of these sensory cells in the skin are connected with large nerve fibres, which conduct signals rapidly. Others are smaller and slower and the finest of all are the so-called free nerve endings, very thin nerve fibres not attached to any definite receptor structure in the skin. For many years it was supposed that each different sort of nerve ending provided signals for a different sensation. This theory of specific neural pathways was the conclusion derived from the traditional practice of neurologists in testing the 'functions' of these receptors, by applying artificial stimuli to the skin of a passive person, say by tickling with a hair or pressing, and then asking him what he perceives. Such data have their uses, but during ordinary life sense organs are not used in this way at all. They are part of the system of exploratory programs which an animal or man continually employs in its life to satisfy its needs. The senses of touch, and of pressure, mostly come into action when we *do* things with our hands and feet. Only occasionally are we passively stimulated, say by a fly or a bee, and then we respond with programs of appropriate intensity.

So the various organs in the skin should not be considered as each having a separate function, but as parts of a system for providing relevant information in the actions of daily life. It is true that each of these types of receptor is activated by a somewhat different sort of pressure or deformation of the skin. Thus the sense of touch is largely the result of bending of the hairs or other special structures in the skin, since there are nerve fibres wrapped around the base of each hair. The whiskers of a rat or cat are moved by air pressures and so can even act as distance receptors, telling the animal when it is approaching objects before it actually touches them. But the various types of sense organ in the skin do not work independently, and the sensations we feel there, such as degrees of smoothness or roughness, pressure, tingling, tickling, or movement are the result of collaboration at both the spinal and cortical levels between the various signals. In particular, signals in many of the large fibres entering from the skin inhibit the cells of the spinal cord, whereas those in the smaller fibres excite them. This is called the 'gating theory' of action in the spinal cord. It was found that noxious stimuli may produce very intense signalling by some cells, whereas tactile stimuli or moderate heat or cold would produce a lower level. Wall's suggestion is that pain is the result of great activity of the small fibres when they are not inhibited by signals in the large ones. He found that stimulating the large ones in the nerve above a painful neuroma stops the pain. They can be stimulated separately because large fibres have a lower electrical threshold than small ones. Numerous patients are now being given little gadgets attached to their painful limbs so that by pressing a button they can stimulate these large fibres to switch off their pain (Wall 1978).

## Cortical areas for touch

Although pain has a peripheral origin it is very greatly influenced by the brain, and we must now follow the pathways from the skin upwards. There are three well-known tracts leading from the skin to the brain. A large area of the cerebral cortex receives the signals from these pathways, all laid out in a regular map, corresponding to the topography of the body surface, but with greater areas for the more functionally important parts (Fig. 11.2). Thus there are huge areas for the fingers in a man and for the whiskers in a rat. These 'somatotopic' maps are a fundamental feature of the cerebral computer, as they are also for vision (Chapter 12). In a mouse or rat the nerves to the whiskers are actually larger than the optic nerves. Each whisker is represented in the cortex by its own group of nerve cells (Figs. 11.3 and 11.4). If a whisker is removed at birth there will be a gap in the series of groups in the cortex. There are connections from these groups to the cells of the motor cortex, which direct the muscles attached to the whiskers. So the mouse scans the world by moving its whiskers as we scan it with our eyes (Chapter 12). No doubt making hypotheses as to which way to move next.

Patients with injuries in these skin areas of the cortex suffer from various defects in the sensation of touch and in the capacity to execute delicate movements, such as writing. But patients with cortical injuries do not suffer errors of pain. They do not feel it either more or less than other people. So it is usually stated that there is no cortical centre for pain. Moreover electrical stimulation of the cortex in patients under local anaesthesia never produces reports of pain. Yet of course experiences of pain must in some way become connected with the cortical analysers, otherwise we should never be able to learn to avoid external events that are likely to be unpleasant.

## Internal pains

These facts give us much to think about, both of the functions of the cortex and of the nature of pain. If pain is not a specific sensation like touching or seeing or hearing, what is its physiological basis? The current view could probably be expressed by saying that pain results from disordered nerve discharges, especially if they involve impulses in certain of the thin nerve fibres called free-nerve endings. These are the simplest of all sensory nerve

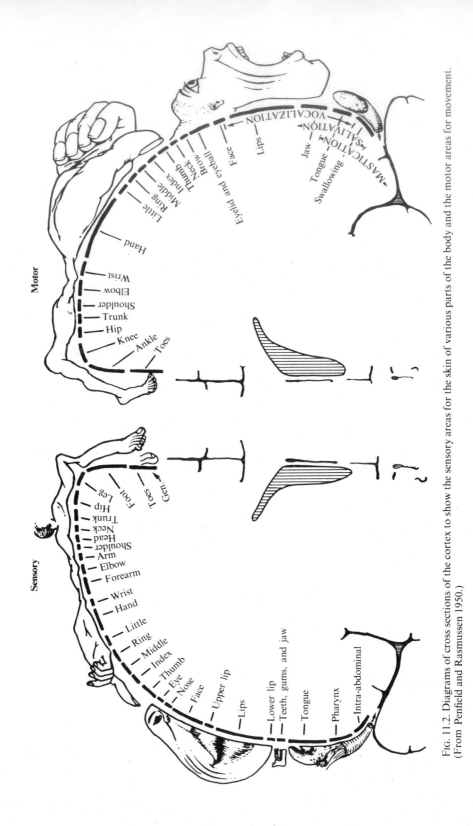

Fig. 11.2. Diagrams of cross sections of the cortex to show the sensory areas for the skin of various parts of the body and the motor areas for movement. (From Penfield and Rasmussen 1950.)

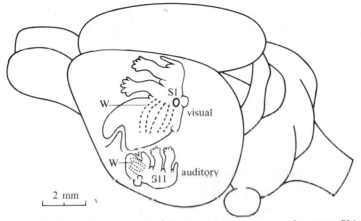

FIG. 11.3. Map of the sensory areas for the skin on the cortex of a mouse. SI is the primary area and SII the secondary. Every part of the surface is represented in each of them. Much the largest areas are devoted to the head, tongue, and whiskers. The lines (W) mark the positions of the five rows of groups of whisker cells shown in Fig. 11.4. The areas for vision and hearing are also indicated. (From Woolsey and van der Loos 1950.)

terminals and they occur not only in the skin but also in some internal organs, especially in the walls of arteries and in the heart. This raises the question of how we feel internal pains. The answer is paradoxically that to a large extent we don't. For instance cutting or pricking the stomach or intestine does not give pain. What does hurt is dragging or pressing them. Presumably the body is not provided by heredity with systems for telling when internal organs are being cut, because this has seldom happened in nature without death. Evolution could not foresee the surgeon's knife. Dragging or pressing of the viscera on the other hand can occur either by a blow or during digestion or 'indigestion' and it is obviously useful to have a mechanism that tells us to avoid this. The significance of pains in the heart is another question that is only partly solved. At least they lead to rest, which relieves the load on the heart. There are important sensory nerves in the heart whose signals are part of the mechanism for adjusting the blood pressure. The pain may involve 'erroneous' signals from these when the heart is not functioning properly. These nerve fibres from the heart enter the spinal cord alongside those from the shoulder and upper arm. When the heart goes wrong the patient may feel the pain in his shoulder. We say it is 'referred' there. Here then we see the phenomena of pain as an error of function compounded by an error of reference. Our nerves are marvellously efficient, but yet far from perfect. They can give false information.

## The pathway of pain to the brain

The pains that we feel as headaches are probably in the blood vessels of the brain. If pain is not felt in the cortex is there any other part of the brain in

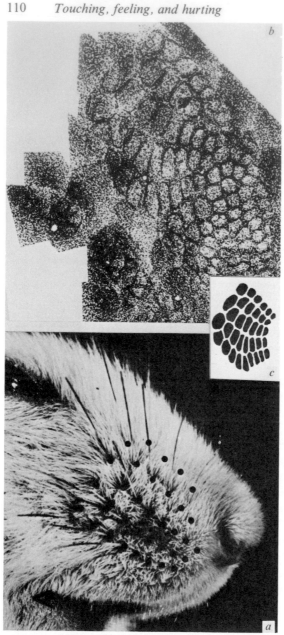

FIG. 11.4(*a*). The head of a mouse seen from the side showing the five rows of whiskers (the mouth is below, nose to the right).
(*b*). Section of the cortex showing the five rows of patches of cells, each corresponding to one whisker.
(*c*). The rows of patches of cells seen in (*b*) are shown diagrammatically. (From Woolsey and van der Loos 1950.)

which it *can* be said to be located? To answer this we must go back to look at the pathways upwards from the spinal cord. The sensory nerve fibres enter the dorsal part of the spinal cord and may there interact with each other and with the local population of nerve cells. From here three main pathways lead upwards to the brain (Fig. 11.5). The anatomical details need not concern us, but each of these paths seems to be responsible for a different aspect of the phenomena of pain and touch. By studying these three pathways, therefore, we get a vivid picture of how the brain combines different sorts of information received along separate paths. The interactions of different combinations of these signals serve to symbolize or encode different external events and so they activate appropriate programs of action, and are reported as particular sensations. Thus some combination of signals will start me scratching and I shall feel what I call an itch, a second combination will give me the feel of a coin in my pocket, and a third will make me scream and suffer pain.

## The reticular formation

One of these three pathways is especially interesting to us. It consists not of long straight-through fibres but of a series of little neurons with axons that are small and short and therefore called 'reticular' or 'net-like'. These polysynaptic pathways of course conduct messages only slowly because there is a delay of one or more milliseconds at each synaptic junction and also small nerve fibres conduct slowly. The pathways reach up through the reticular formation, which is a tissue that occupies the central core of the brain, to the hypothalamus and the limbic system of the cerebral cortex (Figs. 11.5 and 11.6). This reticular system is a very complicated set of cells. Besides the many small ones it includes some that are enormous, with extensive spreading axons (Fig. 11.7). These can send signals to many different areas. The reticular system is thus not only central in position

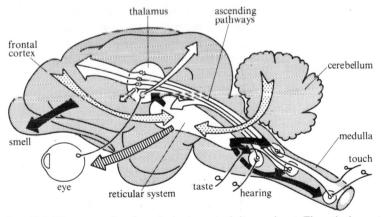

FIG. 11.5. Diagram to show how the brain controls its own input. The reticular system can modify the ascending sensory pathways, including those for touch, taste, smell, and even vision. It is itself influenced by the more basal parts of the cortex, the limbic system and the cerebellum. There is therefore central preconscious modification of sensory experience. (Modified after Hernández-Peón 1955, and see in French 1958.)

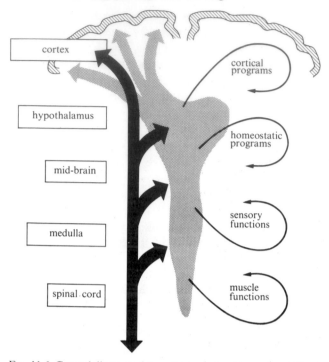

cortex

cortical
programs

hypothalamus

homeostatic
programs

mid-brain

sensory
functions

medulla

muscle
functions

spinal cord

FIG. 11.6. General diagram of the reticular activating system. (After Luria 1973.)

but also in the fact that it communicates information very widely. It is also central in its functions in the sense that it regulates the whole state of activity of the brain, for example in sleeping and waking (Chapter 18). Its more anterior parts and the related hypothalamus are the regulators of what we may call motivation and emotion or affect. Electrical stimulation of this region in cats may lead to responses typical of aversive behaviour to painful stimuli (Chapter 15). Conversely, after they have been damaged, there may be a marked decrease in response to situations that would be expected to be painful. The reticular system includes both ascending and descending pathways and they enter into all the programs of action of an animal or man. Much has been found out by placing electrodes in them and allowing the animal or person to recover. Electrical stimuli can then be given by an experimenter, or it can be arranged that the animal or man stimulates them himself by pressing a lever.

## Programs to switch off pain

Electrical stimulation of certain regions of this central grey matter seems to make rats insensitive to pinching, burning, and even to surgery. The animals are not paralysed but seem instead to be completely oblivious to stimuli that

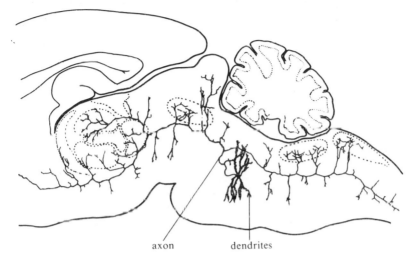

axon          dendrites

FIG. 11.7. Single large cell of the reticular system of the rat, with axon sending signals to many parts of the brain. (After Scheibel & Scheibel from Brazier 1968.)

are normally painful. These nerve cells of the reticular formation contain the substance *enkephalin*, injection of which kills pain in the same way as does morphia (Hughes 1975). Enkephalin is probably the neurotransmitter involved in synaptic transmission in these reticular brain centres. Morphine thus acts by imitating the action of enkephalin in stimulating the nerve cells that switch off the responses to traumatic stimuli, including the subjective phenomena of pain. This is the brain's program for reducing pain.

These actions are due to fibres that proceed from the reticular regions of the brain downwards to the spinal cord (Fig. 11.8). They inhibit the cells that send signals upwards from neurons that respond to noxious stimuli, but they do not inhibit neurons that signal combinations that indicate touch or other non-harmful events (Basbaum *et al.* 1976). There have even been experiments in which stimulation of particular regions of the central grey matter produce analgesia of one particular part of the body. Once again we see how actively the brain regulates everything that is allowed to enter it, even pain.

## Pleasure and pain

Some of these central regions are not concerned with pain but are pleasure centres, which animals will seek to stimulate under suitable conditions (Chapter 13). We do not yet know enough to be able to say whether the pain-inhibiting sets of cells are identical with these that produce pleasure,

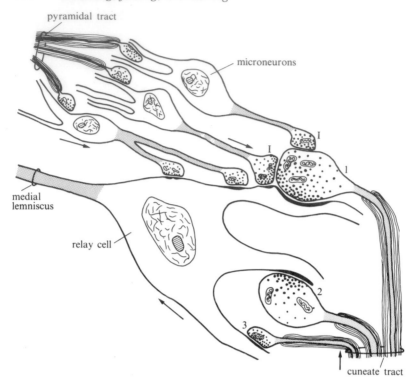

FIG. 11.8. How the brain controls its own input. Diagram of some connections on the pathway from the spinal cord to the brain (cuneate nucleus). The relay cell receives signals from the skin through the synaptic buttons 1–3 and sends them on to the brain by its axon in the medial lemniscus. Some descending fibres from the cortex in the pyramidal tract activate small microneurons. These may make inhibitory synapses (I), blocking some of the ascending pathways. They may also influence the relay cell directly. (After Walberg 1965.)

but we are evidently here close to questions that have long concerned mankind and its philosophers and psychologists such as Freud (p. 164). Is pleasure to be regarded as the absence of pain, or possibly vice versa? Do our programs seek to maximize pleasure or minimize pain, or both? The important point is that there are here what we might call the reference systems that set the course of the whole living control system. Their operation largely determines the ends or aims of the animal or man. These brain regions and the programs they produce are provided by heredity and no doubt modified by experience. Like all other animals we are creatures with built-in aims. These controls are there to provide the objectives that we seek for in life. It is not too much to say that these systems largely determine what human beings do. It is important to emphasize the qualification 'largely', they are powerful influences, but human life is not simple. Other types of program intervene, as it were, on top of these fundamental ones of pleasure and pain that are produced by the actions of the reticular and reward centres.

It is the activation of these central regions that gives to serious pain its unique unpleasant affective quality, demanding attention and driving the animal or person to action to stop the pain. The actions of the anterior parts of the reticular system are also related to those of the cortical prefrontal lobes. After the operation of frontal leucotomy, which separates these lobes from the rest of the brain, patients still feel pricks and pains as much as normally, but no longer complain of 'big' pain, nor do they suffer the anguish they felt before. So evidently there are activities in this part of the brain that regulate what we commonly call emotional feelings.

## Surgical relief of pain

These discoveries about the central grey matter have been used in the relief of human pain. Intractable pains are said to be relieved by lesions in the medial part of the thalamus, or by cutting the cingulum bundle, which connects the frontal cortex to the hippocampus. A person relieved of these agonies is not likely to worry much at theoretical talk about the dangers of considering men as machines. When things go wrong most people want the doctor 'to put it right', rather as they would wish for a mechanic to mend their car. And they want him to deal with their pains and depressions even more than with a broken leg or faulty stomach.

But knowledge and skill are not yet adequate to allow any very sure promise of relief of pain by such surgical and electrical procedures. Surgery is indeed as yet a blunt instrument, but its techniques are becoming more subtle every year. Intractable pain and intense depression are very strong motives for seeking relief. Equally hopeful is the prospect that we may come to understand the chemistry and pharmacology of these pathways and give relief by more flexible means of control than the knife can provide.

It is clear in any case that there is no one single 'centre for pain' in the brain. The cerebral system does not work as a set of boxes each concerned with one of the functions to which we give names. It does have distinct parts, but many of them interact for the performance of each program of action. We have identified three pathways that are concerned with pain, and there may be subdivisions of these, and others besides. In the brain there are many parts concerned with pain. The three pathways show us but a glimpse of how the complicated behaviour and feelings of pain are the product of the combination of many distinct neural activities. The cortex can 'decide' that a particular pattern that was at first disturbing is in fact connected with food—as in the case of Pavlov's dogs. It must then send signals rapidly downwards so that this particular input is prevented from producing the reactions of pain, instead the cortex substitutes appetitive programs appropriate to getting food.

This is clearly only the crudest of summaries of the immense amount of knowledge we have of the pain phenomenon. What we call the sense of touch is the product of a program for exploring the world in the immediate neighbourhood of the skin. Pain is the result of a disordered operation of that program, or of the operations of some internal organ of the body. The disordered signals serve to symbolize that something is wrong and this sets off the programs that may put it right, which in man may be very complex. Pain may initiate the brushing away of a wasp, or be the stimulus for the foundation of a research institute for the treatment of cancer.

# 12 Seeing

## The visual code

It may seem to be a paradox to say that there are programs for seeing. The essence of programs is that they are plans for action, whereas in the conventional schemes of both philosophers and physiologists sensation and action are separated, and a sensation would usually be considered to come first, before action. We are proposing that the reverse is true and that higher animals, at least, go around actively searching for things to see and that they 'see' mainly those things that were expected because the program includes hypotheses and rules for testing them.

To understand this paradox we have to explain why seeing is not like photography and this involves some further rather subtle considerations about symbolism, which even today are not widely understood. When we see a red object, what goes up the optic nerve? It obviously is not red light so what then is it? The physiologist replies, 'a set of nerve impulses'. But nerve impulses are not red either. To express the situation we may say that the nerve impulses are signals that act as symbols of red light, in the sense that they can be decoded by an appropriate brain. Our task is then to explain what is implied by speaking in this way of 'signals', 'symbols', and 'decoding'.

## The retina

Although seeing is not like photography we shall begin by saying that the eye is in some ways very like a camera. It has a lens and a diaphragm (the iris) and a focusing device. What is more, the first step in the process of vision is a photochemical change somewhat like that in a photographic plate. The retina contains a mosaic of more than one hundred million separate receiving elements of two sorts, the rods and cones, each of which detects a tiny part of the image that is thrown on it by the lens, producing a minute electrical or chemical change. Only the cones are sensitive to colours and most of them are concentrated near the centre of the eye. Here there is a small area, the fovea, containing only about 30 000 receptive cones. These perform nearly all the detailed work of seeing, except in dim light. In order to see things we have therefore continually to explore them by minute movements of the eyes around them, examining the part we want to see by the fovea. This is of fundamental importance for our system for thinking about vision because the program that controls these eye movements largely determines what we see.

## Seeking what to see

It is easy to see that a person moves his eyes in jerks, say when he is reading or looking around the room. These large movements are separated by periods of fixation. They occur at a maximum of about five a second (in rapid reading) but often they are less frequent. The movements are ballistic and very fast (1000°/s). Even during fixation the eyes continue to make small tremor movements at about 50/s and 10 minutes of arc, enough to change the position of an image on the fovea by about 30 cones. Both the large and small fast movements are now usually called saccades (from a French word meaning the pull on the reins of a horse). In addition the eyes make slow drifts during fixation, and they may also follow moving targets (pursuit movements) or move to maintain stereoscopy (vergence movements).

No information is received during a saccade, so the large movements divide up the process of seeing into a discontinuous series of packages, and it can be shown that information does in fact reach the cerebral cortex in bursts, corresponding with them. Figure 12.1 shows the sequence of pieces of informa-

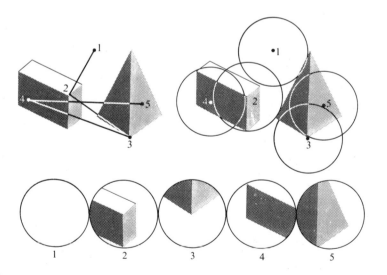

FIG. 12.1 Example of visual discontinuity imposed by large eye jumps. The upper left is a visual scene shown suddenly when the viewer's eye is at fixation 1. He then follows a scanning strategy that takes him to 2, 3, 4 and 5. The central retinal area covered at each of these points is shown at the upper right, and the lower row shows the parts of the scene viewed at each fixation. (After Gaarder 1975, by permission of Hemisphere Publishing Corporation.)

tion that might be sent from the fovea as the eye scans a pyramid. Each jump is towards a point that is likely to be interesting. The direction that is chosen depends on the program in the brain, which makes a forecast on the basis of the information received. In Fig. 12.2(*a* and *b*) the interest is obviously in the human figures, and especially their eyes. Incidentally this is one more example of the propensity of our brain programs to direct attention to human features, a tendency that is probably partly inborn and no doubt accentuated by life as a social creature. In Fig. 12.2(*b*) when instruction was given to search for particular features the program was modified accordingly.

So the programs of enquiry that are learned from childhood onwards dictate what movements are made in response to the information coming in with each jump. Vision is a dynamic process, using a series of scans, but these are not rigidly determined as in a television raster. They are varied according to the nature of the scene itself and the previous experience of the individual. Moreover the scanning does not work by converting the information in the spatial scene into a single channel, but puts it into many parallel channels, which maintain the spatial relations, so in a sense the original picture is reproduced on the cortex, but modified and much expanded (p. 125).

We can thus regard all seeing as a continual search for the answers to questions posed by the brain. The signals sent from the retina constitute 'messages' conveying these answers. The brain then uses this information to construct a suitable hypothesis about what is there and a program of action to meet the situation. As a hungry boy looks around, his eyes may send signals that suggest a fruit tree. Signals go back to the eyes to search for food and if the returning messages indicate 'apples' he starts the climb to pick and eat them.

## Encoding in the retina

The sequence of processes involved in the act of seeing do not therefore really begin in the retina, but involve the brain. Nevertheless it is convenient to ask just how the retina composes its messages. The rods and cones are the light-sensitive elements. They contain special pigments, which change when the intensity of light falling on them varies. This change alters the electrical potentials of the cells, so that the pattern of light thrown by the lens produces a corresponding pattern of electrical and chemical change in the various neurons that make up the retina (Fig. 12.3). Many of these cells are little 'microneurons', which do not send away yes-or-no signals but produce graded changes that increase or decrease the probability that their larger neighbours will set off action potentials. This is a sort of analogue computation, which finally generates discontinuous (digital) all-or-nothing signals in the largest cells of the retina, the ganglion cells, whose axons run to the brain. These impulses in the optic nerve fibres at each moment of scanning a scene are the answers, in code, to the 'questions' that had been asked at the previous moment. Of course if something quite unexpected happens it is seen even though it had not been anticipated. The point is that what goes on in the retina is not the recording of a 'picture', but the detection of a series

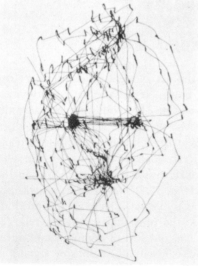

FIG. 12.2(*a*). Eye-movements and fixations during free examination of a photograph for 3 minutes. Fixations are mainly on points that the brain program suggests are likely to provide interesting information. (From Yarbus 1965.)

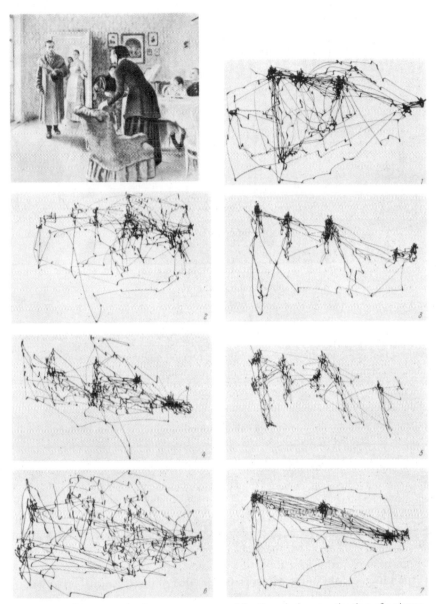

FIG. 12.2(b). Seven records of eye-movements and fixations during examination of a picture. Each record lasted 3 minutes. During (1) the subject was allowed free examination. Before the others he was given the following instructions. (2) Estimate the material circumstances of the family. (3) Give the ages of the people. (4) What were the family doing before the arrival of the 'unexpected visitor'? (5) What clothes were the family wearing? (6) Describe the position of the people and objects in the room. (7) How long had the unexpected visitor been away from the family? The program for eye-movement is adjusted to obtain the required information. (From Yarbus 1965.)

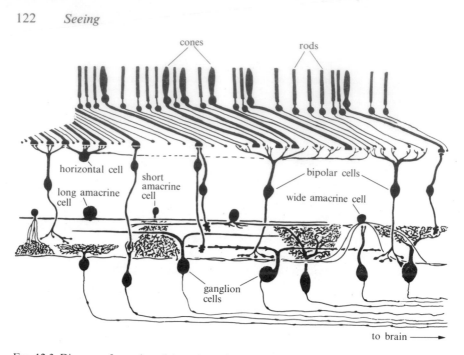

FIG. 12.3. Diagram of a section of the retina, taken across the fovea. Some of the amacrine cells have all their branches in one region, others reach out for long distances. Similarly the dendrites of the ganglion cells may connect with few or many bipolar cells. (After Boycott 1974.)

of items, which are reported to the brain. If the eyes are prevented from moving the signals fade within a second and no picture can be seen.

## Simple programs for seeing

In order to understand what happens along all the multiple lines of communication from the eye and within the brain, we have to go back to real life and examine how vision is used by man and other animals. Vision is not like taking a series of photos but is part of a whole life system. It may perhaps help to think first about the simplest possible sort of seeing, which is responding simply to the presence or absence of light. Animals that live in caves, such as some fishes, or underground, such as moles, are not 'blind', but they cannot 'see' shapes, they need only to 'know' whether light is present or not. If you live in caves and therefore have no use for good eyes it is better to *stay* in the dark, so such animals are actually especially sensitive to light. Some fishes and amphibians can 'see' with their skins, which have receptors that are activated by light. The signals from them simply set in motion the action of swimming, which continues until the animal is again in the dark. In the larvae of lampreys, which live buried in the mud, the tip of the tail is the most sensitive part, so they go on swimming until it is covered. The nerve impulses from the skin may thus be said to symbolize simply the presence of light and they are 'decoded' by the brain to produce swimming. We can say that for these animals light has the same symbolic significance as pain, it is something to be avoided.

## Perceptual hypotheses

Human photoreception is a much more complicated process. We are able to encode all sorts of aspects of the world and to decode the signals and act accordingly. Our eyes have lenses and we examine the pictures or patterns thrown upon the retina. The task therefore is to understand how the brain is able to decide appropriate responses to many different patterns. As Blakemore puts it seeing is not really representational but interpretive (1975, 1977). Gregory has emphasized that the brain picks out features of the pattern that combine with its internal hypotheses to provide programs of action (Gregory 1975). Images are only patterns of light, they cannot be eaten or be dangerous, but they serve as symbols allowing selection among what Gregory calls perceptual hypotheses, to produce what I call programs of action. He calls them perceptual hypotheses to emphasize the importance of prediction, the making of effective decisions with little sensory data.

We cannot possibly have enough storage space to build all possible programs of action for use each time we take in information. Instead we use overall hypotheses about what the world is like, and look for items that assist in carrying out whatever course of action we are engaged in. So perception is an active search for meaningful clues and the brain builds programs that guide the search. These programs may possibly be something like those that artificial intelligence workers devise for pattern recognition with computers. Sutherland (1971) has emphasized that perception involves making structural descriptions from the data and testing inferences as to what these data 'mean' for us. Thus if bodies look heavy our interpretations normally assume that they are supported. When certain contours are presented they are put together in ways that allow us, for instance, to sit down on a horizontal and four vertical lines that we call a stool. Features that are especially used in the analysis are brightness, contours, corners, edges, vertices, nearness, and so on, and there is evidence for cortical detectors for all of these features (p. 50). The brain presumably has programs for examining them, in order to find, as Sutherland puts it, first points, then lines, regions, surfaces, bodies, and eventually objects that have meaning or use. The brain reads the letters, words, sentences, and paragraphs of the visual code (Chapter 7).

## The visual pathways to the brain

The optic nerves carry the information to at least three parts of the brain, the midbrain, cerebellum, and through the thalamus to the cortex. All these parts are interconnected and concerned in any act of vision, but the first two deal mainly with detailed control of the eye movements. After injury to its midbrain a cat will totally ignore the opposite visual field and will walk in circles away from it.

The pattern of ganglion cells of the retina is reproduced by point-to-point connections with the midbrain of monkeys (Goldberg and Wurtz 1972). Deeper in the centre of the midbrain are motor nerve cells each of which has its own 'movement area' so that it sends signals when there is movement in a particular part of the visual field. Its discharge occurs *before* a pursuit jump of one particular direction and extent. So movement in the visual field produces jumps that are appropriate to follow the movement. This midbrain region receives auditory and somatosensory as well as visual inputs and these direct the line of sight to objects heard or touched. So in a general way we can say that the projection from the eye to the midbrain is concerned with 'where' to look, while the cerebral cortex determines 'what' to look at.

## The cerebral cortex and vision

It is the cortex that asks meaningful questions, and so dictates the whole scanning process through its connections with the midbrain. This is well shown in an experiment by Mountcastle and his colleagues (Fig. 12.4). They trained monkeys to take their food from a cup. Then electrodes inserted into the inferior parietal region of the cortex showed that there are movement cells there, which produce impulses only when the monkey moves his eyes to fix upon the cup that he desires. The discharge stops as soon as he gets it. These results suggest that the parietal lobe executes a matching function between the neural signals of the nature of objects and the internal drive state of the organism (Lynch, Mountcastle, Talbot, and Yin 1977). This important experiment carries our understanding of vision one stage further. But the real problem is to find out how the cortex uses the messages it gets from the retina to answer its questions and ask others. This is the serial process that we call visual perception.

The cortex is an immense folded sheet of layers of nerve cells, arranged in columns (Fig. 7.7). The nerve fibres bringing signals from the sense organs, via the thalamus, enter the sheet from the inside. They are arranged in a regular pattern or map, which exactly reproduces every point of the receptive surface of the body, in this case the retina, in the correct relations with its neighbours. Thus there are cortical maps for vision, for hearing, and for

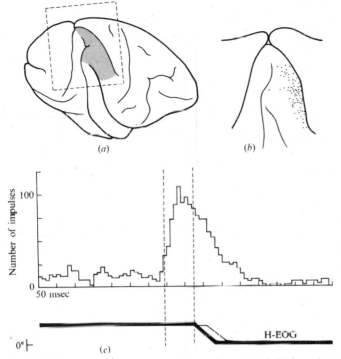

FIG. 12.4. Visual-attention neurons in the monkey. (*a*) and (*b*) show the post-central region of the brain and the positions in it at which electrodes were placed. (*c*) shows the frequency of firing of a single neuron preceding a visually evoked pursuit eye-movement, shown by the lower line by the electrical response (EOG) recorded from the eye muscles. (After Lynch *et al.* 1977.)

touch (Figs. 11.2, 11.3, and 11.4). It is interesting that there are no such detailed maps for smell or taste, which do not have the same power to detect 'shape', at least in man.

The primary visual cortex is in the occipital region at the back of the head (Fig. 12.5). Here the pattern of the retina is enormously enlarged, there are 5000 cortical cells for each cell of the thalamus, which sends on the signals from the optic nerve. The cortex is, as it were, a greatly expanded version of the retina, the fovea being especially extensively represented. Each degree of retinal field at the fovea is represented by 6 mm of this primary visual cortex (Daniel and Whitteridge 1961). But the visual cortex is much more extensive even than this. Beyond the primary visual area is a whole series of 'secondary' areas, each carrying a further full topographical map or representation of the retina and having cells with distinctive functions. Zeki (1974) recognizes at least second, third, fourth and fifth visual areas, probably there are more (Fig. 12.6). The later members of the series receive connections from the earlier ones.

All the areas of the system are made up of columns of nerve cells, each sensitive to some particular visual feature, say a line placed at 30° to the

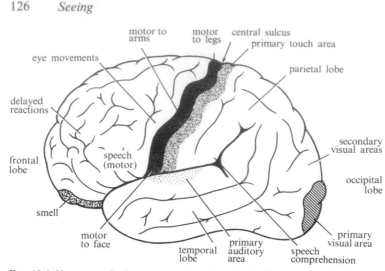

FIG. 12.5. Human cerebral cortex seen from the left side. The primary sensory areas are stippled and the motor cortex is black. (From Young 1971.)

horizontal (p. 50). In some areas there are cells censitive only to one colour. So we can say that the signals sent from the retina by red light are 'decoded' by the fact that they activate certain particular 'red' cells in the cortex. Like all codes this one is pre-established, being laid down initially by heredity and improved by use. A kitten or monkey is born with cells in the brain sensitive to contours set at various angles, but any that are not used will disappear (Chapter 3).

As signals from the retina pass through the various visual areas they are recombined in different ways. This is the process by which the words of the neural language are joined in 'grammatical' ways to give meanings. No doubt there is a hereditary element in the development of the grammar and it is also greatly influenced by experience. As yet all we know about the processes involved is that they somehow depend upon topological relations and that they are disturbed by local injuries to the cortex.

So we have now given some meaning to the statement that the signals from the retina 'represent' visual events and are 'decoded' in the brain. But we have not explained in what sense these activities of the cortical cells can be said to 'interpret' or 'understand' the messages from the retina. Somehow the actions of all these cortical nerve cells must co-operate to receive and 'interpret' the signals. Often they are answers to the questions that the cortex has itself asked, and it goes on to ask others. Notice that this interpretation cannot be instantaneous, since it depends on synthesizing the information from a whole series of pursuit movements. At present we do not know either how the brain asks its questions or how it uses the answers. The knowledge we now have of the principles of coding has been acquired only in the last few years. We may expect that physiologists will quickly

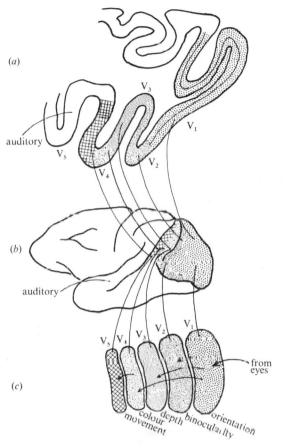

(a)

auditory

$V_3$

$V_1$

$V_5$

$V_4$

$V_2$

(b)

auditory

(c)

$V_5$  $V_4$  $V_3$  $V_2$  $V_1$

from
eyes

colour
movement
depth
binocularity
orientation

Fig. 12.6. Areas in a monkey's
brain for analysis of visual
information. (a) shows a slice
through the brain revealing the
position in the folds of the areas
seen on the left side in (b). (c)
shows the five areas diagrammatically and a very rough
indication of some of the features
detected by each. $V_1$–$V_5$ are the
five visual areas. (From the data
of Dr. S. Zeki.)

pursue the problem further. Perhaps the analogies of language and of questions and answers may help to show what to look for.

## The later stages of decoding

The brain pursues ongoing programs of search for information that will
meet the needs represented by its motivational centres. At each level
through the brain the visual information is packaged into larger and larger
units. First by computing in the retina, which produces nerve impulses in
the optic nerve each carrying a small amount of information, as it were the
letters of the visual code. The cells of the thalamus (lateral geniculate body)
send on information about the distribution of small circular spots of light or
dark, rather like the dots on a photograph that has been screened for reproduction in a newspaper. Then the primary visual cortex uses these spots to compute
edges, which could be compared with words. Further on both in space through

the cortex and in time, the brain interprets a whole 'sentence'—say the sight of a cup or a face, or a letter, word, or larger unit of information that is picked out in reading, perhaps a whole line of print. The process does not continue uninterruptedly for vision, or any other sense. The whole set of brain actions goes on in discrete packages, each of perhaps one-fifth of a second. These may be mainly visual, or mainly auditory, with perhaps mixtures of items from visceral or emotional sources, or of memory records from previous experience. Our own awareness of the stream of consciousness suggests that there is some central processor receiving information at about this rate, which is also the order of frequency of the electroencephalogram.

So each part of the system progressively extracts more and more abstract or general features of the visual information. It combines them with information from other sense organs and of course with the stored information and instructions already in it. Each part from time to time gives outputs producing appropriate actions in the further regions to which it is connected. We are only just beginning to find the details of this web of backward and forward connections. There is some evidence that each of the successive visual areas has its own connections with the thalamus (Diamond 1978).

At present there is no adequate theory as to how the information collected in the various cortical areas interacts to produce actions by the whole animal or man. Some people have supposed that at later stages the process of decoding and re-coding must produce the activation of cells each representing some complex feature of the world. Thus Gross of Princeton believes that he has found cells in the monkey's cortex that respond only when the animal sees a monkey's hand (1972). They do not even respond to a human hand. Such hypothetical cells for recognizing complicated features have been called 'gnostic neurons' or, humorously, 'grandmother's-face cells'. But other people have given different interpretations of Gross's observations. The fact is that there is no agreed hypothesis as to how the signals from the various feature-detector cells interact to constitute complete messages. It can hardly be that there are gnostic neurons representing all the various features of the world as seen from every angle. It is much more likely that the 'putting together' of all the information is a property of *groups* of neurons. Anyhow it is a mistake to try to discover some 'final' stage of synthesis. Each part of the brain continually moves on from one action to another, just as the whole person does in real life.

## Growth of the programs for seeing

A good way to learn about the program for seeing may be to watch how it develops in a child. We can follow the stages by which it learns to use its eyes to conduct a search for features of the world that are significant for its needs and wants and comfort. As already noticed, the earliest features to which attention is directed include the characteristics of other people, especially their faces (Vurpillot 1976). The child must learn to move its eyes systematically so as to examine new objects, to 'feel' with the eyes all round whatever it is examining. The movements of the eyes of an adult are directed by their six muscles to bring them to positions that will provide whatever information is required at the moment (p. 118). These movements reflect the expectation as to what is likely to be interesting. As you look around, you pick out objects, people, furniture, say, but usually pay no attention to the dark and bright areas in between them. So the movements of the eye are dictated by the brain program for exploring the world. This is all the more interesting because although this search is such a personal matter we are not *conscious* that we are using such a program. This is a useful clue when thinking about what is meant by saying we are conscious.

A three-year-old child shows remarkably few eye movements. By 4–5 years he shows twice as many, and the fixations are clustered at distinctive portions of the objects looked at (Day 1975). By 6 years the movements follow a different pattern, they trace around the contours of figures. Further changes then continue for many years. One way to study this progressive change is to show children complicated figures and to ask them to describe what they have seen. There is very marked improvement up to 11 years, as the scanning procedure becomes more systematic. The younger child does not know which features to look for. Up to 7 years he finds it difficult to search for two or more attributes together. With development, the brain acquires a program that makes scanning a purposeful search for relevant information. It becomes continually more systematic and appropriate to the task. It selects the more informative points and so increases the useful field of view. The child no longer needs to concentrate his regard on a few objects.

As the speed and efficiency improves, the time spent with each object decreases. When an object is familiar and corresponds to an internal hypothesis or plan of action, then a few eye movements are enough to allow the appropriate response. One can see this very well in the process of learning to read. At first each letter must be examined separately, then words, phrases, sentences, whole paragraphs or perhaps pages or even whole books, can be in a sense 'comprehended' at a glance by a reader who has learned programs of action that take sufficient account of the probability of what will be found there. One knows pretty well what will be found in any book by P. G. Wodehouse, or indeed in a textbook of anatomy.

So perhaps it is dangerous to speak of maps or models in the brain. The program for seeing each object or type of object probably consists of a routine that dictates a series of operations, guided by subroutines as expectations are examined. Spatial features and distances are dominant characteristics, as we have seen in discussing memory. The 'maps' are not literal topographical plans but schemes of action, coordinated especially to social life and convention. The landmarks and routes are those that the person is familiar with and distances will be judged accordingly, for example, a well-known place downtown will be judged to be nearer than an unfamiliar suburb that is really quite near.

## Brain injuries and sight

Penfield and others have found that electrical stimulation of some of the cortical visual areas in patients under local anaesthesia may arouse visual scenes, often including images of people (Fig. 12.7) (Penfield and Roberts 1959). Perhaps even more revealing are the types of defect seen after injury to the secondary visual areas of the occipital cortex (Luria 1973). Such people with 'visual agnosia' are not blind and they can often recognize features of objects, but they cannot '*deduce* the meaning of the image'. This is an interesting formulation by Luria. The 'image' is there on the retina, but the patient cannot decipher the signals in the code of the nerve impulses that are set up in the optic nerves. Perhaps he cannot do this because he does not scan properly, since his program has been disrupted.

Further clinical problems that throw light on visual programs are difficulties in the analyses of spatial coordinates. Patients with lesions of the occipital cortical visual areas often cannot distinguish right and left or read the hands of the clock. They have special difficulty in finding their place on a map. They cannot copy letters, because they put the lines in the wrong

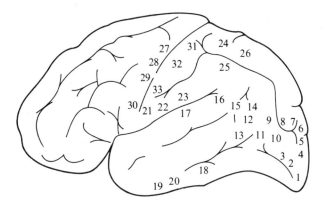

FIG. 12.7. Summary of some effects of electrical stimuli applied to the cortex of patients operated under local anaesthesia: 1–6 flashes of light and coloured spots; 7–11 images of flowers, people, etc., 12–15 sequences of movement; 16–17 sounds of words; 18–23 tongue feelings; 24–6 balancing sensations (vestibular); 27–30 production of sounds and words; 31–3 skin sensations. (Modified from Luria 1973, assembled from data of Foerster, Penfield, Pötzl, and others.) (After Luria 1973.)

places. All this is further evidence that they lack programs for deciphering the code of their own brains. Perhaps, surprisingly, they also have difficulty with speech codes, especially those dealing with relationships, such as the distinction between 'brother's father' and 'father's brother'. It is fascinating that such semantic problems are linked with the mechanisms for judging distances and relationship by vision.

Some of the reports give a vivid idea of how the program of seeing proceeds as the patient tries to guess, 'There is a circle, another circle, and a stick, a cross bar, why it must be a bicycle.' It was a pair of spectacles. 'This is a fire, here are the flames.' It was a coloured picture of a cock. A telephone dial is called a clock and a couch is a trunk and so on. Anything that obscures or complicates the figures makes additional difficulties. A further problem for such patients with visual agnosia is that they can see only one object at a time, rather than a whole field. This is also one of the characteristics of the vision of young children (p. 129). Conversely when such patients are asked to draw or copy they can only draw the parts, and children's earliest drawings show very much the same separation. The child has perhaps learned the program for *seeing* a person, but his brain does not yet contain a program adequate to put the parts together by drawing. Neither in the child or the patient is the internal program what we should ordinarily call conscious.

The most fascinating and instructive of all the clinical studies of vision are those of patients who are born blind but have later recovered their sight after surgical operation. The philosophical implications of the question of what they would see were raised by Bishop Berkeley. The answer has now been given by study of patients by von Senden (1960), Valvo (1971), and Gregory and Wallace (1963). The short answer is that on recovery of vision such patients are able to recognize only some of the objects that they already know by touch. Mostly they see only a swirling mass of colour which they may find very disturbing, so that they quickly shut their eyes again. They have, as we shall now say, no program for seeing. With patience and time they may learn to see, but it is a slow and painful process, unlike the normal acquisition of programs for seeing at the appropriate time of the developmental sequence of a child. This is an excellent example of one of the sensitive critical periods, when the brain is especially ready to develop some particular capacity.

We have therefore a moderately clear idea of what we mean by programs for seeing. They are sets of pathways and activities in the brain, determined partly by heredity but largely by learning, which organize the search for the meaning of the code signals in the visual pathways which are generated by the patterns of light on the retina. Each human individual learns to pick out from the maze of light, shadow, and movement those patterns that symbolize objects of importance for him for life in his social world.

# 13 Needing, nourishing, and valuing

*Do we need a special language to describe emotion?*

With the discussion of needs and desires we reach a central point in our enquiry as to the possible scope and uses of the concept of programs in the brain. From now onwards we shall be trying to discover how far such ways of thinking can help in considering the more subtle activities that we usually associate with peoples minds, such as wanting or loving or fearing. Ways of talking about such things are deeply influenced by culture and are vague and imprecise. The first question is how far is it possible and desirable to translate this ordinary language into a more scientific one. Psychologists and neurologists have not found it easy to produce an exact language with which to talk about needs and desires, loves and fears, beliefs and morals, and so on. New words have been invented and some people claim that a special terminology is essential if psychology is to become precise, just as has proved necessary for mathematics, physics, and chemistry and, to a large extent, biology. There is much in this claim and exact scientific enquiry and language are conferring immense benefits on mankind. Simple distinctions such as heavy/light or loud/soft are usually good enough as measures in daily life, but not for physics. Can we expect that angry/joyful will be good enough for psychology? Moreover common speech is not at all the same in different languages. The Germans speak of 'lust' and 'unlust' meaning (very roughly) pleasure and displeasure, but they have no word for 'emotion'. Again, we certainly need to dissect the ordinary language meaning of such words as consciousness and mind if we are to use them precisely. The old controversies over such concepts still operate powerfully to hinder the work of psychiatrists who try to help people who are mentally sick and distressed. Perhaps nowhere else in human life can clarification of ideas do so much to help.

Nevertheless I believe that it will be unfortunate if the human sciences try to follow the physical too strictly. It is true that ordinary language is redundant, vague, over-inclusive, and ambiguous; while that of mathematics, physics, and engineering seems to be the reverse. But this is partly an illusion produced by considering the scientific workers and their works as if they existed in some abstract stratosphere. As soon as we begin to ask why scientists pursue their activities in the ways they do we have to go back to the 'inexact' language of psychology. Quantum mechanics will not tell physicists why they study it. Yet surely in the best analysis this is the most important question for each science to answer for itself. Some philosophers of science realizing this dilemma take active evasive action. For example Popper (1972, p. 67) claims specifically that 'questions of truth or validity ... must be *sharply distinguished from all genetic, historical, and psychological questions*' (his italics). My thesis is that such evasion is deceptive and dangerous. It takes no account of what we know about the unity of brain action and it leads to reactionary and elitist social and political positions. Above all it is debilitating for the sciences themselves. Of course this does not mean that we should abandon the precise habits of thought that have proved so valuable. But we need to combine them much more readily with considerations of human values (see Polanyi and Prosch 1975).

In any case, no specialist language can really be so abstract that it avoids the burden of the long histories of our various languages and cultures. This does not mean that we must operate with all the old apparatus, for instance, of prior irreducible ideas and feelings and moral judgements. We have to learn to look at language itself; to realize that words are all only arbitrary and relative, and to appreciate what they can and cannot tell us. It is important to ask what we expect from language. It is difficult even to imagine a simple and coherent culture in which all the symbols are related to each other in such a way that no inconsistencies arise. Western thought certainly does not operate with such a single unitary system. It is compounded from many strands, determined by historical accidents and by particular social and political systems and the religious and philosophical explanations of the world that go with them. Most of us are at best only vaguely aware of these influences, but yet they determine the course of our thinking and research. We cannot avoid this and even with our best endeavours we shall remain puzzled mortals, uncertain how best to proceed.

## Are value judgements beyond scientific enquiry?

It will be said that there are much more fundamental reasons why a scientific psychology cannot be fully inclusive as well as exact. It is common to consider that there are as it were fundamentally separate parts of human existence. In particular many people tell us that our capacities for precise logical discussion or scientific experiment and reasoning are distinct from the faculties we use when we decide what to regard as good and bad or speak about our gods. This antinaturalist thesis, that judgements of value are outside the province of science, has been widely held by philosophers. G. E. Moore whose book in 1903 began the modern discussion of this view held that such judgements are in a sense outside nature, the product of a special intuitive human faculty. As Wittgenstein put it the idea was that value is transcendental, that it 'is not in the world' (see Quinton 1973).

My thesis will be that study of the brain and its programs shows that there is no possibility of making such sharp separation of capacities. The parts of the brain that operate when we experience pleasure or love, fear or anxiety are closely linked with all those parts that are used in more intellectual activities and vice versa. The cerebral activities of every man are a unity, many parts being at work at any one time. This implies that each of us can at best only partly separate his simpler satisfactions from his decisions as to which intellectual, social, political, or moral beliefs are good or bad.

## The programs for eating and drinking

Questions about what it is to be good apply to a huge range of judgements from food to philosophies. It may be useful to consider questions of value first in relation to the satisfaction of the *simple* needs of the body. Study of the programs that regulate such lowly wants as eating and drinking provide a basis for examining the higher ones. It may be indeed that many differences of opinion on these questions arise because some people insist on starting at the top, whereas others prefer to decide first the easier questions at the bottom of this scale. We may therefore begin by examining the systems that ensure the genesis of the basic needs whose fulfilment ensures the continued existence of the body. The intake of food and drink is indeed close to the centre of all living, it opposes the tendency to dispersal and uniform distribution of matter. Moreover the amount that we eat and drink is very precisely regulated. During a lifetime each of us consumes several tons of food and thousands of litres of liquid yet, once adult, we remain of about the same size and weight within limits of a few pounds. Where is the reference standard by which the intake is regulated to produce this remarkable result?

For the ordinary individual it is 'natural'. He eats and drinks what he wants, with a rhythm of regular times and if his habits are interrupted he feels hungry or thirsty. Can we find correlations between these rhythms and feelings and any physical events in his body? Such events would represent the written 'score' of the programs that ensure our eating and drinking. Physiologists early noticed that the empty stomach gives waves of contraction and we all vaguely feel hunger in our stomachs. Even more definitely the throat is dry when we are thirsty. But these visceral feelings are not the only sources of the nerve signals that set us off eating and drinking. This is the function of nerve cells in certain regions of the brain, in the hypothalamus, which are programmed to send signals either in a regular pattern of habits or when the composition of the blood indicates that there is a need for food or water (Fig. 9.1). The operations of these parts of the brain, together with those of the stomach, are accompanied by feelings of hunger (Reichlin *et al.* 1977).

In 1952 when I was in Stockholm I was lucky enough to be shown one of the first experiments on the control of drinking. Dr. Andersson had previously inserted under anaesthetic a fine tube into the hypothalamus of the brain of a goat. Whenever a tiny drop of strong salt solution was sent down the tube the goat dipped its head into a bowl of water in front of it and began to drink. If a dilute solution was sent down to the brain the drinking stopped at once. I can remember how the goat shook the drops of water off his beard. The minute injections were imitating the condition in which when the blood becomes more concentrated the goat is thirsty, and the blood then becomes diluted when the animal drinks (Andersson 1953). Incidentally these nerve cells do other things to regulate the amount of water in the body. Besides controlling the intake of water they and their neighbours control the amount of water that is let out, by increasing or decreasing the amount of a hormone sent from the pituitary gland to the kidney, which stops secretion of the urine. The hypothalamus thus controls both the intake and output of water.

These cells serve as the central regulator of the amount of water in the body. The setting of the level of their sensitivity to salt provides the instruction that determines the quantity of water that is held in the body. We can say that the properties of these cells are physical symbols 'representing' the required water content. They do this in fact by actually swelling or shrinking when the salt concentration of the blood changes. The setting of this reference standard of the homeostat has been made by heredity and is no doubt also modified by the subsequent physiological experience of the individuals.

The amount of food intake is also regulated from this same region of the body, the hypothalamus. Animals and humans with injuries to certain 'feeding centres' eat either too little or much too much. Two regions are involved. Rats with injuries to the more medial nerve cells and fibre tracts of the hypothalamus eat far more than normal ones and become very fat. Animals lacking the more lateral region stop eating and drinking and may starve to death. Thus the lateral areas provide the drive to start eating and the medial ones to stop it. Indeed records from electrodes in the hypothalamus show that the lateral regions are active when a normal rat is hungry and the medial ones when it has just finished eating and is satiated. The stimulus that normally sets these cells into action is partly the composition of the blood. Some of the nerve cells here take up sugar from the blood and they send out signals when there is not enough of it there. These cells provide the homeostat's reference standard for sugar. Probably other cells are sensitive to other substances, but many details of the system are still not known. Most of our eating and drinking follows acquired rhythmic programs and control of them is a complicated business, influenced by many higher levels of the brain. One of these centres lying just above the hypothalamus is known as the amygdala, from its shape like a nut. It has effects on various conditions associated with emotion. If it is electrically stimulated in a rat *after* intake has begun the amount eaten will be greatly increased. Pribram (1971) records the case of a girl with injury to the amygdala on both sides, who had become very fat. When he asked her if she was hungry, she said, 'No', but a few minutes later at lunch he saw her pushing the others aside and stuffing the food into her mouth with both hands. Once started she couldn't stop. So he called her back to his room and she repeated, 'No, I'm not hungry.'

In normal people the influences of the cerebral cortex on hunger are still more complicated. We all form habits as to when to eat, and also how much. People can change their habits according to personal and social demands. We cannot pretend that we fully understand even the simpler controllers of the needs for food. Nevertheless in the hypothalamus there are those lateral centres that become operative when we are hungry, they give us appetite. The medial centres send messages when appetite has been assuaged and we are satisfied. The two areas are interconnected and inhibit each other, corresponding, we may suppose, with the mutual interplay of appetite and consummation.

Thus the actions of eating and drinking are certainly programmed largely by the cells of the hypothalamus and fibre tracts that pass through them. Their activities decide when the need for food will be felt and they are also responsible for indicating that the need is satisfied and that consumption should stop. While this is going on we say 'I ate because I wanted to and when I was satisfied I stopped'. Is there a dilemma in this parallelism? Statements about the wants and satisfactions are accompaniments of brain actions exactly as are descriptions of, say, the shape of the moon. The experience of the need for food and satisfaction at eating it are the accompaniments of brain activity and so are experiences of the shape of the moon. In theory the actions of the cells involved could be read off by electrical recordings from the brain. Conversely by activating the appropriate sets of cells it should be possible to produce either set of phenomena. It is however actually easier to stimulate the brain to make an animal 'thirsty', than it is to make it see the moon.

## Self-stimulation of the brain

Feelings of satisfaction are produced by stimulation of some of these very areas injury to which causes error of eating, drinking, and sexual and other behaviour. With the electrodes in some positions the shocks have rewarding effects and are sought for as if they were satisfying. They give positive reinforcements or 'rewarding stimuli', causing an animal to come back for more (Olds 1976, Hall *et al.* 1977). James Olds showed this by implanting wires into the brains of rats. When the animals had recovered from the operation he arranged that if they pressed a lever a weak electric current was passed to the brain. The rats soon learned to do this and evidently obtained satisfaction from the shocks. They would press the lever over and over again a 100 times a minute for hours at a time. They would even neglect food and starve to death while continuing to get the reward. More usually they showed pauses for eating, drinking and sleeping.

Similar observations on humans have been made during stimulation of the brain in therapeutic procedures designed to alleviate the pains of dying patients. Stimulation by electrodes in some regions was reported to give great reduction in pains and sometimes pleasurable feelings, including those of sexual satisfaction.

Experiments by electrical stimulation show that there are some areas of the brain whose activity produces drives to action, others that indicate satiation. Some areas make the animal more active, others make it less. Areas where stimulation produces very active responses may be quite close to others that produce the opposite effects. These are intricate networks of millions of distinct nerve cells, with many different properties and connections. The electrodes used in the experiments are much larger than the cells and are likely to stimulate many neurons at once, including some producing positive and others negative effects if they are close together. In fact we are only able to reproduce the normal actions of the brain very crudely. Nevertheless as we learn more from these experiments we begin to see the operations of the whole system that determines not only how actions are normally related to bodily needs but also in man how the rewards of our most abstract and social satisfactions are influenced by the activities of certain brain areas and the chemical substances that they contain. These areas are responsible for the quality of affect, of pleasure, satisfaction or the reverse that make life worthwhile.

Of course these centres are influenced by signals coming both from outside the body and within it, including for example those from the nose and from the taste buds of the tongue. A specially interesting pathway begins in the cells of the locus cocruleus, lying near the taste centres of the medulla oblongata (Fig. 10.5). If this tract of fibres, running forwards, is interrupted a rat can no longer be taught to run a maze for a food reward (Anlezark *et al.* 1973). There is evidently some relationship between the sensation of taste and the drive to search for food. Perhaps in simpler animals the need for food was indicated by receptors such as those of taste. Then, based on centres for these nerve fibres in the medulla, there developed more sophisticated neural equipment for learning to regulate the programs of eating in relation to whatever sources are available.

## Meeting dietary deficiencies and poisons

In higher animals the systems indicating the needs for food have become very subtle. Animals and men will make special efforts to meet particular deficiencies. Thus if the adrenal glands, which are involved in the hormonal regulation of salt balance, are damaged, the body needs much salt. Rats in this condition stuff themselves with salt, and die if there is not enough around. Richter has reported the case of a boy with diseased adrenals who ate handfuls of salt at home and remained well, but when he was taken to hospital the diet nearly killed him because he got so little salt. If rats are made deficient in calcium they will drink water with calcium and avoid that with none. These and many other such examples depend partly on the sense of taste. If the nerves to the tongue have been cut deficient rats no longer choose calcium water. The effect of the deficiency seems to be to lower the threshold at which the substance in question is detected. This must be the result of some change in the sense organs or brain. There are many examples of people acquiring special appetites for the foods they need. Children deficient in calcium will eat plaster, and anaemic patients are said to crave for liver.

The converse to such food selection mechanisms is the capacity to detect and reject poisons, which is also especially well developed in rats. Solutions of arsenic or mercury are rejected even when they are far too weak to have any physiological effects.

Some of these capacities for selection of what is needed are certainly innate, but others are learned. Thus animals deficient in B vitamins learned to eat food that contained them and was flavoured with aniseed, rather than plain food. When the vitamins were changed over they came to eat the plain food (Scott and Verney, 1947). The animals must therefore learn to associate the taste with some beneficial effect, although this can hardly occur less than 15 minutes after eating—probably much later. Again, we do not know how they do it.

## Is the drive mechanism model adequate?

Studies of eating and drinking during the 1950s and 1960s showed the importance of these peripheral sensory mechanisms as well as of the control centres in the hypothalamus. They led to a theory of the substrates of motivation that has been called the drive mechanism model. In its simplest form it supposed that the impetus for eating and drinking comes from deficit signals sent by the cells of the hypothalamus when they detect that there is an insufficiency, say of sugar or of water. Psychologists soon began to point out however that such an analysis based on specific drive mechanisms is much too simple. Animals do not act only because of their physiological deficits nor, of course, do men and women. In higher mammals, especially, much of the behaviour is for exploration, manipulation, and investigation. Something is known also about the areas responsible for initiation of these latter types of behaviour. We shall consider them in relation to sleeping and waking (Chapter 18). They include the brain stem reticular system or 'core brain' which has enormous cells with spreading axonal fields of influence (Fig. 11.7). These neurons are activated by internal deficit signals and also by signals from the outside world and from the cerebral cortex. They operate to arouse or suppress the activities of large parts of the brain.

## Higher reward centres

There are reciprocal reactions between these lower specific and non-specific activating systems and higher centres in the mediofrontal parts of the cortex. Injuries to these also produce errors of emotion and affect. The individual becomes either too active or totally passive. As Luria (1973*a*) puts it, 'Each human activity starts from a definite intention, directed at a definite goal and is regulated by a definite program, which requires that constant cortical tone is maintained.' When this tone is weakened no organized thought is possible, strong stimuli have little effect and weak stimuli too much. Evidently there is some sense in which these areas are necessary for pleasant experience. They are necessary, but not sufficient for pleasure. We must be careful not to exaggerate, and human satisfactions are very complicated. Nevertheless all these reward centres, are also connected with the operations of the parts of the brain that are involved in the satisfactions we obtain from higher intellectual, social, moral, and even religious activities. One of the greatest advantages of studying the brain is that it begins to show how the simpler and the more complicated human activities relate and interact. Quite a lot has been found out about this, but we can still only say that we *begin* to understand human motivations and drives.

## Pleasure is more than the absence of excitation

Workers as different as psychoanalysts, psychologists, and physiologists have sometimes suggested that the aim of the behaving animal is repose. 'The pleasure principle is then a tendency which subserves a certain function, namely that of rendering the psychic apparatus as a whole free from any excitation or to keep the amount of excitation constant or as low as possible' (Freud 1920). I believe that such a view underestimates the directive or aimed action of the programs that the hypothalamus and core brain dictate. The continuation of life is possible because the actions of the individual are aimed not at reducing excitation but at obtaining those materials and situations that are needed. When such pursuits are effective the individual receives the reward of satisfaction and discontinues that particular activity. The search is not for absence of excitation but for the fulfilment of a need.

## Value judgements

The discovery of the pleasure centres in the brain has fundamental consequences for philosophy and practical affairs. It influences our ideas about the aims of human actions, which are basic to all social, political, and moral theories. It is not possible any longer to consider that human aims and values are set by some transcendent, intuitive process that is as Wittgenstein put it 'not in the world'. We know now that they are basically regulated by the organization and activities of certain parts of the brain, however much they may be complicated and varied by culture and experience. Some recent philosophers have accordingly changed ground from the attack on naturalism, and they see the problem rather as a need to find out what is the special character of *statements* about values. It may help to discuss them. One way of putting it is that if value statements are accepted by the listener it is implied that he will *do* something. Some philosophers have compared statements of value to imperatives, and this agrees with our idea that decisions about value spring from the effort to meet needs. Value judgements include statements about what is *good* and what people *ought* to do. They contrast with statements of fact, whose acceptance does not (necessarily) entail action. 'It is raining' is merely factual. 'You ought not to hit that child' implies a value judgement. One way of putting this is that value statements are prescriptive, not purely descriptive (Hare 1963). Another teminology is that value statements are practical, while purely factual statements are theoretical (Quinton 1973). The great question is then, can we find a basis for prescriptive statements in descriptive ones? Broadly speaking naturalists hold that you can and antinaturalists still maintain that you cannot. Hare says, for example, 'If asked why are strawberries good you can say they taste nice and are sweet, but this does not define goodness.' Moore's way of putting it was, 'If I am asked what is good my answer is that good is good and that is the end of the matter.' Similarly, as he says, one cannot define yellowness—yellow is yellow. But how could one describe it except as that which is experienced with light of a certain wavelength? Instead of trying to define yellowness we search for the conditions outside and inside the body in which we experience it. The whole of physics consists in making such enquiries. Similarly we can look for the conditions that we associate with goodness both outside and inside.

Quinton's reply to Hare's challenge about the strawberries is that by strawberries are good (we mean) they belong to the class of fruit that most people enjoy. He also says:

Most of the judgements of value about which there is some sort of consensus of opinion are just what they would be if to ascribe value to something were to assert that it is such as to give satisfaction to people in general in the long run (p. 366).

To evaluate something is to say something about its capacity for giving satisfaction. This of course is a controversial position, to which many philosophers have objected, and we shall have to take a lot of trouble to defend it, especially when we come to consider judgements about ethics and morals. The point is that the biologist sees that at least part of the basis of judgements of value lies in the *fact* that all living actions are directed towards aims or objectives, which are determined by their fundamental programs. The programs we have inherited tell us to continue to promote life. Every creature organizes its activities so as to attempt to follow this instruction, though it may interpret it in such a manner that its actions even lead to its own individual death.

If we can show that in every human being there are appetitive mechanisms at work in *all* the programs of the brain, then surely we can no longer continue to hold that 'good is good is the end of the matter'. These systems provide the stimulants for all the aims of self-maintenance that constitute living. J. S. Mill's thesis that pleasure alone is the object of desire is an understatement. All cerebral operations are related in some way to the set of standards and aims dictated initially by our genes. But of course the cerebral programs that we learn are so immensely complicated that they may seem to show little connection with the basic standards set by the genes and the hypothalamus. It is characteristic of humans that they learn to obtain satisfaction in many different ways. But if the reward centres are not working even the most refined cultural or religious programs act in vain. The individual becomes unhappy and depressed, useless to himself and others and, ultimately, suicidal.

Many people have a different and less complicated sort of 'belief' about human values, relating them to a divine source. Goodness is what God wills us to do, as he has shown in the Scriptures and life of, say, Christ, Buddha, or Mahomet. All human beliefs are to be respected and studied, but when we look at religious beliefs we shall find that they too are the product of people, which have involved action by many parts of their brains including the reward centres we have been discussing. This does not mean that we shall find them ultimately either right or wrong, there is very little we can say about ultimates. But we can now say something about the *origins* of human beliefs just as we can about the origins of our desires and fears. They are all the products of our human nature and the complicated cultural conditions that this nature has brought about. I am claiming that we are more likely to reach useful and satisfactory conclusions by considering this knowledge about origins than by assuming that our values are set by a divinely endowed inner imperative.

We now know that satisfaction and happiness depend upon the proper functioning of certain reward centres in the brain. If these are not working well, no actions, or indeed thoughts, will produce satisfaction or happiness. These areas are necessary for satisfactory individual and social life, though not of course sufficient in themselves. This does not tell us that happiness *is* in the hypothalamus or that it *is* noradrenaline—we all know that it is simply happiness just as yellow is yellowness. What we now know is a great deal more about its origins and how to obtain it. It may well be objected that there is nothing new in all this, everyone knows that human beings are influenced by needs and desires and seek happiness. What is new is the knowledge of the unity of the whole brain program, and the part that the centres that generate needs play in it. Already with still imperfect knowledge we can see something of the relations between the operations of the hypothalamus and basal forebrain centres and the frontal areas of the cortex. Together these set the 'tone' of operations of the parts of the cortex involved in even the most abstract operations of thinking.

# 14   Loving and caring

## Love of self and of others

Attempting to define love is indeed a hazardous enterprise, more suitable for a poet than for a scientist. Yet in the belief that human capacities should not be considered in separate compartments I hope to show that knowledge about the brain can enrich our loves. Understanding them can make them more fruitful for ourselves and those we care for.

Think first of the many senses in which we use the word: 'I love life'; 'I love the country'; 'I love my country, my work'; 'I love my wife, my mother, my daughter'; 'I love Jesus'. All these are proper uses but have very different emphasis, even different meanings. The *Oxford English Dictionary* has no less than 24 columns of meanings for love. Should we then conclude that the category of loving is too vague for scientific use? That would be a great pity. What would be the use of a neuroscience that cannot tell us anything about love? Surely in common to all these uses is the concept of something especially satisfying about a relationship, something pleasing, something that we hope will continue, whether it is a loving sexual partnership or a blessed belief in the goodness of God. After all the Latin equivalent of to love is *libet* or *lubet*, to please, hence libido or desire. When we love someone we feel happiness in their company and sadness in separation. And as biologists we find a full understanding of this emotion. Our central concept is that the main goal of organisms is to continue to maintain themselves, in simple words to remain in good health. Pleasure and happiness are the signs that a creature is succeeding in this aim, they are the internal signs indicating that its programs of action are working well. What we have to find therefore is the connection between the happiness of loving others and this tendency to continued survival, and this is not immediately quite so obvious as we might hope.

## The hypothalamus and Eros

We have seen already that sensations of pleasure are possible only with proper functioning of certain circuits including the frontal cortex and hypothalamus. People in whom these regions are not working adequately are difficult to please. Indeed they may be full of displeasure and even apt to terminate their life altogether. It is therefore no surprise to find that at least some of the simpler of the activities that we characterize as loving, the sexual ones, are also regulated by the actions of the hypothalamus. Indeed electrical stimulation here in conscious human subjects may produce feelings of general well-being and sometimes sexual pleasure (Chapter 13).

The hypothalamus is the part of the brain whose programs insist upon the performance of self-preserving activities. It makes sure that we eat and drink the right amounts and, with neighbouring regions, it allows us to defend ourselves if attacked (Chapter 15). Conservation over much longer times is also ensured by this part of the brain. Even if the body is very well looked after it cannot go on forever and must ultimately be replaced. Homeostasis conserves not just one body but the whole program for a way of life, which is written in the genes and passed on by reproduction. The hypothalamus contains programs devoted to this longer term conservation. It ensures that after a while the individual comes to sexual development. Many of his or her actions now tend not only to maintain their own genes but also to pass them on. In a bisexual species this involves a co-operation between individuals and the taking of actions that, far from promoting their own lives, may actually endanger them, especially while they care for the young. To ensure such co-operation and altruistic behaviour each species has evolved special and elaborate mechanisms to promote mating and care of the young. In most species individuals for most of their lifetime compete and conflict. Quite fantastic developments such as the peacock's tail may be needed to bring the sexes together. In humans sexual attractions, mating behaviour, and care of the young occupy a major part of our lives and energies. It is proper for the conservation of our kind that such activities should be pleasurable and rewarding, and these are the pleasures of love.

The hypothalamus thus has a central part in directing behaviour towards the goals both of self-preservation of the individual and the reproduction of his genetic program. We often identify the acts of reproduction as the prototype of love, symbolized by Eros. But we can see now that this love is only a special part of the larger program for the conservation of life. Our self-preservative 'selfish' desires are as much a part of this as our altruistic wishes for others. Being directed by the same parts of the brain the two sorts have naturally much in common. Let us then identify Eros not only with sexual love but with the conservation of life, of ourselves, our children, other people, and indeed of all life. This is an entirely appropriate modern version of the old Greek myth. In the Orphic legend of the Titans Eros was the first god, the golden-winged child, hatched from the egg of the black-winged uncreated bird, Nyx. Eros thus symbolized all life and was antecedent to Thanatos, the god of death, brother of Lethe or sleep.

There is no falling from grace in admitting that all love involves an element of self-love. Indeed it is a truism that our needs, motivations and search for rewards move us to actions that are a curious confusion of egoism and altruism. The very activities of sex, which may lead us to all the responsibilities of parenthood, are themselves perhaps the most rewarding of all experiences for the individual. We need all the knowledge we can get about our programs in order to understand such paradoxes and to learn how best to regulate our actions.

## Programs for attachment

The sequence of development of the child shows how these ambiguities begin and develop. We shall follow them in some detail since everyone is agreed about the importance of these early days for the whole of later life, although recent studies have shown that it is possible for people to make surprisingly good recoveries from bad starts (Clarke and Clarke 1976).

We have already examined how the child develops its physical and intellectual skills, as studied by Bruner (1974) and Piaget (1969 and 1971) (Chapter 9). Now we are concerned with the stages of his emotional development. The many different points of view among psychologists make it hard to know how best to organize this description. We shall in the main follow John Bowlby's excellent account of the development of attachment (1969). In spite of some criticisms his general conclusions about the importance of the early experiences of the child have in general been confirmed (see Rutter 1972). Bowlby based them on actual observations of children, as indeed do some of the more psychoanalytical schools such as those of Anna Freud (1974), Klein (1975) and Eissler *et al.* (1977). But these are mainly concerned with the later psychopathological conditions that are supposed to result from early experiences. It is not always easy to discern how far their conclusions depend upon actual evidence from observation of children. We shall discuss them later in connection with fear and anxiety (Chapter 15).

A fundamental difficulty is that the young child cannot tell us about its motivations, pleasures, or fears, we can only deduce them from its behaviour. It is difficult indeed to know what is meant by saying, as Klein does, that the earliest fear is of death and the first desire is to return to the womb. On the other hand the transactions between mother and child that have been mapped by Bowlby and others can reasonably be interpreted to show the growth of loving and also of fearing.

In spite of great differences in the rates of development it seems likely that in humans there is an inherited program that promotes attachment, usually to the mother, between the ages of about 4–12 months. The child needs to form lasting bonds with at least one person. The first year is probably the 'sensitive period', during which such attachments are most readily formed. I shall compare this phenomenon to imprinting, first shown by Heinroth (1910) and later Lorenz (1935) in birds, but now well known also in mammals. The essential feature is that in many species the young are born with a specific learning mechanism, which ensures that they become 'attached' to the first object they see, usually of course the mother. In precocial species, such as sheep or horses, where the newborn is well developed, imprinting occurs immediately after birth, but in non-precocials such as mice and men, only later, as the capacity to discriminate develops. The fact that in humans attachment is late and may be delayed has the important corollary that even with what we conventionally call a bad start a child may yet recover. Some workers would therefore wish not to emphasize the comparison with imprinting.

The child is born with programs that ensure he receives attention, for example, crying, and the mother is also programmed to respond to them. Her brain and her hormones normally make sure that she responds to his cries just as they also ensure that she has the milk to feed him. He cannot run to her like a lamb or even cling continually to her as a baby monkey can, so it is especially important that his cries should be heard and answered. The speed of maternal response is the chief factor in reducing crying (Bell and Ainsworth 1972). Study of a series of children proved that babies cry less if their mothers have been quick to respond. Moreover much physical contact and cuddling makes a 'good' baby. Fears of 'spoiling' miss the point that the child's cries and mother's responses are biologically correct. Here indeed is an area where 'facts' tell us what we 'ought' to do. The idea that it was 'right' not to spoil the baby because it might encourage his 'bad' crying is a good example of where reliance on transcendental intuition can go wrong. On the other hand there is some evidence that mild stressing does increase capacity to resist. Rats isolated for a few minutes every day from their mothers later showed raised corticosteroid levels and increased resistance to stress. No similar observations are available for children. We do indeed need further *facts* in order to decide what it is best to do.

In his early days the child has little capacity for discrimination and attends only to his own immediate needs. It is said that the neocortex plays little part in the control of behaviour for the first 4 weeks. It is difficult to condition a child during the first month and for the first two months 'crying is its only major effort of expression'. It is 'a peremptory message to the mother, "come close, change what is happening"' (Emde *et al.* 1976). The food intake is ensured by programs of seeking for the breast, sucking, and swallowing, which are controlled by the child's internal condition and certain simple external stimuli. His other behaviour in the earliest weeks consists mainly in startle responses to simple visual and auditory stimuli, reflexes, and tracking movements. He cannot properly be said to show love, unless perhaps for himself, for he has not yet the power to discern and distinguish other entities. Nor does he at first show any signs of intentional responses. Transient evidence of smiling occurs from the first days but the 'social smile' appears shortly after scanning of the face and eye-contact with mother begin, at about 7 weeks (Emde *et al.* 1976). At first the smile may be given to any object that shows two black dots on a pale background. Then by 3 or 4 months the image of a full human face is needed to elicit the smile, which says 'Keep up what you're doing, I like it' (*ibid.*, p. 87). The mother, of course, likes it too and it elicits her loving behaviour and prolongs their intercourse. By 5 months the effective stimulus is limited to the smiling face of certain familiar persons and strange faces now begin to produce first close attention, then sometimes reactions of fear. This 'stranger distress' becomes marked at 7–9 months and is a distinct response, not necessarily correlated with reactions to mother loss though these develop at about the same time. The 'stranger distress', like smiling, seems to be the maturation of a specific capacity, in this case, for 'fearfulness' of strange situations.

The baby is now definitely attached to those that he loves and will show a whole series of reactions if he is separated from them. By 4 months he will probably be responding differently to his mother as compared with other people, smiling and following her with his eyes. His attachment is first shown by crying when she leaves and then, when he can crawl, by going towards her. He will smile and crow with pleasure when she returns. From 6 to 9 months onwards he will also follow the father and any familiar figure. A few children still show no attachment behaviour even at 12 months, but nearly all are by then giving a special set of responses to certain individuals. So it is very likely that this is a pre-programmed response, essentially of imprinting, which I take to mean the presence of a neural mechanism ready to respond to certain stimuli by attachment.

## Motherly love

We are apt to take this response by the mother for granted, but think of a situation where as many as half of all children die before the age of 1 year, which was not so uncommon in Europe 200 years ago. The mother can hardly then *wish* to become emotionally attached to children so many of whom seem doomed to die. Yet she is programmed to do so, and if the child lives to remain attached to it. From quite early on the child indeed seems to recognize the effort that is needed on his part and begins to control the mother, rather than simply responding to her as a stimulus. He is not passive but seeks for interaction, by his babblings and many other attractive devices. The actions that lead to attachment behaviour are listed by Bowlby (1969) as sucking, crying, and smiling, then later following and clinging. As communication develops, calling her name becomes important. But a list gives a poor idea of the infant's responses and we also need to know what it is about the mother and her actions that produces this imprinting of her characteristics upon the child. These responses are called out most readily by human features. The human face and human voice are particularly powerful elicitors of smiling and babbling. The touch of human hands and movements of the arms in cuddling and rocking also have obvious specific effects and probably human smells as well.

The best interpretation of these facts is that the child is programmed to respond to human features. We cannot demonstrate that there are cells in the brain ready at birth to do this, as there have been shown to be for recognition of certain visual patterns by monkeys and kittens and for human speech sounds (p. 179). But there is enough evidence to allow us to use as a hypothesis that there are such cells (or combinations of cells) and that they come to full development only if properly stimulated. Moreover I shall hold that such cell systems, programmed to respond to human characteristics, come to be the central elements of the whole neocortical system. It may be that a large part if not the whole of later cerebral organization is arranged to some extent around various human features. Perhaps inputs are recorded in the memory on the basis of their resemblance to human characteristics, and this may provide a large part of the basis of the addressing system by which items are found for recall (Chapter 10). This is only a hypothesis, but we need one to understand cerebral organization. The evidence from childhood certainly shows that humans are born with a propensity to pay special attention to the sights and sounds of each other. Is this the basis of anthropomorphism?

## Adult attachments

It may be that the same neural mechanism is responsible for some characteristic features of later life. Sudden and violent attachments to people are typical in adolescence, and surely falling in love is a real enough phenomenon. Is it very different from the reaction of the child to its mother, whether or not we call it imprinting? Parents, again, fall in love with their children. We have commented on the way that the smiles and babbles of the baby fascinate and capture the mother. Outside the family adults very often become attached to groups or institutions, sometimes focusing only too readily on its leader, president, or king. Attachments to stars of stage, ring, or football fields are commonplace. This very characteristic human feature of attachment must have a specific basis in the brain. Indeed it must have a common basis in all mankind, for most humans respond to leaders, from Indian chieftains to the late Chairman Mao. We do not know when it began to be so, but the earliest known human art includes statuettes that are evidently portraits of persons made by paleolithic hunters more than 30 000 years ago (Fig. 14.1) (Sandars 1968).

## Juvenile sex

We have traced the phenomena of attachment in great detail but the themes we are supposed to be discussing are loving and caring. Are we to conclude

FIG 14 1. Statuette of a man from the Gravettian
paleolithic culture, about 30 000 years ago. It is made of
mammoth ivory and is 25 cm high. It was found in a
grave with the skeleton of a man buried wearing a
head-dress or necklace of 600 shells and polished ivory
beads. Found at Brno, Czechoslovakia and now in the
Moravian Museum there. This is one of the oldest
known artistic products. (After Formanů
and Poulíka 1956, and see Sandars
1968.)

then that the love we have glorified as the supreme human achievement is
nothing but 'attachment'? This would be reductionism indeed. We have to
look for the steps by which selfishness is transformed into mutual delight
and self-sacrifice for others. The newly imprinted child may perhaps be said
to have fallen in love, as the mother certainly has. But there is nothing
altruistic about the child's devotion, it is purely selfish and for long remains
so. As he becomes more skilful in eliciting the responses he requires, he
gradually gains insight into the fact that the mother too requires rewards.
He may offer her his teddy bear to tempt her when she refuses a request. He
is gradually building the model or set of hypotheses about how the social
world works, a model which must serve him in all his later human relations.
Throughout the long years of childhood he is learning how to get on with
people. He develops attachments to seniors and peers, some temporary,
some long-lasting, and of course varied according to the rules of his culture.

  Then with the development of sexuality come new needs. Elements of sexual behaviour are already present in infants of less than one year. Baby boys or girls will throw their arms around mother and nuzzle her with pelvic thrusts. They are manifesting their mutual love in the typically selfish manner of seeking erotic pleasures of touch. A boy and a girl of two or three may excitedly stimulate each other as in coitus. These are early fragments of sexual behaviour, rewarded with partial consummatory results. The capacity to receive pleasure from certain erogenous parts of the body is present from earliest childhood. Before adolescence it lacks the priming effect of the sex hormones.

It may be nevertheless that such juvenile sex is important for the development of full sexual behaviour. There is evidence from the works of the Harlows (1962) with monkeys that fully heterosexual behaviour requires some previous affectionate relations between infants. Unfortunately in spite of endless speculation there is much conflict in the evidence about the conditions conducive to sexual development in man. Certainly the conditions differ greatly with culture. The impetus to sex comes from heredity and hormones, but its manifestations are profoundly influenced by experience. Whether a person becomes 'normally' heterosexual (whatever that means) is certainly influenced by his or her relations with parents and peers. Even animals such as rats and dogs only develop proper sexual behaviour after a period of experiment and learning, and they may become homosexual. This need for experience is much more true of men and women. As Ashley Montagu (1976) puts it, 'the *capacity* to perform sexually is one thing; the ability is quite another' (p. 72). As he points out every gynaecologist knows that 'grown men and women may enter upon marriage without the slightest idea of how to go about sexual intercourse'. It is possible, indeed likely, that experience at certain sensitive periods has especially marked effects—but we do not know when these periods are. Patterns of sexual behaviour once adopted evidently often persist, but we do not know with what intensity, and they certainly can later be changed.

## What is normal human sexuality?

Adult sexual experience undoubtedly shows great variety in all cultures. There is evidence that homosexual feelings are everywhere quite common, among both males and females. The frequency of sexual 'outlets' as they are called by sex researchers such as Kinsey (1948 and 1953) and Masters and Johnson (1966) also varies enormously. In spite of such investigators and of the spate of publicity about sex it remains a very private phenomenon among humans. Most of us would wish it to remain so, yet this very privacy undoubtedly leads to much anxiety and ignorance and to quite unfounded fears of being abnormal.

The conditions of permanent attachment and marriage of course also differ enormously between societies. Investigators have told us little about the sexual activities of societies other than American (mainly white). What is the situation where marriages are nearly all arranged, or where it is uncommon for there to be a permanent male head of the family? It is often said that the fact that sexual activity is not limited in humans to the days around ovulation is another adaptation from our hunting ancestors, and that it serves to keep the family together. But others doubt if in fact it has this effect. The whole question of sexual attractions between permanent partners seems still to need study. Our western theory that we become attached to each other by a biological bond seems to me to be as likely to be right as any other. Whatever anthropologists may say I believe that falling in love is a real phenomenon.

The whole question of sexual relations is peculiar in man today because of our population dilemma. Our sexual capacities were formed in a primitive society where death was so prevalent that our full reproductive powers were needed, as they are still today by such pastoral tribes as the Samburu (see Clark 1967). The attractions and satisfactions to produce and raise these children had to be strong. These programs remain with us although mankind no longer needs to produce so many offspring. Yet individuals and nations are only gradually becoming ready to recognize this, while sexual desires grow if anything more powerful as we become more healthy. The obvious conclusions are that we must both limit numbers and yet find adequate sexual outlets.

Individual sexual attachments are undoubtedly related in some way to those formed in infancy. Psychoanalysts have of course elaborate myths about the various sequences possible for boys and girls in relation to mothers and fathers. These are difficult for the biological psychologist to evaluate. It is interesting that the word Oedipus does not occur in the index to either volume of Bowlby's work (1969 and 1973), though I am sure he would not wish for this to be taken to mean that childhood attachments are without importance for later sexual development. In spite of all the theorizing and therapeutic procedures of psychoanalysts we are left without certain knowledge of the foundations of adult sexuality, because we still lack adequate studies of children or of the development of the brain. Bowlby is probably right to insist that in spite of the similarities between early imprinting and sexual attraction we should be careful to emphasize also the differences. In particular they appear at different times and depend on different stimuli. 'Yet in man the overlaps between attachment behaviour, parental behaviour and sexual behaviour are commonplace . . . clinging and kissing are examples of patterns common to both types of behaviour.' Quite often one individual treats a sexual partner as a parent and the reverse.

## The balance between masculine and feminine

It is important for understanding the varieties of sexual behaviour to recognize that the differences between the sexes are quantitative rather than absolute. Every individual is a human first and a male or female as it were only secondarily. To appreciate the basis for one's own sexual urges it is useful to have some knowledge of the genetic and chemical (hormonal) factors that influence it.

Each of us inherits both maleness and femaleness, in slightly different proportions. In a simple way this is illustrated in the fruitfly *Drosophila*, where the female has two sex chromosomes and six others (autosomes), and thus a ratio of 1X–3A, whereas the male has 1X–6A. Flies have been found with two sex chromosomes and nine autosomes (1X–4·5A) and they are *intersexes*. Thus sex in flies is determined by a *balance* between female genes on the X and male genes on the autosomes. This is an oversimplification, but something similar is approximately true also in man. The chromosomes of course are found in every cell in the body, so we are really bisexual in every part. This fact alone surely throws light on a range of human problems. If sex is is a balance of maleness and femaleness it will be tipped more or less strongly in different individuals, but it is natural for everyone to show some characteristics of the opposite sex, as much physically (as in the breasts) as in their innermost feelings.

Full mutual understanding between men and women is greatly helped by the realization of how similar they are. The woman may like to be dominated but also wants sometimes to dominate, and the man can find that he also wants it this way. Their mutual satisfaction can be increased by the realization that the feelings of the vagina are similar to those of the penis, since both are variants of one set of organs. Finally satisfaction in orgasm is an experience of the whole person, equally in man and woman, an extreme achievement of consciousness, whose physiological basis we still do not understand, in either sex.

## Sex hormones

These hereditary factors influence the sexual impetus in each of us, not only during development but for every day of our lives. Their mode of action is complicated, involving stimulation of the secretion of pituitary hormones, which control the sex glands (ovary and testis), whose secretions in turn influence the brain, which controls the pituitary. This cycle alone shows plenty of opportunity for complications and variations, but the situation of the individual is much more complex. The sex hormones make the brain cells amenable to sexually stimulating situations, but the actual sexual behaviour that results depends largely on the influence of upbringing and the cultural situation.

Both male and female sex hormones are present in every individual, but of course in different amounts. They have effects on many parts of the brain. Female sex hormones (oestrogens) injected into rats are taken up most readily in the cells of the hypothalamus. These hormones also have influences on many other parts of the nervous system. Injection of oestrogen alters the sleeping pattern of female rats, producing the condition normally found on the night before oestrus, when the sleep is of the type without the normal rapid eye movements (Chapter 18). In monkeys the more aggressive individuals have higher levels of testosterone. Hormones certainly exert comparably powerful effects on brain development and functioning in man. An experiment with 27 pairs of male students showed that artificial increase of testosterone in the blood considerably improved the power to do a rather boring arithmetical task.

The relationship between these hormonal factors and the programs of so-called higher parts of the brain is still very obscure. There is no doubt that it is a two-way relationship. Hormones influence thinking and vice versa. To take one extreme example, the false pregnancy syndrome, which is almost certainly a neuroendocrine development. Thinking herself pregnant a woman can so influence her hypothalamus that it makes the pituitary produce bona fide pregnancy changes in the wall of the uterus and ovary and even sometimes the secretion of milk by the breasts.

## Variety of sexual needs

With so many factors acting at all levels of the brain it is not surprising that human sexual behaviour is endlessly varied. Probably no two individuals respond sexually to exactly the same stimuli. Associations are formed between sexual arousal and situations too various to classify. Some people are stimulated mainly by smells others by sounds, sights, or touches, most by combinations of all of these and sometimes by bizarre ones. Innumerable conditions of family and social life add their complications, from the wish to find a partner who represents revenge on a parent to the resolve to sacrifice one's satisfactions for a cause or for love of a god. It is characteristic of humans to be adaptable and to learn, and this is abundantly evident in the variety of their sex life. We are only just beginning to understand how the several reward systems operate. What happens in the network of cells of the hypothalamus when we satisfy our hunger or reach a sexual orgasm? Learning largely depends upon such rewards but neuroscience cannot yet tell us how they act. Indeed to find the nature of reward and its effect upon the memory circuits in the brain is now one of the frontiers of biological research.

The ability to learn does not necessarily mean an equal capacity in all directions. It would be hard to maintain that human sex can be manifested in *any* manner. The variety is not infinite. It may be that the tendencies catalogued by psychiatrists and symbolized in their lore represent certain preferred directions for the human course. Further researches will probably show that development is programmed to proceed in certain sequences. Let us hope that these will be specified rather more clearly than by reference to Greek myths, romantic though they are.

## Psychoanalysis and sex

The knowledge we now have of the neuroendocrine basis of sex provides a much sounder basis than was previously possible for classical psychoanalysis. Probably Freud himself would have been delighted by these discoveries. He seems to have yearned for 'biological' explanations, but lacking them he held that the individual was driven by a force that he called the libido. We can now see something about the sources of sexual and other drives in the hypothalamic centres. Freud's belief that the libido remains as an unconscious force even when its expression is consciously suppressed certainly contains the elements of a truth (1920–2).

It is less easy for the biologist to understand or believe in the more detailed workings of the Oedipus complex. The boy's wish for his mother is clear enough, but girls are also so attached. Children of both sexes might also be supposed to show jealousy of the father as a rival for mother's attention. The complications of the boy's supposed fear of castration by the father and girl's penis envy might be particular forms of learning prevalent at least in some societies, but here we must leave judgement to those with experience of the evidence. Similarly with Freud's view of the stages of sexual development, oral, anal, and genital. He believed that if the output of the libido at any stage is repressed, development is halted at that stage. Further complications come from the fact that there may be developmental programs that actually promote antagonism in the family (Chapter 15). The mother must be free to consider the welfare of later sibs. The child will at first resist this separation, but there comes a time when he must be detached and come to act on his own. Growing up is indeed a complicated matter.

The tentative conclusion may be that as the sexual urge grows the individual seeks satisfaction by attachments having some resemblance to those he has made in the past. This may have changed greatly from the satisfaction that he derived from the early attachments to mother and father, but in many people and cultures it will have grown naturally from it. In particular in our culture the individual will have learned that his satisfaction is not best achieved by selfishness. If his development has gone well he will have learned that his offer of his teddy bear to his mother was a good idea. Brought up in a giving environment he will have learned that to give is better than to receive, or at least provides the best chance of receiving. It is foolish to deny that a large element of selfishness remains in most adult loving. The individual requires satisfaction, the whole brain works that way, although we do not really know yet how consummation and rewards operate. But the supreme achievement of sexual development is to learn to *share* selfishness and so to transcend it. This surely is what we mean by loving and caring in our culture.

# 15  Fearing, hating, and fighting

## Programs for defence

There can be no question that the brain provides men and animals with special programs that alert them to threats to their security and enable them to deal with them. Stimulation of certain regions in the brain of a cat produces arching of the back, bristling of the hairs, baring of the teeth and all the signs of aggression. Conversely after removal of other regions monkeys no longer display the appropriate reaction of fear to a sudden disturbance, and they will pick up and examine dangerous objects such as snakes. Evidence that there are similar centres in the human brain comes from the results of injuries and tumours, which may turn a mild person into an aggressive one or the reverse.

Preparations for defence are a necessity for all animals, in a sense for all life. Every living thing is continually in danger of destruction. Life is a precarious steady state, maintained only by continual activity and preparedness to meet and counter adverse conditions. In higher animals readiness to meet danger is ensured partly by inborn programs, partly by others that are learned. These are the programs that give us fear and anxiety. We shall follow the child's first inborn reactions to possibly dangerous situations, and then see how he acquires later fears and anxieties as he learns that his special problems and difficulties are likely to be personal and social. The physiological responses to clues to danger, whether inborn or learned, prepare the individual to give an appropriately strong response of fight or flight, and suitable responses are as necessary in social life as in physical conflict. The right response may vary from a fight to the death to submission to a superior in the hierarchy of business or any part of social life.

## Preparation for fight or flight

In either case the individual must be prepared. It has been known for a long time that secretion of the monoamines such as adrenaline prepares the body for fight or flight. Quite recently several systems of aminergic nerve cells and fibres in the brain have also been found to be involved in aggressive and defensive actions by men and animals. We begin to see the connections between the programs of fear and anxiety that prepare us for trouble, and those of defence and attack with which we deal with it. This has made possible the beginning of a rational scientific treatment of the excessive fears and anxieties that overcome us in depression.

We have to be careful not to maximize or minimize either the theoretical importance of these discoveries or their practical applications. The actions of these lower parts of the brain are greatly influenced by the higher parts. Experience and learning are such dominant factors that in man the lower centres are largely controlled by cultural and individual influences. It is characteristic of humans that they can be educated. We may have innate capacities for aggression but it does not follow that we need to use them. A great deal has been learned about these responses by the study of the behaviour of animals, especially higher primates, but we have to be continually cautious in comparing animals with ourselves.

No one can deny that anxiety, fear, and aggression exist. They are necessary parts of life, vital to the continued existence of the individual and of the species. We characterize them as evil and wish they could be abolished, but they are the inevitable corollaries of the precarious and unstable nature of life. We cannot avoid meeting destructive conditions and we may need aggressive forces to protect ourselves from some of them. Certainly we can make every effort to minimize conflicts within our species. To do that we shall need to consider what human attitudes and controls are required to regulate our reactions to each other in a growing population with limited resources. The programs for aggression and defence that have appeared during evolution have served the individual and the species well in the past, otherwise we should not be here as we are today. Appropriately controlled they may yet be exceedingly useful. No one should deceive themselves into thinking that all groups of men are going to live contentedly without constraints. There are too many inequalities among us already and those who are deprived will seek for better conditions, which the privileged will deny them. There are certain to be conflicts. Recognition of men's capacities for aggression and defence may at least help to limit and to contain them.

## Brain programs for aggression

Various forms of aggressive or agonistic behaviour can be recognized and each has a different physiological mechanism. In the cat we can distinguish between behaviour that serves for defence, attack, and flight. A cat acts quite differently when attacking a mouse or another cat. Each of these types of behaviour can be produced by stimulation of a different part of the brain. In life each form of aggression is provoked by a different stimulus and they serve the individual in different ways in the struggle for food, social status, territory, or reproduction (see Pradhan 1975). One classification recognizes at least six types of aggression, released by distinct stimuli, each dependent on rather different parts of the brain and chemicals within it. Thus predatory aggression is released by prey objects, internal aggression by members of the same species, fear aggression by a threatening predator, maternal aggression by a threat to the young, and territorial aggression is released by an intruder.

Lesions in various parts of the brain have different effects on these programs. The degree and amount of aggression can be measured in rats after lesions or after electrical stimulation of the brain, or treatment by different drugs, including substances known to occur in these same parts of the brain. The control of even the simplest form of aggression is very complicated. It involves many different brain regions and is influenced by many chemical substances. One type of behaviour that is readily measured has been the tendency of rats to kill mice (muricide). There are three areas whose effect is to increase this tendency and no less than six that reduce it—the latter lying mostly further forward in the brain (Fig. 15.1). These are only the areas in the *basal* parts of the brain. No doubt the neocortex has an equal or greater influence, and in man one would hope that it could dominate these basal zones.

There is a continual interplay between the tendencies to action that spring

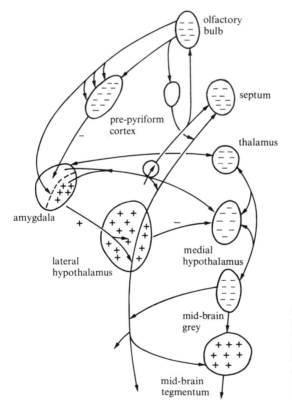

FIG. 15.1. Numerous areas in the basal parts of a rat's brain are responsible for either increasing (+) or decreasing (−) the tendency to kill mice. Many parts are involved in the control of this one type of aggression. (After Pradhan 1975.)

from the lower centres and the restraints imposed by the learned responses of the cortex. Stimulation in the midbrain region will make one monkey attack another—but only if it is a lower member of the hierarchy (Montagu 1976). A remarkable example of inhibition of aggressive behaviour is given by Delgado who inserted electrodes into the brain of a bull and gave the bullfighter a remote-control stimulator with which to defend himself (Fig. 15.2). In man the basal (orbital) zone of the frontal cortex is an especially important inhibitor of these lower regions. People in whom it is damaged show a generalized disinhibition and changes in affect. They may show lack of self-control, violent emotional outbursts and in fact their character seems quite changed.

## The chemistry of some defence mechanisms

Chemical transmitters characteristic of some of these areas have been identified, and their amounts can be altered by several procedures. Thus the levels of the monoamine noradrenaline (NA) in the brain are depressed in rats that readily kill mice, while dopamine (DA) levels are raised. A third amine, serotonin, when injected will depress other forms of aggressive behaviour. So a proper ratio between these amines is important in control of aggression. In a study of two strains of mice the dopamine levels were found to be higher than noradrenaline levels in the brains of the more aggressive strain and vice versa

The discovery that these substances are active in the brain has been made only recently, but for many years it has been known that adrenaline produced by the adrenal gland is involved in reactions of alarm and stress. In the brain amines are 'transmitters' used by one nerve fibre to activate another at synaptic junctions (p. 54). It is very interesting that the central part of the adrenal gland (the medulla) is devoted to producing similar substances and sending them in the blood all round the body. The 'alarm reaction' that they cause was one of the first examples of emotional processes to be studied by physiologists. Stimulation of the nerves to the adrenal gland releases adrenaline, which has the effect of preparing the body for action. The heart speeds up, digestion stops, blood is diverted from the viscera to the muscles, sugar is mobilized as fuel from the liver, and in the cat or dog even the hairs are made to stand up by its action. It is indeed strange that this and the similar substance, noradrenaline, are at the same time at work in the intricate networks of the core brain, making the animal or man alert, attentive, and ready to respond. Both in the brain and body these amines produce rather general effects. These are not the programs that tell the animal or person exactly what to do, only that he should be aroused and ready.

The level of adrenaline in the body can now be studied by following the small amounts that are excreted in the urine (Frankenhaeuser 1975). There is

FIG. 15.2. The bull-fighter entices the bull to attack but then stops him by remote control of stimulation of the brain through electrodes previously implanted. (From Delgado 1965.)

a regular cycle of levels in man, usually lowest at night, highest at midday. Moderate physical or social stress increases the output by 3–5 times. Individuals with higher adrenaline levels were found to be quicker and more efficient at various physical and mental tasks. The level was found to be high in people watching films of violence, while sex films raised the level more in men than women. In general the adrenaline levels are more readily raised in males, which may make them more able to respond to attack. This gives a short-term gain in adaptability but there is some evidence that this ability also increases the risk of longer term weakening and damage to arteries. This may even be part of the reason why women live longer than men.

Preparedness to meet stress is obviously one of the most important of all programs and far more is involved than the production of adrenaline. The longer term mechanism for toning up the body is centred on the outer part of the adrenal gland, the cortex, which produces the corticosteroids, such as cortisone, whose secretion varies in a regular cycle, preparing the body for action each day (p. 67).

## The fears of the child

There are therefore both central and peripheral nervous and humoral programs that prepare the body for action, and these are related to the nervous programs that produce the protective actions of defence and aggression. Fear is elicited in children by a motley list of situations such as 'being lost or alone, sudden noises and movements, strange objects or persons, animals, height, rapid approach, darkness and anything we have learnt can cause pain' (Bowlby 1973, p. 96). Long ago the first behaviourist, J. B. Watson, tried to show that all the child's fear reactions depend upon two basic stimuli, loud sound and loss of support (Watson and Rayner 1920). Freud and his followers hold quite a different sort of view, that what we fear in the external world is a reflection of the dangers we meet in the inner one (see p. 163). Bowlby, with his usual good sense, gives a practical and biological approach. Each of these 'natural' stimuli of fear is a clue. Loud noises or darkness are not themselves dangerous, but they are likely to presage danger. Moreover he notes that in children the intensity of the fear aroused by such primary clues varies enormously according to whether the mother is present or not. Separation is indeed a major source of anxiety from childhood onwards, though of course it is not the only one. But we are all more fearful when alone.

Young children in their first half year show startle reactions and crying but little sign of what could clearly be called fear. Thereafter they begin to show fear to strange persons or objects, especially if large and looming. By the time they can crawl they show fear of empty spaces and will not venture where they are unsure. From two to five years years old the main fearful situations change little and include noise, heights, strangeness, animals, and pain or people associated with it.

## Separation

Yet none of these situations evoke marked fear *if the mother is present*. And her absence alone produces a definite set of reactions indicating anxiety and fear. From the time of attachment at about 4 months onwards nearly all children show a similar series of responses to the absence of the attachment figure (p. 145). After the mother departs, first the child cries, the sign of his anxiety and protest. If she does not return he may become quiet and seem superficially less disturbed, but will not respond to the attempts of others to interest him. This is the stage of grief and despair. If the loved one still stays away despair gives place to detachment and aggression, the child is defending itself against the assault on its needs. When the mother does return she may be greeted coldly and even with aggression. In one study of ten children on reunion after days or weeks of separation, every one 'showed some degree of detachment. Two seemed not to recognize mother. The other eight turned away or even walked away from her. Most of them either cried or came close to tears.' By contrast 'all but one responded affectionately when they first met father again' (Bowlby 1973, p. 12). When a child returns home it often presents a whole set of problems especially to the mother, who is herself disturbed by the situation. Maternal deprivation in fact covers a wide range of experiences, 'it is not a single stress' (Rutter 1972). Disruption of the bonds between mother and child may produce different syndromes, according to whether the child goes to unfamiliar surroundings or the mother goes to hospital and leaves him at home. Once a child has been away it will show signs of fear at any hint that it may be separated again. From about one year onwards, indeed, the child's fear responses tend to be especially to clues that it has learned are likely to indicate danger, as well as to actually dangerous situations.

Bowlby distinguishes three classes of clues to danger; natural, cultural, and learned. The natural clues are probably inborn and include as already mentioned loud sounds, sudden movement, large objects, a visual cliff, perhaps darkness, fear of animals, and of course the fear of separation. These all produce fear also in other animal species. The child acquires cultural clues to fear from the second year onwards by observing parents and others. Truly 'rational' learning of what to fear occurs only in later childhood. Throughout life we are probably as much or more influenced by the natural and cultural clues that were acquired early on than by rational ones. Who is not a little afraid when it thunders?

## The psychoanalytic view of aggression

The development of the child's fears as seen by Bowlby follows what we might call a rational course, easily understood biologically and by all of us. Psychoanalysts believe that the situation is much more complicated. Besides fears of obvious dangers they claim to find evidence from the mental illnesses of adults that leads them to postulate a variety of wishes for aggression in the child that are unconscious, or are suppressed, and so lead to feelings of guilt and of retaliation. It is difficult to know how to evaluate this evidence, but it is sincerely believed by those who have dealt with psychopathology and has great literary and popular appeal.

Some of what seem to be the most extraordinary views come from Melanie Klein (1975). She believes that we are born with a fear of death, and a desire to return to the womb. There is an inherent impulse to eat the mother's breast (oral sadism). The baby's aim is to appropriate the whole contents of the mother and to destroy her, using all its sadistic endeavours. These aims are mixed with desires to consume its own products, the faeces. As the Oedipal period develops the child's first sex theories are that the mother incorporates the father's penis, or all of him. So it wants to eat both its parents and this raises internal anxieties about retaliation. These anxieties are then suppressed and become the basis of the super-ego or conscience. This summary is obviously something of a parody and these extreme early views have been moderated later, but Anna Freud in her closing address to the 28th International Congress of Psychoanalysis in 1971 says essentially the same. She follows the child through various stages of aggression—oral, which is cannibalistic; anal (cruel, sadistic, and possessive); to penetrating or phallic, which is domineering and despotic. The means of aggression develop correspondingly. The child uses first teeth, then excreta (to contaminate), then penis and hands, arms, legs, etc. If the aggression is absent or blocked there is a failure of the oral, anal, or genital pleasure. Anna Freud therefore believes that aggression is a compulsion that is 'innate, primary and independent'. She thinks the evidence for this is (1) the great strength or impetus of the compulsion, (2) the relief obtained by its discharge, and (3) the difficulties that arise if this discharge is blocked. Anxiety, therefore, she believes to be a fundamental, irreducible element in the human constitution.

## Is there a death instinct?

Many psychoanalysts believe that people have an innate impulse to destruction. This is not necessarily the product of early frustrations, but may be increased by them (once again a combination of nature and nurture). The British psychoanalyst Herbert Rosenfeld reports that nearly all his depressed patients had a compulsion for death. The melancholic wants to destroy in the most cruel way all happiness in the world. Rosenfeld says that his patients consciously recognize that they have this compulsion. They are afraid of it and afraid that the analyst will not recognize its genuineness. They cannot bear the thought that they are born with something bad, a need to hurt, or an incapacity to love or appreciate others. They are terribly afraid that they are landed with this original sin or badness, which they can't explain. They may feel unable to remain alive and wish to disappear into nothingness. The destructive self is opposed to the caring self, which seems to have disappeared. This is destructive narcissism, which is opposed to the bonds between mother and child and seeks to destroy them. It may succeed to the point of denial that they have ever existed. Such a patient attacks all evidence that he has need of the analyst, or is helped by him. Any admission of dependence in one session is forgotten by the next. There may even be deceitful false cooperation, by which the aggressive narcissist revenges himself secretly and shows his superiority to the analyst.

Sigmund Freud first postulated such a death instinct in 1920 in his book *Beyond the pleasure principle*. By this he meant, at that time, a very vague 'universal tendency of all living matter to return to the place of the inorganic world'. This was combined with a view that

... for the living organism protection against stimuli is almost a more important task than reception of stimuli ... [Even] the pleasure principle subserves a certain function namely that of rendering the psychic apparatus as a whole free from any excitation, or to keep the amount of excitation constant or as low as possible.

This type of view is perhaps the basis of those oriental cults that seek pursuit of Nirvana or nothingness as the aim of life. For the biologist this cannot be a good description of normal living, which is a continual *activity*, directed to the aim of conserving its own order. If it is true that some individuals seek their own destruction this is an unusual condition for which some explanation must be sought, perhaps in errors of brain metabolism such as those of schizophrenia (p. 166).

These are inevitably simplified but I hope fair samples of the views of distinguished psychoanalysts. Others would probably contest their validity and wish to substitute different versions, for the psychoanalytic fraternity shows an aggressive variety of opinions. Moreover individual workers often change their opinions, which makes most biological psychologists somewhat suspicious of their validity. But they should not be dismissed. These are difficult matters and human beings are indeed very varied. It is not easy for some of us to credit that people really have these bizarre wishes—still less that we *all* have them in suppressed forms. But belief that humans are wicked and evil is not the same as an urge to self-destruction, and goes back far beyond Freud. It is deeply embedded in Jewish–Christian doctrines of guilt and sin. There are endless complications in the human make-up and we are trying to recognize some regularities and their biological basis. Considering all these complications should remind us of the constant danger of over-simplification.

There is good evidence that the child is programmed to be able to form attachments. There is also evidence that he soon begins to show aggression. Many of his early attacks are protests at being separated and are therefore directed against those he also loves. But some capacity to separate himself, and indeed to oppose, is probably necessary if the individual is to develop his own independence and not to remain an appendage attached to his parents. The full dominance of sexuality cannot be reached without the appropriate mixture of aggressiveness, especially in the man, but also in a woman.

If there are these opposing tendencies operating in the brain it is not surprising that they produce conflicts and the accompanying fears. The unfolding of these programs as the child develops is a delicate matter. To ensure what may be called 'normal' independence and sexuality and capacity to reproduce and to rear children, the various stages no doubt require appropriate stimuli at each specially sensitive, perhaps critical period, as in the development of all other parts of the brain (p. 26). We know very little about these stages, but finding out becomes a more practical task as we learn what to look for.

## Adult psychosis and neurosis

The conflicts we have been considering presumably arise in the higher parts of the brain, such as the cerebral cortex, if that is where learning and experience count most. Probably there is not really any clear separation between the operation of these parts and the lower ones, those using the amines, which we considered earlier. They must all work together for proper development. The fact that many parts of the brain are involved is probably the reason that psychiatrists find it so difficult to identify and cure aberrations of its functioning. It may be useful to say something about their approaches to mental illness. A good introduction to this is the book by Stuart Sutherland, himself a Professor of Psychology, about his own recent illness. As he puts it, 'The classification of mental illnesses is itself a furiously contested topic' (1976). The difficulties produced by linguistic obscurity and attempts to maintain the traditional distinction between body and mind are more damaging here than anywhere else. The confusions they produce in the practice of psychiatrists have probably greatly increased the distress of the mentally ill. Some practitioners maintain that a condition is 'functional' or 'purely psychological' and insist on treating it only by talk. Others, considering it purely physical, will provide only drugs or shock treatment. It is hard to know which show the greater ignorance and inhumanity. Let us try to forget the distinction altogether and find out more about the purposeful operations and errors of human brain programs.

Meanwhile we must follow the language that psychiatrists use, though most of them realize its inadequacy (see Sutherland 1976). They recognize psychoses and neuroses as two major categories, distinguished by the evidence that the psychotic is out of touch with reality. But this is such a vague criterion that there is very much overlap. Sutherland puts it, 'I have no idea whether in the statistical returns in which my case figured I was classified as psychotic or neurotic.' Examples of conditions considered as neurotic are 'anxiety neurosis', 'depressive neurosis', 'hysteria' (now uncommon), 'neurasthenia', and obsessive phobias and compulsions. There are all gradations between these conditions and personality disorders, including those that lead to antisocial or criminal behaviour ('psychopaths' or 'sociopaths'). Neurosis is thus undoubtedly a very mixed category of relatively minor deviations from an arbitrary norm. The conditions are serious indeed for the person and for his effect upon others, but not infrequently they are only temporary and recovery is common.

Psychoses, so far as they are really distinct, are more long-lasting, serious, and difficult to treat. They are divided into 'organic' and 'functional', the former being due to known malfunctioning of the brain. Examples of organic psychoses are those produced by tumours, or by syphilis, poisoning by alcohol, drugs, or malnutrition or by the atrophy of old age. 'Functional psychoses' are supposed to be those in which we cannot as yet recognize any abnormality in the brain. However this is no criterion, since biochemical aberrations are already known or suspected in the two most common 'functional psychoses', namely the 'affective psychoses' and schizophrenia. The former involve variations in mood between depression and elation. It seems likely that some aberration of functioning of the now classical determinants of mood in the lower parts of the brain are involved, but the trigger that sets off the condition may be a social or personal condition such as a bankruptcy or loss of a spouse. Once again we see how all parts interact. There is hope that 'considerable progress will be made over the next decade in uncovering more information about the biochemical bases of depressive illnesses and in devising a taxonomy that will be useful in determining the most effective treatment' (Sutherland 1976, p. 81).

## Schizophrenia

In schizophrenia there is definitely some connection with the activity of the aminergic centres of the brain. This is admittedly a very vague and variable condition, often characterized by excessive terrors and unreal fears, in which the person feels that he is being manipulated by malign outside forces (see

Clare 1976, p. 123). He may hear hallucinatory voices talking about him, perhaps broadcasting his own thoughts to others.

There is profound disagreement among psychiatrists as to the genesis of schizophrenia, as indeed of so much 'mental' illness. This ranges all the way from those who regard it as due to an error of catecholamine metabolism, to those like Szasz (1971) or Laing (1960) who consider that it is a purely 'mental' condition, the result of stresses imposed by say family troubles or the capitalist system. It may well be that both interpretations are right.

Children of schizophrenics have a significantly high probability of developing the condition, whether or not they are reared by their natural parents. There is some evidence that the hereditary defect is in the metabolism of biogenic amines. For example dimethyltryptamine (DMT) is a substance that is probably formed in the brain and is a hallucinogen four times more powerful than mescaline. It is present in the snuff used in Haiti to produce mystical states. There is some evidence that this or similar substances may be produced in excess in schizophrenics or that the enzymes for destroying them are defective. But the methods available for estimating small amounts of the amines are still imperfect (see Bradley and Smythies 1976). The quantities of such substances are influenced by diet and other environmental factors, as well as by heredity. As techniques improve we should come to understand better how nature and nurture contribute to produce these very distressing conditions.

## Mental health and brain health

This is an excellent example of the need for a monistic approach to mental health problems. The psychotherapists view is that mental symptoms imply 'a patient's communications about himself, others and the world about him' (Szasz 1960). For these practitioners the symptoms of the 'disease' are social and the psychiatrist should concern himself with the patient's problems of living. The opposite view has been expressed by many physicians from Hippocrates onwards. As Maudsley put it in 1881, 'Insanity is, in fact, disorder of brain producing disorder of mind; . . . it is a disorder of the supreme nerve-centres of the brain . . . producing derangement of thought, feeling, and action, . . . of such degree or kind as to incapacitate the individual for the relations of life.' MacAlpine and Hunter point out, 'The lesson of the history of psychiatry is that progress is inevitable and irrevocable from psychology to neurology, from mind to brain, never the other way round' (1974).

Is there a fundamental theoretical basis for this dispute? I think not, but we must argue the matter further when we deal with higher nervous functions than mere fear. There is certainly a danger that those who use the 'organic model' may oversimplify and even, as their opponents allege, treat their patients 'impersonally'. There are also indisputably differences of social and political approach. How does anyone know what is to be considered a 'disorder of thinking or behaviour'. Have doctors any right to judge such matters, or the training and skill to do it? In a study of the social attitudes and methods of treatment used by 42 British psychiatrists there was found to be a positive association between conservative social attitudes and preference for physical methods of treatment (Pallis and Stoffelmayr 1973). Yet psychoanalysis flourishes in the U.S.A. but is hardly used in the U.S.S.R. Evidently we are very confused in our attitudes to these problems. No one can say that questions of the relations of body and mind are 'merely philosophical'. They are of the utmost practical importance to millions of sufferers, perhaps to all of us.

## Criminal aggression

The various contributions that lead to behaviour classified as 'aberrant' are well seen in the violence of criminal psychopaths. There is evidence that some of them have a definite chromosome abnormality, with an extra Y chromosome (XYY), but it is more likely that this condition leads to sexual and personality difficulties, which then determine the aggression. Not all XYY individuals are aggressive. The liability to be violent no doubt lies both in the genetic background and family upbringing. 'The best "predictor" of violence is still a feeling on the part of the clinician that the patient is cold, irreverent of human life, aloof and emotionally distant' (Lion, and Penna 1974). This is a condition likely to follow from a failure of attachment when young. As they continue, 'crimes of violence occur mainly among intimates—the victim may be a party to the assailant's action—a heritage of family violence, with guns around waiting to be used'. This speaks for itself as a prescription for poor upbringing. And again, 'Aggressive patients are generally very defensive and constantly exert emotional energy to protect a weak, fragile inner core of vulnerability. A great inner emptiness and sadness is the basis of these person's need to be powerful and strong and aggressive. It is always easier for them to be mad than sad.'

This makes a good summary of the evidence we have been pursuing. The programs that lead to excessive violence are probably a compound of hereditary brain defects such as errors of monamine systems, and failure to achieve adequate personal and social attachments. The latter may in turn be a compound of genetic inadequacy and oppressive social conditions. We cannot deal with the genetics easily, if at all, and we are only beginning to understand the amines, but we *can* improve at least some social conditions in a short time and surely should aim to start at once. Obviously the causes of violence are very complicated and it is not limited to those who are 'socially deprived'. There have been recent outbreaks of violence among the progeny of the middle and upper classes in both the U.S.A. and West Germany.

These various pathological manifestations of anxiety, fear, and depression are obviously the result of overactivity of programs that are useful to alert the organisms to possible dangers. Like all other brain programs these have a genetic background but are elicited and reinforced by environment. The pathological overaction may be hereditary or due to past or present stimuli, some of which we have considered.

## Grieving and sorrowing

In most people defensive programs are called forth temporarily when conditions demand them. There are many situations in which these programs of fear, anxiety, and aggression come into operation in normal life. Grief and sorrowing are forms of depression brought on by deprivation and including elements of calling for help, but also of anger, self-pity, and guilt. They are responses to social situations, making use of specific physical reactions, including of course weeping, and are parts of the vast array of programs that determine our reactions to each other. Even sorrow has a large social component. Each culture recognizes appropriate levels of grief for various losses (Lazarus 1975). Thus in Japan it is bad manners to show much grief, it would upset others.

For any individual the breaking of an attachment is bound to be a most serious disruption of the whole brain program, and children seem to have special programs for meeting such deprivation (Chapter 14). Adults show similar responses, first of withdrawal and then compensation, which may take various forms including rejection of life itself. It may be that the variety of responses should be further studied and their relation to childhood memories explored. Everyone is certain sometime to need programs for dealing with grief.

Chimpanzees undoubtedly experience grief. There is a reliable record by Goodall of a young male, $8\frac{1}{2}$ years old, which died of sorrow 25 days after the death of its mother, to whom he was especially attached (see Hamburg *et al.* 1975). The program for being depressed may be part of the socially useful operation of accepting a subordinate social rank, which involves a whole set of external gestures and internal feelings to match. A dominant male vervet monkey shows a blue colour behind, but this fades when he is depressed and he falls in the sexual hierarchy. If a rhesus monkey drops to a lower status level the testosterone level in his blood falls and he becomes less aggressive; we could say he is depressed (Henry *et al.* 1975). A depressed person is often full of inferiority feelings and avoids looking other people in the face.

## Depression and swings of the programs for pleasure

The full manifestation of depressive illness however goes far beyond what could be called the reasonable expression of a fall in dominance. A recent formidable description by Leonard (1975) includes 'Crying, feelings of inadequacy, guilt, hopelessness, suicide, loss of drive and ambition, mental and motor retardation, anxiety, sleep disturbance, loss of appetite and weight and libido, constipation.' Then the mood swings after an interval, varying from every other day to years. The manic is now all too ready for action and interaction with others. Leonard's description includes irritability, grandiosity, rapid speech, flight of ideas, increased motor activity, loss of discretion and judgement, and formulation of unrealistic plans.

The person with cyclic affective disorder thus shows an exaggeration of the changes of mood and behaviour that are appropriate for normal social life. There is reason to suppose that the condition is due to errors of the control mechanism, allowing swings in the activity of the chemical components of the neuroendocrine system and especially the monoamines. One suggestion is that serotonin, produced by the raphe nuclei of the brain stem (p. 159) serves to regulate the production of both noradrenaline and dopamine. High levels of noradrenaline are reported from patients during depression. Errors in the hypothalamus in turn produce excess production of adrenocorticotropic hormone (ACTH) by the pituitary and large amounts of adrenocorticosteroids have been found by several workers in the blood of patients during periods of depression. These are of course the substances that prepare the body for stress, but one of their actions is to decrease the rate of firing of the serotonin cells of the brain stem. It is easy to see how somewhere in the cycle the regulation goes wrong, producing too much or too little of one of the substances that are needed to keep the person stable. There is some evidence that the defect of control is inherited, but stressful situations can no doubt make it manifest.

Psychiatrists use many different techniques in the attempt to help the victims of depression. Electric-shock therapy is certainly sometimes helpful, there is some evidence that it works by an action on the balance of biogenic amines. Tricyclic antidepressants probably work in the same way (their name comes from the presence of three rings of carbon atoms in the molecule).

However the best preventive known for the swings of manic-depressive psychosis seems to be the simple element lithium, a salt similar to sodium (see Bunney and Murphy 1976). This occurs in mineral springs and was actually advocated by the Greeks to reduce mania. Its properties were rediscovered in Australia in 1949 but only widely introduced in 1970. The drug companies are said not to like it because it is very cheap and cannot be patented. Careful blind trials with patients have proved that within a week lithium can completely normalize the manic condition. One patient reported, 'I'm just back to the good old Jane and she's quiet.' Then on the first day with a placebo (a pill without lithium) she began to sing and hum and talk fast; a few days later she said, 'My brain is going so fast I feel exhausted.' She became grandiose and wild, spoke in poems and rhymes, 'Drip, drip, dripping, tap, tap, tapping on its top, top, topping icing on the cake. The President came to see me today and 39 surgeons were here yesterday.' Back on lithium, 3 days later she became and remained the good old Jane (Bunney 1976). The mechanism of action of lithium is not known, but it probably influences the rate of synthesis of one or more of the monoamines. There is evidence that it alters the rate of uptake of tryptophan and its conversion to serotonin, which as we have seen is known to regulate the other amines.

## Anger and aggression

There is obviously an aggressive response ready to be used in every normal adult human. It would be difficult indeed to list and classify all the situations by which it is aroused. But consider the significance of that common phrase, anger has to be 'aroused'. It does not spring up spontaneously, at least in normal people. Once started it may, as it were, reinforce itself—we make ourselves more angry. Everyone has the experience that anger is triggered and grows, almost as a reflex, for instance when driving a car. Attacks on our children or infringement of 'rights' to territory or possessions are potent in eliciting aggression. Frustration is a common stimulus to aggression, whether it is due to circumstances or apparently purposeless opposition. These responses certainly come largely from the activity of the ancient core brain, including the hypothalamus. They are part of the mechanisms that prepare us for daily life, as much as the secretions of corticosteroids or adrenaline.

Many workers have held that beyond such responses to stimuli there is as it were a fund of aggressiveness in each individual that needs to be discharged. They have much evidence to quote. The readiness with which people respond to calls for aggressive war, the universal prevalence of games, often with contents of combat and violence. The interest of art and theatre in war, from sagas to horror films. Is it that people need the discharge of aggression as they do that of sex in orgasm? The fact that some of the brain areas promoting these responses lie close to those for other appetites lends plausibility to the theory.

Nevertheless I think it to be incorrect. Certainly not every individual feels that he has a *need* for aggression, though most are able to be angry when provoked. To show that there is value in such a *fund* of anger we should have to see its biological necessity. There have been attempts to do this by regarding aggression as a legacy from our paleolithic hunting ancestors. But *killing for food involves mechanisms distinct from those for intraspecific fighting, even in cats* (p. 157). Anyhow it is likely that the modifications that turned man into an agricultural omnivore included at least a decrease in the hunting capacity. Man may possibly have an inborn tendency to defend his territory or his young, but that does not mean that he *has* to be aggressive if no one attacks him or incites him to aggression.

Aggression is not universal and there are examples of anti-violent communities where interpersonal violence is controlled by the customs of the inhabitants, without any special laws or police (Paddock 1975). Investigation in Mexico showed various differences between these isolated communities and their more violent neighbours. The attitude of the anti-violent villages to children was a casual acceptance into the group, with minimum emphasis either on misbehaviour or showing off achievements. Adults tended to remain apart, with few close friendships or feuds and 'near absence of machismo'. There was a 'much stronger social role for women'.

## Warfare

Can we find a biological explanation for the marked tendency of humans to form groups that fight each other? One theory turns on the view that in a state of nature altruism will only have evolutionary value if practised towards relatives (Chapter 19). It is suggested that the formation of hostile groups may have ensured the necessary separation, stealing of women and slaves perhaps providing the exogamy needed to prevent excessive inbreeding (Wilson 1975). There are many difficulties in this view, but at least it does not claim, as some do, that warfare is the result of aggressiveness of individuals. 'War,' as Rousseau wrote, 'is not a relation between man and man but between State and State, and individuals are enemies accidentally, not as men . . . Finally each State can have for enemies only other States, and not men; for *between things disparate in nature there can be no real relation.*' The passage here given italics is a classic warning to those who apply biology to human affairs. A state is not ruled by its hypothalamus. 'Aggression does not regulate social conflict, but social conflict does regulate aggression' (Sahlins 1977, p. 9).

It is difficult to imagine that social groups large or small can possibly remain in equilibrium without some antagonism. The interests of individuals and groups are bound to conflict quite frequently. Granted that humans possess the mechanisms of aggression it is not at all likely that they will suddenly cease to use them. Anyhow conflict is not so much the product of aggressiveness as of need and of greed. The aggression comes in the attempt by groups to gain more, or to defend what they have.

Whatever may have been the origins of warfare it is obviously a major continuing danger to all individual human beings, and to mankind. Wars continue to be as prevalent as ever and soldiers take charge of many governments. Wise men may conclude from this that it is important that soldiers should be well informed about biology and about society, as well as about fighting. Do we insist strongly enough that soldiers should be well educated? (See p. 224.)

The question of how conflict may be limited and contained is one of political organization, where biology can be of little help. Like other animals however we have brain programs that can promote the continuance of stable and tolerable hierarchies of dominance and cooperation (Chapter 19). We need all the information we can get to help people to control the dangerous capacities for aggressiveness within themselves and others. Widespread recognition of the obvious facts about our propensity to be aggressive may at least help to prevent exploitation of the tendency by interested parties. The fact that we have these protective and defensive mechanisms does not justify the claims of Freud and others that there is an aggressive death instinct, acting against Eros, as it were on behalf of the second law of thermodynamics. That seems to the biologist to be nonsense. There is no difficulty in seeing the positive survival values of the programs for fearing and fighting. Surely such a view is more sensible. We cannot banish these evils, but at least we can show that they have a proper place in life, and keep them to it.

# 16   Hearing, speaking, and writing

## The dictionary in the brain

In asking whether the brain contains programs for language, are we to look only for the source of the capacity to utter words or are we to try to find how we express a flow of meaningful ideas? No one can doubt that the brain is involved in the act of speaking, although the methods of physiology have so far been too crude to provide a full account of how this is achieved. But really severe difficulties begin to appear if we try to hold that speech is produced by some entity other than the brain, that it is a 'mirror of the mind'. I believe it is possible to avoid or evade this difficulty and to make sense of the concept that what we say is a result of the activities of the brain. Speech is essentially the product of a person and the concept of a person must include his brain. For, unless one believes in disembodied spirits, the continuity of the personality depends upon the store of programs recorded in the brain. These are the only enduring entities able to provide the words we utter and to comprehend speech. If the dictionary is not in the brain where is it? And with the dictionary must surely also be the grammar, and the system that uses both to produce meaningful speech.

We have to try to discover how the alerting system of the brain gets access to the relevant programs as a person uses language throughout his days to think his thoughts and express his intentions (see Halliday 1970). This involves using a much broader concept of a 'brain' than we usually employ. We have to find ways of speaking not so much of its substance as of the modes of activity of its many channels and of all its parts operating together. The study of language is especially useful for this purpose because, as Lashley has said, 'Speech is the only window through which the physiologist can view cerebral life . . . the problems raised by the organization of language seem to be characteristic of almost all other cerebral activity' (Lashley 1950). This remains a useful thought, although we do now have some other 'windows' to the brain.

## What is language?

It may seem at first sight curious that it is difficult to define language. Yet it is really perhaps the strangest phenomenon in our whole experience. 'It is a peculiar kind of entity nowhere all present at once, nowhere taking the form of an object or substance and yet making its existence felt at every moment of our thought in every act of speech.' Jameson (1972) uses these words in discussing the classical concept put forward by Saussure (1916) of *langue,* the total potentiality of a language for expression, in contrast to the *parole* or individual act of speech. The distinction may be made clear by analogy with performances of a piece of music. Each is different (*la parole*), but all have the same structure or organization (*la langue*). The structure would be the same in whatever medium it was performed, and also in writing. The distinction is important for us in trying to find how the brain makes language possible. We must expect to find much more than simple lists of words if we are to understand the ordered system of relations between signs and what they signify (Searle 1971).

Most people hold that language has something to do with communication, but we saw in Chapter 1 that its essence must be a system of organization. Chomsky (1976) has argued that language is a structured system with an independent existence. We are indeed saying that the programs of the brain constitute a structured system written in a 'language'. A further problem is that a major use of language in each of us is internal—for thinking, that is for speaking to ourselves. In spite of these confusions it seems to me rather perverse not to consider human spoken or written language as primarily a functional system evolved for communication (Lyons 1970, 1977). One definition is that 'Language can be operationally defined as a communications system that permits the exchange of new, unanticipated information' (Lieberman 1973, 1975, and 1977). There has indeed lately been much emphasis on the fact that human language enables us to transmit an infinite variety of sentences. Perhaps we could question whether it is right to call the variety infinite or the information totally unanticipated. In any case such a definition would deny that animals have language. This seems unwise, for certainly we have evolved from an animal condition, however sophisticated our language may be today. As Trevarthen has said, 'Biological causes run deep. One does not find complex, highly evolved life processes showing no evidence of their origin from much simpler adaptive functions. To explain language one must therefore attend to apparently unrelated aspects of intentional performance' (1974, p. 570). The brain produces language like other types of behaviour as part of its task to keep the individual and his progeny alive, communication is basically intentional. Someone may object that actions of the brain cannot be intentional because intentionality is by definition a property of the mind consciously foreseeing the results of its actions. Such an attitude dictates a dualist approach without discussion, and that is surely not acceptable. If brain actions are not allowed to be intentional we might ask whether there can be mental intentions without a brain. The concept of intentionality indeed causes much discussion and confusion among philosophers (see Anscombe 1963).

Both linguists and philosophers, following Austin (1962), have become increasingly concerned to emphasize that speech is 'performative'. 'Animal drives are still at work behind the torrent of human speech, but they are seldom clearly to be traced' (Quine 1975). The transmitter, whether human or animal may usefully be said to intend either to produce some action by the listener or to have some effect upon him by provision of information. To do this he uses the equipment with which he is provided, whether he is a baby crying or a professor lecturing. We might therefore define language as 'any species specific system of intentional communication between individuals'. It involves encoding of some desired message by selecting appropriate items from a mutually known set of signs, transmission of these, as by sound, gesture or scent, and decoding by the recipient as evidenced by some response or change in capacity to respond. Even when a person is 'thinking to himself' he still has at least some trace of intention, either to solve a problem or to fulfil some desire in his day-dreaming.

This definition of language will certainly not please everyone, but it is broad enough to cover all species. In most animals the set of signs is very limited and the intention they convey is to elicit performance of some simple function, say to assist an infant or to flee from danger (Thorpe 1974). The languages of monkeys and chimpanzees have as many as 100 distinct signs. But whales have perhaps the most complicated of all animal languages. The song of the humpback whale (*Megaptera*) is said to run for 30 minutes without repetition.

Human language differs from all other systems of communication in that it allows the recombination of symbols to provide for effective transmission of a range of messages so large that many call it infinite. We can talk about (almost) anything. No animals use a signal system that has the phonological, syntactic, and semantic universals that we find in human language. Most linguists would probably reject or at least qualify the claim that chimpanzees have been taught to use American Sign Language, or otherwise to communicate in a way fully comparable to humans, as is claimed by Linden (1976), Kellogg (1968), and Premack (1975). What we have to ask, then, is how do humans achieve the feat of transmitting what Lieberman (1973) called 'unanticipated information'?

## The structure of languages

In order to try to understand the systems used for encoding and transmission it is useful to remember that what is transmitted is mostly a system of relations (Lenneberg 1974, p. 619). Language does not consist only of an arbitrary set of signs that are learned by some process of association or conditioning. All our means of communication, from crying onwards, probably follow certain rules of structure, which we shall try to find out. By these principles and rules the brain selects one sound and rejects another for transmission, or recognizes the intended meaning when it hears them.

Use of language involves selecting speech actions that are likely to be appropriate in the light of external and internal information. In searching for clues as to the brain operations involved we can therefore look towards the parts of the brain that assemble the information of feature detectors and are involved in the recognition of objects and situations in the world around (Chapter 12). We have already seen something of how feature detectors operate and discussed the difficulty of understanding how the information that they provide is brought together to allow recognition—say of a face or a spoken word. This may be described as a problem of encoding and decoding.

Does the 'recognition' consist in the activity of some 'pontifical' or 'gnostic' neuron (the grandmother's-face cell) or in the statistical operations of an ensemble of cells (Chapter 12). The answer to this might help in identifying the encoding process by which words are chosen to express intentions. A good way to approach both problems is to ask the simple biological question, why should the organism recognize certain objects or communicate about them? And the answer is surely because to do so is likely to help with his life. We recognize and speak about those situations that are relevant to ourselves. The brain operations that do this must be those that compute the appropriate relationships Marr and Nishihara (1978). The clue to the operations may be that the information from the senses is laid out on the surface of the brain as a series of maps.

Linguists have recently been asking insistently the question 'Where do sentences come from?' (Osgood 1971). And the answer is that 'many properties of grammar are present in some form in prelinguistic perceptuo-motor behaviour'. Speech, like all motor behaviour, is 'a system or structure of relationships'. Much encoding is done with reference to the system of opposites. Things are above or below, good or bad, fast or slow, large or small and so on. Moreover, the system emphasizes relationships between natural phenomena that are important. We recognize father/mother, friend/foe, day/night, dry/wet and so on endlessly. As Lenneberg puts it 'the human organism is a peculiar sort of "computer"—an object that "computes" relationships'. But he uses the quotes because, he says, there is no agent who 'uses' the biological computer, and he adds a curious coda, 'Brain activity is an end in itself' (1974, p. 620). Surely here he slips. Brain activity is a process with an aim. The relations that it computes are those that may help to further the continuance of life. The rules by which it does this are likely to have a large inherited component and there is strong evidence that human beings are genetically programmed for speech (see Lenneberg 1967, Chomsky 1976a). Indeed there is now evidence that human infants have specific detectors especially sensitive to speech sounds, before they can themselves speak or understand (p. 179) (Eimas *et al.* 1971).

## Hearing

The basic arrangement of the auditory pathways in the brain of a mammal is similar to that for vision (Moore 1977). Information from the ear is relayed through various lower stages and then to the cortex through a set of cells in the thalamus called the medial geniculate body, which is comparable to the lateral geniculate body for vision. The primary cortical receiving area for hearing is along the upper border of the temporal lobe (Fig. 12.5). The receptors for sound in the cochlear organ of the ear are tuned to respond to particular frequencies. Passing through the various links to the cortex the neurons prove to be progressively more likely to be 'deaf' to steady states of tone or intensity and to become responsive instead to *patterns* of timing, and to *transitions*. These are of course the features that occur in sounds in nature, whether accidental, such as the snap of a twig or rustle of a leaf, or the communicative sounds of a friend or enemy. Investigation of the cells of the auditory cortex of the squirrel monkey showed that some of them respond well both to simple auditory stimuli and to tapes of the calls of other monkeys. Other cells responded only to simple stimuli and a few (3·5 per cent) only to monkey calls (Winter 1972).

Here we meet again the question of whether there is a hierarchy of feature detectors ending with a 'pontifical neuron' or 'gnostic neuron' that extracts the biologically relevant features from all the others (p. 128). The relevant features may be said to include constant frequency, amplitude modulation, frequency modulation, and noise bursts (Suga 1972). Human speech is composed of constant frequency components, which are the vowel formants, and noise bursts combined with frequency transients for the consonants.

It is not possible to record the responses of single neurons in the human cortex but linguists have been able to produce evidence that babies as young as one month are more responsive to speech sounds than to others (Eimas *et*

|  | o | a | e | u | ə | i | l | ŋ | ʃ | ĵ | k | z | ẑ | g | m | f | p | v | b | n | s | θ | t | z | ð | d | h | # |
|---|---|---|---|---|---|---|---|---|---|---|---|---|---|---|---|---|---|---|---|---|---|---|---|---|---|---|---|---|
| 1. Vocalic/non-vocalic | + | + | + | + | + | + | + | − | − | − | − | − | − | − | − | − | − | − | − | − | − | − | − | − | − | − | − | − |
| 2. Consonantal/non-consonantal | − | − | − | − | − | − | + | + | + | + | + | + | + | + | + | + | + | + | + | + | + | + | + | + | + | + | − | − |
| 3. Compact /diffuse | + | + | + | − | − | − | + | + | + | + | + | + | + |  |  |  |  |  |  |  |  |  |  |  |  |  |  |  |
| 4. Grave/acute | + | + | − | + | + | − |  |  |  |  |  |  |  |  | + | + | + | + | + | − |  |  |  |  |  |  |  |  |
| 5. Flat /plain | + | − |  |  |  |  |  |  | + | − |  |  |  |  |  |  |  |  |  |  |  |  |  |  |  |  |  |  |
| 6. Nasal/oral |  |  |  |  |  |  |  | + | − | − | − | − | − | − | + | − | − | − | − | + | − | − | − | − | − | − |  |  |
| 7. Tense/lax |  |  |  |  |  |  |  |  | + | + | + | − | − | − |  | + | + | − | − |  | + | + | + | − | − | − | + | − |
| 8. Continuant/interrupted |  |  |  |  |  |  |  |  | + | − | − | + | + | − |  | + | − | + | − |  | + | + | − | + | + | − |  |  |
| 9. Strident/mellow |  |  |  |  |  |  |  |  | + | − |  | + | − |  |  |  |  |  |  |  | + | − |  | + | − |  |  |  |

FIG. 16.1. The phoneme pattern of English; 1–9 are the distinctive features, one or more of which characterize each phoneme. The phonemes are written as /o/-pot, /a/-pat, etc. (From Cherry 1966, by permission of the M.I.T. Press.)

*al.* 1971 and 1973). The investigators used synthetic speech sounds in which the cues that distinguish phonemes with so-called voiced and voiceless stop consonants such as /t/ and /d/ are varied. The chief difference between them is the time of onset of the first formant after the initial noise burst (voice onset time, VOT). Studies with adults show that whereas listeners readily distinguish between synthetically produced consonants, they have more difficulty in detecting differences of similar extent *within* the VOT range of each phoneme. In other words discrimination between phoneme categories was better than discrimination within phoneme categories. These stop consonants and VOT intervals are nearly the same in all languages, so it was very interesting to find that these capacities and restrictions are present in young babies.

In order to show this Eimas made use of the fact that babies show their interest and pleasure in sounds by sucking on a teat, even if it gives no milk. The experimenters arranged that the sucking operated a device that maintained and increased a given sound. After first hearing it the baby is 'interested' and sucks hard for a while. Then gradually he gets tired of that sound (habituates) and stops sucking. If the sound is changed he starts again. In this way we can find out what constitutes for him a change of sound. Differences of 20 milliseconds in the onset of the formants are not recognized if they are *within* the range of one of the phonemes. But if the same change falls across a phonemic boundary it is recognized. Evidently, then, infants already sort acoustic variations of phonemic sounds in the same way as adults do. Similar studies with Kikuyu children and adults, in Kenya, have shown that they also recognize /t/ and /d/ although the Bantu language only has one labial stop, a prevoiced /b/ (Streeter 1976). These studies suggest that all human beings are born with some sets of feature detectors suitable for language although Streeter also found evidence of other discriminations that depended upon exposure to the sounds. No doubt the capacity to recognize the variants of speech sounds is altered in the course of learning of a language. The English vowel sounds that are so easily distinguished in 'red' and 'raid' cannot be separated by many Indian speakers. Conversely Indians require six different /t/ sounds, which are mostly indistinguishable to English speakers.

## Grammar

Valuable as such studies are they do not tell us the answers we need to the very difficult question of what sort of entity it may be that performs the wondrous tasks of speaking and understanding. Chomsky (1976, p. 23) has recently made another powerful appeal that we should be ready to think boldly about the structure of our concepts. 'There is nothing essentially mysterious about the concept of an abstract cognitive structure, created by an innate faculty of mind, represented in some still unknown way in the brain, and entering into the system of capacities and dispositions to act and "interpret".' To the biologist this provides an attractive appeal to consider the structure of the systems that regulate human behaviour. Can any such program of investigation be realized? Chomsky gives many hints of the sort of 'structures' that he implies. 'Grammar is the system of rules and principles that determines the formal and semantic properties of sentences.' What rules does he mean? An example is how to transform a statement into a question. How does 'The man is tall' become 'Is the man tall?' Can the rule be 'Move the "is" to the beginning of the sentence'? Well then, what about 'The man who is tall is in the room'? No child will ever say 'Is the man who tall is in the room?' Why not? The rule must be to locate the *main* verb and move that. What the child acquires is a *structure-dependent rule*, one that involves analysis into words and phrases. We need to seek for some type of brain program that can operate in this way.

## Learning to speak

Wittgenstein believed that we can only understand the complexity of the phenomenon of language when we ask how it is learned (see Wollheim 1973). One approach is to follow the sequence by which a child comes to speak. Babbling is at first random or an expression of satisfaction, partly a form of play. But soon the baby may seem to be asking questions or even making statements, still before there are any individualized words. He then proceeds in his second year to develop rules first for comprehension, then for production of speech. His first words are for familiar things such as: 'mama' and 'dada', milk, ball; or for actions such as 'all gone', or experiences 'bye bye'. His early sentences often consist of a single 'pivot' word or phrase, used in a fixed relation to various 'open' words—thus 'all gone shoe', 'all gone car' (see Garvey 1977 and Greenfield and Smith 1976). Common relationships are of possession (mama shoe), agent–action (mama read), action–object (put book), position (hat chair), or absence (all gone rattle). These relations give us some notion of how the linguistic program is gradually built up as the child learns the symbolic and social expressions of the events of daily life.

   At first he makes many mistakes of pronunciation and grammar. He will pronounce rag and wag the same, but he knows which is which. He begins with a wong wule—namely that 'r' before a vowel is pronounced as a 'w'. Later he discards the wrong rules—a process that is similar to his discarding of wrong bodily movements as he comes to use parts of the body separately (Chapter 4). This is yet another example of the fact that memory is a selective process. Learning is by selection from the initial set of many possible actions (p. 83).

The child's comprehension and use of grammar then develops gradually. At age 2, sentences are interpreted in the plan of actor and action. This can be investigated by giving a child toys and asking him to arrange them according to what we say. (1) 'The cow kissed the horse' is correctly understood, but (2) 'The horse is kissed by the cow' is not. (3) 'It is the horse that the cow kissed' is again understood. The child picks out the action sequence 'cow kissed' that he can follow. By age 4 a new rule develops—'Consider the first noun in a sequence as the actor.' So now (2) and (3) are confused. The capacity to understand elaborately nested statements comes quite late. We might all have difficulty with 'The girl the man the boy saw kissed left'. Evidently the mechanism for understanding involves some process of holding back the decoding process until a satisfactory solution is reached. The young child does not wait long enough and so makes mistakes. After damage to the frontal lobes adults may do the same. The restraint they impose is necessary for many human characteristics.

Study of the development of actual speech production shows similar stages, passing from broad, poorly differentiated action to specific sounds. The speech sounds (phonemes) do not appear at random but as a set of contrasts, relations and opposites (R. Jakobson, see Cherry 1966). The first words are often variants of mum and dad. Later when a word is used another will be chosen to comment or oppose it. But at first words are used in a very general or 'global' way to cover a large area of meaning. Then gradually the use of each contracts and it is applied in its correct semantic relationship. Yet again we see progress by selection from an originally larger set.

## The speech mechanism

The mechanism for the production of speech sounds tells us something more about the brain programs that may be involved. The main parts are the larynx (sound box) and the supralaryngeal apparatus, the pharynx, tongue, palate, and lips. The energy for speech transmission comes from the puffs of air expelled from the lungs. These pass through the vocal cords of the larynx, which are pairs of folds that vibrate to give a humming sound. The frequency (pitch) of this vibration is varied by the speaker (between about 60–350 Hz) by changing the pressure of the air and varying the tension on the vocal cords by muscles in the larynx. The air issuing from the larynx thus vibrates at a fundamental frequency and with various harmonics. Variations in this frequency are an important linguistic agent in Chinese, in English they form the intonation patterns that convey the presuppositions underlying a sentence. Nearly all the detailed information is encoded by the supralaryngeal tract. This acts as an acoustic filter and by varying its shape the speaker alters the sound produced, just as do the length and openings of an organ pipe. The frequencies that are uttered depend mainly upon these features of the airway and are independent of the basic frequency of the vocal cords. These damped resonances of the tract are known as the formant frequencies of speech. The lowest peak frequency is known as the first formant the next peak as the second formant and so on. The vowel sounds are usually recognizable by identifying the relative positions of the first two formants. The vowels are the melodic and hence musical features of speech. Thus /a/ and /i/ have different formant frequencies. It is the *relative* positions of the formants that are important. Each vowel sound can be pronounced at any pitch of the human voice. The vowel sounds are thus the result of the balance of higher and lower frequency components irrespective of pitch-shifts. There may be an analogy here with Land's discovery that colours are reported as the psychophysiological products of contrasts of higher and lower wavelengths irrespective of their position in the frequency spectrum (1959). Perhaps we shall find brain mechanisms that respond to such *relationships* in all the sensory fields (Ohe 1962).

Some consonants also have formant frequencies, for example /b/ and /d/, but most consonants are very rapid and irregular noises, such as /p/ and /s/, produced by air turbulence at the teeth or lips. The actual contractions that alter the shape of the vocal tract are due to about 15 muscles. Like other muscles they are mostly arranged in pairs, acting against each other, or against some elastic restoring elements. As the child comes to speak he has to learn to limit the actions of these pairs of muscles, exactly as he learns to control the paired muscles of the legs when he comes to walk. He learns by selection among the possibilities provided.

Speaking involves selecting those movements of the muscles that produce the conventional sounds of a language in certain conventional patterns of words and phrases. Linguists identify in each language a finite number of speech sounds, or phonemes. There are 40 in English (Fig. 16.1). According to Jakobson the phonemes are produced by selection of one each out of 12 pairs of distinctive features (Cherry 1966). These have not actually been characterized by particular positions of the muscles of the airway, but in principle they could be. Such an analysis certainly does not tell us how the brain produces speech but it gives us an idea of how analysis might proceed. There is some evidence that speech is in fact produced by regulation of these or similar individual features. Thus in some aphasics the mistakes include only one feature. A patient may say 'I got out of ben' (instead of bed) and /n/ and /d/ differ only in the feature of nasality, produced by the position of the velum of the soft palate (Buckingham and Kertesz 1974).

In the daily perception of speech we do not identify the phonemes as separate entities—they are 'squashed together' (Lieberman 1977). Thus in saying 'bat' we begin to put the vocal tract in the position for /b/, but before we ever reach it move on to the vowel /ae/ and then to /t/. The consonants

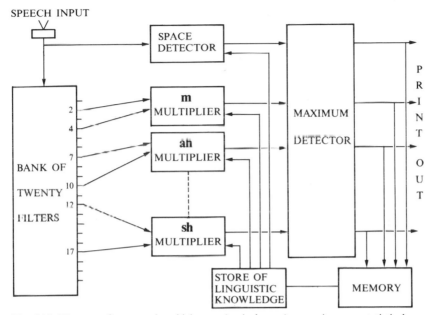

SPEECH INPUT

Fig. 16.2. Diagram of a system by which a mechanical speech recognizer uses statistical information to classify speech sounds. Each phoneme is characterized by two or more sound features filtered from the speech input and combined with linguistic knowledge showing what the word is, given the context. The maximum detector rejects less probable solutions and the output is written and also sent to improve the memory record. (From Fry and Denes 1958.)

thus act as it were to modulate the vowels and the syllable must be heard as a whole. We can only identify 7–9 distinct sounds each second, but the words we can follow may include 20–30 phonemes per second.

## Decoding speech

The whole process of decoding speech depends upon a large set of anticipations and expectancies (Fry 1970). These constraints can be studied by asking a speaker to guess the next letter of a word or word of a sentence. Thus starting with 'Ex' he has several alternatives but after 'Exch' he has fewer and after 'Exche' he has only 'Exchequer'. Full knowledge of a language means being able to anticipate the sequences. Without this knowledge we cannot follow a native speaker even though we could recognize every word individually. The analysis of the process of speech decoding has allowed the production of blueprints for machines that could recognize speech (Fig. 16.2). This serves to emphasize that clues are used to make hypotheses about possible later features of the word or sentence. Recognizing speech, like seeing and other perceptual acts is an active process of *reconstruction*,

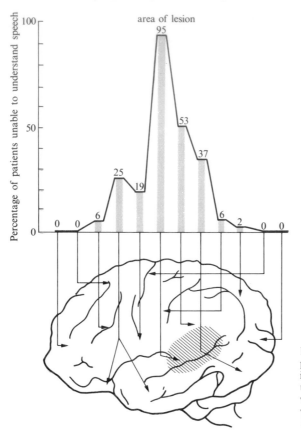

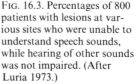

Fig. 16.3. Percentages of 800 patients with lesions at various sites who were unable to understand speech sounds, while hearing of other sounds was not impaired. (After Luria 1973.)

not a mere passive reception. Much of the making of hypotheses or guessing depends upon the individual's knowledge of a particular language. Yet there may be some expectancies that are common to all mankind, especially if we include gesture as part of speech. We all recognize the meaning of loud aggressive speech or the soft words and smiles of love. This may seem trivial, but the learning and understanding of speech certainly depends on the whole social situation, what Wittgenstein called the language game (see Wollheim 1973).

However, most of the decoding of speech depends on 'the store of *a priori* knowledge about the language . . . Every speaker or listener carries in his cortex a vast store of information about any language he uses. This includes the complete inventory of phonemes and words, the rules for forming syllables from phonemes and sentences from words, and in addition a great deal of statistical information about the sequence of units which may occur in the language at various levels' (Fry 1970).

Fry is here telling us what might be in the cortex. Alas we have very little idea of how it is held there. This has led some linguists to feel that neurolinguistics is of little use, 'The facts [about the brain], especially those concerning predisposing factors, are totally unknowable and no more open to observation than the thoughts, images etc. of the mentalists' (Palmer 1976). This is pessimistic, but these are some signs that it will not continue to be true. Linguists and neurologists together are trying to find out what to look for and this should at least help to produce a neurology that is more adequate to describe the human brain (see Laver 1970).

## Language universals

There is increasing evidence that languages share many common features. This may encourage us to hope that we may be able to understand more of the processes by which they are produced. Linguists have been able to identify a number of language universals, in phonetics, in syntax, and in semantics (Greenberg 1975). For example all languages are primarily vocal and all use vowels and consonants. Nearly all also have both stop consonants and nasal consonants. All languages are structured in the same dual way in the sense that they are made up of two sorts of units. The meaningful or primary units are *words*, whether spoken or written. They are composed of lesser units, the *phonemes* or letters, which have no meanings in themselves but are grouped to make the words. In all languages messages are therefore composed by grouping the basic phonemes into definite units, which cannot be broken up. For example 'my new hat' is three words because they can be changed separately and as wholes (cf. your old car).

Messages consist of a kernel structure (deep structure), which may be transformed in various ways to give surface structure. Thus 'John ate the apple' and 'the apple was eaten by John' have different surface structures but the same deep structure. There are said to be universal features also in the development of speech. The child's first vowel is always /a/, although it is never the only vowel. Some linguists also believe that we can find language universals in the construction of sentences. For example the subject–predicate construction is held to occur in all languages examined. But Quine has pointed out that it is difficult to give objective evidence for this (see Harman 1975). Does it merely mean that all languages can be 'however forcibly' translated into English? The evidence is more ambiguous than for the use of particular sounds. Does this 'universal of language' only mean that all humans talk about the same topics? Similar difficulties arise over other semantic universals—for example that all languages use similar relations for expressing kinship and spatial and temporal distinctions.

Finally the most important universal feature of all is the creativity or productivity of language. The fact that we can construct and understand an indefinitely large number of messages is the basis of the freedom of the individual to be different from others. This freedom is in turn the basis of the great adaptability of humans and of their cultures.

## The origin of language

If there are universal features in human language it seems likely that it arose once only, within a single population, or at least that one system has out-lived all the others (Spuhler 1977). Some people suggest that human lan-guage first became possible as a result of adopting the upright posture, perhaps as much as 10 million years ago. Maybe this so changed the position of the upper part of the respiratory tract that it became capable of the alter-ations of shape that we have seen are responsible for controlling the formant frequencies that produce the vowels and the plosive, fricative, nasal, and other noises that provide us with our 40 phonemes. Language depends upon much more than the capacity to utter these sounds, but it is doubtful whether the recombinations of syntax that enable us to synthesize sentences could be *reliably* transmitted without these modifications of the airway. The main differences in the vocal system between man and chimpanzee are the lengthening of the pharynx and the more posterior position of the tongue. It has been argued that the skulls of both *Australopithecus* and Neanderthal man show that the forms of the pharynx and palate were more like those of the ape than man (Lieberman 1971). Others however have disputed this (Le May 1975) and it does indeed seem unlikely that Neanderthal man, living only 50 000 years ago, and with a fully human brain size, could not speak. Others have argued conversely that the capacity to make tools according to a tradition and to use fire indicate that the capacity for speech was already present in *Homo erectus*, and even earlier, that is to say more than a million years ago.

It seems likely that in future we shall be able to say more about this. At present the origin of syntactic speech remains a mystery. Linguists sometimes seem to imply that such a characteristically human feature must have some source and origin that is distinct from other natural processes. Together with some structuralist anthropologists they cling to a romantic interpretation of human origins, part of the view that rejects scientific methods of study as inappropriate to apply to man. Indeed in the academic warfare between arts and sciences the linguists are the shock troops of the arts faculty. Only they have an arcane terminology and grasp of statistics adequate to repel the invasion of scientists into their territory. Unfortun-ately indeed it *has* kept the scientists at bay, pinned down by such labels as 'Behaviourists' or 'Reductionists'.

Seriously, there is no need for any contest, and most linguists and anth-ropologists agree with biologists that it is difficult to believe that so complicated a phenomenon as language arose suddenly. We know that our ancestors were once something like apes and presumably used a system of communication at least as complicated as they exhibit today. We are surely wise to search among them for the first signs of the appearance of the features of human language. It is not appropriate for the linguist to turn his scorn upon such efforts. The biologist can understand perfectly well that the chimpanzee taught to use a gestural 'language' has not the capacity for transformational grammar. That should not prevent us from trying to find evidence of how the human type of communication began. We shall not stop now to consider the various theories that have been advanced, for admittedly none is convincing. For example it might be that song preceded speech, shared rhythms often provide a basis for common action, and children readily speak in chorus. But such a theory does not begin to touch the vast problems about the origins of syntax. What we can be sure is that we are descended from creatures that did not have these facilities. Moreover since it is now shown that part of the basis of human speech is inherited in the DNA there must have been evolution of it by gradual natural selection.

## Aphasia

Language must depend upon the interaction of many processes in the brain. Correspondingly it is found that damage to different parts of the cortex interferes with the language faculty in different ways. It has been known for a long time that after injuries to the brain a person may be 'struck dumb', but there is still much debate as to how to interpret the phenomena of aphasia. In spite of controversy the various symptoms reported can be understood in the light of the conception that the encoding and decoding of information as words and sentences is related to the processes that allow recognition of visual and auditory forms. Admittedly it is not known what those processes are, but we are working on the hypothesis that they involve recoding the information of the feature detectors in such a way as to enable the individual to interact with aspects of the environment that are relevant to his daily life. This is what we mean when we speak of recognizing things. We pick out the visual features that identify a chair as something that can be sat on and a table as suitable to carry things, and in speech choose the forms of words that refer to these objects and actions and so make statements to others about them.

We should expect, then, to find that the operations for the production of speech proceed in parts of the brain somewhere beyond those concerned with the detection of simple features and somewhere near those parts that are involved in producing detailed movements and actions. Moreover we should expect to find not one simple speech centre but that damage to the various parts of the brain concerned with different aspects of coding would be likely to produce different sorts of impairment in the use of language. This variety of response to injury is exactly what has been found by clinical neurologists, and indeed has produced much controversy as to whether language is a unitary or divided activity of the brain.

All aphasiologists agree that the use of language for communication is impaired by injury to the hinder part of the superior temporal gyrus on one side of the brain, usually the left (Fig. 12.5). This area could be regarded as being in a sense the functional centre of the cortex. It lies between visual centres behind, auditory below, tactile and proprioceptive above, and motor areas in front. Lesions extending in different directions from this central area produce differing types of defect. In spite of the controversy among clinicians it is possible to recognize a systematic series of these conditions and we shall follow Lord Brain (1965) in describing them.

*Word deafness* Perhaps the simplest form of aphasia is word-deafness, or acoustic agnosia, in which the patient hears sounds perfectly but cannot recognize them as words, 'I can hear sounds come, but words won't separate'. The patient can speak, read, or write perfectly well but can't repeat words spoken to him. The injury that produces word deafness is in the middle of the left first temporal convolution, close to the auditory cortex (Fig. 16.3).

*Semantic aphasia.* A lesion further back produces the symptoms of semantic aphasia, in which both the understanding and production of speech, by voice or writing are impaired. The patient has the physical power to produce words, but they are arranged ungrammatically and his sentences are without meaning. Thus one man when shown a tape measure says 'a kind of machinery' and then, when shown a bunch of keys, he says 'indication of measurement of piece of apparatus or intimating the cost of apparatus in various forms'. Evidently the whole program for producing intelligible speech is disturbed. This form of defect is also called receptive, sensory, or syntactical aphasia. It is named after Wernicke, who first described it in 1874.

Some of the defects due to injuries in this region lead to a sort of regression to the conditions when the child can only interpret simple word order. He is unable to understand relations or follow inversions. Luria records a case where after a wound in the left parietal region the patient was puzzled by the question 'Is an elephant bigger than a fly?' He knew that elephants were large and flies small but 'I just didn't understand the words *smaller* or *bigger* . Somehow I always think the expression "a fly is smaller than an elephant" means they're talking about a very small elephant and a big fly' (Luria 1973a). We begin to get an inkling of how the mechanism in the brain is 'working over' the coded representations of the names but can't operate the comparatives. If only we knew what physiological processes are involved!

*Nominal aphasia.* Nominal aphasia is the incapacity to find the right word, usually due to an injury also in the left parieto-temporal region, but nearer to the visual area. The person can't give the right name. Shown scissors he says 'It's a nail file'. Told it should be 'scissors' he repeats 'Yes that's right. Of course it's not a nail file, it's a nail file.' For him the wrong word had got the symbolic value of scissors. If we could understand more about how the program for classifying objects operates we might go on to see how it serves to select the right word, as if from a lexicon that is somehow resident in this area.

*Motor aphasia.* Motor or expressive aphasia results from lesions further forwards, in front of the region that directly controls movements of the tongue and lips. This is the classical aphasia first described by Broca in 1861 and often named after him (see Head 1926, Mohr 1976). Unlike the semantic aphasic the person can understand speech perfectly but he can't produce the words. His phonetic disintegration may involve all sorts of difficulties of inflection, stress, and rhythm, so that he speaks, if at all, like a foreigner. Very interestingly the words will be produced more readily in natural situations than when he is artificially tested. 'Can you say no?' 'No, I can't.' 'Can you say goodbye.' 'No, I can't'—but then later 'Goodbye Doctor'. Swear words may also come readily. Often the sentence structure is less impaired than the words, unlike the semantic aphasics. So surely this region of the brain is involved in organizing the programs for the actual production of words. At the same time inner speech and thinking are impaired. The person cannot speak to himself. In many aphasics writing is also disturbed (agraphia).

The programs that produce writing are of course learned laboriously long after those for speaking have appeared in the child. Perhaps they are a different sort of program. Whereas we speak only with the mouth we can write, more or less well, with either hand, or by moving the head, or indeed with the big toe. This illustrates dramatically that the action program involved is not the serial activation of particular motor neurons. It involves translating the concept that is to be communicated into certain visible shapes. For example when asked to write the number six the aphasic patient simply produces six dashes.

The opposite of agraphia is alexia, or word-blindness, the incapacity to recognize the visual symbols. Although all other speech functions are intact and the patient can write, he cannot read what he has written. The confusions that he makes are between the visually more similar forms: P and R, D and O, M and N, and the reversed ones: d and b, p and q. Other patients have more complicated difficulties, they may be able to read whole words but not the letters of which they are composed! The characteristic injury is further back in the occipital lobe than those we have been considering, between them and the primary visual cortex. This must include the region that is necessary for the extraction from the information of the simpler feature detectors of those aspects that characterize the letters.

We are sometimes told by neurologists that we must not try to use results such as these to seek for centres in the brain for particular functions. In the light of the evidence I think this admonition should not be given too much weight. There is little danger we shall forget that all parts of the brain are continually interacting to produce a single line of behaviour by the individual. The evidence of aphasia begins to tell us how each of several parts contributes towards the interactions that allow a person to produce or understand speech or writing. The areas for speech production are to some extent distinct entities. A case has been described where after a brain lesion the whole speech region was isolated and the patient became a talking machine who would repeat everything said to him but without any of the words having the least effect on him otherwise (Geschwind *et al.* 1968).

An important clue is that none of these areas has been shown to have any particular features of the cells or nerve fibres. Of course we don't really know what to look for, but it seems that the production and recognition of language does not depend upon some wonderful new sort of nerve cell. This can at least encourage us to look for its secret in an extension of the humbler operations of encoding and decoding already considered, and particularly in the topological arrangements revealed by the anatomy of their connections.

We also have continually to remember that many parts of the brain must work together. For example injuries to the frontal lobes may also produce impairment of speech, along with difficulties in other activities that we shall discuss as 'thinking' (Chapter 17). The whole reticular system indeed is involved in all 'conscious' behaviour. Furthermore all cortical behaviour implies continued activity also in the thalamus and midbrain colliculi so these too must be involved in speaking. It is quite likely that each and all of these parts perform actions in a speaking person that are different from those in any animal. In this sense they are all specialized 'speech centres'.

It is this need to consider the operations of many parts together that makes it so difficult to give precise meaning to the concept of a program for speaking, or almost any other brain activity for that matter. Nevertheless, some areas can be recognized as nodal points in the process. One sort of evidence about this comes from electrical stimulation of the cortex of patients under operation for the cure of epilepsy. Penfield and Roberts (1959) found that mild electrical stimuli delivered to the temporo-parietal region sometimes led to the emission of speech sounds, though never of connected speech. More recently Fedio and van Buren (1974) have stimulated these areas while the patients were performing the task of recognizing and naming a number of pictures shown one after the other for short periods. In all 19 patients studied there was one or more naming errors during periods of stimulation of the left temporal-parietal cortex, whereas this never occurred on the right. Stimulation near the area that produced actual errors often caused delay in response. The stimulus is thus somehow preventing access to the subject's verbal information store. The stimulus also interfered with recording in the memory. The patients were unable to repeat later the name of the picture that was shown at the moment of stimulation at the front of the temporal lobe (anterograde amnesia). After stimulation further back patients sometimes failed to repeat the name of the picture seen *before* the stimulus (retrograde amnesia). Evidence from injuries to the temporal lobe has already shown that they are involved in the formation of verbal memories.

Analysis of these various parts of the brain thus gives us glimpses of how the programs for producing language are organized. Perhaps one day physiologists will develop methods for investigation of the interactive processing that must go on between these various parts of the brain (see Arbib 1976). To understand language we need to know how to relate it to the brain processes that occur as the individual goes about his daily life. The programs that produce grammatically correct speech must somehow be linked to those that determine the semantic intentions of the speaker. The planning of speech like that of other actions is greatly influenced by the frontal lobes. Patients with injuries to these can speak quite correctly but may seldom do so spontaneously. In response to a question they may simply echo it. They will answer the question 'Were you drinking tea?' but can make no reply to 'Where have you been today?', which requires that they should think about things. In answering questions about the brain programs for language we are all of us rather like such patients. We can answer simple questions such as 'What is the effect of a lesion in the angular gyrus?' but are baffled by questions such as 'How do the various parts cooperate to produce cognitive concepts?' Such questions involve bringing together so many sorts of data that our poor frontal lobes give up. Obviously we are going to tax them still more when we search in the next chapter for the programs for thinking.

# 17   Knowing and thinking

## The store of knowledge in the brain

Our search for the details of the programs in the brain becomes harder and harder. When we began to enquire about 'speaking' we could ask about things and events we can easily explain to each other, such as auditory feature detectors, muscles for producing sound, and analysis into phonemes. But how can we start to examine thinking, which is conscious and goes on only in our heads? Yet each person undoubtedly has his particular way of thinking, part inherited, part learned, and the program for this must be there, recorded in his brain, waiting to be used, otherwise where is it when he sleeps? It is strange, as the neuropsychologist Luria notes, that 'From the very beginning of philosophy and psychology, the concept of the "brain" has always been so opposed to the concept of "thinking"' (1973, p. 323). Is it because we find it hard to imagine how the brain functions in thinking? Yet where can we suppose that the characteristic powers for thinking are stored if not in the brain? And if they are there then study of the brain should be of great help in identifying them and we should devote ourselves to that study, philosophers and neuroscientists together, perhaps even as one discipline not two. But of course until recently so little has been known about the brain that study of it has not been of much help, and philosophers have had to do it all themselves.

Can the brain be said to contain knowledge? The verb 'to know' has many and muddled uses. Do we 'know' a given fact all the time or only when asked about it? Use of the concept of memory records in the brain helps us to handle such problems. It can also reconcile various uses of the concept of 'knowing' such as 'knowing that' (of propositions, French con-nâitre) 'knowing how' (of things or events, French savoir) (see Rozeboom 1972). Just as knowledge can be recorded in books or in computers so 'knowledge' of all these sorts is encoded in the brain all the time. We need to find out how it is written there and how the record is consulted when we think.

## Thinking

What do we mean by thinking? The word seems originally to have meant 'to cause something to seem to appear to oneself' and we shall try to keep to this meaning and its natural extensions to cover all forms of conscious awareness. Many psychologists prefer to use 'thinking' only for some form of problem-solving (see Hebb 1949, Bartlett 1958). This may seem restrictive, but a great deal of conscious life consists of testing simple hypotheses. Vision and hearing involve continual asking of questions about the world (Chapters 12 and 16). Conscious activity without perception is an internal questioning process of the same sort. If the store of information that we call knowledge is in the brain, then thinking involves the process by which some items are temporarily called from the store and used to solve a problem, perhaps only the simple one of identifying what is being seen or heard. Even complicated internal thinking probably involves processes similar to the active search for the meaning of sights or sounds.

## The daily run of thoughts

Throughout the day we think a series of thoughts, one at a time. They may be aroused by stimulation from outside or by the internal operations of the brain. The thoughts that are thus called up may be visual or auditory or perhaps of smell, taste, or touch. They need not be verbal, though often they are. With this definition we must agree that animals think. But they cannot be said to think *about* things in the sense that we do in verbal thought, because their brains lack our verbal codes. They are 'dumb animals'.

So we pass through our days, with a succession of thoughts. They follow a program that is recorded in our brains as a combined product of heredity, the custom of our tribe, and our individual experience. The human dilemma is that we find it hard to express the relation between our thoughts and the world. The problem has been put in many ways. A biologist who was also a logician expressed it as follows: 'The ingredients of our days are not the houses, or mountains or even persons around us, but are the looks, feels and sounds etc. that are *of* such objects' (Woodger 1952). A different formulation is that the paradox of man is that 'he lives in two environments, in two worlds: as a "body" or extended thing he is among objects, as a "mind" or thinking thing he lives and converses with objects of a different kind, which he also perceives, holds and offers to other minds' (Vendler 1972, p. 39). We are trying to probe this paradox, and for now we will note again that all the thinking depends upon the organization and activity of materials stored in the brain. Without a brain there is no thought.

## The structure of thinking

Thinking is organized partly around signals received from the objects that we encounter, partly by signals arising from our memories. It is influenced all the time by signals indicating our inner needs. It is a curious assumption of much philosophy that cognitive activities are qualitatively distinct from the rest of our lives, that thinking is something special not involving wants or satisfactions (see Gellner 1973). This separation is contrary to all experience, but is basic to the logic and mathematics of western civilization. Yet the symbolic systems that we use to describe our perceptions and handle our problems are a combination of positional concepts and emotional responses to the objects perceived. Many common physical oppositions also have psychological flavours, for example solid/fluid, closed/open, behind /ahead, fast/slow. Colours are widely regarded as related to emotional experience. The structuralist such as Lévi-Strauss (1963, 1977) tries to find behind the chaos of rules and customs the single structural themes such as relationships of correlation and opposition. These are likely to be most helpful in discovering how the brain operates to relate thinking and speaking to the facts of the world. Psychoanalysts such as Ferenczi go so far as to suggest that in all naming the child tries to relate objects to parts of his own body and its functions. Others hold that objects are judged to be similar because they give rise to similar pleasure or to anxiety (for instance if they are somehow like a penis). The point for us is that *even the simplest act of comparison involves emotional factors.*

In building up categories for communication all languages use some common antitheses, as we have seen, such as good/bad, strong/weak, past/future, or bright/dull. This suggests again that the brain acts as an analogue with certain built in ways of collecting data, especially by use of the spatial brain maps of our surroundings. Such bipolar antitheses are often given a spatial reference (good is above bad, and so on). Similar terms are used about music, in relation to position (high or low tones), and to emotions (cheerful, sad, etc.) (Chapter 20). Verbal operation often uses a visual–spatial process, we 'move through an argument', we make 'progress' with our studies. Perhaps such clues can be used to understand how the brain operates in the 'search' for solutions.

## Fundamentals of thinking

It has been said that man classifies and captures nature in terms of his own feelings. To do this it may be that all people everywhere use certain powers or attitudes which can be said to be '*a priori*', given by our nature as humans. Thus the philosopher Vendler tells us that we do not have to be taught to know 'what it is to assert or request or to believe or decide. What is truth or necessity, what is a person, an object, a process or a state. What are change, purpose, causation time, extension or number. These are clear and distinct ideas' (Vendler 1972, p. 141). Perhaps the author has been overbold, and the list could be faulted or expressed otherwise. But the concept is important. 'A people not understanding say negation, identity and noncontradiction could not be said to think' (Lukes 1973). These are ultimate constraints to which all human thought is subject. 'They represent the basic adaptive mechanisms for any human society'. We return to this problem in discussion of belief (Chapter 21).

Such constants and constraints are of course the basic components of logic and it is important to define them. They have to be accepted as such by the philosopher as much as by the neuropsychologist. Even with all the developments of modal logic it is admitted that there is 'no systematic and universally acceptable account of this connection: "*p* follows from *q*"; no agreement, therefore, on what the formal pattern supporting correct inference is' (Jager 1972, p. 136).

## Do people of different cultures think differently?

An ancient and worrying question is whether logical powers vary genetically, as they certainly do between cultures. One might define logic as the process by which human beings arrange symbols in ways that compel agreement. This acceptability of particular types of argument will obviously vary with custom, as will the verbal forms. Yet if some of the basic principles of language are common to all mankind it seems likely that this may also be true of modes of reasoning. Indeed it should be profitable to keep before us all the time the clue that there are likely to be ties between natural phenomena and the operations that go on in our heads, as in the rest of our bodies. We cannot defy gravity, and all languages must describe up and down. The structure of our brain programs must truly represent that of the world, and this encourages us to rely upon their conclusions.

Many studies have tried to answer the question whether pre-literate cultures differ from western in their rational operations (Lévi-Strauss 1963, 1977) or whether we can find a 'psychic unity' in mankind, as many anthropologists propose (e.g. Boas). Psychologists, with their batteries of tests, are apt to postulate many different categories and modes of thinking. It used to be thought that pre-literate people are less intelligent (as measured by 'intelligence tests') or that they cannot or do not 'think rationally'. But most psychologists now agree that I.Q. tests cannot be culture free. The very concept of 'testing' in an arbitrary situation is a feature of western culture (and perhaps a dangerous feature at that). Many psychologists following Spearman (1932) have attempted to extract a general intelligence factor ($g$) by statistical analysis of a person's performance with different types of test. But this empirical procedure cannot disguise the fact that we have no valid scientific concept of efficiency of brain function or intelligence in man (or indeed in any animal). So of course we cannot measure it.

## The earliest thoughts of the child

How people attack problems depends very much on the context in which they are set. Anthropologists and psychologists in their attempts to collect data that are 'objective' and 'repeatable' often face people with unreal situations. It may be useful to consider that a person's 'natural' method of thinking is usually 'situation bound', whereas when tested he is expected to use 'rational' or 'logical' methods that may seem to him inappropriate. There is good evidence that children in the pre-operational stage (up to 7 years) are limited to thinking and speaking about the type of operation involved in *simple* situations as expressed in kernel sentences. They are incapable of indirect or reversal thinking (Chapter 4). At first they classify perceptually, thus a cow is not 'food', but a stuffed animal is an 'animal'. Meals are 'food' but the odd bar of chocolate is not, later both are. The young child undergeneralizes, which after all is a safe technique, less likely to confuse (Saltz, Soller and Sigel 1972). But for us the point is that all concepts are complex. Think of all the concepts, abstractions and properties that we imply when we speak of a simple object such as a cup. It is a hollow vessel, used for drinking, probably fragile and with a handle; often on a saucer, white or coloured, and so on. These have all been added by accretion as life goes on, and each property attaches to many objects. All of these concepts must be held by whatever brain structure or process constitutes the record, for this is the *only* persisting entity that continues to represent a concept when it is not recalled for thought or speech.

Besides additions to the child's store of concepts there are great changes in the way they are used. Sometime after the age of seven, something happens in his brain, or is added to its store of programs, that makes analysis of reversal and other complex problems possible (see p. 181). But even adults resolve complex problems more readily by situation-bound than logical solutions. For example it has been shown that reasoning even by 'highly intelligent' people is influenced by content in systematic ways (Wason and Johnson-Laird 1972). Even in those who have matured to the possibility of performing what Piaget calls formal operations content has not become fully subordinated to structure (Beth and Piaget 1966). People in any culture may use the immediate apparent content of a problem more readily than a logical analysis (Cole *et al*. 1971). This does not necessarily mean that they are incapable of rational thinking. The stages postulated by Piaget are evidence of upper bounds of competence, which may or may not be expressed in performance.

The conclusion from all this would be that the natural programs for thinking are those that run every day to promote the life of the individual in his culture. He will of course use the methods, verbal and otherwise, that have been learned by virture of inheritance of human capabilities and the environment in which he has been reared. A library of such programs is stored in the brain.

## Induction and deduction

One important sense of the verb 'to think' implies prediction. We cannot yet say how the brain operates to make comparisons possible and hence becomes capable of both induction and deduction. The nature of the problem recalls that of recognition of complex visible features—once again the grandmother's face cell. Induction, as Quine (1972) reminds us, is an extrapolation by resemblance, the power for which must be partly innate, or we could never have begun to learn, 'Innate standards of resemblance have been according to us and other animals better than random chances in anticipating the course of nature—this thought somewhat alleviates the discomfort of the problem of induction.' A biologist will heartily agree, and anyway he has probably never experienced the disquiet felt by some philosophers because they cannot *prove* that the sun will rise tomorrow.

Logicians and linguists give us some insight into the types of comparison that must be involved in these innate standards of resemblance. There is no reason in principle why we should be unable to find out how the brain operates to produce them. Surely physiologists should be ready to ask the help of philosophers in framing experiments to answer such questions, as they have when dealing with problems of perception. Once again the spatial organization of the 'words' of the cortical language may provide a clue.

## Thinking by machines

Problem solving obviously involves coding of the data into appropriate categories and then operating with them, and this may be done in many ways. Experts with computer languages and artificial intelligence have tried to write programs that will solve problems as humans do. Perhaps their most general conclusion is that human brain operations are even more complicated than had been supposed. The cleverest program writers have only been able to imitate brains when they are acting under some relatively restricted set of rules, such as games of noughts and crosses or, at most, of chess. They have not been able to incorporate to an appreciable extent our use of analogy or metaphor. But it does not follow that we never shall simulate thought on a computer, 'The question is empirical' (see Sutherland 1976b). The magnitude of the problem becomes clear when one considers what would be involved in giving a computer all the experience of a human upbringing. This thought indeed reminds us how complicated the brain programs are, and that they have grown slowly and differently in each of us. It is amazing that we begin to be able to describe how they are written by using the new discoveries about the nervous system.

## Thinking by logicians

Systems of computerized thinking have mostly followed logicians in assuming that the processes of the brain can be usefully categorized by abstract entities. How many arguments begin with a form such as 'if $p$ entails $q$ then ...' Indeed modern logic has evolved a whole special symbolism for the extraction of truth functions. The assumption involved in such a method is that the essential features of statements whose truthfulness is in question can be captured in simple symbols. We try to define our terms to ensure this, but the biologist, like the sociologist, finds many situations so complicated that simplification produces distortion. There are no simple answers to most of the questions that arise in everyday life. Indeed some logicians seem to feel that ordinary language is so 'fuzzy' and imprecise that it can never be described in a system of precise logical symbols and rules (Fodor 1970, p. 204). The corollary would be that the job of the logician is not to capture the complex logic of ordinary language but to construct a consistent and precise alternative for scientific purposes.

The use of abstract classes has obviously given sensational increases in control of nature, especially through mathematics. Perhaps the brain operations that are involved may not be such a very great extension beyond the classifying capacities that we have already considered. The concept of a class is itself a category. Use of complex and novel abstract classes involves performing operations that are proper only to the content of the class. This is not essentially different from correctly naming a chair as something to sit upon. The subject seems complicated because logicians and mathematicians reformulate their problems using what Quine has called logical paraphrases, such as regarding time as a fourth dimension, or eliminating it altogether and regarding it as on a par with place (1960). This helps wonderfully in discovering truth functions, for which tense may be a triviality. But it can lead to absurd conclusions such as Quine quotes, 'George V married Queen Mary. Queen Mary is a widow. Therefore George V married a widow.' The point is that if we simplify problems by logical or mathematical analysis we are liable to lose as well as to gain. Logicians will of course object that they are continually aware of such dangers and indeed there is a system of 'tense logic' that overcomes the difficulty about George V's wife. But I wonder if the results of their simplifications are really discounted in a culture that is increasingly based upon them. Logic, mathematics, and computers represent potentially dangerous reductionisms.

## Thinking and satisfaction

Society is obviously not likely to give up the use of these analytical tools, such as mathematics. Indeed previously illiterate and anumerate societies may increasingly try to acquire them, envying the material riches that they seem to produce. But there are plenty of signs already that the literate and numerate societies are themselves finding such abstract conceptions unsatisfying. This will not surprise the biologist. He may not be able to describe fully how the brain operates in thinking, but he feels fairly sure that its calculations have something to do with the satisfaction of needs. The very fact of separating out precise logical propositions about complex situations presupposes that such separations are possible without loss of some features that are essential for the solution of real human problems. Gellner (1973) has called it 'the bureaucratisation of nature'. Not only are such separations held possible, it is further assumed that logical operations show them to be desirable. Popper goes so far as to seem to wish to exclude what he calls 'psychological questions' from considerations of truthfulness (1972). The conclusion that Gellner draws is that three centuries of empiricist propaganda, insisting on 'such separation of classes of propositions, has established the Autonomy of Fact ... Greater and greater expanses of truth acquire an autonomy from the social, moral and political obligations and decencies of the society' (p. 180). Looking at the way the brain actually works as enabling a person to live in society seems to me to be a help in avoiding this separation, which people of many sorts increasingly deplore. Biologists are the great antireductionists. They emphasize that it is not possible to separate the question of how people think from what they think about. Presumably everyone will agree that thinking is not the same as formal logic or even problem solving. We must be ready to acknowledge the importance of the alogical content of human experience.

## Brain operations in problem solving

The routines used in thinking about a problem involve first identifying a goal or end and then choosing a method or program to reach it. In the program we often explore a network of possibilities or contingencies and at each branch point we apply a test to see whether we are getting nearer to the goal (see Bartlett 1958). The process includes many references back for checking (recursive loops). In this serial operation different parts of the brain may be involved one after the other, though there is no direct evidence of this yet. It is certain that immense numbers of nervous channels are used throughout, many *in parallel*. This fundamental difference from the operation of an artificial computer may explain how we sometimes seem to reach the solution of complex problems quickly, as we say by intuition. Some of these parallel processes can be simulated on a serial computer, but only because it goes through many possibilities very fast. It may be that the brain can bring a number of variables together and match them in parallel with those of the desired solution. This analogue system of calculation recalls us to the concept of a model in the brain. It has a firm basis in our anatomical knowledge of the multiplicity of channels, but as yet no sound physiological basis. The major problem of brain physiology is to discover how the model is embodied.

## Electrical changes in the brain during thinking

Although we cannot analyse thinking in terms of nerve impulses and synapses, we can already begin to study the electrical brain events that accompany it. From the earliest days of electroencephalograms it was found that the wave-forms changed when an intellectual or perceptual task was begun. Special techniques have been used to try to identify specific electrical events that occur during thinking. The technical problem is to obtain a series of runs that can be averaged to allow any change at the moment of thought to be distinguished in the wavy electroencephalogram. It is then possible to pick out from the averaged electrical change those events that were associated with the thinking. In one such experiment Chapman (1973) asked his subjects to look at a screen upon which a ran-dom sequence of letters and numbers appeared. The subject then had to say on each run either, which of two numbers was the larger, or which letter was earlier in the alphabet. Thus at some times during each run he had to think, at other times not. It was found that the patterns of potential change were quite different according to whether he was thinking, that is storing infor-mation about a number or letter in memory in order to make the compar-ison. Now of course we do not know what these changes mean in terms of brain activities; though they enable us to decide from the record whether the subject was thinking or not. In a sense therefore they illustrate the weakness of our knowledge of brain programs, but at least they show that whatever it is that goes on in the brain can be studied, though we certainly can't read off what a person is thinking from his electrical brain record.

However a subject can be trained to control his own brain waves (Kamiya 1969). People can learn to produce at will bursts of the particular type of electrical activity known as alpha waves. These bursts can be made to be long or short, and so serve (within limits) as elements of the Morse code. The subject can thus send out messages from his brain without speaking. At first this sounds sensational, but is it really different in principle from tap-ping out Morse with a finger?

## Meditating

After they had learned, people could then bring on or suppress their alpha rhythm and when asked how they did the suppression they mostly replied that it was by concentrating on a visual image, say of a person's face. It has long been known that there is a connection between the alpha rhythm and seeing. Several workers claim that they can detect people who are 'visualizers' by their alpha rhythm (though others have denied this). In any case it is shown that people can learn either to turn the rhythm on or off, and it was interesting that they mostly said that they enjoyed more making it come than making it go away, even although suppression was easier. Turning on was reported as 'a general calming down of the mind—where you stop being *critical* about anything' (Kamiya 1969, p. 514). The people who were best at producing alpha rhythms were reported to be good at visual imagination and also to be good meditators. There is indeed evidence that when a person successfully undertakes a Zen Buddhist meditation (Zazen), by breathing exercises, his brain shows much alpha rhythm. During this time, while he is in the state of Satori or enlightenment, he will report various mostly pleasant sensations, such as drowsiness and relaxation (non-striving) and physical feelings of waves, vibrations, and dizziness. The successful meditator says he becomes fully aware of his inner self (Kasamatsu and Hirai 1969). During the whole time of meditation a Zen master shows large alpha waves, first fast, then slower, in spite of the fact that his eyes are open.

## Brain lesions and thinking

Evidence about how parts of the brain operate in thinking comes from studies after brain injury (Gardner 1975). The difficulties of these patients help to identify the steps by which we proceed in solving a problem. Lesions in various parts of the brain interfere with the process in different ways (Luria 1973). Knowing these steps we can look for the programs that produce particular operations, rather than for a cerebral substrate for some vague general process of thinking or the formation of abstract ideas. Even if we cannot specify how the brain produces these operations we shall have identified some features of them. This provides many advantages. It helps the logician in his analysis of thinking and the patient and his doctor in managing the results of cerebral injury. Those concerned with artificial intelligence and the simulation of thought by computer have had to make similar analyses of the stages of thinking.

All analysis of problems depends upon the logical structure of speech, which is itself related to the structure of the world, to our place in it, and to the problems that we meet there. Thinking is an adaptive process, directed to meeting our needs. The first stage of problem solving is thus recognition that there is a problem. The individual must be motivated to attend to the situation, recognize the uncertainty in it, and suffer for failure to resolve it. Disturbances of this goal-seeking capacity may follow lesions deep in the brain or in the frontal lobes. When patients with such lesions are given a written problem they do not recognize it; instead of answering they will simply restate part of it, without noticing their mistake. How far has mankind's discernment of great problems had to wait for the growth of brain powers and programs of motivation that will even recognize them? Apes are not motivated to recognize problems of philosophy, ethics, or science.

The second stage in a program for solving a problem is to identify its conditions and components, and this involves waiting and restraint until they are all realized. Patients with frontal-lobe lesions lack such restraint; they impulsively give fragmentary solutions. Thus one patient was asked 'There are 18 books on two shelves and twice as many on one as on the other, how many are there on each?' He quickly replied, 'Easy, 18 + 36 = 54.' We have seen that from the octopus onwards a mechanism ensuring *restraint* is a necessary component of any system with alternative possibilities of action (p. 90).

Once the problem has been recognized the third stage is to select an appropriate strategy from among the network of possible alternative hypotheses and methods. There are of course programs available to the individual as a result of his innate and acquired capacities, largely verbal. Different cultural situations produce different sets of solutions and indeed may determine whether a problem is recognized at all. We know only a little about how such a search is undertaken. It resembles the searching for items in the memory and it is likely that some form of content addressing is used. That is we try to identify the problem as similar to some familiar situation, in fact to see its relevance to our whole life program as represented by a model in the brain that is unitary rather than fragmented. Some neurologists believe that the requisite recoding and cross-correlations may be achieved by operations 'in the holographic mode', but it is not easy to see exactly what brain operations this would involve (see Pribram 1971).

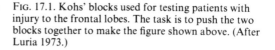

FIG. 17.1. Kohs' blocks used for testing patients with injury to the frontal lobes. The task is to push the two blocks together to make the figure shown above. (After Luria 1973.)

This process of selection from the repertoire of codes is disturbed by a lesion of the left parieto-occipital region, which seems to cause distortion of the recognition of relations, both spatial and logico-grammatical or numerical (Fig. 12.5). The patient can recognize the problem and is motivated to solve it but cannot put the elements correctly together. Very simple problems are soluble. 'Jack has two apples, Jill has four—how many have they together?' can be answered. But 'Jack has two, while Jill two more' gives confusions. He asks, 'While? More?, what does more mean?' Again with a visual problem such as that shown in Fig. 17.1 the patient turns the blocks helplessly and without plan. The intention to solve is there and attempts continue. With a few spatial hints he will find the answer, unlike frontal-lobe patients who push them together impulsively and can only be helped by dictating a rigid program of procedure.

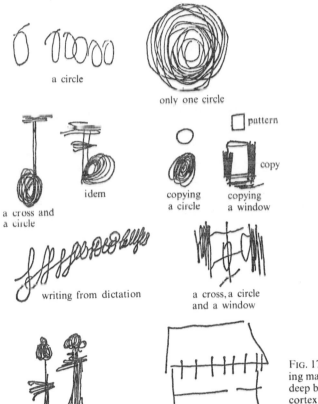

a circle

only one circle

a cross and a circle

idem

copying a circle

copying a window

pattern

copy

writing from dictation

a cross, a circle and a window

two circles and a cross

a house

FIG. 17.2. Mistakes in copying made by a patient with a deep brain lesion of the cortex and basal ganglia. Among other defects he was unable to recognize when his task was completed (After Luria 1973.)

The final stages of problem solving involve not only finding an answer but comparing it with the conditions and deciding whether it is correct. Failure to take these very necessary steps may occur in people with either too little motivation or lack of capacity to identify a correct solution. One form of this failure is not to recognize that the problem has been solved and in fact to *repeat* the solution over and over again (Fig. 17.2).

These observations tell us at least something about the components of the procedure of problem solving, as well as of the different parts of the brain that are involved. Of course the actual operations in the brain do not follow quite such simple sequences. Many parts of the brain interact throughout and our problem in discussing it is to try to find useful ways to conceptualize the interaction of such vast systems of channels.

Thinking is a serial activity of fitting things together into a pattern. We continually try to reconcile all our sensations with the model in the brain. Every act of perception is an act of thinking. Conversely puzzles of many sorts can be considered as extended perceptions. Solving them is a pleasure; we enjoy puzzles, from jigsaws to crosswords.

So we can at least begin to describe how the brain operates in thinking. The process involves the motivations for search and exploration, including functions of the frontal lobes, the perceptions of the sensory cortex, the study of relations by the association cortex, and the satisfactions of achievement, that are linked ultimately with those life promoting activities of the hypothalamus and reticular system that are at the centre of all consciousness.

# 18   Sleeping, dreaming, and consciousness

## The program for sleeping

Many major problems of philosophy and science revolve around the relations between the concepts of brain, mind, and consciousness and the fact that we sleep provides a valuable insight into all of them. At least once a day we cease to be conscious, the mind no longer operates, and only the brain remains active as the guardian of our personality and the guarantee of its continuance. When we wake up we are still the same person as before. So if consciousness and mind can come and go it is very difficult to see how they can be the carriers of our character and individuality. What *does* persist is the organization and continuing activity of the brain, and it is these that provide the unified program of that single entity 'myself'. At intervals the program wakes me up for a period of conscious mental activity. There is therefore a wonderful opportunity to study the parallel changes in brain and mind as we fall asleep each night and in the morning wake again. By following electrical changes and reports of consciousness we can see how the activities that we call those of the brain and the mind are related, providing together the entity that we call a person, sometimes conscious, sometimes not. Finally, as a further study of this conscious entity we shall show how both brain and mind can actually be divided by the surgeon's knife, and also how consciousness is altered by brain injury.

Knowledge about sleep is therefore important for the study of programs of the brain for several reasons. First sleep is certainly a state both of the brain and of consciousness. Secondly no one will question that it occurs following a rhythmic program. Thirdly it involves a simultaneous *change* of activity of the whole brain and of the condition of consciousness.

Understanding of sleep has been revolutionized by the discovery that electrical activities in the brain indicate that there are two main types of sleep. It was first shown by Berger, who discovered the electroencephalogram (EEG) in 1929, that when a person falls asleep the EEG changes from the 10 cycles per second of people with their eyes shut (alpha rhythm) to very large slow waves at 1–3 per second (Adrian and Matthews 1934). This is the EEG characteristic of *quiet sleep*. (QS). Later it was found that about once every $1\frac{1}{2}$ hours while we sleep the EEG changes, passing through several stages. The waves get larger and slower but with bursts of higher frequency, known from their appearance in records as spindles. At the same time the eyes make rapid jerky movements. This is the condition known as rapid eye movement or REM sleep, sometimes called paradoxical sleep, or perhaps best of all active sleep (AS). If a person is woken up during active sleep he will often report that he had been dreaming, whereas this is less common when someone is woken out of quiet sleep. Even a few minutes after a period of active sleep he will not remember that he had dreamt. Here then we have a means of discovering something about the relations between the electrical activity of the brain and the dreaming mind, for surely we regard dreaming as a mental activity. These two types of sleep have been found in nearly all mammals and birds, but not apparently in reptiles or other lower vertebrates or in invertebrates, though many of these show periods of inactivity (Oswald, 1966).

## The core brain and the script for dreaming

The program of sleep that is written in the brain thus involves a much more complicated score than would be needed for a mere alternation of sleeping and waking. We begin to know a little of how this score is embodied in the activities of parts of the core brain, the reticular system ('net system' from the form of its cells, see later) lying at the centre of the grey matter of the brain (p. 111). This system acts as a unifying entity, setting the level of responsiveness and activity of all other parts. It probably represents what Penfield called the 'centrencephalic system' when he wished to emphasize the significance of influences outside the cortex (1975). The integration of the whole personality and the control of its waking or sleeping is produced by this complicated set of reticular neurons. Some are very large, with axons proceeding to many parts of the brain (Fig. 11.7). Others are small and with short axons—hence the reference in the name to a net-like organization. The ascending reticular pathways pass up from the spinal cord and medulla to the midbrain, hypothalamus, and cortex. The descending reticular system allows the cerebral cortex, especially the frontal and medial parts, to influence the rest of the system.

Two regions particularly involved in sleep are called the raphe nucleus and locus coeruleus, near to each other in the medulla oblongata at the hind end of the brain (Fig. 10.5). The cells of the raphe nucleus (p. 159) produce the amine serotonin (5-hydroxytryptamine, 5-HT) and deliver it along their axons to nuclei further forward. It is probably released in the thalamus (the gateway to the cortex, (Fig. 11.5) and acts upon the cells there to produce the synchronized activities of the cells of the cortex that give the slow waves of quiet sleep. Destruction of the raphe nucleus in a cat produces insomnia, as do drugs that inhibit the action of serotonin.

The locus coeruleus and nearby nuclei produce the opposite effects by the noradrenaline of their cells and fibres. We have already met this pathway as part of the reward system (p. 89). Studies are beginning to show how these two sets of cells interact to produce the rhythm of waking and sleep and the detailed pattern of quiet sleep and active sleep throughout each night. A suggestion is that neurons producing serotonin induce the quiet sleep and then the catecholamines set in action a series of neurons that is called, rather alarmingly, the ponto-geniculo-occipital system (PGO). This set begins with cells in the pons (bridge), an area of tissue below the cerebellum (Fig. 9.1). These send fibres to the geniculate body (knee-like, from its shape) and cells from this proceed to the occipital part of the cortex (i.e. that lying at the back of the head). The curious names indicate one of the difficulties we have in neuroscience. Only in the last few years has it been found that the PGO neurons could be better called 'the dream-producing neurons'.

## The programs for dreaming

The effect of stimulating the geniculate cells of this set is to produce activity in the occipital and other parts of the cortex, which we experience as dreaming during active sleep (see Resnick 1972, Jouvet 1975). This is especially interesting to us because we can see here something of the actual physical changes that constitute the program by which dreams are produced, though not of course yet in the detail we should wish for. The pacemaker for active sleep is in the lateral part of the pons, which is the first element in the PGO sequence. This is itself controlled by activation and inhibition of the mono-amines of the locus coeruleus, which as we have seen depends upon some interaction with the serotonin of the raphe nuclei.

In his dream a person may be running fast, or doing all sorts of things, but his only actual movements are at most a few jerks. So the great cortical activity must be accompanied by an *inhibition* of the motor centres. It has been found that this inhibition is initiated from a special hinder part of the locus coeruleus. If that region is destroyed in cats then motor activity is *not* inhibited when they dream. Indeed they may 'suddenly leap up, and either display some aggressive behavior or play with their front paws as they might play with a mouse, or they show a rage behavior or a defense reaction against a large predator' (Jouvet 1975). Yet all the time the cat's eyes are shut and the animal may bang into anything it touches. Finally it may either wake up or return to sleep. Presumably a similar failure of inhibition of movement occurs in sleep-walking in man.

So the programs for sleeping and for dreaming are quite complicated, and seem to involve periods of activation of the brain but inhibition of the movements that would be expected from their activity. The actions of these various cells of the core brain thus constitute the physical basis or 'script' of the program of sleeping and waking.

## Functions of sleep

If there is a program for sleeping, what is its aim and are there feedback mechanisms to ensure that the aim is achieved? Are there some minimum necessary amounts of sleep and of dreaming, and if these are not allowed is there full compensation by more sleep and dreaming later on? It seems at first obvious that sleep is for rest and recuperation—but why should the brain alone need to recuperate rather than other tissues? The heart for instance never rests. Many suggestions have been made by those who investigate sleep, but they seem to be influenced by rather simple-minded human reactions to this important part of our lives. Thus Dement (1968) suggested that quiet sleep serves to store 'nervous energy' (since none is then expended) and that active sleep is a 'safety valve' to allow discharge when the store is full. Other suggestions are that sleep in some way allows for the reorganization or reprogramming, of cortical circuitry. It may be that there will be found to be something in such suggestions, when we know more clearly what we mean by 'nervous energy' and 'cortical circuitry'.

Perhaps it is a mistake to look at sleep only or mainly as a rest for the brain. It is reasonable to think that many bodily activities require periodical recuperation and that providing for this is the reason for the physiological changes that accompany the various sorts of sleep. Now that it is possible to assay hormone levels in the blood it has been found that several of the master hormones of the pituitary gland show daily fluctuations. The best known are the changes in adrenocorticotropic hormone (ACTH), which controls the secretion of cortisol by the adrenals, so that it is three times higher on waking in the morning than at midday (p. 67). This, like other cycles is reversed by change in sleeping habits, the change taking 1–2 weeks. Since the adrenal cortex is responsible for promoting many activities that are responses to 'stress' we have here real evidence of the filling of a sort of 'reservoir' during sleep. It seems not to be known during which part of sleeping this filling happens, but it is said that after a stressful day people show an increase in active sleep.

Equally interesting are the fluctuations in production of growth hormone (somatotropin), which is said to be at a maximum during the first hours of sleep, that is during a period mainly of quiet sleep. After a day of heavy bodily exercise there is increased quiet sleep. Somatotropin promotes many synthetic metabolic processes, in the nerve cells and elsewhere in the body. If the cells of the cerebral cortex really have a special need for 'restoration' then somatotropin will assist it. On the other hand the sleep of infants both before and after birth seems to be mainly of the active variety! Possibly other factors are involved here—thus the flow of blood to the brain, and its temperature, are increased during active sleep but not quiet sleep, and the growing infant's brain requires an especially good supply of blood.

## Sleep deprivation

The program for sleeping is so insistent that it is very difficult to deprive people of sleep. Dr. Oswald records how in an experiment he walked the streets of Edinburgh with two sleep-deprived volunteers, one on each side, and saw their eyelids closing until they walked unseeing in light sleep (1966). In spite of the demand for sleep the effects of deprivation are sometimes not so marked as one might expect. After three days and nights without sleep volunteers were found to exert a grip that was as strong as before, and arithmetical tasks and reaction times were as quick as ever. There was however some increase in tendency to make mistakes, perhaps mainly because of little catnaps of sleep. After very long deprivation people suffer from hallucinations and paranoia, thinking they are being persecuted. This perhaps confirms the idea that some sort of reprogramming goes on in the brain while we sleep.

Whatever it is about sleep that is important partly relates to active sleep. To test this people can be deprived of it by waking them whenever their EEG shows that they are about to dream. After deprivation in this way for a night people show more active-sleep periods the next night and so on, until after several nights 30 or more wakenings were necessary in a night. On the other hand volunteers deprived of all sleep for three nights have mostly quiet sleep on the fourth, but more than usual active sleep on the fifth. So it seems that both sorts are necessary.

## Dreaming

The fact that we need active sleep and that it is associated with dreaming has been considered to support the idea that the benefits of sleep come from dreams. It is interesting that dreaming is initiated by the monoamine systems of the locus coeruleus, which also influence the reward centres of the hypothalamus (Chapter 13). This may be a significant connection, since dreams are so much concerned with wish-fulfilment The stereotyped behaviour of cats that is released during dreaming after lesions (p. 207) is highly organized, it is not a set of epileptic discharges, but indicates that the brain activity evoked by the sleep program is itself following some program. This suggests the idea that dreaming fulfils some special function in relation to instinctive behaviour (Jouvet 1975). The active sleep in infants before and after birth might be connected with the fact that their 'instinctive' neural mechanisms are actively maturing, with but a minimum of external influence. Dreams could thus be regarded as providing for better building of the memory model by continued operation of the mechanism for memorizing during the night, even when no further information from external sources is available. The newborn rat, which has a very immature brain, has much active sleep, but the baby guinea-pig, whose brain is mature at birth, has little. The function of dreaming may thus be to stimulate the unfolding of the genetically programmed patterns of the neurons, linking this with the information that has come in during the previous day (see Jouvet 1975).

A dream is a sort of extension and fantasy of life, often expressing urges that are suppressed or disguised during the day. Can it be that fulfilling our wishes in dreams is in some way beneficial? We live out our fears in dreams too, and perhaps we get over them in this way. I do not think that anyone can give a sure answer to these questions. Nor is it really known what determines the elaborate symbolism that is used in dreams. If they are in some way an attempt to act out what we desire or fear, why should the hopes or anxieties be disguised in symbols? Is it because the implications of our fears are too traumatic to be fully faced? As a small example—when I was about to retire from University College I dreamed with dread of having to give a lecture in Helsinki. 'Why in Finland?' I asked my wife. She saw the symbolism at once, 'Its the finish of life!' People who have lived through battles or other terrifying experiences certainly relive them in dreams for long afterwards, but it is not clear whether this somehow relieves their pain.

The subject-matter of dreams is influenced by sounds heard during sleep. The ring of the alarm clock often enters into a dream. In an experiment by Berger (1963), names were introduced from a tape recorder during active sleep and the sleeper then awakened and a report of his dream recorded. There were many associations, some only by the sound or rhyme—thus with the name Robert the dream was of a 'distorted rabbit'. Jung has called these 'clang responses'. Other associations were more complicated; thus to 'Naomi'—'We travelled north with an aim to ski'. The theory that dreams are wish-fulfilments is not borne out by hungry or thirsty people, they do not have obviously relevant dreams. Psychoanalysts will find symbolic references in all such situations, but it is hard to establish their validity. Sexual wishes are actually fulfilled by orgasm in wet dreams, and when symbolism accompanies them it can be used to support Freudian interpretations. But why are an individual's sex dreams sometimes open and sometimes symbolically disguised?

## Freud's interpretation of dreams

The classic analysis of dreams is, of course, that of Freud and it has been, as he himself noted, one of the most successful outcomes of the psychoanalytic method. He proceeded, very logically, from the fact that 'The young child always dreams of the fulfilment of wishes which were aroused in him the day before and were not satisfied' (in *The interpretation of dreams* 1900). In adults 'you must distinguish between the *manifest dream-content*, which we remember in the morning only confusedly . . . and the *latent dream-thoughts*, whose presence in the unconscious we must assume'. By analysis one finds out the 'real sense of the dream . . . as the fulfilling of an unsatisfied wish'. He explained the change and the disguise as the result of the operation of the 'defensive forces of the ego, of the resistances', which he supposed had been developed during the conflicts of upbringing and socialization. More important for our view of the brain is his concept that 'During the night the train of thoughts succeed in finding connections with one of the unconscious tendencies present ever since his childhood in the mind of the dreamer but ordinarily repressed and excluded from his conscious life' (1912). How interested he would have been to hear about the importance of the locus coeruleus in reward systems as well as in control of sleep. His *Project for a scientific psychology* written in 1895 has recently been called 'a kind of Rosetta stone for those interested in communication between neurologists and psychoanalysts' (Pribram and Gill 1976). Freud knew that great secrets were to be discovered 'there is the opportunity to learn what we could not have guessed from speculation . . . that the laws of the unconscious differ widely from those of the conscious . . . and we may hope to learn still more about them by a profounder investigation of the process of dream-formation'. And he adds, 'This enquiry is not yet half finished'. Unhappily that is still so more than 60 years later.

## Resting

It may be that in looking for complicated explanations for the significance of sleep in ourselves we are missing its most obvious biological feature which is *stillness*. Animals tend to sleep in places and postures where they are secure (see Meddis 1975). Herbivores, which have to eat a lot, sleep little. They are also liable to attack and must be ready to escape. Carnivores feed rapidly and can defend themselves, and they sleep a lot. The cat is the champion of dreamers, with up to 200 minutes of active sleep a day. The times of sleep are often those at which food cannot be gathered and the animal then economizes energy and runs less risk by retiring to a safe home or nest, or at least remaining still. Circadian rhythms thus concentrate activity at the most profitable times of day. There are a few species of animals that seem never to sleep, including high-flying swifts, albatrosses, and some dolphins, and these species are relatively safe from enemies.

According to this view the significance of the recurrent periods of active sleep is that they provide occasions on which thresholds of response are lowered and the animal is ready to wake if there is danger or conditions have changed. This may seem rather far-fetched, but we should not exclude the possibility that there is no unique physiological benefit to be derived from sleep, beyond keeping the animal or person inactive. This view of sleep as nothing more than as it were a 'spare time activity' hardly explains the insistent demand for it, nor (perhaps) its association with fluctuations in hormone levels. On the other hand many human beings have learned to do with far less sleep than a simple circadian rhythm suggests. There are reports of regular sleepers for whom an hour or even 15 minutes each night is enough (Meddis 1975).

So it may be that there is no basic physiological need to spend so much of our lives in an unconscious state. This in itself throws light on the significance of consciousness. It is the state in which a man (or animal) is active and ready to react. At times of day or night when there is no advantage in being alert then there is no consciousness of the surroundings, but some programs are rehearsed and perhaps reinforced by dreaming.

## Divided consciousness

Studies of sleep tend to emphasize the unity of consciousness. We may speak of being half-awake, but we don't mean awake on the left side only. The results of operations in which the corpus callosum has been divided do indeed show that one's awareness can be divided into two separate and different parts. The division is done to prevent the spread of epileptic fits from one side of the cortex to the other, the rest of the brain remaining undivided. Careful tests after the operation show that the result is a split personality (Sperry 1967). Neither he himself nor those around them notice this because the two persons in one body share so much that for most purposes they behave as one. For instance since only the cortex is divided they share a single reticular system and wake and fall asleep together. But when they are awake only sights seen with the right eye can be described verbally, because all (or nearly all) the speech capacity depends upon centres in the left cortex, which alone receives visual signals from the right eye (Fig. 18.1). If an object (say a watch) is shown to the left eye the left brain will say it has seen nothing, but if the left hand (which is controlled by the right brain, the 'minor' hemisphere) is allowed to feel various objects it will correctly pick out a watch. The left brain which *can* speak cannot say what the left hand is holding. So the right brain is not stupid: but is it conscious? If it cannot speak is it the seat of a mind? Although the right brain cannot speak it is not devoid of verbal understanding. If it hears the word 'pen', then the left hand, which it guides, can pick out a pen from a group of objects. It can do this even if the instruction is quite complicated, say 'Find the writing instrument' (for a pen) or 'Unlocks doors' (for a key) or 'Inserted in slot machines' (for a coin). This hemisphere can even spell simple words like 'hat' by picking out letters with the left hand. As this goes on the left hemisphere may be making critical and erroneous comments, the two are truly separate. Finally the minor hemisphere can also show emotion. If different pictures are flashed to the right and left visual fields only

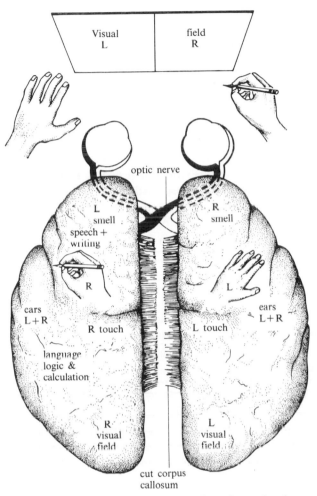

FIG. 18.1. Diagram of the situation in a patient after cutting the corpus callosum. Only the right part of the visual field is now connected to the left hemisphere, which controls speech and writing. Things seen only in the left visual field cannot be described, but the left hemisphere may 'know' what they are and the left hand can identify them. Note that the fibres in the optic nerves cross in a way that ensures that each half of the visual field is represented in one hemisphere. The right half-field is seen by the lateral half of the left retina and the medial half of the right retina. (After Sperry 1974.)

those seen by the right eye are named. But when one young woman was shown pictures to the left eye of a nude man and to the right eye of a horse, then while the left hemisphere said 'horse' the voice changed and there was a flush and an embarrassed grin. Asked why she smiled, the speaking part of the patient said, 'I don't know, Oh that bright light'! As a general summary we can say that the left hemisphere is the seat of most of the capacity for language, calculation, arrangement in order, and logical analysis. The right hemisphere is better than the left at spatial perception, recognition of faces and maps, and at musical appreciation.

Split-brain operations are only one of the ways in which we learn about the strange variations that there are in the states of consciousness. Patients with injuries to the occipital cortex may be nearly 'blind' or have blind patches in their field of vision. Yet they can show by pressing buttons that they can discriminate between shapes, though when asked what they see they say 'nothing at all' (Weiskrantz *et al.* 1974). They may remark that they have a vague 'feeling', although they cannot see. Some people may like to suppose that similar 'feelings' are the basis on which people react to each other, or to things, by one of the various suspected sorts of extra-sensory perception. But the suggestion should not be taken up without very critical examination of any alleged evidence for such powers. The evidence I have seen has not convinced me of the existence of any extensive capacities of this sort.

## Drugs and consciousness

It is obvious that a wide range of altered states of consciousness can be induced by drugs or meditation, or by the influence of one person on another as in hypnosis (see Tart 1969). The fact that under mescaline one may see strange visions does not mean that these are nearer to some special world truth than is normal seeing. What it does show is that conscious experience is so dependent on the activity of the brain that it is changed by many drugs. Some of these drugs produce hallucinations very like those that are experienced in schizophrenia, and these are now known to be due to errors of the working of adrenaline, dopamine, and other amines in the brain (Chapter 15). So these visions tell us more about ourselves than about the world or the heavens. They emphasize once again that what we consciously experience is closely related to the activities of our brains. Should we say that the brain 'produces visions'?

## Brain damage and consciousness

The brain's influence on personality is shown dramatically when it is damaged. In a little book called *The man with a shattered world*, Luria (1973a) reports the long-term results of a war wound in the left parietal area. The patient suffered severe loss of memory and had all sorts of difficulties with vision, speech, reading, and writing. He was just able to speak and could write well enough to describe his experiences and to try to reconstruct his life. But he suffered, even years later, from what we should call strange illusions:

I'll look to the right of me and be horrified to discover half of my body is gone. I'm terrified—sometimes when I'm sitting down I suddenly feel as though my head is the size of a table, every bit as big—while my hands and feet and torso become very small—Another annoying thing that happens is that sometimes when I'm sitting on a chair, I suddenly become very tall, but my torso becomes terribly short and my head very, very tiny—no bigger than a chicken's head. You can't imagine what this is like even if you tried—it's just got to happen to you.

Of course we don't know what is happening, or not happening in his brain to produce these peculiarities. But they illustrate that what one calls the normal flow of consciousness is the result of the program that maintains one's relation to the world, including its spatial features and one's own bodily form. Notice that he 'suddenly' began to experience these forms of consciousness. We might consider this comparable to the way we 'suddenly' fall asleep or wake up as the program changes.

## What is consciousness?

So the various aspects of consciousness we have considered emphasize first its dependence on the brain and secondly its unreliability for description of the world. Each of us feels sure that we really know what we experience. It is often said that subjective reality is the only 'real' reality. Yet if the brain is altered by drugs or a bullet the experiences of the person give what normal people regard as a very misleading account of the world. The programs of the brain usually provide us with a view of the world that agrees with that of others and is 'correct' enough to allow us to stay alive. But individual consciousness certainly cannot guarantee correctness.

What do we know then about consciousness? It is the name that we apply to the condition of ourselves that we experience and report for most of the day. We realize that there are serious difficulties in specifying the use of the word. Our language is designed to describe our experiences of the world to each other. We get into difficulties when we try to use language to describe the user. But once this is appreciated there is no reason why we should not go on to frame a better language. We are learning how the brain operates, by continually making hypotheses about what it is best to do to meet the needs that its control centres indicate. These continuing operations are thus related to evidence about the body itself and about events and persons around. The person 'myself' is a compound of activities that has grown gradually from my heredity and experience. These activities constitute my mind, which has an amazing unity and continuity in spite of the fact that from time to time it ceases to have the character that we call consciousness. Both the continuity and the consciousness depend upon the continuing operations of the brain. As we learn more about these activities we may hope to become better at describing ourselves both to ourselves and to each other.

So with the assistance of the evidence we have collected let us again examine the concepts that are needed to describe oneself and other persons. In saying that one is conscious one means awake and aware and open to receive and give out information. The capacity to do this depends upon the operations of a system in the head called the brain. One is not directly aware of this brain but the information about its nature and properties is objective and generally available and agreed upon. Use of this new information gives a fresh dimension to our thinking and substantial clarifications in the language by which we describe persons.

## Is the mind a single entity?

The operations of the brain during periods of awareness are commonly referred to as constituting an entity called the mind. Neither the individual himself nor others have any direct perception of this as an entity and in some senses we know even less about it than about the brain. One cannot see or hear or touch a mind, it is not that sort of 'thing'. It clearly has no physical dimensions but is useful as a description of the general mode of operation of the brain. The mind is sometimes described as the functional organization of the brain, but the brain performs many functions of which one is not aware. The entity we refer to as the mind is perhaps that part of the brain's functional organization of which we are conscious. But it is really at best a vague concept. Further information should allow us to replace the single concept of mind and mental activity by others more fully descriptive of the modes of action of brain processes. It is already clear that in the right and left sides of the brain each of us has as it were two minds, with rather distinct capacities. A person may be good at mathematics with his left side but a poor artist on the right. Extending this we know that different parts of the hypothalamus and frontal cortex provide different emotional and motivational capacities. These may control behaviour to varying extents at different times. The conception that each of us has a single entity called the mind already appears over simple. The philosopher Nagel suggests the possibility that one day it will seem quaint that we ever held that a human being is a single person. I think here he is carrying analysis too far. The brain has indeed many parts, and different combinations of them may operate at different times. But the whole system is controlled by one central reticular system and produces in each of us a single stream of consciousness. From moment to moment a single entity 'myself' has to make those decisions about the future course of action upon which life depends.

# 19   Helping, commanding, and obeying

## The evolution of altruism

From the fables of Aesop to the fables of Orwell, men have tried to learn and to teach by using animal analogues of social organization. With the rise of ethology the urge to make such comparisons has recently been very strong, and we have been introduced to a new science called sociobiology (Wilson 1975). But there are risks in this procedure and we must be careful. Our human cultural organizations depend upon a fluent language, which animals do not have. Our societies are regulated by custom, which can be altered in a few years and not only by the slow changes of genes. For these and other reasons it is not easy to draw valid lessons for the present from our pre-human ancestry. The biologist has to be especially careful because questions about our relations to each other are matters of intense concern to everyone, individually and politically. Superficial analogies about ethical questions such as freedom and equality, rights and duties can be misused by interested parties to do great harm.

Yet when this has been said there is no doubt that all our social systems are possible only because we have certain biological characteristics. Cultural evolution cannot be independent of its biological substratum. 'Thus we would expect the genetic system to have various inbuilt safeguards and to provide not a blank sheet for individual cultural development but a sheet at least lightly scrawled with certain tentative outlines' (Hamilton 1975, p. 134). This is, if anything, too cautious. No human societies would exist without the special features of our brains, bodies, and glands. Especially we are all influenced by the pattern of slow growth and long childhood that has been already discussed (Chapter 4).

All social animals have a genetically controlled system of ethics that regulates their responses to each other. This may involve altruism, in the sense either of taking action on behalf of the group although it endangers the individual, or by failing to be selfish, say over the consumption of food or escape from enemies. Biologists differ somewhat in their opinions as to the conditions needed for the evolution of altruism (see Wilson 1975). Wynne-Edwards (1962) has postulated that many animal species have what he has called 'density-dependent conventions', by which they regulate their numbers and prevent over-exploitation of limited food resources. These conventions include the massed daily gatherings of birds such as starlings (known as epideictic displays) and the nesting of sea-birds on particular cliffs, where only those who find a place can reproduce. Individuals are thus held to adopt behaviour that limits their own chance of reproducing but increases the fitness of the group.

In the controversy over this theory geneticists emphasize that only actions that increase the probability of survival of the *individual's* own genes will be selected. There is no such thing as selection for genes just because they are of advantage to the *species*. So altruism will not further the survival of the altruist's own genes unless practised for the benefit of relatives (Chapter 4). Sexual sharing of course has precisely this effect, but how widely can habits of co-operation be spread without corruption by the parasitic actions of non-relatives (Dawkins 1976)? Of course it is doubtful how far human loving and caring as we ordinarily understand them are the products of specific hereditary factors. They are the results of particular personal and social experiences, though there must be some hereditary influences providing the capacity to learn from experience. The question is whether it is proper to insist, as reformers do, that the behaviour of human beings is mainly the result of social and cultural influences and that these can and should be changed? We must not use theories about possible genetic influences in the past to be an excuse for delaying social advances today. Yet it may be that the human patterns of interbreeding have in the past been influenced by the advantage of being altruistic only to those who propagate similar genes. This would be achieved if mating was restricted to small groups, while still allowing for some interchange of individuals between groups. It has been pointed out that carnivores that co-operate in hunting breed mostly within the pack, but that some unmated males change packs, so avoiding excessive inbreeding. Before adoption to his new pack the newcomer must pass a probationary period—to show that he behaves altruistically. Man was probably once a group-hunting carnivore, but this hardly justifies us in concluding that all his elaborate marriage customs and taboos were necessary for the evolution of altruism.

'Kinship' is indeed the dominant structure in the culture of many peoples but it often has little or nothing to do with blood relationships. 'No system of human kinship relations is organised in accord with the genetic coefficients of relationship as known to sociobiologists. Each consists . . . of arbitrary rules of marriage, residence, and descent, from which are generated distinctive arrangements of kinship groups and statuses' (Sahlins 1977, p. 57). Cultural practices involve the relations of human beings to each other and are symbolized in many ways, including kinship. Economic, religious, and other relationships may be much more powerful than selectionist factors, which can only operate slowly. Therefore we can neither discard nor prove the possibility that some human habits have survived because they promoted the spread of genes for altruism.

Geneticists have tried to work out what are the sizes of population, and other conditions, that would be needed to counter the effects of individual selection, which tends of course to break any altruistic convention. It is unlikely that altruism can spread through large, widely interbreeding populations. In general the requirement is that the altruistic act should tend to provide in the next generation a greater proportion of an individual's genes than a selfish act. This is obviously most likely to occur by selection for altruism among relatives, the process called by Maynard Smith 'kin selection' (see Smith 1964 and Hamilton 1975). Altruism is at a maximum among the social insects, where all the members of each colony are descended from one queen and therefore closely related. They help each other and may die in defence of the colony, but they fight members of other colonies, even of the same species. Moreover most of the workers and soldiers are sterile, so their altruism or death does not directly lessen reproductive potential.

Genes for altruism will spread if by the sacrificial actions of an individual more of them are passed on than would have been left without the sacrifice. Thus if a man by his action saves his brother's life but sacrifices his own he must more than double the latter's fitness for reproduction. For a cousin he would have to make an eightfold increase (Haldane 1932). A child seeks to increase its chance of survival by eliciting altruistic behaviour from its parents (see Chapter 9). But this *parental investment* will cease to be of advantage to their shared genes if it becomes so great as to prejudice the parents' ability to invest in *other* offspring (Trivers 1972). It is therefore likely that there has been selection to ensure scaling of the degree of parent–offspring conflict (weaning conflict) to ensure the maximum reproductive success of the family. Further complications arise from the fact that earlier children help in the rearing of sibs. This will also promote their own genes, but the situation will vary according to the attitude of the culture to marriage. Differences in extent of parent-offspring conflict and help given to sibs have been found by some investigators, corresponding to the attitude of cultures to extra-marital coitus (Textor 1967, Hartung 1977). The interconnections of cultural and genetic influences are indeed complicated.

It is clear that true altruism can spread within a species only among those who share genes. This is most likely to occur in semi-closed societies such as packs of hunting carnivores. Dogs and wolves provide some of the closest analogies to human altruism. Apart from helping each other in hunting, orphaned puppies may be cared for by males of the pack. However there are many examples of unselfish behaviour among animals as diverse as termites, ants, birds, and chimpanzees.

It is still a problem how the initial stages of altruism began in nature. In evolutionary terms it only pays to be altruistic if the sacrifice is somehow reciprocated. If the characteristic is due to mutation there is little chance of two mutually helpful individuals meeting, except in small groups. Such genes would perhaps spread well only by genetic drift, a process that occurs in small isolated populations (Wright 1943). This is also the situation in which reciprocal altruism is most likely to be recognized. Moreover cheating is more easily detected in a small group and forms of behaviour likely to limit it can appear (for instance blushing) (see p. 71). Cheating and lying are in fact far more prevalent in man than in animals—speech provides exceptional opportunities for them. If detected and punished within a group they can yet be of advantage to it as against other groups.

One of the ways of increasing the spread of altruism is to decrease the chances of reproduction in unrelated individuals, the process that Wilson calls 'spite'. He suggests that the fact that humans are particularly prone to such behaviour and to lying and deception may be among the factors that have actually promoted the spread of altruism. 'Human beings are keenly aware of their own blood lines and have the intelligence to plot and intrigue.'

Understanding of the theory of group selection and kin selection is still imperfect and we can hardly use it to provide prescriptions for human behaviour. What we do know provides some suggestive insights into the reasons for our tendency to divide into groups. It is clear that the advantages of altruism over selfishness for evolution depend upon many circumstances. This corresponds with our feeling that we are often 'forced to make imperfect choices based on irreconcilable loyalties—between the "rights" and "duties" of self and those of family or tribe, . . . each of which evolves its own code of honor' (Wilson 1975, p. 129).

Biology and especially genetics can thus provide some suggestions about possible reasons for human divisions in the past. I do not see that it can be used to define the proper limits of altruism today. Biology tells us that the duty is to act so as to preserve ones own life and to propagate ones genes. It does *not* tell us how this can best be achieved. Many species of animals and plants achieve success by co-operation, indeed all the colours of flowers proclaim it. Rational human beings have discovered how to save themselves by promoting the lives of other men and of animals and plants, carrying this to the limit that 'all men are brothers'. Geneticists may laugh at this, but neuroscientists, like others who study actual human interactions, will know that we have programs to ensure that we propagate our own genes by recruiting the assistance of others (Chapter 14). To quote Thomas Hobbes, who was keenly aware that natural selfishness is best served by altruism, 'Whosoever therefore holds that it had been best to have continued in that state in which all things were lawful for all men, he contradicts himself. For every man by natural necessity desires that which is good for him: nor is there any that esteems a war of all against all . . . to be good for him. And so it happens, that . . . we get some fellows, that if their needs must be war, it may not yet be against all men, nor without some help.' ((see Milo 1973).

## Kinship systems in animals

Mankind was almost certainly once a group hunter and, as we have seen, this habit provides the situations in which altruism might be expected to evolve. Wolves have a social system similar in some ways to that of man. It is no accident that dogs certainly have an inherited capacity to show recognition that they have done wrong, but cats never show guilt. More relevant is recent evidence that the basis for our own system is to be found among other primates. There is no justification for the attitude that regards 'culture' as a sort of artificial intrusion separate from 'nature' (Fox 1975). 'Our primate cousins have "kinship systems" which contain the elements of human kinship systems.' Studies of monkeys and apes in recent years have shown the great complexity and variety of their social systems, each adapted to a particular way of life. In some species there are polygamous groups, each with one male in dominant control. In others the males associate as a unit with a hierarchy, and there are no breeding units, all the females in the group belong to all the males. Yet in these species, although sexual relationships are brief and promiscuous, the animals fall into clear-cut groups on a *matrilineal* basis. In macacques and chimpanzees these groups of relatives, an old mother and her daughters and sons and their children, are the units that live together, feeding and grooming and so on.

These various forms of social grouping provide in different ways for the spread of genes mainly within small groups, but with provisions for exchange between neighbouring populations. This is just the sort of system that is likely to allow for the spread of altruistic practices and the development and use of new methods of communication. The provisions for the avoidance of incest are particularly interesting in societies that form small groups and families. In animals that live in large herds close inbreeding is unlikely and there is no evidence of incest avoidance. In all higher primates on the other hand a recent study has shown that there are provisions that prevent mating between near relatives (Bischof 1975). There is no need to explain this avoidance as produced by any special capacity to recognize blood relatives. It seems to depend upon a maturational device that provides at adolescence for avoidance of those with whom childhood has been spent, whether parents or sibs or unrelated individuals. Thus in chimpanzees, where sexual play is common among juveniles, when females reach sexual maturity they begin to repel their brother's approaches, but display keen interest in males of other groups.

Incest avoidance in man has the curious characteristic that it is both universal and dependent upon rules, which are often held to be the criteria of 'natural' as opposed to cultural features of man (Lévi-Strauss 1969). Lévi-Strauss explained this by saying that the incest taboo was the step by which the transition from nature to culture was established 'the prohibition of incest is where nature transcends itself'. We can now suggest the possibility that this was a natural transition based on the methods of gene interchange needed to allow the spread of altruism and communication. Curiously enough we may also see here light on the omnipresent features of the Oedipus complex. The fight of the young man with his father may spring from the mechanism that actually ensures the *avoidance* of incest (Bischof 1975). Once again, however, it is necessary to remember that human patterns of culture are regulated by far more complex and immediate concerns than the proper distribution of genes.

## Learning submission and leadership

During the long period of childhood prior to sexual maturity the individual is bound to be subservient to adults, if only because he is genetically programmed to be smaller. It is during this period that the capacity to learn ethical concepts develops (Waddington 1960). If we have innate tendencies to learn the order of words in a sentence there are surely likely to be equal capacities to learn the proper ordering of society. Heredity gives us the outward powers to smile or to frown, and the mood to be happy or angry. It probably also gives us the equipment by which we learn what is considered in society to be right or wrong in our relations with others. It is also likely that all these capacities vary between individuals. What heredity does *not give us is our particular conceptions of morals, rights, and duties.*

The child early learns that his first selfish attitudes must be modified. The sequences by which he does so have been studied by many people from Piaget to the psychoanalysts. The demands for self-sacrifice will seem at first to conflict with his needs for food and comfort, love and sex. Psychoanalysts tend to dramatize these conflicts and it may be that in some individuals they leave traumatic scars, but there is no reason to think that it is 'natural' for them to do so. If the brain has the right capacities to learn, and the environmental conditions provide suitable teaching, then the individual can come to realize that altruism helps him to fulfil his needs within society. This may seem to be facile optimism, but the psychoanalyst deals almost wholly with those in whom the adaptation has been faulty. 'Weaning conflict' is a necessary and 'natural' corollary of the genetic and family situation. Once recognized there is no reason for it to leave scars, especially in small families, where the parents can continue to give sufficient attention to the older children.

## Power

The particular patterns learned in youth of appreciation of the nature of hierarchies, of rights and duties, submission and dominance remains to a large extent throughout life, and all cultures are built upon them. One of the basic experiences is of course of the power of the parent, as the larger creature. This introduces the concept of power, which pervades many cultures, perhaps all of them. It is true that agreement is the basis of social organization and there may be some fully egalitarian democracies. But leadership and the exercise of power are also conspicuous features of human relations, as they are of some animal altruism. As a small example, I recently startled a group of guinea-fowls in the woods and watched the male chivvying the females to safety in the bushes and even turning back to collect a laggard, at potential risk to himself. More relevant are recent studies by Chance (1975) of leadership in primates. He distinguishes between agonistic and hedonic cohesion in a group. Among baboons the leader establishes discipline by neck-biting and other punishments. But among chimpanzees the leader is the one who displays most enthusiasm when they find fruit, and they all jump about and shout and kiss (like footballers after a goal). This system of selecting a leader is probably more flexible and allows changes of leaders without the disruption of a fight.

Some sociologists argue that in man the power to make decisions must come from individuals, and that leadership is inevitable. We have seen several reasons for believing that human beings may be specially programmed to recognize and respond to others (p. 9). Carved symbols of individuals are among the oldest known artistic objects and these may represent leaders or even symbolize leadership (p. 148). The concept of power in western society is still surprisingly crude. 'Many Americans equate masculinity with power' (Kaplan 1964). No doubt this is true of other societies too, and it probably has its basis in the extra growth of both sexes at puberty and especially of the male. Power has been defined as the ability of a person to influence the behaviour of others. It is held to be something that can be exercised by coercion or reward, as Chance would say, either agonistically or hedonically (see Kahn 1964). The attitude that power is essential implies that 'disagreement over goals is typical of human organizations', and that 'power begets conflict'. If it is true that we are so prone to disagree it is curious that we have evolved so far. And yet we see such assumptions and attitudes all around us.

## Types of leadership and loyalty

Recent experimental studies of various ways of exercising power and of reducing conflict tend to modify these attitudes. Investigators of leadership in business management now often emphasize that its success depends on the acceptability of the personality of the leader, and his 'attraction', and that both of these are reduced by 'coercive power' (French 1964). There is considerable evidence that sharing of managerial responsibility throughout a factory can give gains in productivity (though it also raises difficulties). A few studies even emphasize the paradox that the 'leader' gains in power from adopting a position of subordination:

> A leader is best
> When people barely know that he exists
> Not so good when people obey and acclaim him
> Worst when they despise him
>
> (*Lao-Tzu on Taoism*, trans. W. Brynner; see Waddington 1960)

Another emphasis of sociologists is on the need for common goals and values throughout an organization. For the biologist and perhaps the anthropologist these may seem to be nearer to 'natural' forms of human organization than the competitive model that has been the basis for much western industry. Max Weber, the father of sociology, classified types of authority into charismatic, traditional, and rational (or legal). We have seen reason to think that response to a person may be as it were biologically deeper than to a system. Payment by results, for example by money, may be less satisfying than by the reward of acceptance by individuals or groups, which is called by Gellner (1959) the 'ethic of loyalty'. There are signs that these factors are becoming increasingly recognized, in the organization of work, for instance in China and Japan. Bureaucratic organization, with monetary rewards, may be 'rational', but it is not necessarily efficient.

If we must have leaders can we say anything about ways of improving them? I do not think we are in a position to say much about the characteristics of their brain programs. Military leadership that is charismatic may be successful in war, but the training of soldiers in peace time often attracts bureaucrats. Moreover the authoritarian is often a person unable to accept his own sexual and other desires and hence comes to suppress them and disapprove of them in others (see Rothenstein 1960). Paradoxically authoritarians often have suppressed feminine characteristics that lead them to submit all too readily to superauthorities and directors. The education of military men should be an important priority for all societies. Provision of insight into themselves for potential leaders might do something to alleviate the dangers of our future (see p. 173).

Professionalizing violence involves legitimizing and controlling patterns of behaviour that are normally taboo in civilized society (see Dixon 1976). There is evidence that, as one would expect, there is a relationship between the type of personality that is ready to accept this situation and a liking for soldiering. But, further, the trait of 'authoritarianism', as measured by a standard test was found to be correlated with obsessive traits and rigidity of opinions. In a study of military disasters Dixon found that such characteristics in the leaders were among the chief factors responsible for defeat. Failure of decision and leadership in a crisis may sometimes be due to the fact that some of the people attracted to soldiering have personalities that are not really suited for warfare.

## Obeying

Whatever may be the features that characterize a leader it is certain that human social order depends upon acceptance of rules by the led. Obedience is the 'dispositional cement' that binds society, and the capacity for it presumably has a hereditary background. 'The functioning of a social system as a moral order requires a capacity for self-objectivication on the part of the actor, self-identification with his own conduct over time, and appraisal of his own conduct and that of others in a common framework of socially recognised and sanctioned standards of behaviour' (Hallowell; see Waddington 1960, p. 169). Unfortunately these fine words outline a characteristic that may yet undo us all. It has been proved in a well-known experiment that people will readily perform tasks even though they believe them to be very hurtful to others (Milgram 1974). In this study the majority of the subjects were found to be ready to inflict pain (as they supposed) when instructed to do so by an authority. This unpleasant experiment underlines the dangers, now that with modern technology the soldier has become an automaton. His killing is done not in anger but in *inhumanity*. People may *say* that disobedience to immoral orders is proper, but the majority of them act differently and will obey. This may yet prove to be the 'fatal flaw that nature has designed into us, and which in the long run gives our species only a modest chance of survival' (Eibl-Eibesfeldt 1971).

The existence of moral rules is one of the universals of human cultures and behaviour, but the details of them vary greatly. The capacity to respond socially is probably genetically inherited, but particular customs are transmitted culturally. So the capacity to learn during the long period of childhood appears once again as a central human feature. Culture is transmitted by virtue of this genetically determined pattern of growth and development of the brain.

The factors that ensure the development of an ethical sense are thus both external and internal. It certainly does not mature spontaneously as do the capacities for walking and to some extent for talking (Chapter 16). As Piaget puts it, 'The individual must receive a command from another individual', but there must be a capacity to accept it, 'unilateral respect or the respect felt by the small for the great plays an essential part' (see Waddington 1960, p. 156).

Psychoanalysts have investigated how this 'respect' develops to become conscience, and the basis of moral behaviour. This building of the personality is at the very centre of the system of hypotheses and actions that constitutes the model in the brain, which we are holding to be organized around the attributes of persons. The child recognizes the 'goodness' in those around him, when it assists him, and the 'badness' when his parents frustrate him. According to Klein he projects these feelings on to the others and then introjects their characteristics into himself. 'The child's mental capacity establishes people, in the first place his parents, within his own mind, as if they were part of himself' (Waddington 1960). (I would say within his own brain.) And so by a series of steps are built up the child's knowledge of the concepts of good and evil and also his tendencies to aggression and to guilt. According to Klein the self-condemnation for this aggressiveness is the basis of conscience. Like all other sorts of knowledge these must depend upon organizations of the nerve cells in the brain. Even the disposition to act conscientiously must have a physical basis, how otherwise does it persist when we are not being conscientious or are asleep?

The strains and conflicts that build up around the ambiguities of good and evil are the price that men have had to pay throughout the ages since the power to acquire self-knowledge first evolved. If it is true that such self-knowledge is an essential element in social behaviour then it is also the basis of all culture, as Waddington has emphasized. He concludes that the efficiency with which differing ethical beliefs function to allow cultural evolution is a criterion by which we can decide upon their 'value'. Needless to say he rejects the charge that this is a 'fallacy of naturalism' (see p. 140).

## The ethics of human variety

Particular notions about such fundamental matters as rights and duties, freedom and equality vary with cultural patterns and are certainly not mainly determined by genetic inheritance. However once again we have to remember that the very capacity to transmit culture depends upon our long period of development, and the particular capabilities we may have for learning. There are certainly genetic differences that will affect such capacities. Characteristics that are known to have an inherited factor are tendencies to dominance, introversion/extroversion, physical strength, neuroticism, and schizophrenia (see Wilson 1975, Lerner and Libby 1976). It is impossible at present to say whether selection for particular capabilities has influenced the direction of cultural growth in the past or whether it still does so now. It is sometimes objected that the period of human cultural evolution has been too short for there to have been much basic genetic divergence in cultural capacity. But physical adaptation to particular conditions has certainly occurred relatively recently. Presumably all human beings had dark skins until one million years ago, perhaps much less. Selection that has produced the genes needed to allow synthesis of vitamin D in the skin may also have modified learning capacities to make them more suitable for the

rigors of northern climates than for life in the warm conditions in which
man began.

We do not yet understand what determines the direction of cultural
evolution. For instance many cultures have division into classes, each playing a different role in society. But it is very doubtful whether these classes
have a genetic basis. In India there is little difference in blood groups
between castes that have been distinct for centuries (Sanghvi 1966). Classes
usually have different rights, duties, and rewards in society. Notoriously
some classes may be very poor, very unhealthy, and have much shorter lives
than others. This is not a characteristic only of 'backward' societies. In the
U.S.A. in 1973 non-whites had an expectation of life at birth about *seven
years less than whites* (Honderich 1975). In England and Wales the poorest
of our five classes of people (those classed as 'unskilled') had in 1971 a *life-
expectancy, at age 25, 3·5 years less* than those in the richest (professional)
class. If all men are brothers it is difficult to feel that such condemnation to
early death is justified on the basis of the functions that people in different
classes perform. Honderich notes that we are not shocked by such differences, as we are by, say, violence or disorder, because they are less visible.
We take them for granted as entrenched in the order of society, but biology
certainly does not tell us that it is right to do so.

Variety, whether inherited or acquired, is indeed a valuable feature for the
continued survival of man. Many different sorts of people are needed for
life in different parts of the world and for the functioning of society, beginning with differentiation into males and females. Man is a polymorphic
species, genetically and culturally, and for survival we require that this shall
continue to be so. But we are almost wholly ignorant about the genetical
foundations for the classes that we reward so unequally. Nor have geneticists
any reliable programs for improving us. The mixture of genes is so wide that it is
not possible to give more than a very general forecast as to the effects of
particular social practices on the gene pool. If a geneticist was given dictatorial
powers over reproduction in order to improve the population he would not
know how to begin. So called positive eugenics is not now feasible and perhaps
never will be.

## The right to life

The corollary of the value for mankind of this great variety and our ignorance of its basis seems to be that all individuals have equal rights to life. But
this implies that they have the responsibility and capacity to make some use
of life for the benefit both of self and society. Is it humane or sensible to
extend this right to a creature that shows no sign that it is ever likely to
develop these capacities even to a minimum extent? Of course the problem is
to decide who should be the judges in such matters. Equally difficult prob-

lems arise over questions of the right to reproduce. If all variety is valuable, then all have a right to reproduce. Yet some heritable conditions, such as haemophilia, impose such handicap and suffering that disincentives to their propagation seem to be both humane and biologically sound. Such questions largely revolve around the methods used for restraint. Granted the essential rights to life and reproduction, compulsory birth control is repellent. Persuasion and disincentives may not seem logically better, but do not raise the same revulsion.

A society whose medical and other welfare procedures lead to unacceptable population increases needs somehow to introduce restraints on the right to reproduce. All species regulate their numbers, mostly by inherited devices. In man the 'natural' way to do this is to use the brains with which we are so amply provided. Even if it be agreed that limitation is sensible there remains the very difficult question of whether it should be differential. It is true that we do not know enough to practise negative eugenics, but equally there is no guarantee that welfare practices will not increase the prevalence of 'undesirable' genes, or decrease desirable ones, for example those providing immunity against diseases. These are risks that we must simply be prepared to face. This is not an excessive price to pay for preventing people from suffering and dying from these diseases. Moreover in some cases we can eliminate the disease itself, as is happening with malaria (see Medawar and Medawar 1977).

Of course it is important to think about the effects of reduced selection on the future. But those who profess most alarm about this often have a disguised interest, say against state medicine or in favour of the belief that illness is God's punishment for sin (again see Medawar and Medawar 1977). In at least one case where such deterioration would be expected if poorer classes are 'genetically inferior' there has been actual improvement instead. Poorer people have larger families, in Scotland as elsewhere. But the study of a large number of children there showed that the average intelligence had not decreased, as would be expected, but actually increased substantially over ten years (if I.Q. tests have any value as measures of this) (Thomson 1949). These are all matters about which biological knowledge can be helpful. But decisions as to how such knowledge is to be applied depend upon individual and collective decisions as to the weight to be given to many considerations.

## Rights, duties and freedom

As social creatures we obviously all have duties and obligations to our groups. These are defined by custom, as also is the extent of the individual's right to be sustained by group facilities. The particular details of the extent and availability of both duties and rights are decided by each culture and the biologist cannot give very much help in the difficult problems that they raise. Whether a culture is authoritarian or democratic there will inevitably be conflicts between the desires of its individuals and the requirements of the group. It is especially important to emphasize that there are no simple biological criteria by which to decide the proper limits of disagreement on such fundamental questions as liberty and freedom to criticize. The communication of information about an endless variety of matters is perhaps our most fundamental biological feature, differentiating us from all other species. This does not establish, however, any principle by which we can decide the proper limits of protest or violence when freedom of communication is denied.

The problem of the source of the authority of governments and the limits of the duty to obey them has occupied a great part of political thought. Anyone who accepts the benefits of society has obviously some duties towards it. But this extent will surely vary with the *fairness* of the society. The duties of a slave are not the same as those of a company director (see Honderich 1975). No society is perfect or eternal and all will have to change and to evolve. Privileged classes will resist change, and violence may be justified if not practised for its own sake but because it is sincerely believed to be necessary to promote aims of equality and freedom. Clearly freedom is not absolute. A social creature cannot expect to be allowed to try to destroy his society without opposition. But the biologist can only emphasize that the development and transmission of new ideas is the very essence of the human method of evolution. Human individuals differ from animals in being able to act according to information received not from two parents only, but from many sources. The wide spreading of information and ideas, and their continued refreshment from many new sources, is the only guarantee that future human development and evolution will avoid the dangers that we face. If men are above apes it is because of this dissemination of new sorts of information. Failure to allow discussion of possible ways to change our cultures is the surest recipe for guaranteeing that we shall be damaged by their inadequacies

Perhaps the most difficult of all the questions that face us are those concerned with equality and opportunity, both within cultures and between them. It is obvious that every individual has some right to the facilities of society, and the easy extension is that in principle each has an equal right to all facilities. It is not obvious whether or not this is the best prescription for success within a culture now, or in future. Still less is it clear that we can attach any meaning to the concept of the 'rights' of larger components of the human race, such as nations. Can it be 'right' that life-expectancy at birth is 37 years in Nigeria but 75 in England (for females)?

There are certainly genetic differences between different parts of the human population and some of these have in the past provided effective adaptation to climatic and other conditions. Dark skins have been better for life in the tropics and light skins where there is little daylight, but do such restrictions need to continue now? The variations in our characteristics may have been the secret of much of human success in living in all parts of the world in the past, and may continue to be so. Circumstances change and loss of variation is likely to be dangerous for any species. We certainly should not aim to become one homogeneous human mass. The inherent conflicts within and between individuals and groups are themselves suffi-cient to prevent this from happening. For this reason we can welcome competition, provided it does not endanger us all. But competition alone certainly does not provide a realistic biological basis for a social species such as man. In fact once again we meet the ambiguity of the two types of human need, for his own advancement and for that of those around who support him. This conflict has to be resolved within each individual and each society and throughout the world. Some hold that social inequality is an inevitable feature of social organization and that the repeated revolutionary revolts of the underprivileged ensure continual change (Dahrendorf 1969). Such cyclical views are a pessimistic contrast to the optimism of Marx that we can achieve 'The genuine resolution of the conflict between man and nature and man and man' (see Billig 1976). Perhaps sociology and biology together will some day provide a science that tells us which forecast may be expected to come true.

# 20   Enjoying, playing, and creating

## The necessity of art

In these next two chapters we have special opportunities to test whether study of the programs of the brain can really help us to understand ourselves. Art and religion are surely among the most truly characteristic human activities. Can we learn anything from the actions within the brain that accompany them? Aesthetic pleasures and religious beliefs are very precious, and some people probably feel that these are parts of life that cannot and indeed should not be subjects of scientific enquiry. I sympathize with their fears, but believe to the contrary that knowledge about the brain can enlarge our capacities for imagination and perception, for appreciation, for understanding the significance of our lives, and for deepening our religious beliefs. Proper study of the organization of the brain shows that belief and creative art are essential and universal features of all human life. They are not mere peripheral luxury activities. They are literally the most important of all the functional features that ensure human homeostasis.

I must explain and defend these large statements. The next chapter will examine some of the ways in which beliefs operate, and will discuss why they are so important. In this chapter I suggest that aesthetic creation and enjoyment are fundamental features of human life. They are activities in which the brain is operating in the same way as it does in daily life, but as it were at a higher level of intensity. All human perception is a form of creative activity. The notion that seeing or hearing consist only in receiving messages from the outside is a great mistake. In seeing we are not looking at the image on the retina in the same way as we look at a picture on the wall. In all perception we are engaged in creating images from the few clues that the senses provide (Chapter 12). The products of artists are symbols of this continuous creative activity of our lives. We appreciate them because they express and amplify these constructions that we all make every day.

## Measuring appreciation

The question of the nature and significance of art has puzzled thinkers at least since Plato and Aristotle (see Wollheim 1968, 1976). We cannot hope here to do justice to all the many views that have been put forward. Psychologists have recently tried to make the subject more precise by obtaining quantitative data about the shapes and sounds that people prefer. In this way they hope to provide objective measurements instead of the usual subjective appraisals about art. We shall follow this science of aesthetics so far as possible, but the subject is so complicated and the workings of the brain so little understood that it is often still necessary to rely on vague opinions and judgements rather than on precise measurements.

The science of aesthetics, stemming from the work of Wundt (1874) and Fechner (1876) in the last century, tries to express the degrees of pleasure that any situation gives in terms of the amount of *arousal* that is produced (for summaries and history see Berlyne 1971, Pickford 1972). Their studies showed that increased interest and excitement in anything gives pleasure, but if it becomes too intense it is painful or distasteful (Fig. 20.1). The electroencephalogram (EEG) has often been used in the attempt to measure the degree of arousal. This provides direct experimental evidence for Wundt's curve and it may result from the operations of the activating reticular formation of the core brain and the reward systems (Chapter 14). In this way we certainly gain the beginnings of a basis for a scientific study of aesthetics, but unfortunately there is still very little precise quantitative information about these activating and reward systems in humans. Our daily lives and perceptual activities continue satisfactorily because of the rewards that come from those pleasure systems. They are the guarantors for the continuation of life. They alone can provide the smooth and integrated working of the whole brain program that ensures a successful life. They are continually influencing our thoughts, words and actions, urging us, as it were, to do things that are satisfactory.

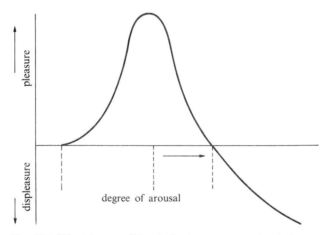

Fɪɢ. 20.1. Wundt's curve. The relation between arousal and pleasure or displeasure. (After Berlyne 1967.)

## The search for satisfaction

The production of satisfying situations or stories, objects, pictures, buildings or clothes is clearly an active process. It may be less obvious that pleasure in them, and indeed all enjoyment of the situations around us, is also not passive. It involves a search for the structure, meaning, and significance of the object for oneself. The significance may be intellectual or emotional or both of these. This search for satisfaction goes on continuously all day. Often it follows a routine program under the control of the activating system, so that we hardly notice our daily surroundings. But we are quickly alerted by new and interesting objects or occurrences. There is a continuous interaction between signals flowing up and down these immensely intricate nervous pathways, the activating system keeps the sensory system alert, looking all the time for interesting data in what goes on around. The whole brain operates first in inborn patterns and only gradually develops its individual program of life by personal experience and cultural influences. The reward systems monitor and select what is to come in and criticize what goes out, ensuring that the actions performed from moment to moment are appropriate and effective in relation to the overall life plan that has been devised over the years.

Many of our actions as the days proceed involve continual search by the eyes, ears, nose, and brain for items of interest or satisfaction. The eyes in particular are never still while we are awake. The brain programs cause them to search the world for information that suits us (Chapter 12). We spend our lives trying to fit the events that we see to the programs of our expectations. Works of art are the symbols that this process of living is proceeding satisfactorily. Some of them serve to confirm our expectations, for instance 'naturalistic' or religious pictures, or well-known music. They reassure us that things are ordered as we supposed. Many people who understand little of composition or style yet find great satisfaction in pictures of familiar things, say of faces, or of horses or of landscapes. The movement in a ballet together with the perfection of sound of the music is a wonderful symbol of what life should be like. Other works provide the stimulus that awakens new interest in the search, for example cubist pictures that introduce us to new perceptions of space, or the emotions and trains of thought aroused by a good poem or novel, or the puns and paradoxes of James Joyce.

The activities that go to the creation and enjoyment of works of art are thus quintessentially those by which the brain, working every day as a creative agent, synthesizes input from the world to make a satisfactory life. This is why I say that for human societies the creative aesthetic and artistic activities are among the most important things that we do. Of course without simpler biological homeostatic functions such as eating and reproduction there would be no life. But these are actions that we share with the millions of species that have no art. In man the mundane daily activities themselves depend upon the special cerebral powers that allow communication and thus social life. The creations and satisfactions of art include and symbolize both our individual acts of perception and the expression to others of what we perceive. These are the very brain actions that give us the powers of communication by which we obtain all the rest, food, shelter, sex, and social life.

These are large claims and the artist himself may be disposed to repudiate them. He does not write poems or paint or compose music or design a building with such thoughts openly before him. He says that he produces his works 'because he wants to'—and this is just the point. His creation is valuable *because* it is pleasing or significant for him. The results of his choice symbolize the active achievement of satisfaction, which is the essence of living. Incidentally it is easy to see why dogmatists, whether religious propagandists or politicians of the right or left, tend to dislike new forms of art. Art embodies the rival doctrine that life is worth while for its own sake, irrespective of any ideology.

It is difficult to know how best to express the depth of this relationship between artistic creation and the daily programs of the brain. Most of us have an awareness that the relationship is there, at all levels from the most abstract to the most practical. Even the most philistine person, or the poorest, has feelings for design and even symbolism, for instance in clothes or cartoons, in advertisements or dance music. Questions of symbolism, design, symmetry, and balance enter into the production of almost any of the objects around us, for whatever sort of use.

Some anthropologists suggest that brain programs with certain structural characteristics can be found in all the different walks of life (see p. 12). Such structures are made especially apparent in the creations of artists, since these symbolize living. Edmund Leach (1977) puts it like this, 'The mental operations of any human designer are circumscribed not only by the qualities of his materials and by his objectives but by the design of the human brain itself.' My contention will be that works of art satisfy in proportion as they epitomize and bring to the surface these basic features of our life programs, and also find new features that we had not recognized before.

## Symbolism and reality

One of Freud's pronouncements was that the artist moulds his fancies into 'truths of new kind, which are valued by men as precious reflections of reality' (1911). He emphasized that such reflections are not less true because they are metaphorical or symbolic, finding exciting similarities rather than stating logical propositions. My love is indeed like a red, red rose. The question why this is true and in what sense it is true is near the centre of our enquiry and I believe that the study of the brain can help us to find an answer that will satisfy both the philosopher and the artist. I suppose many of us who think about life feel that one of our ambitions is to learn how to combine exact thinking with the symbolism that satisfies emotion. To combine metonymy or logic with metaphor, one might say. We try to understand the relation of these two sorts of truth. One of the values of works of art is that they make us face this problem. Reading, or hearing music, or looking at pictures can help us to understand the twin mysteries of exact description and symbolic representation. Is Picasso's representation of a toad more or less like one than a photograph? (Fig. 20.2). Which of these two statues gives a fuller representation of femininity? (Fig. 20.3). As Picasso himself once said, 'Reality is more than the thing itself' (see Collier 1972). An excellent analysis of such problems is given by Collier in discussion of Picasso's *Guernica*. Here we have a representation of all the horrors of war, hatred, and destruction (Fig. 20.4). Among the many symbols that he uses to rouse these responses look at the horse: see the simplicity of the clues, and how his imagination and feelings of horror work upon yours.

FIG. 20.2. *The Toad* by Pablo Picasso. (1949), lithograph. (Arts Council of Great Britain; © by S.P.A.D.E.M. Paris, 1978.)

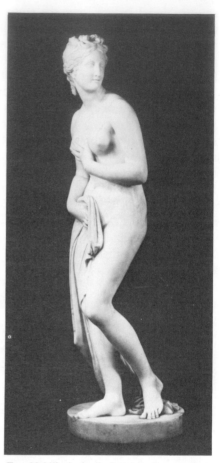

FIG. 20.3(*b*). A classical statue of a nymph (a copy in white marble in the Wellcome collection. Reproduced by courtesy of the Wellcome Trustees.)

FIG. 20.3(*a*). Pre-dynastic Egyptian figurine (30 cm high). (Reproduced by courtesy of the British Museum.)

You instantly recognize a horse, but how distorted. Twisted head, nostrils distended with agony. Why are the teeth all wrong? The eyes are pinpoints of fear. At the centre of all the tongue, not soft, but a sword. It is the very image of violence and a violent response to it.

In thinking about such questions we learn what is involved in communication, in coding, and in abstraction. Thus we examine the nature of reality itself and our relation to it, which is entirely by coded signals and their

Fig. 20.4. *Guernica* by Pablo Picasso (1937, May – early June). Oil on canvas, 11′ 5½″ × 25′ 5¾″. On extended loan to the Museum of Modern Art, New York from the artist's estate; © by S.P.A.D.E.M. Paris, 1978.

interpretation by our emotions (Chapter 7). These are the very questions that have come up over and over again in our examination of the programs of life and of the brain. This is what I mean when I say that the work of the artist is at the very centre of human activities.

How then does he manage to perform his wondrous functions? There is of course no one single way. We are all creating new forms every day, and at the most general level the artist simply helps with the act of perception. He gives us new ways of seeing or hearing or thinking. 'We know only two realities: the one around and the one within us. The first reality is the Universe; the second is the life of the psyche. Outside is in space, inside is in time, art brings them together. The work of art, far from being an ornament, . . . lies at the heart of the mystery of Being.' By art man's 'inner life . . . becomes inscribed in space . . .' (Huyghe 1972, p. xi). These are perhaps somewhat poetical and even obscure metaphorical dicta, but they try to formulate the problem of consciousness that we have skirted around so often. The bringing together of universe and psyche goes on every minute of the day in each of us. The artist cannot solve the mystery any better than the rest of us but he brings it to our attention and gives us some satisfaction by showing and sharing this puzzle of what is 'real'.

## Symbolism in the brain and in art

When we perceive anything we respond only to a small selective sample from all the possible combinations that could be recorded from the sights and sounds of the world around. As we look or listen the sample of inputs that we choose is actively selected because it speaks of people or objects that concern us (Chapter 12). Each object is separated from the lights and shadows around it because we have learned its significance as an object. These selected complexes of nerve signals serve as symbols of those features of the world that interest us. It is useful to use the word symbol in this context as a name for the nerve impulses and brain processes that occur during perception (Chapter 7). It is indeed a word used in many senses, but one useful connotation is that it is a sign that has emotional importance. Firth (1973) gives as a definition, '*Symbol*—where a sign has a complex series of associations, often of emotional kind, and difficult (some would say impossible) to describe in terms other than partial representation.' He is speaking here as an anthropologist, about religious symbols, but we need exactly that concept to express how certain sets of nerve processes come to represent events in the world. Once we realize that the brain itself works all the time with arbitrary symbols we begin to understand how all works of art can be understood. They are symbols, in spoken words, or on canvas, or in musical sound that somehow correspond to the code of the symbolism of the brain. That code is partly innate, but also largely learned. Similarly some of our responses to works of art are immediate and universal, but most of them depend upon learning the code that the artist is using. Every painter uses a code that is partly conventional and partly his own, Gombrich (1972) quotes Sir Winston Churchill's remarkably acute understanding of the importance of coding:

> The canvas receives a message dispatched usually a few seconds before from the natural object. But it has come through a post office *en route.* It has been transmitted in code. It has been turned from light into paint. It reaches the canvas as a cryptogram. Not until it has been placed in its correct relation to everything else that is on the canvas can it be deciphered, is its meaning apparent, is it translated once again from mere pigment into light.

The process of painting is thus an extra stage between looking and understanding. The coding and symbolism of the painter must correspond to that which goes on in the brain. We refer to the signs on canvas or in words as symbols *because* they arouse interest in us on account of their connection with our life pattern or program, which is guided by our emotional needs. In short, we make each moment of perception part of the *structure* of our thinking and feeling.

## The creation of abstract representations

Our thesis has been that this structure of the operations going on in the brain is one unified whole, all its many parts related, and to some extent interdependent. The whole program has a tendency to relate its operations to features of human beings and particularly to the real or imagined characteristics of one's own body, mind, or brain program. Man is both a symbol-using creature and also a fabricator, both of words and objects. The things that he makes inevitably reflect the operations of the needs of the symbol-using system within. If it was useful for paleolithic men planning a hunt to think and speak about game, then it was also 'natural' for them to try to 'make' animals by carving or painting upon the walls of the caves. Similarly today, those whose brains are full of concern for sex or of violence introduce symbols of them in their paintings or poems or films, or perhaps by graffiti on the lavatory walls. Representation, like thought, is a substitute for reality. As Gombrich has pointed out a child makes a hobby horse out of a stick for *use* (1972). It is not at first for communication, though it comes to be an image of a horse. Substitution may precede portrayal, and creation precede communication. After all the meaning of 'imagination' is the making of an image. And, further, the hobby horse need not have all the features of a horse. Indeed all it needs at the absolute minimum is the capacity to be made to *go*. It can be effective even if it is exceedingly abstract, provided that its symbolism stimulates the necessary imagination and action.

There are, incidentally, lessons here for those who are trying to unravel brain functions. The symbolic representations *in* the brain are probably themselves very abstract, no more than just sufficient to carry their meaning. Every cartoonist knows how to play upon such simple clues. Whatever the cells are that serve to represent grandmother's face they do not have to indicate every wrinkle (p. 128). They might outline the merest hint of granny's features and the structured operations of the brain do the rest, using all the other information to create the image of that particular old lady.

## Principles of aesthetics

The artist joins us, then, in the activity of perceiving, in our search for relevant features of the world. Psychologists, from Fechner, in the last century onwards, have been able to provide some clues as to the features that are generally found to be satisfying in the visual arts (for review see Pickford 1972). Indeed this has been a subject of study by artists through the centuries. One of the very well-established preferences is for the ratio known as the golden section. If people are asked to divide a line so as to give the most pleasing proportions their choices will tend to be like this:

A                              B                                                      C

where BC is 62% of AC. This ratio appears in many different forms, though the reasons for it are not clear.

By study of such preferences Fechner and his successors have as it were codified the principles of experimental aesthetics. He suggested that 'the fundamental principle of aesthetics may be briefly summarized by saying that human beings in order to enjoy the contemplation of some object require to find therein a kind of unified variety'. Many studies since have verified and amplified this view. Eysenck (1968) and Eysenck and Castle (1970) for instance, investigated it by asking people to look at various polygonal shapes and to place them in order of preference (Fig. 20.5). These figures were produced earlier by Birkhoff (1933) to test his theory that $M$, the 'aesthetic measure' is proportional to the degree of order in the elements of a figure (symmetry, equal sides, etc.), divided by its complexity (number of sides, angles, etc.). He expressed this as $M = O/C$ but Eysenck found that the results for 90 subjects he tested agreed better with $M = O \times C$. That is to say preference is the *product* of the elements of order and complexity. In a somewhat similar study Smets (1973) found that subjects preferred a moderate degree of complexity (Fig. 20.6).

There have been many investigations of this sort. Some of them have

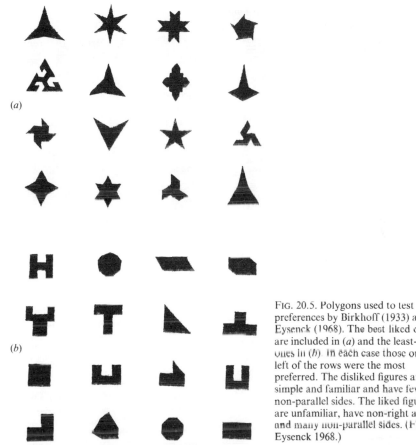

FIG. 20.5. Polygons used to test preferences by Birkhoff (1933) and Eysenck (1968). The best liked ones are included in (*a*) and the least-liked ones in (*b*). In each case those on the left of the rows were the most preferred. The disliked figures are simple and familiar and have few non-parallel sides. The liked figures are unfamiliar, have non-right angles and many non-parallel sides. (From Eysenck 1968.)

related the preferences of their subjects to their culture. In the project known as Cantometrics, the songs and dances preferred by societies from different parts of the world were analysed in relation to their modes of life (hunting, fishing, farming, industry, etc.). Relationships were found between singing and economic organization. Where men and women work together in complex groups there is rhythmic and melodic polyphony in their songs. In stratified, male-dominated communities people do not sing together. Other studies have shown that there is a preference for complex art in rich urban societies and for simpler forms in more isolated communities (Kavolis 1968). This rather obvious conclusion can be related to the degree of arousal and information intake, which was mentioned earlier. In cities arousal is already high, so the art forms preferred are those that make it higher still. But high stimulation is too much for simple people (see Berlyne 1971).

"Complexity"
(*a*)  Information H=225 bits  (=Redundancy)   (*b*) Information H=900 bits

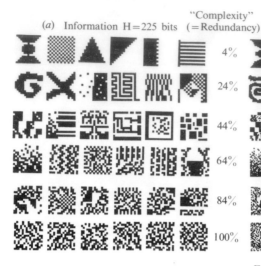

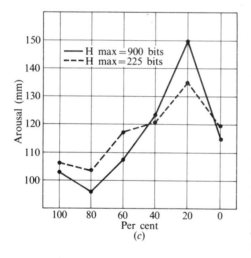

FIG. 20.6. Experiment to show arousal by figures of different degrees of complexity (redundancy). The figures are designed to show differences in amount of information (*H* = number of squares filled to make the pattern) and redundancy (*R* = regularity, symmetry, continuity, etc.). The figures in (*a*) have $H = 225$ bits, in (*b*) they have $H = 900$ bits. In each figure the redundancy increases from above downwards.

The 'arousal value' of the figures was measured by showing them one at a time to 85 people and recording for how long the alpha wave in the EEG was blocked (desynchronized. In (*c*) the time is shown as mm of distance on the polygraph recorder. The figures with 'complexity' measured at about 20 per cent gave the maximum arousal, as measured by the duration of the EEG blocking, the very complex ones much less. (After Smets 1973.)

These are just some examples of experimental aesthetics. They provide quantitative measures of some aspects of preference and some information about the principles of satisfactory design. They may not seem to be very profound, yet such studies and principles can provide useful guidance for those who design to please. They may be helpful for instance in the design of clothes or house furnishings or wallpapers, for users in different communities, and also in advertising. Many people certainly prefer systems of moderate complexity to those that are either very simple or very elaborate. They like variety, but also regularity, symmetry, and continuity of line.

Obviously this is only a very small sample of some of the cruder features of visual art that are found to be attractive. Much of the appeal of a picture, poem, or song depends upon its particular metaphoric or symbolic evocations, for instance of family or country, religion or sex. To reduce these to formulae would be an impossible task. Gestalt psychologists, such as Arnheim (1954), believe that some forms express emotional states because they share human postures. Thus weeping willows are droopy and sad (Berlyne 1971). I have often wondered whether there is a special affinity in our brain programs for tree shapes, which for me have a particular attraction. This is one of the reasons that I enjoy studying the tree-like forms of nerve cells. There may be more in this sort of view than is usually allowed. Appreciations of metaphorical symbols may be related to inborn emotions and the attitudes that express them, for instance of sorrow or of joy. Concepts of opposition and balance, again, and of golden means may be part of the fundamental structure of our brain programs as they are also of our bodily structure. Many people have called attention to the relationship of forms and colours. Curves are serene, but angles are active. Red is slow but blue is fast, and this has even been held to be related to the wavelengths of the colours. It is not wise to dismiss such ideas until we know more of the structure of the human brain program and the way it develops. It may be that a lot of our responses to shapes and colours and sounds depend basically on inborn capacities, but of course immensely modified by cultural influences. Some of these stimuli and responses may be looked upon as similar to the sign stimuli and releasers of ethologists, particularly those connected with human features.

By playing upon these and many other responses artists have stimulated and assisted mankind in many ways over the centuries. If the primary aim of art is to please it also has an endless series of secondary uses. 'Practical' functions of art are more prevalent today than ever. We need only think of the immense numbers of people who still worship, or at least give respect to, visual images, such as those of the Virgin or the Crucifixion. Advertisers are continually searching for new ways to attract us to their products, and I do not need to emphasize how well they understand that the human brain program is especially attracted by human features, especially those of pretty girls. Fabrication of all the goods of modern commerce involves design, whether of clothes, motor cars, houses, or anything else. The design of each product may become a symbol, useful alike to manufacturers and consumer.

## Pleasure in music

To speak of music is surely to speak of pleasure. It exists only to be enjoyed. Almost all human beings are affected by patterns of tunes and rhythm. To be moved by them is a characteristic trait of our species. The patterns that are preferred vary with culture, but some features are universal and they help us to understand the fundamental structuring of human brain processes. A child indeed responds to music without being taught. Everyone can recognize a march, or tell the difference between a dirge and a dance. It is curious that although the more sophisticated patterns of music can be appreciated only after much experience, yet music (of a sort) is played in almost every public place, and presumably gives some pleasure. What is it that makes some sounds pleasing to so many people?

Music has been called the language of emotion. It is a language that is sensuous rather than factual. It suggests and portrays emotions. Any emotional response is a combination of sensation and the response to it. For example certain stimuli arouse say fear, sadness, or sex, and in each case the particular emotion is accompanied by physical changes such as increased heart beats, weeping, or sexual response. Music produces a partial or symbolic emotional response. When we hear it we do not necessarily recognize or identify the emotion. We may feel a sort of faint sadness without weeping, or joy without laughter. It has been said that through music we experience the elements of emotion by metaphor (Ferguson 1960). In fact Ferguson suggests that the elements of music, which are melody, harmony, and rhythm, produce musical tension and emotion. A simple example of tonal stress is the contrast between rising and falling pitch, expressing changes of mood. The very words correlate with the effort needed to rise and the release of falling. The subtleties of harmony and dissonance provide endless variations of such 'nervous tension'. Rhythm plays such a large part in music that its connection with action hardly needs further emphasis.

The pattern of a composition is thus able to arouse what might be called abstract complexes of emotion and action, without necessarily indicating any particular events. Nevertheless we may quickly begin to imagine a story 'association, drawing from some few suggested data the obvious inferences, erects the emotional characteristics which are promptly translated into successions of physical event; and lo! in the twinkling of an eye that which once was music has become a story' (Ferguson 1960). Such an operation performed by the listener may be neither the intention nor the fault of the composer. Musical semantics is concerned with the grouping of sounds to produce emotional effects not stories. Music has its own language with which to illustrate the abstract qualities of human experience, rather than particular facts. These qualities are fundamental features of the whole cerebral organization, therefore inevitably, when say sadness or joy are suggested, whole complexes of associated details may follow. The cerebral organization operates as one single whole.

Every composer has his own characteristic groupings of sounds. His composition can be recognized from these, just as the works of an author can be identified by analysis of his words, or of a painter by his stylistic tricks and his themes. In each case these are external manifestations of the internal brain programs of the individual. Yet there are some common groupings of sounds that are used by different composers to indicate particular feelings or meanings. Such common features have been identified by some critics as the language of music (Cooke 1959). If we wish to make comparison with speech we can say that notes or chords are like phonemes, whereas a unit or cell of music is like a word. But only several words together make a morpheme or unit of meaning.

Neurologists have made some progress towards understanding the parts of the brain that are involved in musical appreciation (see Critchley and Henson 1977). The capacity to appreciate music is lost after injuries to some cortical areas. This condition, known as amusia, may take various forms, as does aphasia (Chapter 16). There may be an incapacity to understand the arrangement of the notes, which may be called semantic amusia. After a stroke a trained musician may find himself unable to play, which is the condition of musical apraxia.

The areas especially concerned with music lie around those in the temporal lobe that are responsible for hearing (Fig. 12.5). Recent work has shown that the areas for musical appreciation are mainly in the right cerebral cortex, whereas those for speech are in the left (Chapter 16). Thus the left ear (connected to the right cortex) is the better receptor for melodies, and injury to the right temporal lobe has the greater effect on musical appreciation. The difference appears strikingly when for diagnosis neurologists produce temporary paralysis of one side or the other by injecting barbitone into a carotid artery. This produces aphasia on the left but amusia on the right (again see Critchley and Henson 1977).

The temporal lobes of the cortex lie close to the hippocampus and other basal parts of the cerebral hemispheres that are connected with reward systems and emotional responses. We cannot yet do more than point to the relationship in the hope that our successors may discover more about it and perhaps learn how to further increase appreciation of the charms of music.

## Playing

All art forms, whether visual or musical, try to introduce us to fresh ways of perceiving and feeling. This question of the search for novelty may lead us to the relations of art to play. Playing is pleasant, interesting, and creative. Yet it is also partly innate and conventional. Lambs frolicking on the little hills or kittens playing with a ball of wool are using inborn patterns, but also enjoying themselves and learning to be good sheep or cats. Human children play many sorts of games with language, either alone or with others. First they babble, then repeat words over and over again, experimenting with rhythm, pronunciation, grammar, and meaning. A child's talk to himself at bedtime is quite different from his use of it for communication in the day-time (Garvey 1977). Much play also involves experiments in socialization, as in the traditional games of early school years. It is successful in so far as it is pleasurable, and this makes it effective as an introduction to social life. In laughter we have a pre-programmed sign to use in order to show that life is proceeding well. It represents the successful termination of an episode—it is a relief and a consummation, a symbol of the triumphs of the pleasure principle, of Eros, that is, of life (see p. 143).

The special feature of human play is that it and our laughter are not restricted to youth. We are lucky that our program dictates that through life we remain juveniles (Chapter 4). Even as 'adults' we can laugh and have pleasure in following the rules of the game. Moreover we add to the old rules and have special joy in new creations, perceptions, and discoveries. Some of the features that art and play have in common have been listed by Dissanayake (1974). Both activities are in a sense 'non-serious' and 'non-functional' but are not therefore unimportant. Both are self-rewarding, but are often enjoyed with others. Play and art both express a need for surprise and for change. This feature is especially important if we are looking for the emotional basis for originality. Art and play are pleasant for the par-ticipants, and this relates them to the fundamental aims and satisfactions of life, and emphasizes that they are in fact important components of the homeostatic system. Finally art and play are symbolic of life, and what could be more important than that? These are indeed striking similarities and they convinced Dissanayake that art must have evolved from play.

## Art and discovery

Perhaps we shall never know how art began, but we are surely lucky to have brain systems that urge us on to continue to look and listen, to play, to experiment, to enquire, to imagine and construct, and to find satisfaction in what we have made or discovered. These are the activities that have made man what he is, and they have been especially evident in both art and science in recent times. We can rejoice that man has made new discoveries, not only of new ways of making things, but also of new ways of thinking, of seeing, and of hearing. Of course all codes have to be learned, new ways need practice before they are satisfying. Many people do not take to them readily but wish to return to older programs of thinking and perceiving, as also of believing. This is natural enough, but there may be comfort in the fact that the finding of *new* ways is in fact an *old* and well-tried way for man. In developing new forms of abstraction painters and thinkers are continuing man's long search for symbols that give satisfactory and useful clues to reality. For example religions emphasize that life contains evil as well as good, and art also brings these realities before us, whether in the symbolism of the Cross or of Picasso's *Guernica*. Again, although Chagall's colours and composition give us pleasure his world is ambiguous and partly upside down (Fig. 20.7). But isn't that true for all of us? So he shares with us our worries about the incoherence of the world, but asks us to join him all the same in celebrating its beauty and colour. Certainly we often cannot explain precisely what it is that satisfies us by any art. Purely abstract composition of planes and colours and textures fits with something in our visual system, as music does for our hearing (Fig. 20.8). Kasimir Malevich, who in 1918 first exhibited a pure white square on a white ground, later described 'a blissful sense of liberating non-objectivity drew me forth into the "desert", where nothing is real except feeling. . . . This was no empty square which I had exhibited but rather the feeling of non-objectivity' (see Collier 1972). This may seem puzzling, alas we know so little about our brain programs. Artists are continually finding keys that fit into them and may open new doors for us.

FIG. 20.7. *I and the Village* by Marc Chagall (1911). Oil on canvas, 6′ 3⅝″ × 4′ 11⅝″. Collection, The Museum of Modern Art, NewYork. Mrs. Simon Guggenheim Fund; © by A.D.A.G.P. Paris, 1978.

FIG. 20.8. *Abstract* by
Raymonde Parsons (1978).

Of course the discovery of new ways of understanding the world is not the exclusive privilege of either the exact method of the scientist or the imagination of the artist. This is curiously illustrated by the discoveries early this century about the relativity of space. Einstein (1905) showed by rigid reasoning that we must doubt our naïve concept of space. It is not just emptiness, but is altered by the objects in it. What a strange coincidence that the cubists Braque and Picasso at about the same time taught us how to look at things from several directions at once, to see more than the camera sees. Our brain programs do this for us all the time. When the eye detects a few lines the brain constructs a chair that can be sat upon. From the shape of the back of a head we reconstruct a whole familiar face.

## Architecture and symbolism

I hope to have convinced you that pursuit of the fine arts is indeed close to the core of the structure of culture, at least in its modern forms, perhaps in all communities. The message is that proper living depends upon the presence of suitably satisfying sights and sounds, and indeed touches, tastes,

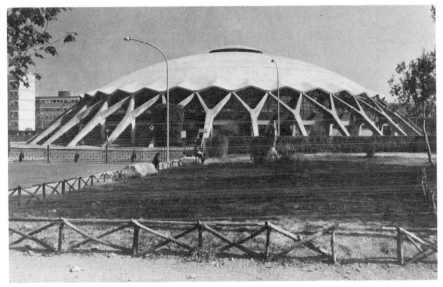

FIG. 20.9. The Olympic Sports Hall in Rome. Engineer and architect, Pier Luigi Nervi. (Studio Ingegneri Nervi, Ranc.)

FIG. 20.10. The Arena in Raleigh, North Carolina. Engineer, Matthew Novicki. (From Hesselgren 1972.)

and smells too. For architects and planners the message is equally clear. Humans need buildings and objects around them that suit the structures of their brain programs. Of course we must add at once that the structure of what they see will greatly influence their brains. We grow to have our preferences, say for Classic or Gothic architecture, and some come to like angular modern buildings. People can learn to live with almost anything, and even to like it. But that does not mean that the architect can plan without thought for those who will have to see his building. It is for him to imagine and search and discover significant symbols for us all, like any other artist. Indeed many architects realize this and still do great things for us (Figs. 20.9 and 20.10). They often succeed in breaking old conventions and teaching us to enjoy new ones. Unhappily there are some architects who ignore the importance of visual design. They claim to think only 'functionally', not understanding that *the most important functional activities of the human brain are symbolic*. The architect has indeed a special responsibility to us all. No one is compelled to look at pictures that he doesn't like, but we all have to look at the buildings around us. Architects, developers, and planners have the responsibility at least to try to give aesthetic satisfaction to the lives of those who will use or pass their buildings. The very fact of an obvious attempt at novelty is likely to please some people, but the failure to try to produce satisfying shapes is a scandalous insult to one's fellows.

Tastes differ and no one can please everyone by the style of their life and ideas, or the forms or sounds that they produce. Variety of life styles is one of the features of human life that the biologist can recognize as part of the secret of man's success. Man is far more varied than other mammals, in brain programs and behaviour, if not in physical structure. Tolerance and understanding of different styles of life and of taste is not easy. This fact alone indicates how deeply important their symbols are to us. A proper understanding of the brain shows that cultivation of the arts is of profound practical and emotional importance. The artist arouses needs and satisfies them. His work is not an impractical luxury, but is closer than that of any other labourer to meeting the continuing long-term needs of man. We are all symbol-creating creatures by the very working of our brains. Art assures us that our activities are proceeding satisfactorily, it symbolizes the central fact that life is worth living.

# 21   Believing and worshipping

## Knowing depends on believing

The capacity to believe includes much more than religious belief. Belief is necessary before we can use and accept the fundamental concepts upon which all logical discourse depends. Acquisition of knowledge in the human, rational way depends on the capacity to recognize certain logical truths (p. 194). Our whole method of reasoning depends on putting things into classes and then identifying certain truths about them. For example we need to recognize what is meant by asking a question and giving an answer. Then we must agree about the nature of truth and falsehood, equality and difference, the meaning of 'more' and 'less', 'before' and 'after', and many more such relationships. In fact we have to have faith in the intelligibility of discourse. It is true that we learn this reliance in childhood, but like all other memory processes this must depend upon the presence of a particular *capacity* to learn. Apes do not have the capacity to ask questions or to learn to have faith in true statements (though we might identify the rudiments of it)

'Critical thought is analytical and discursive. It rests upon an assumption of order that it cannot prove' (Bellah 1970, p. 165). Without belief we could not have trust in either analytic propositions, such as $2 + 2 = 4$, or synthetic ones such as that the sun will rise tomorrow. I take it that this is what Immanuel Kant meant by the capacity to make synthetic *a priori* judgements. Beliefs are thus essential to all reasoning, but they are not achieved by reason. They are, quite simply, the result of the trusting capacity of the human brain, which allows the individual to build up programs that use such beliefs. Of course it is hard to know just how much of any particular belief is due to training and how much to heredity. But the basic capacity to believe is essential to the functioning of every individual, and, like the capacity to speak, it must have a fundamental inherited background.

Everyone uses his capacity to learn the language of his culture, and similarly he uses the capacity for believing to acquire a set of beliefs that guide him through his life. These will include the whole range from belief in the truths of logic and the theorem of Pythagoras to belief in the virgin birth. The essential feature of all his beliefs is that he believes in them, they are the props and stays of his brain program. The very word belief implies love and trust. The German version of it is *Glauben* and both words come from the Aryan root *lubh* to 'hold dear', in fact to love. We love our beliefs.

The capacity for believing is a mode of operating that is not learned by experience. As Quinton (1973) puts it, beliefs like 'the concepts of logic are *a priori* not empirical, they are not learnt by correlation with empirical things or states of affairs . . .'. Of course this does not mean that a baby is born with any particular system of logic or of religious belief, but that its brain will develop a power to operate with complete reliance on certain concepts. Without the capacity to believe it could not function at all. 'Our systems of belief are those that the mind as a biological structure is designed to construct' (Chomsky 1976). The development and construction of the whole human brain model depends upon this capacity to accept or have faith in certain fundamental methods of operating. It is a fascinating paradox that believing produces both the essential foundations of logic and all the many schemes, extravagant, metaphysical, and even irrational, by which men explain their universe. Perhaps it is not really so paradoxical, for the faculty of believing considered in this way is as characteristic of man as is language. Animals do not believe either in logic or in God. As Bertrand Russell said 'believing seems the most "mental" thing we do' (1921, p. 231).

Another way of putting this is that 'A profoundly non-rational order and form is the necessary precondition for the emergence of rationality at all' (Bellah 1970, p. 165). We are, all of us, therefore, much more credulous creatures than we perhaps like to think. Even the most sceptical have to take many things on faith. Emphasizing like this that we are all in the same believing boat has, however, the disadvantage that it seems to evade the genuine distinction between what are usually called religious and non-religious attitudes. The psychologist William James deals with a similar problem in the very first of his famous series of Gifford Lectures on *Varieties of Religious Experience*, given in Edinburgh in 1902. The title of that lecture, interestingly for us, was Religion and Neurology. In it he deals with various medical interpretations of religious and similar phenomena, how Saint Paul's vision was said to be epileptic and Carlyle's 'organ tones of misery were due to gastro-duodenal catarrh' and so on. This was equivalent to our stories about reward systems and reticulo-activating centres of the core brain. But he goes on to warn us against treating 'our own more exalted soul-flights as "nothing-but" expressions of our organic disposition'. Such an attitude would be an outrage and would make us 'wish that all this medical materialism would hold its tongue.'

I do not reach the same general conclusion as James, who if I understand him, remains, at the end, at least in part a Christian believer, but I have equally no wish to seem to dismiss or denigrate anyone's religious beliefs. The fact that they are examples of a more general human capacity seems to me to increase rather than reduce their significance. We all need belief where knowledge fails us. But it is degrading to continue to use detailed beliefs that have become inconsistent with knowledge.

## Mystical belief

Of course much of what people usually call belief has little or no logical basis and indeed is frankly mystical. It is no surprise after what we have seen of brain processes that many people have experiences that are not rooted in the common observations of daily working life. For instance, as we know too well, psychodelic practices, whether by drums or drugs, can produce all sorts of hallucinations, and some of them are said to be experiences of God. Indeed some anthropologists have held that the discovery of hallucinogenic drug plants was the origin of mystical religion, that 'God grew in a flower pot' (see Mary Barnard in Bowker 1973). I do not propose to pursue the endless manifestations of mystical experience, whether western or oriental. There is no doubt that they are genuine and for us it is important that there is good reason to think that they are generated by states of the brain sometimes chemically induced. That they should often be labelled as 'a sense of God' confirms that such a faculty of belief is near the centre of the brain program. That they are blissful confirms how important such a centre is to humans.

## The function of belief

To fulfil their tasks beliefs have to assist the individual through all the difficult phases of life. It is obvious that the capacity of the brain to operate satisfactorily for this end must have been subject to natural selection in the past, and probably still is today. The individual has to face a very wide range of eventualities and anxieties, and his own detailed knowledge and information is usually supplemented by a set of categorical beliefs, whether scientific, political, or religious. We all need beliefs. A characteristic of our method of brain modelling is that we require what we call 'explanations' for all the occurrences around us. We expect them to fit into one coherent scheme. Yet all of us, however wise, reach, in the end, points where our knowledge and understanding fail and some form of hypothesis, or guess, or faith, or religion becomes the only possible way to provide the explanations. This is therefore the mode of brain activity that relates a man to ultimates that he cannot know about logically. Many people believe that they can do this by cultivating modes of mystical experience, which they enshrine in beliefs about some spirit or god. Others may find that a logical belief in the unity of nature is sufficiently satisfying. Neither of them can *prove* that they are right.

The capacity to frame and to accept faith in religious beliefs almost certainly has its inherited background in the tendencies to respond to persons, which we have noted so often before. It is reasonable to say that men have an innate tendency to theism, to believe in God. The actual forms of religion have of course varied very much with the mode of life of societies. There is no doubt a form of group selection among sects so that some gain attention and interest at the expense of others that provide less benefit for their practitioners (Wilson 1975, p. 561). It has often been noted that one of the functions of religion is to establish the relations between things, as Durkheim (1915) put it. The individual needs a picture of a harmonious universe in order to calm his many anxieties and feelings of guilt: we all need repeated reassurances in the face of our fears of the unknown. When the child wakes in the dark he's frightened, his mother doesn't hesitate to tell him 'It will be all right'. The death-bed convert is comforted by belief when he is faced with the uncertainty of his future.

To provide the required security in face of the dark, night-side of life and of evil and of death, the brain program of course reverts to the basic features of childhood. Extension of the earliest security provided by the first parent helper, provides safety for the whole life-time. One great strength of monotheistic religions lies in this emphasis on a father figure (for the one god is always male). Nearly all monotheistic religions have arisen among pastoral peoples, notably the Hebrew, Christian, and Moslem, the shepherd providing the symbolic father. Our brain programs are so highly organized around concepts of persons that gods (whether many or one) are nearly always personified (though not strictly in Buddhism or in China). To form a concept of God in non-personal terms may be a rational aim but as La Barré (1970) says it is 'a difficult piety'. Perhaps it is also not a very effective piety either. It is not surprising that people prefer to believe in the operation of agents who are receptive to human communication.

## Religion as a social phenomenon

We have so far considered the belief of individuals, but of course religion is a fundamentally social phenomenon. As social creatures men get their gods and protection from anxieties, like their goods, from other people. Moreover religion gives a man protection not only against nature, but also *against* society. Men impose painful restraints on each other, but God sanctifies these, makes them acceptable, and helps as a friend to make them bearable. The Christian God has been called 'the ground of nature, the ground of morals, the basis of law ... and a friend' (Skorupski 1976). An important feature of the gods in many religions is that they are accessible and also have access to still greater powers. Thus in Christianity, Jesus and the Virgin are in a sense more important to individual men and women than the Father or Holy Spirit, who are remote. Most effective religions contain an element of magic. They express 'a cosmology based on agencies responsive to human communication, and equipped with powers to act on the world' (Skorupski 1976, p. 164). When Saint Christopher was recently demoted to the second division of saints, Catholic wits said that the saint complained to the Almighty that this was out of keeping with modern times, 'As the patron saint of motorists I often need instant access to your infinite powers.'

In examining religions we therefore have to look at the relationships between the needs and anxieties of individuals and the organization of the societies of which they are part. Religions serve to maintain the equilibrium both of the individual and of his society. The relationship is complex and still not clear in spite of all the efforts of theologians and anthropologists. Firth (1971, p. 221) exclaimed 'No really satisfactory theoretical classification of religious behaviour has yet been made.' In order to begin to understand religion we have to look both at the part it plays in the programs of individual people and the way it serves to regulate their relationships to each other.

This dual character of religion explains the paradox that it is both a public and a very private activity. Many people today probably feel that a man's religion is his own affair. As Thomas Paine put it, 'My mind is my church' and Thomas Jefferson said, 'I am a sect myself'. But to the anthropologist (and also to many theologians) the conception of a private religion is an absurdity. Perhaps indeed it is true that for social man the satisfactory conduct of his life requires a degree of shared belief and some participation in collaborative ritual. The tendency to meet together in large or small gatherings is even more widespread than particular religions, and survives when religion is discarded. People who never go to church are often ready for a party or a scientific meeting or a football match. Probably the very act of coming together symbolizes communication. A symbol is a sign that points to some state that is of emotional importance. The very fact of assembly gives reassurance that we are part of a larger whole and the individual's life is strengthened thereby. The tendency to come together in large groups was evidently one of the earlier forms of behaviour of neolithic man (and of course may have been present much earlier than that). I have suggested that the building of large structures as meeting-places has for long served as a symbol of communication, of belonging (Young 1951). Silbury Hill in Wiltshire, which I understand is the largest prehistoric man-made artefact, at least in Europe, seems to have had no other function. We may call it the first cathedral. And what is more comforting and symbolic than to rejoin the dead with the living by burying them in the meeting-place, as we do in every village churchyard?

## Ritual

This interpretation emphasizes that ritual is more important than particular beliefs. As Edmund Leach (1954) puts it, 'Ritual actions and beliefs are . . . forms of symbolic statement about the social order.' This is not necessarily incompatible with the view that men use ritual and magic in the hope of influencing the course of nature. The earlier generation of anthropologists such as J. G. Frazer and E. B. Tylor took it as axiomatic that sympathetic magic was used for its supposed practical value in improving the fertility of crops, the success of the chase, the cure of illness, or for any end not otherwise easily achieved. According to this view the ritual practised by the shaman or priest symbolizes natural forces and assists them in their tasks. Tylor and E. E. Evans-Pritchard were able to show some of the reasons why people continue to use such rituals and do not perceive the futility of their magic. One fundamental point is that in a traditional society there is no sharp distinction such as we should make between an activity, say sowing seeds, and the mystical practices and the prayers that accompany it. One simply does the two together, they are the same activity. As Tylor put it, conservatism and unreflectiveness are two major features of savagery. Our whole system of separating life into parts is absent and without it our method of making hypotheses and trying to verify or falsify them simply never gets considered. Curiously enough anthropologists often report talking with individuals who do hold beliefs divergent from their fellows. But the traditional society does not allow such deviations to spread. Just as in our scientific society those who do not subscribe to what Kuhn (1962) has called the current paradigms, are dismissed. For example not many physiologists will be ready to accept the wide interpretations I am giving about the programs of the brain.

However, to return to the question of the meaning of religious rituals. Recent anthropologists have held that it is wrong to consider that they are irrational or pre-scientific attempts to explain the world. Instead we should regard them as a special sort of social language, serving to symbolize society. Ritual often serves more for showing and saying than for actually producing some particular effect. Magic and symbolization are by their very essence confused and all-embracing rather than logical and detailed. The purpose of participation in a rite is to do the right thing. The savage may say that he acts out a ritual to get power over game, but his 'real' reason is to show respect for the social order. Also his own upbringing and method of brain-working insist that he *must* do it. Just as the superstitious 'touch wood', or refuse to walk under a ladder, or to pass on the stairs, or when they spill salt throw some over their shoulder. The very acts and beliefs reduce tension and anxiety. The individual does not participate because he believes in the details of the ceremony but because it is the correct thing to do in the circumstances. This is very evident in modern Christian religious practices, for instance in the United States, where going to church is still an almost obligatory social convention in some parts of society. To say, 'I don't believe in God' is more bad manners than bad metaphysics.

Humans probably need some formal rites both for individual development and to call attention to their responsibilities in society. Religious experience and moral conscience take many forms and are undoubtedly engendered or helped in many people by rites, whether in communal gathering and worship or individual meditation. Members of societies that are democratic need to renew their common identity as much as do totalitarians In fact, *more* symbols of communication are probably needed where there is less authority. Human beings are, as we have often emphasized, especially programmed to be indoctrinated. They do not operate most effectively when every action of the individual is minutely regulated, but shared participation even in simple social units furthers mutual cooperation. At the lowest level we still make much use of simple rituals, for instance many levels of eating together persist, from the Mass to the Banquet or the family breakfast or supper. Each has its proper procedure.

Communal acts, including singing and worship, sanctify endeavours and transform the arbitrary restrictions of social life into acceptable and necessary conventions. As Durkheim put it, rites serve to label, reaffirm, and rejuvenate moral values (see Wilson 1975). Every school knows that its assemblies, concerts, and other ceremonial occasions have their value beyond the words spoken or music heard. Religious rites indeed still have many functions even in societies where the associated beliefs are weakened. They still serve as signs of passage from one state to another, from child to adult, from single to married, and from alive to dead. Religions may be said to map the life program of the individual. They provide as it were route-finding activities, charting the general path along which human beings can trace their way from birth to death and through death (Bowker 1973, p. 83).

## Personal religion

To emphasize the social function of religion is not to minimize the genuine importance of its personal and emotional content. Such a force cannot be a 'tissue of illusions' as Durkheim (1915) said long ago. Religion, ceremonial and worship indeed have fundamental parts in the life of the individual in many societies. Ceremonies provide ideals of perfection. They say, 'Look this is how things should be'. I remember my clerical uncle telling me that his High Anglican ceremonies with vestments and incense were the only beautiful reality in his slum parish in Cardiff. To put it another way, 'worship attempts to break the hold of the ordinary and the usual' (Bellah 1970, p. 209). Ecstatic experience opens us to the mystery that surrounds us (Berger 1969).

It is important that we should not try to make too sharp a separation between logical reasoning and these imaginative ways of knowing and symbolizing the world. Jung in a similar thought said 'You can't tear people into two parts and assign one of them to the doctors and the other to the theologians.' I have emphasized already that to do so violates what we know of the way the whole brain program acts as a unity. The attempt to sever rationality from its deeper roots in nature is probably part of the reason for the malaise and alienation that it is often alleged that people feel about modern life. Worse still this separation sanctifies the wicked actions of those who are allowed to manage peoples' material lives without considering their real human and emotional needs.

Studies of the sociology of religion give us plenty of insight into its function in society but what does this leave of religious truth for the individual? Many of us can no longer believe in the literal truths of traditional religions, whose human origins have become only too plain. Nor is it easy to accept the rejection of the world of intellect which has been characteristic of so many religions including Buddhism, Mohammedinism, and Christianity. Nor, again, can we accept beliefs that insist on the presence of immaterial spirits around us, intervening in our affairs. Whatever God or the meaning of the universe may be we should use all our knowledge to understand them as clearly as we can. This is indeed what men have been doing through the centuries, using human symbols such as fatherhood, but to continue to limit ourselves to these obvious symbols is surely blasphemous. We should be able to improve our symbolism to match our widening knowledge of the universe. This is a challenge to the imagination of artists, scientists, and theologians and all of us.

How may it be attempted? We are not gods and have no comprehension of ultimates. But as modern men we have learned to see something of the order and even the purpose of life on earth. We can see human brains and societies as the latest products of thousands upon thousands of years of gathering of order and information. Surely this gives us the outline of a marvellous hypothesis or map by which to guide our lives. And if a map is too impersonal a helper for some of us, how are we to embellish and ornament it to make it fit adequately to our emotional needs and programs? For many people the program cannot be wholly logical. Perhaps from the very structures of our brains we need to use symbolic and analogical modes of thought. It has been said that one of the functions of religion is to give a face to the universe; perhaps for some people it needs literally to resemble a human face. Many people find analogies and metaphors more persuasive and creative than the accuracies of positive logical statements. It is important to remember that pleasure and pain, the most fundamental truths of life, are not logical. The richness and value of life lie in achievement of aims, in appreciation of beauty and worth, in consummation and fulfilment, and these are not logical either. The beauty of study of the brain in the way that we suggest is that it shows us the fundamental relevance to life of both methods of functioning. We inherit emotional attitudes and aptitudes and we learn them. Our religion or our irreligion are social. Yet we are each alone with the universe.

## A religion of life

How then can we best express the richness of our awareness and knowledge of life and yet be humble in the acceptance of our ignorance? We can each make the effort to see ourselves more or less clearly as individuals and as part of human life and of all life. We all have our awareness of what the theologian Tillich called 'the depth of your being, of your ultimate concern, of what you take seriously without any reservation' (1949). This is what I mean by the experience of the central part of life, which is perhaps as close as we can get to an understanding of God. Yet as Tillich goes on, 'Perhaps, in order to do so, you must forget everything traditional that you have learned about God, perhaps even that word itself.' My belief is that we should each of us trust in the vision of the depth of our own life and being. To do this is to use sound knowledge of mankind and of his brain. What each of us feels as a worthwhile aim for life is for that very reason worthwhile. It becomes an effective system of thought or religion when we find that we can use it as a unifying principle for our thinking and combine it with the beliefs of others. This knowledge of life as a whole is well tested now in experience and covers many of the happenings of our individual lives. It does not explain everything, but we are ready to live with our ignorance and try to reduce it. The knowledge we have allows us to understand the aims of our lives and yet recognize our weaknesses and imperfections. It suggests that we can continue to try to improve on them and gives us the faith to do so.

We can join together in using old and new forms of symbolism and worship. We can unite in celebration of the glory of life and in commiseration for its sadness. And if we need a central symbol I suggest that it should be life itself, which is the most enduring organized reality that we know on earth. As William Blake said in *The Marriage of Heaven and Hell*, 'For everything that lives is Holy.' Life throughout the ages is indeed our father figure, the generator of all our programs. 'Man's creator becomes the vast interdependent and interwoven matrix of all evolving nature ...' (Sperry 1976). We shall not go far wrong if we keep respect for life as the central criterion by which every man's life can be judged.

## Worshipping

Some people will no doubt find such a conception over fanciful and others that it is unacceptably pagan or, conversely, purely humanistic. Everyone has their own ideas about proper levels of symbolism and sentiment. But I hope that there are few of us who do not feel something of the need for worship, whatever may be our religious belief or disbelief. Throughout this analysis our idea has been that believing is a characteristic feature of the human brain. The same is true of worshipping. It is not something that is done only with ritual solemnity in church. It is the product of a need in every human being. Most of us have programs of some sort for thoughts and actions that provide fulfilment and satisfaction of the need to worship. We have the power to rejoice and to be glad to be alive. We are all faced from time to time with the need, as it were, to identify ourselves and our relation to the world. It may range from the gladness of a personal reunion to the joy of a spring morning or simply to the sensation of awe that strikes us at the *mysterium tremendum* of the existence of ourselves and the universe around us. We sometimes feel the need to do something to express such feelings of wholeness, of awe, of gladness, or of sadness, to sing for joy or to join in an act of worship. Public expressions of worship, as in singing, may have this effect of release, whether as part of religious symbolism or simply in a concert. But we can also worship and rejoice alone or with the world around us, as I often do in the open country, on the downs or in the woods. Religious symbolism helps many people with worship and so of course can painting or verse. Remember Robert Browning's early poem 'Johannes Agricola in Meditation':

> There's heaven above, and night by night
>    I look right through its gorgeous roof;
> No suns and moons though e'er so bright
>    Avail to stop me; splendour-proof
>    I keep the broods of stars aloof:
> For I intend to get to God,
>    For 't' is to God I speed so fast,
> For in God's breast, my own abode,
>    Those shoals of dazzling glory passed,
>    I lay my spirit down at last.

So I believe that we can identify worshipping as a very real program of the brain. It can be either an internal or an external act, producing a confirmation and re-ordering of experience and giving an element of consummation and fulfilment. It is an activity that, in Blake's words, does not have 'philosophical or experimental character'. It has a different kind of perception that Blake called 'Poetic or Prophetic'. In today's terms some people might regard worship as a symbolic 'trip', a 'descent' into the depths, the caves of mystery, or an 'ascent' to the realms of light 'above'. The effect of 'The experience of worship should produce an influx of life and power, a feeling of wholeness, of the grace of God, of being at the still center of the turning wheel' (Bellah 1970).

All this may seem to be exaggerated and poetic language, but it is quite close to our concept of the general program of the brain as an integrated action pattern for life. We have repeatedly emphasized the unity of the program. From time to time it needs to be exercised and tried out as a whole. This is what happens when we worship, whether in quiet contemplation of a landscape or in a religious ceremony. We allow the reward systems to pour their gladness over the whole range of the cortical programs. It is not wholly fanciful to imagine that as we feel the effects of gladness and of worship there are literally streams of nerve impulses pouring along the channels of reward, releasing little floods of the chemical messengers that open useful pathways to the cortex and within it. Why should we not be poetic about this? Asking what are the effects of joy and worship should stimulate physiologists to think more deeply and broadly about what goes on in the brain during these, its most important activities.

Study of belief and worship emphasizes once again that the brain program of each person is to a great extent one undivided whole. For many people its relation to the world and to society is expressed in the symbolism of religion, whose practices help them in many phases of life. For those who hold such beliefs, their concept of God is the centre and pivot of their brain programs. But for many others religious symbolism and its social expressions have become too archaic to be useful. Conscious of their ignorance they may feel unwilling to express their general knowledge of the world in terms of any one model, and more and more people find this attitude satisfactory. It is uncertain whether it will be possible or desirable to recapture something of religion by a new symbolism, such as that based on life itself and 'increased respect and reverence for all nature' (Sperry 1976). But whether organized religion survives or not, worship and praises will continue. Happily, in spite of all our discontents, there is no lack of people who are ready to express the joy in their lives, to celebrate the success of life's program, to assert its reality and its ability to guide them through the world.

# 22 Concluding and continuing

## *Life progresses*

Can finite mortals have any proper understanding of infinites? Just as we have no clear knowledge of the Beginning so we cannot with certainty foresee the Ending of man or of the only universe he knows. It may be that we shall in future have knowledge of these matters, but it is not even possible to prophesy this. What we *can* see is that life never stops. Individuals die but their genes go on. The information and order that is stored in their brains is mostly dispersed, yet some of it continues in the remembrance of them by their children and by others, more of course if they have produced writings or works of art. It is an interesting thought that every individual plays a small part in the transmission of culture. He provides the plan of life that orders the future of his family and of people with whom he comes into contact.

Cultures survive longer than the individuals who embody them and genes provide memories of an altogether different scale of permanence. The characteristics of man, like those of other animals and plants alive today embody information that has been accumulated during a history of perhaps 3000 million years. This is such an exceedingly long time that, from our brief perspective, we should indeed say that *life does not conclude*—it goes on and on, essentially for ever, without stopping for a moment.

But what continues is never quite the same. Information is being added during every moment of time. The search by organisms for ways to conduct their lives never stops. Evolutionary change is not something that only happened in the past, it is going on now from second to second, leading to the appearance of more and more complex systems, by which organisms come to live in ever more diverse ways (Chapter 3). This conception of *progress in evolution*, by accumulation of information, is especially revealing to mankind because humans have achieved an exceptional capacity for gathering information. By speech and writing men collect and store information faster by many orders of magnitude than any other organism. In recent years the precise language of science has allowed the growth of agreed, certain, knowledge to go on even faster than has ever been possible before.

So the biologist, looking at the whole history of life, can confirm the contemporary feeling or opinion that we do indeed live in an exceptional period, with great responsibilities and opportunities. Studies of the evolution of vertebrate animals, for instance, provide direct evidence that life has been progressing through the ages, by accumulating more information about how to live (Young 1962). We are in a position to continue that process at a much increased rate. This challenge provides us with an aim that is indeed worthwhile. To meet it we need all the knowledge we can collect about ourselves and our propensities for good and evil. We can see the biological foundations for these, but for wisdom about how to act we must continue to look largely to the traditional skills of philosophy, theology, and politics and the newer ones of anthropology, psychology, and sociology. These are cultural problems, and they require investigation mainly by those who study people as individuals and in groups, and their relations to each other.

## New knowledge of the brain programs

Yet underlying all cultural studies are questions about the nature and tendencies of the individuals who compose societies. It is here that the neuroscientist can contribute. All these special human powers of gathering information come from the properties of the brain. The information about its activities that has been collected in recent years now makes it possible to speak more precisely than in the past about the factors that influence the aims and actions of individuals. This book is an attempt to bring this knowledge together, by comparing the way information is recorded in the brain with programs written in a language. It would be possible to use many other sorts of terminology to describe the brain, its reflexes and conditioned reflexes, electrical waves, feedbacks and so on, with various formal and mathematical complications. But the concept that the brain carries information and instructions written in a language seems to come close to the description we require. Since language is the special human characteristic it is altogether appropriate that we should compare our brain processes to it.

The conception of brain programs can indeed be professionally helpful to physiologists. We need ideas for a specific physiology of the *human* brain. There is a temptation to arrest progress at the level of the wonderfully interesting facts that are collected by current techniques, such as the microelectrodes that Mountcastle and Hubel and Wiesel and many others have used in the cortex (Chapter 7). Generalization from such results to the working of the whole human brain is of course largely guesswork, but it can be stimulating. It involves trying to think about how the interactions of thousands of nerve cells, are so directed as to maintain life. The physiologist can at present only study one of them at a time, but the microscopist has the advantage that he can actually see all the millions of cells together (Fig. 7.1). He can count them and measure the sizes of their parts. With the electron microscope he can determine the finest details of their connections. Indeed the results of anatomical studies provide the most valuable of all clues to the functioning of the cortex. They show that the information about the features of the world is projected on to the cortex and recombined in a series of detailed *maps*. This analogue or model of the world is the basis of all our powers of computation. So we can combine the detailed knowledge of the sequence of events in a few nerve cells that is given by the microelectrode, with the knowledge about the arrangement of many of them that is provided by the microscope. We may thus begin to decipher how individual cells and groups of them interact to provide the coded script in which the programs of the brain are written.

The basic system of connections laid down before birth by heredity determines what may be called the pre-programs. Some of these provide for immediate needs such as for breathing or sucking. But a great number of other systems of connection are pre-programs for social life. The theory of memory as a selective process assumes that the baby already possesses the outline features of the connections that will be needed for all the skills it later acquires. Its particular capacities and knowledge will then be developed by selection of some out of the many possible courses of action (Chapter 10). As more is learned of these processes of selection of pathways at critical or sensitive periods this point of view should help to resolve many old problems of nature and nurture. Even more important—it should provide a factual basis for deciding when, how, and what to teach to children.

Of course each set of nerve-cell structures is only a framework within which varied programs of activity can circulate. The brain networks are literally never in a state of rest. Their activities change and recur in sequences that provide the pattern of life for the individual, indicating his needs and searching for ways to satisfy them. To describe and understand this intensely active network will require techniques of analysis and synthesis far more powerful than any we have been able to use in this book. Practitioners of artificial intelligence are working towards these, making up algorithms that simulate some aspects of brain function and can be tested on computers. They are trying to decipher the code of the brain by imitating small parts of it. They may help to find a notation with which to describe the patterns of brain activity. Until this is achieved the conception of brain programs serves at least for the identification of groups of cerebral processes whose actions are directed to particular ends.

## The unified brain program

It is characteristic of the algorithms of computer languages that they are programs specifying in great detail the logical operations that are required at each step towards the solution of a problem. There are no short cuts. It may be that the brain operates in a different way. Perhaps the wide extent of the interactions between its parts somehow allows it to find analogies between situations, and so to jump to conclusions without going through all the elaborate processes of calculation and testing of every possibility. Of course until it is known how this is done there is little use in speculating, or even in trying to make detailed comparisons with modern computers. When appropriately programmed these machines can change their course and their aims in the light of the results of previous decisions. How do the millions of cells in the brain, in spite of their slow working, reach the conclusions that the computer achieves by its rapid testing of many possibilities?

Instead of providing detailed algorithms I have tried to discuss some of the broader features that are characteristic of human brain programs. One such feature is that they are specially designed by natural selection to recognize and react to features of human beings themselves, such as facial expressions and the sounds of speech. Another of the particular properties of the brain programs is the extraordinary facility to transmit and to receive information of the most varied sorts by the external codes of speech and writing. A special feature is the power to organize information into consistent and coherent patterns by the operations we have called believing, whether in gods or in logical truths. Perhaps most important of all is the idea, still vague, that all the programs of the brain constitute one single model or structured system, whose parts are interrelated. Anthropologists and psychologists are learning how to detect structural relations where they are far from obvious. The brain has many distinct parts but there is increasing evidence that they are interrelated to make one functioning whole, which gives a unique and characteristic direction to the pattern of life of that one individual.

## Are these really new views of man?

Philosophers and psychologists may not think very much of this approach to the brain. They will say that all we are doing is to take what they have known for years and make the obvious point that it comes from the brain. I can imagine many people dismissing all I say as the feeble best of a callow scientist. For instance, I am sure this would have been the view of my old friend C. S. Lewis, with whom I had many arguments on such matters in the past. People like Lewis, whose brains work imaginatively, if perhaps in a rather old-fashioned way, can readily produce fantasies that are widely pleasing, such as those of the Narnia series of stories. They speak to us with well-tried codes. Is it possible to produce equally attractive stories that include the symbolism of science? The criticism that the new language is only a rather complicated and cumbrous translation of the old one is fair enough. But I hope that the objection becomes less cogent year by year, as the interest of new facts becomes plain, and the means of describing them become familiar and even pleasing. For me there is intense beauty in the forms of the cells of the brain and the wonders of their intricate activities. Knowledge of these now gives a vivid new picture of the nature of man, about how he sees and hears and how he feels and fears. There is a rather better understanding of how his tendencies for good and evil arise in the operations of the brain. Questions about the proper conduct of human life have been discussed in the past by philosophers, moralists, and others, largely theoretically. The only factual data have been disputable interpretations of history. Now scientists can join in with some statements of fact about the origins of human behaviour that are agreed by everybody. For instance the discovery that moods of joy and sadness are influenced by the chemistry of the brain helps not only to cure the sick but sometimes to understand and control the deviant who threatens society.

The facts known about the brain are not sufficient to decide all problems or even many of them. The business of life continues to involve making repeated difficult decisions and choices about what is best to do, without adequate information. Living is choosing. But in conducting his life the individual can now use a somewhat more detailed picture of what he is. He can know more of the history that has led to his present state and of the values and goals at which he can aim. Of course most of his aims will be determined by the cultural influences implanted in him by the society in which he has been reared. But the knowledge of himself that biology can give shows the fundamental influences of his long history and at the same time the importance of his own unique individuality.

## What is meant by 'brain' and 'mind'?

We asked very early in our enquiry how far the process of studying the brain can go. Is there any sense in the question whether there are limits to the amounts of information, or type of information, that brains can contain about themselves? What would it mean truly to understand the brain? Perhaps the main value of such an enquiry is in making us ask what is meant by 'minds', 'brains', 'information', and 'understanding'. It is clear that these words are symbols whose significance like that of all words relates to the knowledge and culture of whoever uses them. A brain to me means a set of nerve cells of immense complexity whose intense activity is continually directed to furthering the life of a particular individual. For us to agree on a precise meaning for the concept 'brain' we must agree about the methods by which all these cells can be seen and their activities studied. I have tried to give such a description in this book, but the outcome is that even the best physiological and anatomical techniques still leave us very ignorant about the brain.

This is the difficulty with the whole scheme we are trying to realize. A lot is known about the brain, but not enough to allow detailed descriptions of the cerebral counterparts of our most interesting activities. For each of us there is a continuous flow of experience that we call mental life. Our language consists largely of descriptions of this. If we have some knowledge of the anatomy and physiology of the brain then this small scientific part of our experience tells us that accompanying our mental life there is a series of electrical and chemical events in our heads. These are very interesting, but even the best physiologist can only give crude descriptions of them. For instance I can say that I know the date of the Battle of Waterloo or that apples are good to eat. I have evidence that each of these pieces of knowledge depends on my brain, but I do not know how the brain holds the information in the memory. To say that the brain 'knows about apples or Waterloo' would be at best a sort of metaphor. Probably many philosophers would say it is not even a metaphor but simply a mistake, because the verb 'to know' should be used only of mental experiences. But language changes with new information. The point is that to say 'my brain knows' in 1977 has more sense than it would have had in 1907, even to Sir Charles Sherrington, who had then just published his *Integrative action of the nervous system*, which contains the foundation of so much of our knowledge of the brain. We can begin to give a meaning to the idea that mental events are *in* the brain in something the same sense that programs are in a computer (though with many differences). As we have seen there is some evidence that information is stored by a switching system that alters the probability of future action of neurons. In the octopus brain we can even localize the regions where this switching occurs, though we do not know how the new connectivity is produced (Chapter 10). Does it make sense to say that an octopus 'knows' that rough spheres mean food and smooth spheres shocks? Does its inferior frontal lobe know this? Obviously our language needs to be improved to deal with such new information.

## Knowing and choosing

Knowledge about the brain is growing, and inevitably this brings changes in the way we speak about ourselves. The meaning of key words such as 'knowledge' or 'mind' changes with the culture that uses them. I find that the usages we have suggested help me to understand people better than was possible when I was young. They obviously do not tell us all that we should like to know. How strange it would be if we *did* have complete knowledge and certainty about values and what we should do. We should indeed then be subject to a strong form of determinism. What would our worlds be like if we all knew exactly what we had to do from minute to minute throughout the day? The idea is absurd, living simply is not like that. We 'know' that we have to choose, just as we know that we see the sun or indeed that we are hungry or sad. These are the 'facts' of our existence, but beyond them we can only obscurely see *why* the world appears like this.

Surely our great gain in recent centuries has been that we have begun to learn how to free ourselves from the tyranny of those who claim *absolute* knowledge of the principles that should control action. It is tragic that in this century there are still individuals and systems that claim this certainty. Although some of us have learned to live with the essential uncertainty and limitations of empirical knowledge, there are still many others who find such a sceptical approach difficult and ask for dogma. Perhaps, even, it is wrong to be critical of this. We all need some plan, program, or scheme of action by which to live. One of our conclusions in the previous chapter was that we are all more credulous than we like to think. What we can do is to try to construct systems of belief that are consistent with the greatly increased knowledge that is now available.

Instead of dogmatic principles and certainties, based largely on guesses and simple metaphors, we have learned a great deal about the influences that constrain us as they do all living creatures. But we decided, I hope, that it is not sensible to pretend that we can say that in principle living things are rigidly deterministic (Chapter 3). Such words have meaning only in relation to rather simple collections of small numbers of particles or molecules, whose history is well known. The essential variability of all living things means that there can never be enough information to say exactly what any one of them will do. But of course the more that is known the more accurate can the forecast be. The 'decisions' of even the simplest bacterium can be forecasted only approximately and those of a man will depend upon the particular information available from his own life and that of the long, long line of his ancestors.

## Difficulties of communication

Although we have learnt very much we know also that we are uncertain creatures, rather ignorant, who must yet decide what to do today and throughout our days. How can knowledge about the brain help in the decisions that have to be made? I think that we may be much better off when we have come to learn how to use what we have and to gain more knowledge about how information is recorded in the brain and retrieved from it. In particular it may be that agreed knowledge about the brain will help with the most serious of all our problems, how to get on with each other. To a great extent this problem depends upon how widely forms of symbolism can be used and understood. There are many practical reasons why we quarrel and these will not go away. But difficulties would be much easier to resolve if there was more uniformity in the approaches used to discuss them. I do not mean that people should all speak the same language, but that they could all have some familiarity with the sources of knowledge that are relevant to the problems. The key example is of course the way in which all scientists can readily understand each other in spite of their different cultures and languages. In the same way improved knowledge of the brain and of human biology can provide a common code in which people can express their needs and motivations, and understand those of others. The sceptic will say that the languages we have are good enough for that already. But think what an influence the work of physiologists and psychologists has had already on understanding of human problems. We need only to mention a few words that are in common use, however distorted; conditioned reflex, anxiety neurosis, intelligence quotient, Oedipus complex, neurotic, psychopathic and so on, the examples spring to mind from all the various schools of psychology. The attitudes behind these attempts to explain ourselves have surely helped us towards a more humane treatment of each other. All these are aspects of brain programs; how much more powerful would be a language that could really describe our brain actions in detail. The conception that our various activities are the result of the operation of programs of the brain is an attempt to provide a basis for this.

To look at it another way. How can we expect to get on well together when we know so little about the mechanisms by which we interact? What are the barriers that prevent people from understanding different modes of symbolism, say religious or political? Can all human beings respond equally to the same symbols? Perhaps too little attention has been paid to the question of whether there are great differences in the operating procedures of the brain. Because it is a socially loaded question people are unwilling to consider the origins of difficulties of communication. Since the basic capacities upon which communication depends are innate it is possible that there are inherited differences in the facility with which logical or more metaphorical forms of symbolism are used, but we do not know whether this is so.

Some of the tendencies to the division of mankind and the Babel of languages may be connected with the evolution of the very faculty of altruism, which has been the secret of man's success (Chapter 19). We cannot be sure how far it is true that our divisions have been beneficial for human survival in the past, still less whether it continues to be so. But it is important not to be frightened by the questions. Our very survival depends upon learning the sources of the difficulties that lie in the way. Many parts of the brain's programs certainly tend to promote collaboration, not only between relatives, but also with people of different cultures. We can build securely on this foundation of capacity to co-operate, but of course there are other programs that tend to make us spurn altruism and to produce aggression and discord. We shall surely be wise to look hard at the background in our constitutions to try to find the source of these tendencies to evil as well as for good. As we learn to understand the brain better we can recognize that even if these tendencies have hereditary backgrounds they are not therefore equally and forever immutable. We are no longer apes, or paleoliths. Human nature has changed in the past and is likely to change even more rapidly in the future. Our lives have become very different from those of our ancestors and our descendants will be different from us again. Multi-parental inheritance of information will produce much more rapid change than the genetic evolution that has transformed ape into man.

But first we have to ensure that we do indeed have descendants. If we are not to blow the world up we must try to transcend the natural tendency to limit our concern to those near to us. It is easy to love our relatives and those that we know, and to feel for their suffering, but equally easy to ignore those who are distant or unknown to us. The thousands of millions who are going to inhabit the earth will have to face this question and its inverse. Why do we find it so easy to fight each other and to destroy the very land upon which we all depend?

It is easy to be alarmist and pessimistic, but perhaps the signs if properly read are not all unfavourable. Capacities for communication and for production have certainly greatly increased in recent times. Why should this not continue? The massive populations which seem to constitute the threat are themselves a tribute to man's skill in earning a living on earth, and avoiding early death. It is illogical to assume that this tendency to increase human capacity for survival will suddenly be reversed. What we need is further information about how to communicate better and to produce better. Skill of many sorts will be needed, but human brain programs for co-operation and acquiring knowledge should be adequate to show how to conserve depleted resources and to find substitutes.

## The power of scientific language

The question of how fast changes can take place in human attitudes is also very relevant to the general problem of whether there is any sense in saying that brains can understand brains and whether a suitable scientific language could dispense with the distinctions of body and mind. Are these perhaps really one single question? How far will changes in the use of language go? I suggested earlier that the conception of the mind as a little person in the head seemed to be a product of the general tendency of the brain to explain all phenomena as due to the operation of persons. Even if we dispense with this simplistic concept, which Ryle (1949) has so aptly called the ghost in the machine, we are still left with no clear way of describing the phenomena that we call our mental life. Perhaps this is because the human brain organization *must* operate in this way. It may seem a strange idea that men are genetically programmed to use concepts of body and mind. No one can be sure that this is the answer. But then no biologist can give a precise account of how the brain comes to be able to use concepts at all. If, as the evidence suggests, its programs tend to refer everything to human models it is possible that the ghost is part of the machine all the time.

If this is so it is not surprising that we cannot answer these questions that perplex us. Perhaps this is another way of saying that they are not properly formulated questions at all, within the present usages of human brains and language. It suggests that we should try to find ways in which description could be improved. In particular, while we all think that we know our own minds most people do not attach an adequate meaning to the word brain. This book has been an attempt to improve this situation and to show the brain as a functioning part of each human person. So my hope is that the application of scientific language to describe ourselves may lead to an improvement in powers of communication and co-operation, perhaps even to a revolution in their effectiveness.

The invention of speech depended on using sounds to represent categories of events, which could then be combined to give endless different shades of meaning and information. This provided mankind with an entirely new potential for change, by the accumulation and transmission of knowledge and information by multi-parental inheritance. The new categories of science have produced a further tremendous extension of this power of language. In a sense the ancient dream of a universal medium of communication is coming true in the language of science. The application of it to describe the activities of the brain is producing a revolution in every aspect of our lives. This may lead not only to new concepts with which to talk about ourselves but also to new artefacts, new computers perhaps, with which our descendants will more freely communicate. As signals pass by as yet unknown means between the heads of some future historians and then to their computers and back again, perhaps a new form of laughter will also echo through the system, as the information comes up that in 1978 the best way the ancients had to describe these processes was to call them Programs of the Brain.

# Bibliography

ADRIAN, E. D. and MATTHEWS, B. H. C. (1934). The Berger rhythm: potential changes from the occipital lobes in man. *Brain.* **57**, 355–85.

ANDERSON, J. R. and BOWER, G. H. (1972). Configural properties in sentence memory. *Journal of Verbal Learning and Verbal Behavior.* **11**, 594–605.

ANDERSSON, B. (1953). The effect of injections of hypertonic NaCl-solution into the different parts of the hypothalamus of goats. *Acta Physiologica Scandinavica.* **28**, 188–201.

ANLEZARK, G. M., CROW, T. J., and GREENWAY, A. P. (1973). Evidence that the noradrenergic innervation of the cerebral cortex is necessary for learning. *Journal of Physiology, London.* **231**, 119–20P.

ANSCOMBE, G. E. M. (1963). *Intention.* Blackwell, Oxford.

ARBIB, M. A. (1972). *The metaphorical brain.* Wiley-Interscience, New York.

—— (1976). Neurolinguistics must be computational. Working Paper, Department of Computer Science, University of Massachusetts at Amherst, November 1976.

ARNHEIM, R. (1954). *Art and visual perception.* University of California Press, Berkeley.

AUSTIN, J. L. (1956). Ifs and cans. *Proceedings of the British Academy.* **42**, 109–32.

—— (1962). *How to do things with words: the William James lectures delivered at Harvard University in 1955.* Clarendon Press, Oxford.

BADDELEY, A. D. (1976). *The psychology of memory.* Harper & Row, New York.

BARTLETT, F. C. (1932). *Remembering: a study in experimental and social psychology.* Cambridge University Press.

—— (1958). *Thinking: an experimental and social study.* Allen & Unwin, London.

BASBAUM, A. I. and WALL, P. D. (1976). Chronic changes in the response of cells in adult cat dorsal horn following partial deafferentation: the appearance of responding cells in a previously non-responsive region. *Brain Research.* **116**, 181–204.

BEARD, R. M. (1969). *An outline of Piaget's developmental psychology for students and teachers.* Basic Books, New York.

BELL, S. M. and AINSWORTH, M. D. S. (1972). Infant crying and maternal responsiveness. *Child Development.* **43**, 1171–90.

BELLAH, R. N. (1970). *Beyond belief. Essays on religion in a post-traditional world.* Harper & Row, New York.

BERGER, H. (1929). Über des Elektrenkephalogram des Menschen. *Archiv für Psychiatrie und Nervenkrankeiten.* **87**, 527–70.

BERGER, P. L. (1969). *A rumour of angels. Modern society and the rediscovery of the supernatural.* Penguin, Harmondsworth.

BERGER, R. J. (1963). Experimental modification of dream content by meaningful verbal stimuli. *British Journal of Psychiatry.* **109**, 722–40.

BERGSON, H. (1907). *L'évolution créatrice.* Alcan, Paris.

BERLYNE, D. E. (1967). Arousal and Reinforcement. *Nebraska Symposium on Motivation.* University of Nebraska Press, Lincoln.

BERLYNE, D. E. (1971). *Aesthetics and psychobiology*. Appleton-Century Crofts, New York.

BERNAL, J. D. (1967). *The origin of life*. Weidenfeld & Nicolson, London.

BETH, E. W. and PIAGET, J. (1966). *Mathematical epistemology and psychology*. (translated by W. Mays). Reidel, Dordrecht.

BILLIG, M. (1976). *Social psychology and intergroup relations* (*European Monographs in Social Psychology*, **9**. Series editor H. Tajfel). Academic Press, London.

BIRKHOFF, G. D. (1933). *Aesthetic measure*. Harvard University Press, Cambridge, Mass.

BISCHOF, N. (1975). Comparative ethology of incest avoidance. In *Biosocial anthropology* (ed. R. Fox), pp. 37–67. Malaby Press, London.

BLAKEMORE, C. (1975). Central visual processing. In *Handbook of psychology* (ed. M. S. Gazzaniga and C. Blakemore), pp. 241–68. Academic Press, New York.

—— (1977). *Mechanics of the mind*. Cambridge University Press.

—— and COOPER, G. (1970). Development of the brain depends on the visual environment. *Nature, London*. **228**, 477–8.

BLISS, T. V. P. and GARDNER-MEDWIN, A. R. (1973). Long-lasting potentiation of synaptic transmission in the dentate area of the unanaesthetized rabbit following stimulation of the perforant path. *Journal of Physiology, London*. **232**, 357–74.

BOWKER, J. (1973). *The sense of God. Sociological, anthropological and psychological approaches to the origin of the sense of God*. Clarendon Press, Oxford.

BOWLBY, J. (1969 and 1973). *Attachment and Loss*. Vol. I, *Attachment*, and Vol. II, *Separation: anxiety and anger*. The International Psycho-Analytical Library No. 79 and No. 95. The Hogarth Press and The Institute of Psycho-analysis, London. (Penguin, Harmondsworth, 1971 and 1975.)

BOYCOTT, B. B. (1974). Aspects of the comparative anatomy and physiology of the vertebrate retina. In *Essays on the nervous system: a festschrift for Professor J. Z. Young* (ed. R. Bellairs and E. G. Gray), Clarendon Press, Oxford.

BRADLEY, E. A. and YOUNG, J. Z. (1975). Comparison of visual and tactile learning in octopus after lesions to one of the two memory systems. *Journal of Neuroscience Research*. **1**, 185–205.

BRADLEY, R. J. and SMYTHIES, J. R. (1976). The biochemistry of schizophrenia. In *Biological foundations of psychiatry* (ed. R. G. Grenell and S. Gabay), pp. 653–82. Raven Press, New York.

BRAIN, LORD (1965). *Speech disorders: aphasia, apraxia and agnosia*. Butterworths, London.

BRAZIER, M. A. B. (1968). *Electrical Activity of the Nervous System* 3e. Pitman Medical, Tunbridge Wells.

BRUNER, J. (1974). *Beyond the information given: studies in the psychology of knowing*. Selected and introduced by J. M. Anglin. Allen & Unwin, London.

BUCKINGHAM, H. and KERTESZ, A. (1974). A linguistic analysis of fluent aphasia. *Brain and Language*. **1**, 43–62.

BUNNEY, Jr., W. E. (1976). Acute behavioral effects of lithium carbonate. *Neurosciences Research Program Bulletin*. **14** (No. 2), 124–31.

—— and MURPHY, D. L. (1976). The neurobiology of lithium. *Neurosciences Research Program Bulletin*. **14** (No. 2), 207 pp.

CANNON, W. B. (1932). *The wisdom of the body*. Norton, New York.

CHANCE, M. R. A. (1975). Social cohesion and the structure of attention. In *Biosocial anthropology* (ed. R. Fox), pp. 93–113. Malaby Press, London.

CHAPMAN, R. M. (1973). Evoked potentials of the brain related to thinking. In *The psychophysiology of thinking: the study of covert processes* (ed. F. J. McGuigan and R. A. Schoonover), pp. 69–108. Academic Press, New York.

CHARLESWORTH, W. R. and KREUTZER, M. A. (1973). Facial expression of infants and children. In *Darwin and facial expression: a century of research in review* (ed. P. Ekman), pp. 91–168. Academic Press, New York.

CHERRY, C. (1966). *On human communication: a review, a survey, and a criticism.* MIT Press, Cambridge, Mass.

CHOMSKY, N. (1976a). Language and the mind. In *Current perspectives in social psychology: readings with commentary* (ed. E. P. Hollander and R. G. Hunt) (4th edn), pp. 183–8. Oxford University Press.

—— (1976b). *Reflections on language.* Temple Smith, London.

—— (1976c). On the biological basis of language capacities. In *The neuropsychology of language: essays in honor of Eric Lenneberg* (ed. R. W. Rieber), Plenum Press, New York.

CLARE, A. (1976). *Psychiatry in dissent: controversial issues in thought and practice.* Tavistock Publications, London.

CLARK, C. (1967). *Population growth and land use.* Macmillan, London.

CLARKE, A. M. and CLARKE, A. D. B. (1976). *Early experience: myth and evidence.* Open Books, London.

COLE, M., GAY, J., GLICK, J. A., and SHARP, D. W. (1971). *The cultural context of learning and thinking: an exploration in experimental anthropology.* Methuen, London.

COLLIER, G. (1972). *Art and the creative consciousness.* Prentice-Hall, New Jersey.

CONRAD, R. (1964). Acoustic confusions in immediate memory. *British Journal of Psychology.* **55**, 75–84.

COOKE, D. (1959). *The language of music.* Oxford University Press.

COON, C. S. (1963). *The origin of races.* Cape, London.

CRAGG, B. G. (1967). The density of synapses and neurones in the motor and visual areas of the cerebral cortex. *Journal of Anatomy, London.* **101**, 639–54.

CRAIK, K. J. W. (1943). *The nature of explanation.* Cambridge University Press.

CRICK, F. H. C. (1968). The origin of the genetic code. *Journal of Molecular Biology.* **38**, 367–79.

CRITCHLEY, M. and HENSON, R. A. (1977). *Music and the brain: studies in the neurology of music.* Heinemann, London.

DAHRENDORF, R. (1969). On the origin of inequality among men. In *Social inequality* (ed. A. Beteille). Penguin, Harmondsworth.

DANIEL, P. M. and WHITTERIDGE, D. (1961). The representation of the visual field on the cerebral cortex in monkeys. *Journal of Physiology, London.* **159**, 203–21.

DARWIN, C. (1872). *The expression of the emotions in man and animals.* Murray, London.

DAWKINS, R. (1976). *The selfish gene.* Oxford University Press.

DAY, M. C. (1975). Developmental trends in visual scanning. *Advances in Child Development.* **10**, 153–93.

DELGADO, J. M. R. (1965). *Evolution of physical control of the brain.* James Arthur Lecture on the evolution of the human brain 1965. American Museum of Natural History, New York.

DEMENT, W. C. (1968). The biological role of REM sleep. In *Sleep an active process* (ed. W. B. Webb). Scott Foresman, Glenview, Illinois.

DIAMOND, I. I. (1978). Subdivisions of the neocortex: the traditional classification into sensory, motor, and association areas and a proposal for an alternative classification. In *Progress in psychobiology* (ed. J. Sprague) (in press).

DISSANAYAKE, E. (1974). A hypothesis of the evolution of art from play. *Leonardo.* **7**, 211–17.

DIXON, N. E. (1976). *On the psychology of military incompetence.* Cape, London.

DOMAGK, G. F., ALEXANDER, W. R., and HEERMAN, K. H. (1976). Transfer of learned tactile discrimination in *Octopus vulgaris* by means of brain extracts: negative results. *Journal of Biological Psychology*. **18**, 15–17.

DOSE, K., FOX, S. W., DEBORIN, G. A., and PAVLOVSKAYA, T. E. (1974). *The origin of life and evolutionary biochemistry*. Plenum Press, New York.

DRIESCH, H. (1927). *Mind and body: a criticism of psychophysical parallelism* (translated by T. Besterman). Methuen, London.

DURKHEIM, E. (1915). *The elementary forms of the religious life. A study in religious sociology* (translated by J. W. Sain). Allen & Unwin, London.

EBBINGHAUS, H. (1885). *Über das Gedächtniss*. Dunker, Leipzig.

—— (1913). *Memory: a contribution to experimental psychology* (translated by H. Ruyer and C. E. Bussenius). Teachers College Press, Columbia University, New York.

EIBL-EIBESFELDT, I. (1971). *Love and hate: on the natural history of basic behaviour patterns* (translated by G. Strachan). Methuen, London.

EIMAS, P. D., COOPER, W. E., and CORBIT, J. D. (1973). Some properties of linguistic feature detectors. *Perception and psychophysics*. **13**, 247–52.

——, SIQUELAND, E. R., JUSCZYK, P., and VIGORITO, J. (1971). Speech perception in infants. *Science, New York*. **171**, 303–6.

EINSTEIN, A. (1905). Zur Elektrodynamik bewegter Körper. *Annalen der Physik*. **17**.

—— (1923). In *The principle of relativity. A collection of original memoirs on the special and general theory of relativity* by H. A. Lorentz, A. Einstein, H. Minkowski, and H. Weyl (trans. W. Perrett and G. B. Jeffrey). Methuen, London.

EISSLER, R. S., FREUD, A., KRIS, M., and SOLNIT, A. J. (1977). *An anthology of the psychoanalytic study of the child. Psychoanalytic assessment: the diagnostic profile*. Yale University Press, New Haven.

ELSASSER, W. M. (1975). *The chief abstractions of biology*. North-Holland Publishing, Amsterdam.

EMDE, R. M., GAENSBAUER, T. J., and HARMON, R. J. (1976). Emotional expression in infancy: a biobehavioural study. *Psychological Issues*. **10**, No. 1, Monograph 37.

ERIKSON, E. H. (1977). *Toys and reasons: stages in the ritualization of experience*. Boyars, London.

EYSENCK, H. J. (1968). An experimental study of aesthetic preference for polygonal figures. *Journal of General Psychology*. **79**, 3–17.

—— and CASTLE, M. (1970). Training in art as a factor in the determination of preference judgements for polygons. *British Journal of Psychology*. **61**, 65–81.

FECHNER, G. T. (1876). *Vorschule der Ästhetik*. Breitkopf & Härtel, Leipzig.

FEDIO, P. and VAN BUREN, J. M. (1974). Memory deficits during electrical stimulation of the speech cortex in conscious man. *Brain and Language*. **1**, 29–42.

FERGUSON, D. N. (1960). *Music as metaphor: the elements of expression*. Greenwood, Westport, Connecticut.

FIRTH, R. (1971). *Elements of social organization: Josiah Mason Lectures delivered at the University of Birmingham*. Watts, London.

—— (1973). *Symbols public and private*. Cornell University Press, New York.

FLAVELL, J. H. (1963). *The developmental psychology of Jean Piaget*. Van Nostrand Rheinhold, New York.

—— (1977). *Cognitive development*. Prentice-Hall, New Jersey.

FODOR, J. D. (1970). Formal linguistics and formal logic. In *New horizons in linguistics* (ed. J. Lyons), pp. 198–214. Penguin, Harmondsworth.

FORBES, A. (1922). The interpretation of spinal reflexes in terms of present knowledge of nerve conduction. *Physiological Reviews*. **2**, 361–414.

FORMANŮ, W. A. B. and POULÍKA, J. (1956). *Pravěké umění.* Státní Nakladatelství Krásné Literatury, Hudby a Umění, Praha.

FOX, R. (1975). Primate kin and human kinship. In *Biosocial anthropology* (ed. R. Fox), pp. 9–35. Malaby Press, London.

FOX, S. W. (1976). The evolutionary significance of ordering phenomena in thermal proteinoids and proteins. In *Protein structure and function* (ed. J. L. Fox, Z. Deyl, and A. Blazej). Marcel Dekker, New York.

FRAIBERG, S. and ADELSON, F. (1973). Self-representation in language and play: observations of blind children. *Psychoanalytic Quarterly.* **42**, 539–62.

FRANKENHAEUSER, M. (1975). Experimental approaches to the study of catecholamines and emotion. In *Emotions—their parameters and measurement* (ed. L. Levi). Raven Press, New York.

FRENCH, J. D. (1958). Cortifugal connections with the reticular formation. In *Reticular formation of the brain* (ed. H. H. Jasper, L. D. Proctor, R. S. Knighton, W, C. Noshay, and R. T. Costello). Churchill, London.

FRENCH, Jr., J. R. P. (1964). Laboratory and field studies of power. In *Power and conflict in organizations* (ed. R. L. Kahn and E. Boulding). Tavistock, London.

FREUD, A. (1974). *Introduction to psychoanalysis: lectures for child analysts and teachers 1922–1935.* International Psycho-analytical Library No. 99. The Hogarth Press and the Institute of Psycho-analysis, London.

FREUD, S. (1900–1). *The interpretation of dreams:* and *On dreams* **I** and **II**. *The standard edition of the complete psychological works of Sigmund Freud* **4** and **5**. The Hogarth Press and the Institute of Psychiatry, London.

—— (1911). Formulations on the two principles in mental functioning. *The standard edition of the complete psychological works of Sigmund Freud.* **12**, 213–26. The Hogarth Press and the Institute of Psychiatry, London.

—— (1912). A note on the unconscious in psycho-analysis. *The standard edition of the complete psychological works of Sigmund Freud.* **12**, 255–66. The Hogarth Press and the Institute of Psychiatry, London.

—— (1920). Beyond the pleasure principle. *The standard edition of the complete psychological works of Sigmund Freud.* **18**, 1–64. The Hogarth Press and the Institute of Psychiatry, London.

—— (1921). Group psychology and the analysis of the ego. *The standard edition of the complete psychological works of Sigmund Freud.* **18**, 65–143. The Hogarth Press and the Institute of Psychiatry, London.

FRY, D. B. (1970). Speech reception and perception. In *New horizons in linguistics* (ed. J. Lyons), pp. 29–52. Penguin, Harmondsworth.

—— and DENES, P (1958) The solution of some fundamental problems in mechanical speech recognition. *Language and Speech.* **1**, 35–58.

GAARDER, K. R. (1975). *Eye movements, vision and behavior: a hierarchical visual information processing model.* Wiley, New York.

GARDNER, H. (1975). *The shattered mind: the person after brain damage.* Routledge & Kegan Paul, London.

GARVEY, C. (1977). Play with language. In *Biology of play* (ed. B. Tizard and D. Harvey). (*Clinics in Developmental Medicine* No. **62**.) Heinemann, London.

GELLNER, E. (1959). *Words and things: a critical account of linguistic philosophy and a study of ideology.* Gollancz, London.

—— (1973). The savage and the modern mind. In *Modes of thought: essays on thinking in western and non-western societies* (ed. R. Horton and R. Finnegan). Faber & Faber, London.

GERARD, R. W. and YOUNG, J. Z. (1937). Electrical activity of the central nervous system of the frog. *Proceedings of the Royal Society of London* B, **122**, 343–52.

GESCHWIND, N., QUADFASE, F. A., and SEGARRA, J. M. (1968). Isolation of the speech area. *Neuropsychologia.* **6**, 327–40.

GILBERT, P. (1975). How the cerebellum could memorise movements. *Nature, London.* **254**, 688–9.

GOLDBERG, M. E. and WURTZ, R. H. (1972). Activity of superior colliculus in behaving monkey. *Journal of Neurophysiology.* **35**, 542–59, 560–74.

GOMBRICH, E. H. (1972). *Art and illusion. A study in the psychology of pictorial representation.* Phaidon, London.

GRAY, E. G. (1973). The synapse. *Oxford Biology Readers.* No. 35, 16pp.

GREENBERG, J. (1975). Research on language universals. *Annual Review of Anthropology.* **4**, 75–94.

GREENFIELD, P. M. and SMITH, T. H. (1976). *The structure of communication in early language development.* Academic Press, New York.

GREGORY, R. L. (1969). On how so little information controls so much behaviour. *Towards a theoretical biology.* **2**, 236–47. (An IUBS Symposium ed. C. H. Waddington.) Edinburgh University Press.

—— (1975). Do we need cognitive concepts? In *Handbook of psychobiology* (ed. M. S. Gazzaniga and C. Blakemore), pp. 607–28. Academic Press, New York.

—— and WALLACE, J. G. (1963). Recovery from early blindness. *Experimental Psychology Society Monograph*, No. **2**.

GROSS, C. G., ROCHA-MIRANDA, C. E., and BENDER, D. B. (1972). Visual properties of neurons in inferotemporal cortex of the macaque. *Journal of Neurophysiology.* **35**, 96–111.

HACKING, I. (1975). *Why does language matter to philosophy?* Cambridge University Press.

HALBERG, F. (1977). Implications of biologic rhythms for clinical practice. *Hospital Practice.* **12**, 139–49.

HALDANE, J. B. S. (1932). *The causes of evolution.* Longmans Green, London.

HALL, R. D., BLOOM, F. E., and OLDS, J. (1977). Neuronal and neurochemical substrates of reinforcement. *Neurosciences Research Program Bulletin.* **15**, No. 2, 133–314.

HALLIDAY, M. (1970). Language structure and language function. In *New horizons in linguistics* (ed. J. Lyons), pp. 140–65. Penguin, Harmondsworth.

HAMBURG, D. A., HAMBURG, B. A., and BARCHAS, J. D. (1975). Anger and depression in perspective of behavioral biology. In *Emotions—their parameters and measurement* (ed. L. Levi). Raven Press, New York.

HAMILTON, W. D. (1975). Innate social aptitudes of Man: an approach from evolutionary genetics. In *Biosocial anthropology* (ed. R. Fox), pp. 133–55. Malaby Press, London.

HARE, R. M. (1963). *Freedom and reason.* Clarendon Press, Oxford.

HARLOW, H. F. and HARLOW, M. K. (1962). Social deprivation in monkeys. *Scientific American.* **207** (November), 136–46.

HARMAN, G. (ed.) (1975). *On Noam Chomsky: critical essays.* Doubleday, New York.

HARTUNG, J. (1977). An implication about human mating systems. *Journal of Theoretical Biology.* **66**, 737–45.

HEAD, H. (1926). *Aphasia and kindred disorders of speech* (2 vols). Cambridge University Press.

HEBB, D. O. (1949). *The organization of behavior: a neuropsychological theory.* Wiley, New York.

HEINROTH, O. (1911). Beiträge zur Biologie, namentlich Ethologie und Psychologie der Anatiden. *Verhandlungen des V. Internationalen Ornithologen-Kongresses in Berlin 30 Mai bis 4 Juni, 1910.* Deutsche Ornitologische Gesellschaft, Berlin.

HENRY, J. P., ELY, D. L., WATSON, F. M. C., and STEPHENS, P. M. (1975). Ethological methods as applied to the measurement of emotion. In *Emotions—their parameters and measurement* (ed. L. Levi). Raven Press, New York.

HERNÁNDEZ-PEÓN, R. (1955). *J. Latinoam.* 1,256.

HESSELGREN, S. (1972). *The language of architecture*, Vol. 2. Applied Science Publishers, London.

HOFFMANN, K. (1960). Experimental manipulation of the orientational clock in birds. *Cold Spring Harbor Symposium for Quantitative Biology.* 25, 379–84.

HONDERICH, T. (1975). On inequality and violence and the differences we make between them. In *Nature and conduct* (ed. R. S. Peters). Macmillan, London.

—— (1978). On determinism. In *Philosophy as it is*. Penguin, Harmondsworth. (In press.)

HORRIDGE, G. A. (1968). *Interneurons: their origin, action, specificity, growth, and plasticity*. Freeman, London.

HUBEL, D. H. and WIESEL, T. N. (1968). Receptive fields and functional architecture of monkey striate cortex. *Journal of Physiology, London.* 195, 215–43.

—— (1977). Ferrier Lecture. Functional architecture of macaque monkey visual cortex. *Proceedings of the Royal Society of London.* B, 198, 1–59.

HUGHES, J. (1975). Isolation of an endogenous compound from the brain with pharmacological properties similar to morphine. *Brain Research.* 88, 295–308.

HUYGHE, R. (1972). Introduction, pp. ix–xii. In *Art and the creative consciousness* by G. Collier. Prentice-Hall, New Jersey.

JAGER, R. (1972). *The development of Bertrand Russell's philosophy*. Allen & Unwin, London.

JAMES, W. (1890). *The principles of psychology* (2 vols). Macmillan, London.

—— (1902). *The varieties of religious experience. A study in human nature. Being the Gifford Lectures on Natural Religion delivered at Edinburgh in 1901–1902.* Longmans, London.

JAMESON, F. (1972). *The prison-house of language: a critical account of structuralism and Russian formalism*. Princeton University Press.

JOUVET, M. (1975). The function of dreaming: a neurophysiologist's point of view. In *Handbook of psychobiology* (ed. M. S. Gazzaniga and C. Blakemore), pp. 499–527. Academic Press, New York.

KAHN, R. L. (1964). Introduction. In *Power and conflict in organizations* (ed. R. L. Kahn and E. Boulding). Tavistock, London.

KAMIYA, J. (1969). Operant control of the EEG alpha rhythm and some of its reported effects on consciousness. In *Altered states of consciousness: a book of readings* (ed. C. T. Tart). Wiley, New York.

KAPLAN, A. (1964). Power in perspective. In *Power and conflict in organizations* (ed. R. L. Kahn and E. Boulding). Tavistock, London.

KASAMATSU, A. and HIRAI, T. (1969). An electroencephalic study on the Zen meditation (Zazen). In *Altered states of consciousness: a book of readings* (ed. C. T. Tart). Wiley, New York.

KATZ, B. (1966). *Nerve, muscle and synapse*. McGraw-Hill, New York.

KAVOLIS, V. (1968). *Artistic expression—a sociological analysis*. Cornell University Press, Ithaca.

KELLOGG, W. N. (1968). Communication and language in the home-raised chimpanzee. The gestures, 'words', and behavior signals of home-raised apes are critically examined. *Science, New York.* 162, 423–7.

KINSEY, A. C., POMEROY, W. B., and MARTIN, C. E. (1948). *Sexual behavior in the human male*. Saunders, Philadelphia.

——— ——— ——— and GEBHARD, P. H. (1953). *Sexual behavior in the human female.* Saunders, Philadelphia.

KLEIN, M. (1975). *The writings of Melanie Klein* (4 vols). The Hogarth Press and the Institute of Psycho-analysis, London.

KRAMER, G. (1950). Orientierte Zugaktivität gekäfigter Singvögel. *Naturwissenschaften.* **37**, 188.

KUHN, T. S. (1962). *The structure of scientific revolutions.* University of Chicago Press.

LA BARRE, W. (1970). *The ghost dance: origins of religion.* Doubleday, New York.

LAING, R. D. (1960). *The divided self: a study of sanity and madness.* Tavistock, London. (Penguin, Harmondsworth, 1965.)

LAND, E. H. (1959). Experiments in color vision. *Scientific American.* **200**, (5), 84–99.

LASHLEY, K. S. (1950). In search of the engram. *Symposia of the Society for Experimental Biology.* **4**, 454–82.

LAVER, J. (1970). The production of speech. In *New Horizons in linguistics* (ed. J. Lyons), pp. 53–75. Penguin, Harmondsworth.

LAZARUS, R. S. (1975). The self-regulation of emotion. In *Emotions—their parameters and measurement* (ed. L. Levi). Raven Press, New York.

LEACH, E. R. (1954). *Political systems of Highland Burma: a study of Kachin social structure.* Bell, London.

——— (1977). Michaelangelo's *Genesis.* Structuralist comments on the paintings on the Sistine Chapel ceiling. *Times Literary Supplement* (18 March).

LEAKEY, R. E. F. (1976). New hominid fossils from the Koobi Fora formation in Northern Kenya. *Nature, London.* **261**, 574–6.

——— and LEWIN, R. (1977). *Origins: what new discoveries reveal about the emergence of our species and its possible future.* Macdonald and Jane's, London.

——— and WALKER, A. C. (1976). *Australopithecus, Homo erectus* and the single species hypothesis. *Nature, London.* **261**, 572–4.

LE MAY, M. (1975). The language capability of Neanderthal man. *American Journal of Physical Anthropology.* **42**, 9–14.

LENNEBERG, E. H. (1967). *Biological foundations of language.* Wiley, New York.

——— (1974). Language, speech and speakers. *Neurosciences Research Program Bulletin.* **12**, 619–36.

LEONARD, B. E. (1975). Neurochemical and neuropharmacological aspects of depression. *International Review of Neurobiology.* **18**, 357–87.

LERNER, I. M. and LIBBY, W. J. (1976). *Heredity, evolution, and society* (2nd edn). Freeman, San Francisco.

LÉVI-STRAUSS, C. (1963). *Structural anthropology,* Vol. I (translated by C. Jacobson and B. G. Schoepf). Basic Books, New York. (1977). *Structural anthropology,* Vol. II (translated by M. Layton). Allen Lane, London.

——— (1969). *The elementary structures of kinship* (translated by J. H. Bell, J. R. von Sturmer, and R. Needham). Eyre & Spottiswoode, London.

LEWIN, W. (1976). Changing attitudes to the management of severe head injuries. The Victor Horsley Lecture 1975. *British Medical Journal.* **2**, 1234–9.

LIEBERMAN, P. (1971). On the speech of Neanderthal man. *Linguistic Inquiry.* **2**, 203–22.

——— (1973). On the evolution of language: a unified view. *Cognition.* **2**, 59–94.

——— (1975). *On the origins of language: an introduction to the evolution of human speech.* Macmillan, New York.

——— (1977). The phylogeny of language. In *How animals communicate* (ed. T. A. Sebeok). Indiana University Press, Bloomington.

LINDEN, E. (1976). *Apes, men and language*. Penguin, Harmondsworth.
LION, J. R. and PENNA, M. (1974). The study of human aggression. *Advances in Behavioral Biology*. **12**, 165–82.
LIVINGSTON, W. K. (1943). *Pain mechanisms*. Macmillan, London.
LORENTE DE NÓ, R. (1933). The interaction of the corneal reflex and vestibular nystagmus. *American Journal of Physiology*. **103**, 704–11.
LORENZ, K. Z. (1935). Der Kumpan in der Umwelt des Vogels. *Journal für Ornithologie*. **83**, 137–213, 289–412. (English translation in *Instinctive behavior* (1957), ed. C. H. Schiller. International Universities Press, New York.)
LUKES, S. (1973). On the social determinism of truth. In *Modes of thought: essays on thinking in western and non-western cultures* (ed. R. Horton and R. Finnegan). Faber & Faber, London.
LURIA, A. R. (1968). *The mind of a mnemonist. A little book about a vast memory* (translated by L. Solotaroff). Basic Books, New York and Penguin, Harmondsworth (1975).
—— (1973). *The working brain: an introduction to neuropsychology* (translated by B. Haigh). Penguin, Harmondsworth.
—— (1973a). *The man with a shattered world* (translated by L. Solotaroff). Cape, London.
—— (1973b). The frontal lobes and the regulation of behavior. In *Psychophysiology of the frontal lobes* (ed. K. H. Pribram and A. R. Luria). Academic Press, New York.
LYNCH, J. C., MOUNTCASTLE, V. B., TALBOT, W. H., and YIN, T. C. T. (1977). Parietal lobe mechanisms for directed visual attention. *Journal of Neurophysiology*. **40**, 362–89.
LYONS, J. (1970). Introduction. In *New horizons in linguistics* (ed. J. Lyons). Penguin, Harmondsworth.
—— (1977). *Semantics*. (2 vols). Cambridge University Press.
McCLOY, J. (Ed.) (1964). *The Science of Man 2*. BBC, London.
MACALPINE, I. and HUNTER, R. (1974). The pathography of the past. *Times Literary Supplement* (March 15), 256–7.
MACKIE, J. L. (1977). *Ethics: inventing right and wrong*. Penguin, Harmondsworth.
MACLEAN, C. (1977). *The wolf children*. Allen Lane, London.
MARK, R. (1974). *Memory and nerve cell connections: criticisms and contributions from developmental neurophysiology*. Clarendon Press, Oxford.
MARR, D. and NISHIHARA, H. K. (1978). Representation and recognition of the spatial organization of three-dimensional shapes. *Proceedings of the Royal Society of London*. B, **200**, 269–94.
MASTERS, W. H. and JOHNSON, V. E. (1966). *Human sexual response*. Little, Brown & Co., Boston.
MAUDSLEY, H. (1881). *Responsibility in mental disease* (4th edn). Kegan Paul, London.
MAYR, E. (1961). Cause and effect in biology: kinds of causes, predictability, and teleology are viewed by a practising biologist. *Science, New York*. **134**, 1501–6.
—— (1976). *Evolution and the diversity of life: selected essays*. Belknap Press, Cambridge, Mass.
MEDAWAR, P. B. (1952). *An unsolved problem of biology*. An inaugural lecture delivered at University College, London, 6 December 1951. Lewis, London.
—— and MEDAWAR, J. S. (1977). *The life science: current ideas of biology*. Harper & Row, New York.
MEDDIS. R. (1975). On the function of sleep. *Animal behaviour*. **23**, 676–91.

MELZACK, R. (1973). *The puzzle of pain*. Penguin, Harmondsworth.
—— and SCOTT, T. H. (1957). The effects of early experience on the response to pain. *Journal of Comparative Physiological Psychology*. **50**, 155–61.
MILGRAM, S. (1974). *Obedience to authority: an experimental view*. Tavistock, London.
MILNER, B. (1970). Memory and the medial temporal regions of the brain. In *Biology of memory* (ed. K. H. Pribram and D. E. Broadbent). Academic Press, New York.
MILO, R. D. (1973). *Egoism and altruism*. Wadsworth, Belmont, California.
MOHR, J. P. (1976). Broca's area and Broca's aphasia. In *Studies in neurolinguistics*, Vol. I (ed. H. Whitaker and H. A. Whitaker). Academic Press, London.
MONOD, J. (1970). *Le hasard et la nécessité essai sur la philosophie naturelle de la biologie moderne*. Le Seuil, Paris.
—— (1972). *Chance and necessity: an essay on the natural philosophy of modern biology* (translated by A. Wainhouse). Collins, London.
MONTAGU, A. (1976). *The nature of human aggression*. Oxford University Press.
MOORE, B. C. J. (1977). *Introduction to the psychology of hearing*. Macmillan, London.
MOORE, G. E. (1903). *Principia ethica*. Cambridge University Press.
MOUNTCASTLE, V. B. (1957). Modality and topographic properties of single neurons of cat's somatic sensory cortex. *Journal of Neurophysiology*. **20**, 408–34.
MÜLLER, J. (1848). *The physiology of the senses, voice and muscular motion with the mental faculties* (translated by W. Baly). Taylor, Walton, & Maberly, London.
MUNTZ, W. R. A. (1961). The function of the vertical lobe system of octopus in interocular transfer. *Journal of Comparative and Physiological Psychology*. **54**, 186–91.
OHE, S. (1962). Land's experiments in color vision and the mathematical structure of our sense-perception. *Annals of the Japan Association for Philosophy of Science*. **2**, 65–69.
OLDS, J. (1976). Behavioral studies of hypothalamic functions: drives and reinforcements. In *Biological foundations of psychiatry*, Vol. I (ed. R. G. Grenell and S. Gabay). Raven Press, New York.
—— (1977). *Drives and reinforcements: behavioral studies of hypothalamic functions*. Raven Press, New York.
OSGOOD, C. E. (1971). Where do sentences come from? In *Semantics: an interdisciplinary reader in philosophy, linguistics and psychology* (ed. D. D. Steinberg and L. A. Jakabovits). Cambridge University Press.
OSWALD, I. (1966). *Sleep*. Penguin, Harmondsworth.
PADDOCK, J. (1975). Studies on antiviolent and 'normal' communities. *Aggressive Behavior*. **1**, 217–33.
PAIVIO, A. (1969). Mental imagery in associative learning and memory. *Psychological Review*. **76**, 241–63.
PALLIS, D. J. and STOFFELMAYR, B. E. (1973). Social attitudes and treatment orientation among psychiatrists. *British Journal of Medical Psychology*. **46**, 75–81.
PALMER, F. R. (1976). *Semantics: a new outline*. Cambridge University Press.
PATTEE, H. H. (1961). On the origin of macromolecular sequences. *Biophysical Journal*. **1**, 683–710.
PEIRCE, C. S. (1931–5). *Collected papers of Charles Sanders Peirce*, Vols I–VI (ed. C. Hartshorne and P. Weiss). Harvard University Press, Cambridge, Mass.
PENFIELD, W. (1975). *The mystery of the mind: a critical study of consciousness and the human brain*. Princeton University Press.
—— and RASMUSSEN, T. (1950). *The cerebral cortex of man: a clinical study of localization of function*. Macmillan, New York.

—— and ROBERTS, L. (1959). *Speech and brain-mechanisms.* Princeton University Press.

PHILLIPS, C. G. (1977). On integration and teleonomy. *Proceedings of the Royal Society of London*, B. **199**, 415–24.

PIAGET, J. (1969). *The mechanisms of perception* (translated by G. N. Seagrim). Routledge & Kegan Paul, London.

—— (1971). *Biology and knowledge: an essay on the relations between organic regulations and cognitive processes.* University of Chicago Press.

PICKFORD, R. W. (1972). *Psychology and visual aesthetics.* Hutchinson, London.

PITTENDRIGH, C. S. (1958). Adaptation, natural selection, and behavior. In *Behavior and evolution* (ed. A. Roe and G. G. Simpson), pp. 390–416. Yale University Press, New Haven.

—— (1974). Circadian oscillations in cells and circadian organization of multicellular systems. In *The neurosciences: third study program* (ed. F. O. Schmitt and F. G. Worden). MIT Press, Cambridge, Mass.

POLANYI, M. and PROSCH, H. (1975). *Meaning.* University of Chicago Press.

POPPER, K. (1972). *Objective knowledge: an evolutionary approach.* Clarendon Press, Oxford.

POPPER, K. R. and ECCLES, J. C. (1977). *The self and its brain.* Springer International, Berlin.

PRADHAN, S. N. (1975). Aggression and central neurotransmitters. *International Review of Neurobiology.* **18**, 213–62.

PREMACK, D. (1975). On the origins of language. In *Handbook of psychobiology* (ed. M. S. Gazzaniga and C. Blakemore). Academic Press, New York.

PRIBRAM, K. H. (1971). *Languages of the brain: experimental paradoxes and principles in neurophysiology.* Prentice-Hall, Englewood Cliffs, New Jersey.

—— and GILL, M. M. (1976). *Freud's project reassessed.* Hutchinson, London.

QUASTLER, H. (1965). General principles of systems analysis. In *Theoretical and mathematical biology* (ed. T. H. Waterman and H. J. Morowitz). Blaisdell, New York.

QUINE, W. V. O. (1960). *Word and object.* MIT Press, Cambridge, Mass.

—— (1972). Epistemology naturalized. In *The psychology of knowing* (ed. J. R. Royce and W. W. Rozeboom). Gordon & Breach, New York.

—— (1975). Mind and verbal disposition. In *Mind and language: Wolfson College Lectures 1974* (ed. S. Guttenplan). Oxford University Press.

QUINTON, A. (1973). *The nature of things.* Routledge & Kegan Paul, London.

REICHLIN, S., BALDESSARINI, R. J., and MARTIN, J. B. (eds) (1977), *The hypothalamus.* Raven Press, New York.

RESNICK, O. (1972). The role of biogenic amines in sleep. In *Sleep and the maturing nervous system* (ed. C. D. Clemente, D. P. Purpura, and F. E. Mayer). Academic Press, New York.

ROMANES, G. J. (1882). *Animal intelligence.* Kegan Paul, Trench, London.

ROSENWEIG, M. R., BENNETT, E. L., and DIAMOND, M. C. (1972). Chemical and anatomical plasticity of brain: replications and extensions, 1970. In *Macromolecules and behavior* (ed. J. Gaito) (2nd edn.), pp. 205–77. Appleton-Century-Crofts, New York.

ROTHENSTEIN, R. (1960). Authoritarianism and men's reactions to sexuality and affection in women. *Journal of Abnormal and Social Psychology.* **61**, 329–34.

ROUTTENBERG, A. (1976). Doubts about the role of the locus coeruleus in learning and the phosphorylation mechanism engaged in the cerebellum. *Nature, London.* **260**, 79–80.

ROZEBOOM, W. W. (1972). Problems in the psycho-philosophy of knowledge. In *The psychology of knowing* (ed. J. R. Royce and W. W. Rozeboom). Gordon & Breach, New York.

RUSSELL, B. (1921). *The analysis of mind.* Allen & Unwin, London.

RUTTER, M. (1972). *Maternal deprivation reassessed.* Penguin, Harmondsworth.

RYLE, G. (1949). *The concept of mind.* Hutchinson, London.

SAGAN, C. (ed.) (1973). *Communication with extraterrestrial intelligence (CETI).* MIT Press, Cambridge, Mass.

SAHLINS, M. (1977). *The use and abuse of biology: an anthropological critique of sociobiology.* Tavistock, London.

SALTZ, E., SOLLER, E., and SIGEL, I. E. (1972). The development of natural language concepts. *Child Development.* **43**, 1191–1202.

SANDARS, N. K. (1968). *Prehistoric art in Europe.* Penguin, Harmondsworth.

SANDERS, F. K. and YOUNG, J. Z. (1940). Learning and other functions of the higher nervous centres of *Sepia. Journal of Neurophysiology.* **3**, 501–26.

SANGHVI, L. D. (1966). Inbreeding in India. *Eugenics Quarterly.* **13**, 291–301.

SAUSSURE, F. DE (1916). *Cours de linguistique générale.* Lausanne, Paris.

SCHEIBEL, M. E. and SCHEIBEL, A. B. (1967). Anatomical basis of attention mechanisms in vertebrate brains. In *The neurosciences: a study program* (ed. G. C. Quarton, T. Melnechuk, and F. O. Schmitt), pp. 577–602. The Rockefeller University Press, New York.

SCHWEBEL, M. and RAPH, J. (1974). Before and beyond the three R's. In *Piaget in the classroom* (ed. M. Schwebel and J. Raph). Routledge & Kegan Paul, London.

SCOTT, E. M. and VERNEY, E. L. (1947). Self selection of diet. VI. The nature of appetites for B vitamins. *Journal of Nutrition.* **34**, 471–80.

SEARLE, J. R. (1971). *The philosophy of language.* Oxford University Press.

SEBEOK, T. A. (1977). Zoosemiotic components of human communication. In *How animals communicate* (ed. T. A. Sebeok). Indiana University Press, Bloomington.

SHERRINGTON, C. S. (1906). *The integrative action of the nervous system.* Scribner's, New York.

—— (1925). *The assaying of Brabantius and other verse.* Milford, London.

—— (1940). *Man on his nature. The Gifford Lectures, Edinburgh 1937–1938.* Cambridge University Press.

SKORUPSKI, J. (1976). *Symbol and theory. A philosophical study of theories of religion in social anthropology.* Cambridge University Press.

SMETS, G. (1973). *Aesthetic judgement and arousal: an experimental contribution to psycho-aesthetics.* Leuven University Press.

SMITH, J. MAYNARD (1964). Group selection and kin selection. *Nature, London.* **201**, 1145–7.

SOMMERHOFF, G. (1974). *Logic of the living brain.* Wiley, London.

SPEARMAN, C. E. (1932). *The abilities of man: their nature and measurement.* Macmillan, London.

SPERRY, R. W. (1974). Lateral specialization in the surgically separated hemispheres. In *The neurosciences: third study program* (ed. F. O. Schmitt and F. G. Worden), pp. 5–19. MIT Press, Cambridge, Mass.

—— (1977). Absolute values: problem of the ultimate frame of reference. *International Conference on Unity of the SCIS, 1976.*

—— and GAZZANIGA, M. S. (1967). Language following surgical disconnection of the hemispheres. In *Brain mechanisms underlying speech and language* (ed. C. H. Millikan and F. L. Darley). Grune & Stratton, New York.

SPUHLER, J. N. (1977). Biology, speech and language. *Annual Review of Anthropology.* **6**, 509–61.

STEINER, G. (1975). *After Babel: aspects of language and translation.* Oxford University Press.

STERNBACH, R. A. and TURSKY, B. (1965). Ethnic differences among housewives in psychophysical and skin potential responses to electric shock. *Psychophysiology.* **1**, 241–6.

STREETER, L. A. (1976). Language perception of 2-month-old infants shows effects of both innate mechanisms and experience. *Nature, London.* **259**, 39–40.

STRUMWASSER, F. (1974). Neuronal principles organizing periodic behaviors. In *The neurosciences: third study program* (ed. F. O. Schmitt and F. G. Worden). MIT Press, Cambridge, Mass.

SUGA, N. (1972). A conceptual model of feature detection. *Neuroscience Research Program Bulletin.* **10** (1), 75–7.

SUTHERLAND, N. S. (1971). Object recognition. In *Handbook of perception*, Vol. 3 (ed. E. C. Carterette and M. P. Friedman). Academic Press, New York.

—— (1976a). *Breakdown: a personal crisis and a medical dilemma.* Weidenfeld & Nicolson, London.

—— (1976b). The electronic oracle. *Times Literary Supplement* (July 30), 957–9.

SZASZ, T. S. (1960). The myth of mental illness. *The American Psychologist.* **15**, 113–18.

—— (1971). *The manufacture of madness: a comparative study of the Inquisition and the mental health movement.* Routledge & Kegan Paul, London.

SZENTÁGOTHAI, J. and ARBIB, M. A. (1974). Conceptual models of neural organization. *Neurosciences Research Program Bulletin.* **12**, 307–510.

TART, C. T. (ed.) (1969). *Altered states of consciousness: a book of readings.* Wiley, New York.

TAYLOR, C. (1964). *The explanation of behaviour.* Routledge & Kegan Paul, London.

TAYLOR, W. K. (1964). Cortico-thalamic organization and memory. *Proceedings of the Royal Society of London*, B. **159**, 466–78.

TEXTOR, R. B. (1967). *A cross-cultural summary.* HRAF Press, New Haven, Connecticut.

THOM, R. (1975). *Structural stability and morphogenesis: an outline of a general theory of models* (translated by D. H. Fowler). Benjamin, Reading, Mass.

THOMSON, G. M. (1949). *The trend of Scottish intelligence.* University of London Press.

THORPE, W. H. (1974). *Animal nature and human nature.* Methuen, London.

TILLICH, P. (1949). The depth of existence. In *The shaking of the foundations.* SCM Press, London.

TREVARTHEN, C. (1974). The psychobiology of speech development. *Neurosciences Research Program Bulletin.* **12**, 570–85.

TRIVERS, R. L. (1972). *Sexual selection and the descent of man.* Aldine-Atherton, Chicago.

TRUMAN, J. W. (1974). Circadian release of a prepatterned neural program in silk-moths. In *The neurosciences: third study program* (ed. F. O. Schmitt and F. G. Worden). MIT Press, Cambridge, Mass.

TULVING, E. (1972). Episodic and semantic memory. In *Organisation of memory* (ed. E. Tulving and W. Donaldson). Academic Press, New York.

UNGAR, G. (1972). Biological assays for the molecular coding of acquired information. In *Macromolecules and behavior* (2nd edn.) (ed. J. Gaito). Appleton-Century Crofts, New York.

UNGERSTEDT, U. (1971). Stereotaxic mapping of the monoamine pathways in the rat brain. *Acta Physiologica Scandinavica.* **82**, Suppl. 367, 1–48.

VALVO, A. (1971). Sight restoration rehabilitation. *American Foundation for the Blind.* **15**. New York, W.16 St. N.Y. 10011.

VENDLER, Z. (1972). *Res cogitans: an essay in rational philosophy.* Cornell University Press, Ithaca.

VON FRISCH, K. (1950). Die Sonne als Kompass im Leben der Bienen. *Experientia.* **6**, 210–21.

VON SENDEN, M. (1960). *Space and sight.* Methuen, London.

VURPILLOT, E. (1976). *The visual world of the child* (trans. W. E. C. Gillman). International University Press, New York.

WADDINGTON, C. H. (1960). *The ethical animal.* Allen & Unwin, London.

WALBERG, F. (1965). Axoaxonic contacts in the cuneate nucleus, probable basis for presynaptic depolarization. *Experimental Neurology.* **13**, 218–31.

WALL, P. D. (1978). The gate control theory of pain mechanisms: a re-examination and restatement. *Brain.* **101**, 1–18.

WASON, P. C. and JOHNSON-LAIRD, P. N. (1972). *Psychology of reasoning: structure and content.* Batsford, London.

WATSON, J. B. and RAYNER, R. (1920). Conditioned emotional reactions. *Journal of Experimental Psychology.* **3**, 1–14.

WEINBERG, S. (1977). *The first three minutes.* Deutsch, London.

WEISKRANTZ, L., WARRINGTON, E. K., SANDERS, M. D., and MARSHALL, J. (1974). Visual capacity in the hemianopic field following a restricted occipital ablation. *Brain.* **97**, 709–28.

WELLS, M. J. and YOUNG, J. Z. (1966). Lateral interaction and transfer in the tactile memory of the octopus. *Journal of Experimental Biology.* **45**, 385–400.

WERNICKE, C. (1874). *Der aphasische Symptomenkomplex. Eine psychologische Studie auf anatomische Basis.* Cohn & Wright, Breslau.

WILLIAMS, B. A. O. (1956–7). Personal identity and individuation. *Proceedings of the Aristotelian Society.* **57**, 229–52.

WILLIAMS, G. C. (1957). Pleiotropy, natural selection, and the evolution of senescence. *Evolution.* **11**, 398–411.

WILSON, E. O. (1975). *Sociobiology: the new synthesis.* Belknap Press, Cambridge, Mass.

WINTER, P. (1972). Primates. *Neuroscience Research Program Bulletin.* **10** (1), 72–4.

WOLLHEIM, R. (1968). *Art and its objects: an introduction to aesthetics.* Harper & Row, New York.

—— (1973). *On art and the mind: essays and lectures.* Allen Lane, London.

—— (1978). Adrian Stokes, critic, painter, poet. *Times Literary Supplement* (February 17), 207–9.

WOODGER, J. H. (1952). *Biology and language: an introduction to the methodology of the biological sciences including medicine. The Tarner Lectures 1949–1950.* Cambridge University Press.

WOOLSEY, T. A. and VAN DER LOOS, H. (1970). The structural organization of layer IV in the somatosensory region (S1) of a mouse cerebral cortex. *Brain Research.* **17**, 205–42.

WRIGHT, L. (1976). *Teleological explanations: an etiological analysis of goals and functions.* University of California Press, Berkeley.

WRIGHT, S. (1943). Isolation by distance. *Genetics.* **28**, 114–38.

WUNDT, W. M. (1874). *Grundzüge der physiologischen Psychologie.* Engelmann, Leipzig.

WYNNE-EDWARDS, V. C. (1962). *Animal dispersion in relation to social behaviour.* Oliver & Boyd, Edinburgh.

YARBUS, A. L. (1967). *Eye movements and vision* (translated by B. Haigh). Plenum Press, New York.

YOCKEY, H. P. (1977). A calculation of the probability of spontaneous biogenesis by Information Theory. *Journal of Theoretical Biology*. **67**, 377–98.

YOUNG, J. Z. (1938). The evolution of the nervous system and of the relationship of organism and environment. In *Evolution. Essays presented to E. S. Goodrich* (ed. G. R. de Beer). Clarendon Press, Oxford.

—— (1951). *Doubt and certainty in science: a biologist's reflections on the brain. The B.B.C. Reith Lectures 1950*. Clarendon Press, Oxford.

—— (1960). The visual system of *Octopus*. (1) Regularities in the retina and optic lobes of *Octopus* in relation to form discrimination. *Nature, London*. **186**, 836–9.

—— (1962). *Life of vertebrates*. Clarendon Press, Oxford.

—— (1964). *A model of the brain*. Clarendon Press, Oxford.

—— (1971). *An introduction to the study of man*. Clarendon Press, Oxford.

—— (1974). The George Bidder Lecture 1973. Brains and worlds: the cerebral cosmologies. *Journal of Experimental Biology*. **61**, 5–17.

YOUNG, T. (1802). The Bakerian Lecture. On the theory of light and colours. *Philosophical Transactions of the Royal Society of London*, 12–48.

ZEKI, S. (1974). The mosaic organization of the visual cortex in the monkey. In *Essays on the nervous system: a Festschrift for Professor J. Z. Young* (ed. R. Bellairs and E. G. Gray). Oxford University Press.

# Glossary

*Abstraction.* A representation in a selected code, not directly reproducing the features of its model. See: *Isomorphic*; *Model*; *Representation.*

*Acetylcholine.* A rather simple amine, derived from ethanolamine. Active in very small quantities as a neurotransmitter at many synapses. See *Transmitter.*

*Action potential.* See *Nerve impulse.*

*Address.* The indication of the place in the memory of a computer or brain at which the record of a particular item of information is to be found.

*Adrenal.* An endocrine gland near the kidney. Its outer part (cortex) produces steroid hormones such as cortisone, which influence many bodily activities and are essential for life. The central part (medulla) produces adrenaline, which prepares the body for attack or defence.

*Adrenaline.* A catecholamine derived from the amino acid tyrosine. Secreted as a hormone from the adrenal gland and as a transmitter at many synapses Noradrenaline is a modified derivative. See: *Catecholamine, Transmitter.*

*Aesthetics.* The study of responses to the forms of sounds, signs, or objects that are perceived. See *Art.*

*Agnosia.* Inability to interpret sensory input (e.g. visual agnosia).

*Agreement.* The adoption by two or more people of the same interpretation of a set of code signs.

*Aim* (objective). The target to which actions are directed, as specified by the operations of a program. See *Program*; *Purpose*; *Standard*; *Homeostasis.*

*Alerting system.* See *Reticular system.*

*Algorithm.* A program by which a complicated calculation is reduced to a long series of simple ones that a digital computer can perform.

*Alpha rhythm.* See *EEG.*

*Altruism.* The performance of actions that promote the survival of other individuals rather than oneself.

*Amacrine cells.* Neurons that have no axon. Their processes make synaptic contact with those of neighbours and may influence them without propagating action potentials, e.g. in the retina.

*Aminergic synapses.* Those at which the transmitter is a monoamine such as noradrenaline. See: *Cholinergic synapses*, *Synapse.*

*Amines.* Substances derived from ammonia, especially those containing the amino group, $NH_2$, e.g. amino acids such as glycine $NH_2.CH_2OOH$. Many amines are used in minute concentrations as transmitters at synapses, e.g. adrenaline, acetylcholine, serotonin.

*Amino acid.* A simple organic molecule able to act both as an acid and a base and so to join with others to make the long chains of proteins. The same 20 amino acids occur in all animals and plants.

*Amygdala.* A basal part of the brain, injury to which may cause changes in aggressiveness and other emotional behaviour. (The name means an almond.)

*Analgesia.* Incapacity to feel pain.

*Analogue.* A representation whose parts have the same relations as those of its model.

*Analytic propositions.* Those that are necessarily true because of the programs that determine the use of the words (e.g. this square has four sides). See *Synthetic propositions.*

*Anthropomorphism.* Ascribing human characteristics to animals, physical events, or gods. Perhaps a clue to an inherited brain program.

*Aphasia.* A speech defect following damage to the cortex. Shows either as an inability to speak (motor aphasia, Broca's aphasia) or to understand what is heard (sensory or Wernicke's aphasia).

*Art.* The creation of signs, sounds, or artefacts that are pleasing, stimulating, or symbolically satisfying. See *Pleasure.*

*Artificial intelligence* (A.I.). The making of computer programs or machines that imitate human problem-solving. Logicians and engineers have devised robots that can recognize and select parts and assemble them into structures. Some robots can learn, generalize and predict, but only within specified limits.

*Australopithecus.* Somewhat human creatures living about 1–2 million years ago, with brains of ape size and with a partly upright gait.

*Awareness.* See *Experience.*

*Axon.* The fibre that carries nerve signals away from a nerve cell body, often for a long distance. See *Neuron.*

*Bacteria.* The simplest living organisms, consisting of single cells, with the DNA not concentrated within a nuclear membrane.

*Ballistic.* A movement powered and guided only when it is begun, as in throwing, or firing a rocket.

*Behaviourist.* A term used vaguely and often derogatively, to describe those who try to understand the programs of the brain solely in terms of the behaviour of the organism.

*Belief.* The use of certain rigid programs of thinking, sometimes even although their premises cannot be proved to be valid.

*Binary code.* Expressing numbers to the base 2, using 0s and 1s only. Thus $1 = 1$, $2 = 10$, $3 = 11$, $9 = 1001$. This allows mechanical devices to calculate very quickly. See *Computer.*

*Bit.* Short for 'binary digit', the unit that represents a single yes/no decision, hence the basic unit of information (p. 42).

*Body.* Materials programmed to constitute a living organism.

*Boutons.* The presynaptic nerve endings filled with vesicles of transmitter substance. So called because the buttons first became well-known through the French translation from Spanish of the work of Ramon y Cajal.

*Brain.* A set of nerve cells providing the programs of action that ensure survival of an individual by detecting relevant internal and external events and comparing them to its set of standards and to its memory record of previous events and actions.

*Catecholamines.* Amines containing the catechol ring, e.g. adrenaline, noradrenaline, and dopamine, which are used as neurotransmitters.

*Cause.* An event that produces or is regularly followed by another. The concept of caus-

ality is bound up with the programs that allow induction, which by some philosophers is considered to be a mysterious principle of necessity, but perhaps is an inherited brain capacity.

*Cerebellum.* Large lobe at the back of the brain. Concerned with the proper performance of movements, and perhaps with their timing. Has close interrelations with the cerebral cortex.

*Cerebral cortex.* The sheet of nerve cells and fibres that occupies the top of the brain. It receives signals via the thalamus from all the senses and sends signals to the thalamus and to the lower centres. Each neuron of its receptive areas represents some external feature and those of its motor areas represent movements of muscles (p. 64).

*Choice.* The act of selecting one of two or more programs of action.

*Cholinergic synapses.* Those at which the transmitter is acetylcholine. See: *Acetylcholine; Aminergic synapses.*

*Cingulate cortex.* The middle part of the cortex (where the two sides lie against each other). It is concerned largely with emotional programs, but is little understood.

*Circadian.* Occurring rhythmically about once a day.

*Cochlea.* The spiral structure in the ear that is activated by sounds to send signals to the brain.

*Code.* A set of visible signs, sounds, or other physical events adopted to form a system of communication of messages. See: *Language; Genetic code; Nucleic acids; Nerve impulse; Communication; Digital; Analogue; Message.*

*Coeruleus.* See *Locus coeruleus.*

*Cognition.* The process of using programs for acquisition of information and operating with it.

*Computer.* An artificial device for processing information. Analogue computers work by rearranging some mechanical or electrical system that represents units of information (e.g. a slide rule). In a digital computer a code is used to represent the information in such a form that the machine can perform the operations indicated by the program supplied by its user. Using a binary code the program (algorithm) operates by making decisions between 0 and 1, which can be done at rates of 1 billion per second. See: *Bit; Binary code; Algorithm; Program.*

*Computer memory.* Information is stored by altering the states of a large set of mechanical or electrical devices, usually essentially by on/off switching. The 'meaning' of the information at the address of each point thus depends on the program arranged by the operator.

*Computer program.* A list of signs in some language, which causes the computer to carry out a logical sequence of calculation to answer a question relating to the real world, which the program represents by means of an algorithm.

*Communication.* The interaction between systems or parts of a system using a pre-arranged code.

*Concept.* The learned program for the use of a word or set of words, i.e. its meaning.

*Concrete operations.* In Piaget's terminology the period from 7–11 years of age when the programs come to allow logical operations such as classification, abstraction, and generalization. See: *Pre-operational thought*; *Formal operations.*

*Conditioned reflex.* The setting up of an association by pairing of some arbitrary (conditional) stimulus, say, a sound, with the unconditional stimulus of an inborn reflex, say, of salivation to meat.

*Consciousness.* The state of a person in which the activating programs of the brain allow experiencing and thinking. See: *Experiencing*; *Mind.*

*Conservation, concept of.* The program that allows recognition that quantities or relations are preserved in spite of differing appearances. Develops after 7 years of age.

*Consummation.* The achievement of the aim of a program by a certain act, e.g. eating or sexual union. See: *Reinforcement*; *Reward centre; Standard; Aim.*

*Control.* The regulation of the operation of a system by a program of instructions, often using sensors to detect deviations from a reference standard and initiate corrections. See: *Homeostasis; Feedback; Standard.*

*Core brain.* The central part running the whole length including the reticular system, and those regulating sleeping and waking and emotional responses.

*Corpus callosum.* The band of nerve fibres from one side of the cortex to the other.

*Cortex.* See *Cerebral cortex.*

*Cortical map.* The display of receptor neurons over the cortical surface in the relative positions that they occupy on the body surface.

*Corticosteroid.* One of the steroid hormones produced by the cortex of the adrenal gland.

*Critical period* (sensitive period). The time at which the nervous system is ready, if given a suitable input, to develop a program provided by its inherited capacity, for instance for vision or language.

*Culture.* The particular system of symbols, ideas, values, and artefacts used by a group of people.

*Cytoplasm.* See *Nucleus.*

*Darwinian evolution* proceeds by natural selection of heritable variations.

*Decision.* The process of choosing between alternative programs of action. See *Choice.*

*Deduction.* Strictly, in logic, a program for recognizing that a proposition is necessarily true (analytic). Loosely used for conclusions that are true if their premises are true.

*Deep structure.* See *Generative grammar.*

*Dendrites.* The receptive branches of a neuron. See: *Neuron; Synapse.*

*Determinism.* The theory that the behaviour of living things including humans can, in principle, be precisely and fully forecasted. Considered here to be meaningless because no such principle can be demonstrated (p. 20). There is therefore no basis for the alleged consequence that people are not responsible for their actions. Nevertheless as knowledge of the operations of the brain grows it becomes possible to forecast more precisely what people are likely to do.

*Dialectic.* A method of operation of programs for thinking in which contradiction is supposed to reveal new knowledge. The word has changed in use from Kant through Hegel to Marx and more recently.

*Digital.* A system of coding using only a few clearly defined signs, usually only two, indicating presence or absence, 0 and 1. See: *Coding; Computer.*

*Dizygotic.* Fraternal twins derived by fertilization of separate ova and hence not more alike genetically than any brothers and sisters. If they *are* more alike than this is due to their similar environments.

*DNA.* See *Nucleic acids.*

*Dorsal.* The back side of the human body or the upper side of an animal.

*Drive.* A vague term for the programs producing tendencies to act in a certain way, e.g. hunger drive, sex drive.

*EEG*. Electroencephalogram, the waves of change of electrical potential recorded by electrodes attached to the scalp. In a quiet person with eyes shut the changes are regular at about 10/sec (alpha rhythm). While thinking, the potentials are irregular. See *Sleep*.

*Élan vitale*. The life-force postulated by Bergson as necessary to explain the continuation of life. See: *Entelechy*; *Vitalism*.

*Electrode*. A wire used for carrying an electric current. Sometimes used for the stimulation and recording of events in the brain.

*Element*. One of the 92 basic types of atom, such as oxygen or iron, which make up chemical molecules. Atoms can be broken down only by high energy into their ultimate particles such as electrons, neutrons, and protons.

*Emotion*. The condition of a person when programs are activated that especially concern him, e.g. programs for fearing or loving. They are often accompanied by physical signs.

*Empiricism*. The theory that all programs for describing the world are derived from experience. Locke, Berkeley, and Hume were empiricists of different kinds in contrast to seventeenth-century 'rationalists'. See *Rationalism*.

*Entelechy*. The life force as postulated by Driesch. See: *Élan vitale*; *Vitalism*.

*Entropy*. The amount of disorder in a system, which by the 2nd. law of thermodynamics will tend to increase unless the system is open to receive negentropy, which is information. See: *Information*; *Order*.

*Enzyme*. A protein acting as a catalyst by virtue of its folded structure, which brings reactants close together and allows them to combine at low temperatures. Enzymes may break molecules down (e.g. pepsin in the stomach) or build them up to make proteins, carbohydrates, or fats. See *Protein*.

*Epideictic*. Programs by which, according to V. C. Wynne-Edwards, animals come together in displays so that their numbers are regulated, e.g. starlings in central London.

*Epistemology*. The study of the programs by which we acquire beliefs and knowledge and the capacity to use them. See *Knowledge*.

*Ethnology* has various uses, for some it equals social anthropology, the study of cultures, for others it means study of the history of peoples.

*Ethology*. The study of animal behaviour in natural conditions.

*Evolution*. The change of the genetic programs of populations by natural selection. It has resulted over the ages in the addition of information, giving organisms the capacity to survive in conditions less favourable to life. See: *Genetic program*; *Natural selection*; *Mutation*; *Progress*; *Darwinian evolution*.

*Experiencing*. The condition of a person when he is using his programs for sensing, thinking, or dreaming. See: *Consciousness*; *Person*; *Mind*.

*Explanation*. The process (or result) of answering a question in a form that is consistent with the program of thought of the questioner. See: *Thinking*; *Understanding*.

*Exteroceptors*. Sense organs that detect changes in the outside world (e.g. by vision, hearing, or smell).

*Eye movements*. (1) High frequency tremor during fixation (about 50/s); (2) slow drifts during fixation; (3) rapid flicks between fixations; (4) pursuit movements (tracking); (5) vergence movements for stereoscopic vision. See *Saccades*.

*Feature detectors*. Cells in the brain that are especially sensitive to certain external events, e.g. to a visible contour set at a particular angle or to a particular speech sound (p. 86).

*Feedback*. The use of part of the output of a regulated system to compare with the standard set for its program and produce appropriate change of input. Positive feedback increases and negative feedback decreases the input. See: *Control*; *Homeostasis*; *Standard*.

*Flexor reflex*. The simple program that ensures withdrawal from harm, e.g. by bending an arm when the hand touches a flame.

*Follicle-stimulating hormone* (FSH). Produced by the pituitary, it causes the development of the follicle in the first half of the menstrual cycle before ovulation.

*Foraminifera*. Single-celled protozoans with a calcareous shell that live in the sea. Their shells fall to the bottom and form chalk.

*Forebrain bundle*. An important tract of fibres carrying signals up and down from the basal parts of the brain, such as the hypothalamus.

*Formal operations*. In Piaget's terminology the final stage from 11 years of age onwards in which programs develop allowing inference, and hypothetical and deductive manipulation of symbols. See: *Concrete operations*; *Pre-operational thought.*

*Fovea.* The central part of the retina, composed largely of cones, sensitive to colour and the main agent for detailed vision.

*Free will.* The choice between alternative programs of action, which is performed by the human brain using all the information it has about the probable course of events in the world. See: *Choice; Determinism.*

*Frequency modulation.* A system for communication in which sound signals are transmitted by varying the number of beats (frequency) of a carrier wave.

*Frontal cortex.* The anterior part, not concerned with any particular sensory or motor function but important for its general inhibitory actions, especially repressing inappropriate programs. When overactive it may be involved in depression and hence sometimes has been surgically separated from the brain by frontal leucotomy. Its more medial part (orbito-frontal) is especially concerned with emotional programs.

*Frontal lobe.* See *Frontal cortex.*

*Ganglia.* Collections of nerve cells.

*Gene.* The unit factor of Mendelian inheritance. The region of a chromosome which when transcribed specifies a particular product (usually an enzyme). Genes occur in pairs (alleles), one from each parent, either the same (homozygotic) or different (heterozygotic). One gene may be dominant and prevent the manifestation of the other, recessive. Genes change by mutation.

*Generative grammar.* The brain programs that are followed in generating the sentences in a language. A set of phrase-structure programs provides the deep structure and transformational programs generate various surface structures. Thus the deep structure, 'Cows eat grass' can be transformed to 'Grass is eaten by cows' or 'Can cows eat grass?' etc. See *Grammar.*

*Genetic code.* The language composed of an alphabet of four letters (nucleotides) arranged in sequences of triplets each ensuring the attachment of a particular amino acid as a protein grows. The information in the code thus controls the properties of the enzymes whose actions ensure living. See:

*Genetic code*; *Code*; *Language*; *Protein*; *Enzyme.*

*Genetic drift.* Variation in gene frequencies in a population by chance rather than by natural selection. Probably occurs only in small isolated populations.

*Genetic program* (genotype). The set of genes in an organism determining its development and provide the standards and actions that enable it to learn how to survive.

*Genotype.* The inherited program of instructions that controls the development and life of an individual. See *Phenotype.*

*Glucose.* The commonest form of sugar, $C_6H_{12}O_6$.

*Gnostic neuron* (pontifical neuron, grandmother's face cell). A cell of the cerebral cortex that responds only to a complex set of features (p. 128). See *Feature detectors.*

*Gonadotropic hormones.* Secretions of the pituitary gland serving as signals that activate the gonads, e.g. follicle stimulating hormone (FSH) and luteinizing hormone (LH).

*Grammar.* The set of brain programs by which sentences are generated. Linguists recognize morphemes (words) the lowest units of meaning, which are joined according to grammatical rules to make discourse (sentences). See: *Generative grammar*; *Languages*; *Linguistics.*

*Grandmother's face cells.* See *Gnostic neuron.*

*Hardware.* The actual material of a computer. See *Software.*

*Hard-wired.* Programs incorporated into the structure of a computer and therefore not variable by the software program. In the body, reflexes are 'hard-wired' and so are other connections formed by heredity and not subject to modification by learning. See: *Software; Reflex.*

*Hedonic.* The program for giving pleasure or satisfaction.

*Hedonism.* The theory that human programs are activated by drives to seek pleasure or avoid pain.

*Hermeneutics.* The study of the supposed fundamental significance of human thoughts, utterances, actions, and institutions. Originally used by theologians for the interpretations of the truths of the Bible.

*Hippocampus.* A part of the brain (shaped like a sea-horse) lying close to the cerebral cortex. It is concerned with programs that enable learning to take place (p. 89).

*Hologram.* A photographic image produced by the interference of coherent light reflected from an object with the light waves of a reference source. When the hologram, or even part of it, is illuminated by the reference wave a three-dimensional image of the whole object is reconstituted. It is suggested that neural memory records may be holograms (but where are the coherent waves?).

*Homeostasis.* The tendency or disposition of living' things to maintain a steady state in spite of changing conditions. Depends upon control by inherited programs chosen by natural selection. See: *Control*; *Feedback*; *Standard.*

*Hormone.* A chemical substance secreted into the blood by an endocrine gland (e.g. the thyroid) and providing a signal to the target organs sensitive to it. Hormones provide long-lasting signals suitable for the control of slow processes such as growth or reproduction.

*Human being.* An individual whose genetic program provides a certain type of body and programs that allow experiencing. See: *Person*; *Body*; *Mind*; *Brain*; *Experiencing.*

*Hypothalamus.* The region at the base of the brain containing the reference systems or standards of the programs for ensuring homeostasis, such as those for eating, drinking, and sexual reproduction. Through the pituitary gland it regulates slow processes such as growth.

*Hypothesis.* A program for thought or action based upon certain beliefs and assumptions about facts.

*Icon.* An image. Hence in semiotics a sign that has some natural resemblance to.what it signifies. *Iconic vision* is the immediate impression produced by a scene, which can be remembered by some people who have *iconic memory*. See: *Semiotics*; *Symbol.*

*Idealism.* (1) In philosophy, a general program for thinking, based on the belief that the fundamental realities are minds or ideas, objects being only our constructs from appearances. (2) Used more colloquially of people whose programs are largely influenced by evaluative theories about socially desirable behaviour. See *Realism.*

*Indeterminacy* (uncertainty principle). The fact that it is possible to measure the position and momentum of a particle such as an electron only within certain limits.

*Induction.* The program that allows the forecast that sequences of events that have been repeatedly connected in the past will (probably) be connected in the future (e.g. the sun will rise tomorrow).

*Information.* The ordered features of an external situation or within a living system that enable decisions to be made between action programs. Can be measured in 'bits', units allowing one decision between equiprobable alternatives. See: *Bit*; *Entropy*; *Order.*

*Instinct.* A vague word now little used by biologists, covering approximately programs of behaviour that are inherited but not learned. A dangerous concept because nearly all behaviour patterns in fact include both these influences. It is still sometimes useful to speak of the instinctive components of behaviour.

*Instruction.* A set of signs that arranges the sequence of operations of a system. See: *Information*; *System*; *Sign*; *Control.*

*Intension.* See *Intention.*

*Intention.* Commonly means the aim or purpose of an agent or the sender of a message. 'Intensionality' is a technical term referring to the sense of an expression.

*Isomorphic* (realistic). A model that is an exact copy of as much detail as possible of what it represents. See: *Model*; *Abstraction*; *Representation.*

*Isotopes.* Elements exist in varying states, having the same chemical properties but different numbers of neutrons in the nucleus. Thus carbon exists as $^{12}C$ and $^{14}C$. Use of isotopes has allowed biologists to follow the course of materials as they turnover during metabolism.

*Knowledge.* The information acquired by use of the programs for learning.

*Lactose.* A double sugar found in milk, made of glucose and galactose.

*Lamarckian evolution* is supposed to proceed by the inheritance of characters acquired by the parents. See *Darwinian evolution.*

*Language.* A system of signs used for intentional communication by one or more codes. See: *Linguistics*; *Code*; *Grammar*; *Meaning*; *Intentional*; *Translation*; *Communication.*

*Learning.* The process of adding information to the programs that are available to ensure self-maintenance. See *Memory.*

*Life.* A condition known at present only on Earth in which certain elements have been organized for over 3000 million years into systems of increasing complexity maintained by the information in control programs encoded in nucleic acid molecules. See: *Entropy*; *Information*; *Code*; *Control*.

*Ligase*. An enzyme that allows two molecules to join together.

*Limbic system*. The hippocampus and related centres, concerned with programs for reward and learning. (Limbus means a border or limit.)

*Linguistics*. The study of language. Diachronic linguistics studies the history and synchronic linguistics the present use of language. A person's brain programs provide the linguistic competence (Chomsky) or *langue* (Saussure) which underlies his performance (or *parole*).

*Locus coeruleus* (the blue nucleus). A pigmented region of the brain. Sends aminergic fibres forwards to the medial forebrain bundle and the hypothalamus. Probably concerned with programs that provide rewards for eating.

*Logic*. The study of the brain programs that enable people to make statements that are valid conclusions and hence convincing.

*Logical thought*. The use of programs that produce statements whose truth is agreed to be convincing. See: *Agreement*; *Truth*.

*Luteinizing hormone* (LH). Produced by the pituitary, it causes development of the corpus luteum during the second half of each menstrual cycle and throughout pregnancy.


*Macromolecules*. Substances made of very large and complicated molecules.

*Manic*. Suffering from disordered emotional programs.

*Masochism*. Obtaining sexual pleasure in suffering pain.

*Matter*. Useful only in common speech as a general term for the materials of the universe, of which physical science has made a detailed analysis into ultimate particles and forms of energy.

*Meaning*. A sign has meaning when a group of people has adopted a particular program for using it. Hence the meaning of a word is defined by the rules for its use and the circumstances under which it can be verified. See: *Language*; *Sign*; *Code*; *Intention*; *Concept*.

*Medial geniculate body*. The part of the thalamus that receives acoustic signals and sends them on to the auditory cortex of the temporal lobe.

*Medulla oblongata*. The hindmost part of the brain, containing the cells that provide the programs regulating essential activities such as breathing.

*Melatonin*. An amine found in the pineal body, derived from the ring compound tryptophan.

*Memory*. The set of brain programs that allows addition of information to the programs available for self-maintenance. See: *Homeostasis*; *Learning*.

*Menopause*. The stopping of menstrual cycles. Occurs usually at around 45 years of age.

*Mescaline*. An alkaloid, peyote, said to produce visions of great beauty.

*Message*. A set of code words transmitting an item of information or instruction.

*Metalanguage*. A code used for speaking of or studying another language.

*Metaphysics*. The investigation of the basic programs by which we try to study the fundamental nature of the world and of ourselves. See *Epistemology*.

*Metasociety*. A group of people able to study society from the outside.

*Metonymy*. The use of words in some transferred or oblique sense.

*Microneurons*. Small nerve cells that have no long axon carrying signals away to a distance. The amacrine cells of the retina are one type of microneuron. See *Amacrine cells*.

*Mid-brain*. The region behind the thalamus. In lower vertebrates it contains major centres for vision and hearing. In mammals it is concerned with programs for visual and auditory search.

*Mind*. The system of operations of the programs of the brain of a person during conscious experience. The concept is not precise and a person may perhaps be said to have more than one mind (p. 216). See: *Brain*; *Consciousness*; *Experience*; *Human being*; *Person*.

*Mitochondria*. Little sacs found in all cells, whose folded walls carry enzymes, especially those concerned in respiration—hence 'the power-houses of the cell' (Fig. 7.9).

*Mnemon*. A suggested unit of memory, the system of neurons whose switching alters the probability of initiation of a given action by a feature detector.

*Model*. A representation of something by a process of mapping of its characteristics, often describing them in a special language for some purpose. See: *Isomorphic*; *Abstraction*; *Representation*.

*Molecule.* The smallest unit of a substance that can enter into a chemical reaction. Molecules are made up of atoms, sometimes many thousands as in macromolecules such as proteins, but often fewer, as in adrenaline, or very few as in water.

*Monoamine.* A derivative of ammonia ($NH_3$) where a hydrocarbon radical (R) substitutes for one of the hydrogen atoms—$RNH_2$, e.g. adrenaline.

*Monozygotic.* Identical twins, derived by separation of the two cells produced by the first division of the egg. The twins are thus of the same sex and have identical genetic programs. Any differences between them must be due to environment.

*Multichannel system.* The system used by the brain for transmitting information about the features of an object or situation by using many lines, (nerve fibres) each indicating one feature only, e.g. redness.

*Natural selection.* The differential survival and reproduction of some genotypes and phenotypes, often leading to evolutionary change.

*Naturalism.* The belief that all human faculties are emergent from the rest of nature and not dependent upon some special operations of a *supernatural* agency. Hence in ethics the belief that reliable criteria for right actions can be founded on factual observations, including facts about people.

*Needs.* The requirements for the continuation of life. Needs are indicated by sensors when bodily conditions begin to deviate from standards set for the programs, e.g. in thirst. See: *Control*; *Aims*; *Standards*.

*Neocortex.* The most recently evolved part of the brain, essential for much of the special human programs such as those for seeing, thinking, speaking, and planning.

*Nerve impulse.* The signal that passes without decrement along a nerve fibre, also called an action potential.

*Neuroendocrine systems.* Programs of combined nervous and hormonal action, usually controlling slow processes such as growth. Used especially for the interactions of the hypothalamus and pituitary gland.

*Neuroma.* The lump that forms on the end of a severed nerve and may give rise to pain.

*Neuron.* A nerve cell, including a cell body with nucleus, receptive dendrites and (usually) an axon carrying nerve impulses away. See: *Amacrine cell*; *Dendrites*; *Microneuron*; *Synapse*.

*Neuroscience.* The study of the programs of the brain.

*Neurosecretion.* The process by which some nerve cells carry a chemical signalling substance, used mainly to control slow processes, as by the nerve fibres of the hypothalamus that regulate the pituitary gland. See *Neuroendocrine systems*.

*Nocifensor reflex.* A program, initiated by pain, which protects the body against damage, as by drawing away a hand or foot. See *Flexor reflex*.

*Noise.* A random non-rhythmic disturbance in a communication channel.

*Noradrenaline.* A catecholamine used as a transmitter, especially by post-ganglionic sympathetic pathways, related to adrenaline. See: *Monoamine*; *Catecholamine*.

*Nucleic acids.* Very long molecules containing four sorts of units, the nucleotides, arranged in series to constitute the genetic code that organizes the programs of development. It arranges the sequence of amino acids in proteins and so gives them the properties as enzymes that are able to maintain life. See: *Nucleotide*; *Amino acid*; *Genetic code*.

*Nucleotides.* Units of nucleic acids. Each contains: (1) one of four bases (e.g. adenine); (2) a sugar (ribose in RNA, deoxyribose in DNA); and (3) a phosphoric acid. Thousands of nucleotides are strung together by union of the sugars with the acids. Each sequence of three bases determines the attachment of a particular amino acid to a growing protein chain. See: *Code*; *DNA*; *Genetic code*; *Transcription*; *Translation*.

*Nucleus.* The centre of every cell, containing the DNA, separated by a membrane from the rest of the cell, the cytoplasm.

*Oestrogen.* A steroid hormone (e.g. oestrone) produced during the first phase of an oestrus cycle while the ovarian follicles are ripening.

*Oestrus.* The period of ovulation. In many mammals the only time when a female will accept a male.

*Order.* The state of arrangement of the parts of any system. See: *Entropy*; *Information*.

*Oscillograph* (oscilloscope). An instrument that amplifies electrical oscillations and records them on the face of a cathode-ray tube.

*Parietal lobe.* The side of the cerebral cortex. It includes the areas concerned with touch and with programs involving several senses together, such as language.

*Peptide.* A short sequence of amino acids—fewer than a protein.

*Person.* A whole human being, including the brain and its programs for unconscious and conscious operations. See: *Consciousness; Mind; Experiencing; Body; Human being.*

*Phenotype.* The features that an individual develops by the interaction of its genetic program with its environment. See *Genotype.*

*Phonemes.* The smallest sound units that can change meaning in a language (e.g. in bit /b/, /i/, and /t/). A phoneme may be pronounced in several ways, called allophones. See *Phones.*

*Phones.* The sound features used in language, not themselves carrying meaning. See *Phoneme.*

*Pineal.* A small body in the brain, produces a hormone called melatonin that inhibits sexual development and so may be responsible for the long period of childhood in humans (p. 67).

*Pituitary gland* (hypophysis). It lies below the hypothalamus by which it is controlled. It produces many hormones that regulate slow processes such as growth and reproduction.

*Placebo.* A pill or other medicine that unknown to the recipient does not contain any active substance.

*Pleasure.* The condition produced by a reward program during the successful performance or completion of a program that fulfils some need, or meets an expectation, or ends a search for intellectual or emotional significance. See: *Reward centre; Reinforcement.*

*Polymerase.* An enzyme involved in making the macromolecules that are composed of many repeating parts, polymers such as DNA, RNA, or proteins.

*Polymorphism.* The persistent presence of genes producing different types of individual in a population. Man is a polymorphic species.

*Polysynaptic.* A pathway in the brain involving many neurons and hence delay at many synapses.

*Pons.* The band of tissue below the cerebellum containing many important groups of nerve cells. The term means literally a bridge.

*Pontifical neuron.* See *Gnostic neuron.*

*Prebiotic.* The supposed stage in which organic molecules of various sorts were present but not yet aggregated into organisms.

*Precocial.* Born in a fully developed state (as in lambs and foals).

*Prefrontal cortex.* The most anterior part of the cortex. See *Frontal cortex.*

*Pre-operational thought.* In Piaget's terminology the period from 2–7 years of age in which a child acquires the programs for symbolic representation and language, but signs remain attached to obvious properties and cannot be used for indirect logical operations. See: *Sensori–motor intelligence; Concrete operations.*

*Program.* A set of code signs that indicates the actions to be performed by a living system or artefact in order to achieve its purpose. In living systems the aim is the continuation of the individual and/or his programs. See: *Control; Homeostasis; Purpose; Standard; Aim.*

*Progress.* An evaluative word implying improvement. Can be said to have occurred during evolution by the increase of information in genetic programs and hence of capacity to survive in conditions less favourable for life.

*Proprioceptors.* Sense organs that record the state of the organism itself, especially the position of its limbs and tension in its muscles.

*Protein.* A macromolecule made up of a sequence of amino acids. Many proteins are enzymes (e.g. pepsin) but others are not e.g. egg-white (albumin) or tendon (collagen) See *Amino acid; Enzyme; Macromolecule.*

*Purpose.* The aim or objective of a living system (or artefact) as indicated by the standards embodied in its program of controls, including those standards acquired by learning. The concept can be applied to all living things (p. 18) but its application to the Universe is not clear. See: *Aim; Standard; Homeostasis; Control.*

*Raphe.* The region where the two halves of the medulla oblongata are joined. The name means literally a seam.

*Rationalism* (apriorism). The theory that

there are brain programs for thinking not wholly derived from experience. Some seventeenth-century metaphysicians are called rationalists because they believed that the nature of the world can be described by reasoning (e.g. Descartes, Leibniz).

*Realism*. A general program of thought based on the belief that material objects exist apart from our awareness of them. See *Idealism*.

*Realistic*. See *Isomorphic*.

*Reductionism*. Replacing statements by others that are simpler or generally used in a different context, e.g. describing mental events as programs of the brain. Often used as a term of abuse by those who think that brains are simpler than minds or who wish to continue to believe in spirits.

*Reflex*. An inherited program for performing a single action in response to an external change (stimulus).

*Reinforcement* (reward). A program that allows the consequences of some program of action to increase (or decrease) the probability that it will recur. Food operates a program for positive reinforcement, shock for negative reinforcement. (Removal of shock is also sometimes called negative reinforcement.) See: *Consummation*; *Pleasure*; *Learning*; *Memory*; *Reward centre*.

*Relativity*. The statement of the laws of motion of bodies in terms that do not depend on their motion relative to observers.

*Releaser*. A stimulus that sets off an inherited program of behaviour.

*Releasing factors*. Chemical substances (peptides) produced by the hypothalamus and carried in the blood to the pituitary gland where they control the release of various hormones.

*Representation*. A set of signs for communication of the features of some entity or system (the model). A naturalistic representation is similar to its model, whereas an abstract one uses an arbitrary code.

*Reticular system*. A network of short neurons running up and down near the centre of the brain and responsible for the programs of arousal to action and sleep.

*Reward centre*. If electrodes are put in some regions of the brain a rat will press a lever repeatedly to stimulate himself through them. See: *Pleasure*; *Reinforcement*; *Consummation*.

*Ribosome*. See *Translation*.

*RNA*. See: *Nucleic acid*; *Transcription*; *Translation*.

*Saccades*. Fast eye movements. Now generally used to include both the large flicks between fixations and the rapid small ones during fixation (about 50/s and 10 min of angle). The large flicks vary in extent (1–20 min) and frequency (0·25–5/s), are ballistic and very fast (1000°/s). No information is received during the saccade. See: *Ballistic*; *Eye movements*.

*Satisfaction*. The result of a program indicating conclusion of a successful operation for fulfilment of a want or need. See: *Consummation*; *Pleasure*; *Reinforcement*.

*Schema*. In Piaget's terminology, 'a cognitive structure which has reference to a class of similar action sequences'. Read in our terminology, 'A class of brain programs producing certain types of action.'

*Script*. A physical record of information or instructions in a code.

*Semantics*. The study of the meaning of words, more particularly their referring aspects.

*Semiotics*. The study of signs and symbols and the way they program behaviour, whether transmitted as language or by gesture, smell, touch, or in any other way.

*Senescence*. The decrease with time of the physical powers of an individual and increasing probability of death; presumably this is part of the inherited program for life (p. 27–9).

*Sensori–motor period*. According to Piaget the period up to 2 years of age when a child learns that the world contains stable objects but its brain programs cannot yet perform operations involving symbolism or principles of classification, number or quantity.

*Serotonin* (5-hydroxytryptamine, 5HT). An indoleamine derived by hydroxylation from the aromatic ring compound tryptophan. Used as a transmitter by some synapses involved in the program for sleeping.

*Sex hormones*. Steroids produced by the gonads under the influence of the pituitary. They control the physical and behavioural characters of the sexes (beard, ovulation, etc.). The male hormones are androgens, the female oestrogens and progestagens, but both sexes produce all sorts, in different proportions.

*Sign* (signal). A physical event used as a

means of communication in a code. See *Semiotics*.

*Software*. The programs devised to make the hardware of a computer solve the problems set by the user. See: *Program*; *Code*; *Hardwired*.

*Somatosensory cortex*. The part that deals with signals sent from the skin, e.g. for touch.

*Somatotopic maps*. Groups of nerve cells arranged on the surface of the brain in a pattern that corresponds to the sensory surface of the skin or retina (see Figs. 11.2 and 11.3).

*Spirit*. A non-material entity, often assumed to have power to control matter.

*Standard* (goal, set-point, reference point, aim). The coded instructions that indicate the level of operation to be maintained by the programs of a controlled system. Hereditary standards are basically defined by the genetic program and then embodied in certain parts of the brain, for instance the hypothalamus. Humans have learning mechanisms by which standards of more complex personal and ethical social behaviour are acquired. See: *Aim*; *Purpose*; *Control*, *Homeostasis*.

*Statistics*. The study of the probability of occurrence of events.

*Steroids*. A group of fatty substances, some acting as hormones. Derived from cholesterol and containing a five-membered ring. Include the sex hormones, adrenal cortical hormones, and vitamin D.

*Structure* The framework expressing the relation of the parts of a system. Originally used of physical systems such as buildings or bodies, but now also for many other systems (e.g. social, musical, chemical, etc.).

*Structuralism*. A movement in social science originated by Claude Lévi Strauss, which supposes that social structures depend upon certain basic characteristics of human brain programs, especially attention to binary operations that are used in communication. 'Structuralism' is also sometimes used to define the type of linguistics that studies surface structures rather than Chomsky's more abstract deep structure. See *Generative grammar*.

*Sucrose*. A double sugar made of glucose and fructose.

*Surface structure*. See *Generative grammar*.

*Symbol*. This term has many uses, here we take it to mean a sign that is not wholly conventional but carries some indication of its significance, often emotional. See: *Icon*; *Sign*.

*Symbolic logic* (mathematical logic). The system by which arguments are made exact by using precisely defined symbols in place of words.

*Synapse*. The terminal knob (bouton) by which the end of a presynaptic axon comes into contact with the dendrite of a post-synaptic nerve cell (Fig. 7.9). The joint effect of many of these knobs activates the post-synaptic cell, usually by releasing a chemical transmitter. See: *Bouton*; *Transmitter*.

*Synthetic propositions*. Those that are not true *only* because of the program for the use of the subject word (e.g. this square is large). See *Analytic propositions*.

*System*. Any group of entities that influence each other. In living systems there is control by inherited instructions, which ensure that the actions of the parts tend to perpetuate the system and especially its instructions. See: *Control*; *Instruction*; *Life*.

*Systems analysis*. The procedure of studying systems by identifying their limits and parts (sub-systems), their aims, programs of instruction, and effectiveness. Can be applied to social systems, machines, or living things.

*Teleology*. The study of goals, ends, or purposes, now sometimes called teleonomy (p 16)

*Temporal lobe*. A part of the side of the brain (Fig. 12.5) containing the temporal cortex on the outside (largely concerned with hearing) and certain basal lobes within that are concerned with emotion.

*Testosterone*. The male sex hormone, a steroid produced by the testis and causing the development of masculine characters.

*Thalamus*. A group of cells at the centre of the brain, which send signals from the various sensory systems to the cortex. Also has other functions. The name means literally a chamber.

*Thermodynamics*, laws of: (1) No system can continue to do work without an energy source. (2) The entropy of a closed system never decreases. (3) No system can be cooled to absolute zero. See: *Entropy*; *System*.

*Thinking*. The use of perceptual or logical programs to answer questions about information coming from sense organs or from internal sources. See *Logical thought*.

*Tissue culture*. Keeping cells alive outside the body in an artificial medium.

*Transcendental questions* are those about ultimates, which can be posed but not answered by human cerebral programs, e.g. What is God? *or*, Has the universe a Meaning? The capacity for logical thought is called transcendental by some philosophers (Kant).

*Transcription* (in genetics). The process by which the information in a section of the DNA of a chromosome is copied into a different nucleotide, messenger RNA, which is carried from the nucleus to the cytoplasm and there translated to make a protein. See: *Translation*; *Nucleotide*; *Protein*.

*Translation*. In general, the re-coding of a message from one language to another. In genetics, the process by which the information carried from the nucleus by messenger RNA is made to produce a particular protein by enzymes associated with special granules the ribosomes.

*Transmitter*. The chemical substance contained in little sacs (vesicles) at synaptic nerve endings and released either to excite or inhibit the post-synaptic cell. Transmitters are mostly small molecules such as acetylcholine or noradrenaline.

*Truth*. The agreement of utterances with facts observed. See *Agreement*.

*Turnover*. The process by which the materials of the body are continually broken down and replaced by fresh.

*Understanding*. The process by which a word or concept is accepted as able to operate with others to control the programs of a person. See *Explanation*.

*Value*. The capacity to satisfy the needs and wants of people, which are indicated by the various standards written in their control programs. See: *Standards*; *Needs*; *Wants*.

*Ventral*. The belly side of the human body, or lower side of an animal.

*Vesicles*. Small sacs within the presynaptic boutons, filled with transmitter substance. See: *Transmitter*; *Synapse*; *Bouton*.

*Viruses*. Bodies containing nucleic acid and some protein, which influence living cells to make copies of the virus. They are destroyed by heat, but not by antibiotics.

*Vitalism*. The theory that life is maintained by some special force that cannot be explained by the principles of physics and chemistry. See: *Élan vitale*; *Entelechy*.

*Want*. The condition experienced and reported by an individual when some need is not satisfied. See: *Need*; *Experience*; *Standard*.

*Will*. The program that initiates the making of choices between programs of action. Probably encoded partly in the reticular activating system.

# Index of Names

*Bold type indicates entry in the Bibliography*

# Subject Index